Praise for *The First-Year Teacher's Survival Guide, Fifth Edition*

"In this book, Michelle not only guides first-year teachers on how to survive, she also shows all teachers how to thrive! Everything from the step-by step-practicalities to the helpful reflection questions at the end of each section, she covers a variety of topics that help empower educators with the tools they'll need to be successful in the classroom."

—**Tanya Marshall,** founder and CEO of The Butterfly Teacher

"Michelle Cummings is a brilliant and committed educator who captures the essence of what new teachers need as they embark on their professional journeys. *The First-Year Teacher's Survival Guide* is a must-read and will be an invaluable resource during the first year of teaching!"

—**Brian Shumate,** Superintendent, Troup County School District (GA)

"*The First-Year Teacher's Survival Guide,* simply put, belongs on the desk of every beginning teacher—especially those who want to hone the reflective and practical skills required for professional practice. Cummings wisely reminds us that what and how we teach depends on why we teach. With that in mind, she offers a one-of-a-kind treasure trove of resources and strategies for ensuring every child's achievement. I just wish I had had access to this guide when I started out!"

—**Vicki A. Jacobs,** Former High School Teacher and Faculty Director, Harvard Teacher Education Program

"This latest edition of *The First-Year Teacher's Survival Guide* is a comprehensive resource, rich with current, relevant, and invaluable content essential for every new educator. This book will be well-loved with dog-eared corners and starred passages that will stand the test of time."

—**Tisha Richmond,** Educational Consultant, Author, and International Speaker

"What an incredible gift to the next generation of teachers! This survival guide is overflowing with practical insights, easy-to-implement strategies, opportunities for reflection, and actionable advice for today's classroom. As an educator for over 20 years, I can assure you that you will return to this invaluable companion again and again as you navigate the teaching journey, accelerating your and your students' success."

—**Erika Bare,** Assistant Superintendent of Ashland Schools and Co-author of *Connecting Through Conversation: A Playbook for Talking with Students*

"Michelle Cummings breaks through the mold of prescriptive teaching advice, delivering a nuanced and flexible guide for educators. With a keen awareness of the diverse cultural landscapes in the United States, her wealth of information becomes an indispensable asset for teachers navigating the intricacies of their profession."

—**Clifton Wallace,** Social-organizational Psychologist and Education Consultant

"*The First-Year Teacher's Survival Guide, Fifth Edition* has thought of everything that new teachers will need to consider and implement. Where was this book when I started teaching 20 years ago? This fantastic guide is practical, easy-to-read, and designed for busy teachers. It will serve as an invaluable resource—full of oh-so-many tools, strategies, and templates that are sure to lay the foundation for every new teacher's practice."

—**Tiffany Burns,** Elementary School Principal and Co-author of *Connecting Through Conversation: A Playbook for Talking with Students*

"Thank you, Michelle Cummings, for opening up valuable space on my bookshelf. This is THE single book I will share with all of my new teachers, mentors, and administrators. Both a practical guide, and a trusted friend, this book feels like a warm, weighted blanket to calm the anxieties of new teachers and those who support them."

—**Jennifer Jones,** Mentor Program Coordinator, Southern Oregon Regional Educator Network

THE
First-Year
Teacher's
SURVIVAL GUIDE

Fifth
Edition

THE
First-Year
Teacher's
SURVIVAL GUIDE

*Ready-to-Use Strategies,
Tools and Activities
for Meeting the Challenges
of Each School Day*

Michelle Cummings
Julia G. Thompson

JB JOSSEY-BASS™
A Wiley Brand

For my children, Maya and Skylar,
who are also my greatest teachers.

Contents at a Glance

Contents

Section Two: Develop Professional Productivity Skills

Section Six: Cultivate Positive Classroom Relationships 161

Section Thirteen: Engage in Responsive Discipline 375

Please visit www.wiley.com/go/fyt4e for free online access to templates, checklists, and additional bonus content.

About the Author

Michelle Cummings taught secondary English and social studies in the United States and Switzerland. She served as an elementary principal, high school principal, and assistant superintendent before moving into education technology as the Chief Academic Officer at Teachers Pay Teachers (TPT). Cummings earned her B.A. at Brown University and her Ed.M. at Harvard Graduate School of Education. As a consultant, author, and public speaker, Cummings champions the power of educators and technology to uplift the lives of students and address local and global challenges. Author of *The First-Year Teacher's Survival Guide, 5th Edition*, Cummings can be contacted for workshops and speaking engagements through her website michelle-cummings.com where she also shares insights on a wide-range of educational topics.

No longer an active educator, **Julia Thompson** retired after 40 years as a classroom teacher. She remains steadfast in her belief that the most significant determiner of student success is a capable teacher who faces sometimes overwhelming daily challenges with ingenuity, professionalism, and optimism.

Acknowledgments

We accomplish nothing alone, and this book is no exception. I am grateful to Julia Thompson for entrusting me to update her beloved and enduring book. I have a lifetime of gratitude for my parents who were my first teachers and valued education both in and out of the classroom. Cleo inspired my career in education; John taught me the power of storytelling to amplify muted voices, and Donna's encouragement makes everything seem possible. I would not be who I am today without the love and the many adventures I've shared with my seven siblings. My heartfelt gratitude to Steve for his incredible support. To Elizabeth and Jana, thank you for coaching me on the writing process and cheering me on.

I have been blessed with many mentors who are deep thinkers in the world of education. I heard their voices in my head and on the phone throughout the writing process; I have so much appreciation for Anton Treuer, Carlos Cortés, David Davidson, Elliot Washor, Sonal Patel, and Vicki Jacobs who make the world a better place with their big ideas and leadership.

I am indebted to my professional network for sharing their collective wisdom during interviews, through quotes, and feedback. I am immensely grateful for the insights and inspiration of Clifton Wallace, my trusted reader for the entirety of the book. My profound thanks to the early readers of several chapters, Allison French, Chantae Campbell, Estefanía Pihen González, Jay Schroder, Margaret Wang, Nneka McGee, Tisha Richmond, and Yohanna Hailegebriel.

Special thanks to the incredible educators and leaders who shared expertise to inspire and encourage first-year teachers everywhere:

Alex MacQueen, Angela Fulton, Anna Aslin Cohen, Anthony Rebora, Becca Laroi, Betsy Bishop, Betsy Jones, Brian Shumate, Camila Thorndike, Christiana Kwauk, Colleen Seivright-Crawford, Courtney Roberts, Deborah McManaway, Eduardo García, Edward Gardner, Elaine Makarevich, Evalaurene Jean-Charles, Gail Hislop, Glenna Rost, Hayley Brazell, Jane Goette, Jared Sronce, Jay O'Rourke, Jeff Vande Sande, Jenni Jones, Jennifer

Burns, Jennifer Gonzalez, Jessica Statz, Jocelynn Hubbard, Joseph South, Karen Dalrymple, Kate Kennedy, Kathi Bowen-Jones, Kathy Schrock, Kevin Healy, Kinsey Rawe, Kirstie Christopherson, Kristin Highland, Lana Wong, Laura Moore, Laura van Dernoot Lipsky, Lennart Kuntze, Lisa Roth, Liza Talusan, Luann West Scott, Lynette Stant, Margaret R. Scheirer, Marsha Benjamin Moyer, Mary Landis, Meryl Roberts, Michael A. Barrs, Nickia Burgess, Nikki Darling, Paul Santos-Boulet, Rebekah Ralph, Richard Culatta, Rick Thomas, Rosary Beck, Sarah Bestor, Shelby Moffitt, Shelly Sambiase, Susan Johnson, Tania Tong, Tanya Marshall, Tracy Patterson, Vivian Jewell, and Yen-Yen Chiu.

To all the folks working on this book behind the scenes at Jossey-Bass, I see you and thank you. And, finally, to Amy Fandrei—thank you for inviting me to become an author and providing such helpful guidance throughout the process.

About This Survival Guide

Congratulations on your choice of profession! Every day that you are a teacher, you will know you are making a difference in the world. Something will make you laugh every day, and you will never be bored—guaranteed. Teaching can also be very complex and a stressful career. My hope is that you will find, in this extensive reference book, the strategies, tools, and activities you need not just to survive, but to thrive in a long career as an educator.

This is the book that I needed as a first-year teacher when I was establishing myself as a professional, and learning the art and science of teaching. This book has ready-to-use strategies for you, whether you teach in elementary, middle, or high school, regardless of the subject area you teach or the type of school in which you teach: urban, suburban, rural, private, public, parochial, or charter schools. The purpose of this book is to help you enjoy and succeed in the first years of your career.

Because the word *courage* is nestled inside of the word *encouragement*. My hope is that this book speaks courage into the hearts of first-year teachers. May the encouragement you find in this book give you the courage and the confidence to teach in a way that uplifts all of your students. There is a great deal of new material in the 5th edition. I have updated all sections and included current information and resources about such timely topics as:

- 4Cs: Communication, Collaboration, Critical Thinking, Creativity
- Artificial Intelligence (AI)
- Calming Spaces
- Civil Discourse
- Culturally Responsive Teaching
- Digital Tools
- Growth Mindset
- Inclusive Practices

- Multi-Tiered Systems of Support (MTSS)
- Positive Behavior Interventions and Supports (PBIS)
- Professional Learning Networks (PLN)
- Responsive Discipline
- Restorative Practices
- Self-Care for Teachers
- Social-Emotional Learning
- Standards-Based Grading
- Sustainability, Climate, and Energy Education
- Universal Design for Learning (UDL)

The First-Year Teacher's Survival Guide is designed to be a helpful resource tool for busy teachers to meet the challenges that each school day brings. You may choose to start at page one and read it through to the last page, but this volume is not a compelling work of fiction. It does not exactly have a narrative arc. Instead, think of this book as a reference or guidebook—a resource filled with classroom-tested knowledge for teachers who need answers and advice in a hurry. Here's how to get started.

Skim through the table of contents and the index to get an idea of what the book offers. Use sticky notes to mark the sections that will address information that you know will be helpful to you and that you would like to come back to later. You'll notice that there's a title bar across the top of each right-hand page to indicate just where you are in the book and to make it easier to pick and choose information as the need arises. You'll also find that the book is divided into five categories:

- Learn the Skills Necessary to Become a Professional Educator: Sections One, Two, and Three.
- Establish a Productive Classroom Environment: Sections Four, Five, and Six.
- Teach the Whole Child: Sections Seven and Eight.
- Use Engaging Instructional Practices: Sections Nine and Ten.
- Apply Effective Classroom Management and Discipline Strategies: Sections Eleven, Twelve, Thirteen, and Fourteen.

After you have a good idea of the layout of the book, you can then find the specific information that you want to explore. However you choose to use this book, it is designed to be an interactive experience. Use a pencil to fill in the assessments, set your goals, and scribble notes as you read each section. Highlight. Underline. Annotate information about the links and resources. Dog-ear the pages. Place page markers in the sections that speak to you.

The information in these pages is here to help you become the effective and inspiring educator that you and your students dream of. Thank you for choosing this profession even though you know it will be difficult; it will also be worth it. Thank you for bringing your fresh ideas and perspectives to the profession to continue improving the field of education. Thank you for bringing your energy, enthusiasm, and idealism to the most important job in the world; teachers make all other professions possible. May you not merely survive, but thrive as a teacher.

Best wishes for a wonderful first year!

Michelle Cummings

To contact me and continue exploring a wide range of education topics, visit my website at www.michelle-cummings.com.

SECTION ONE

Begin Your Professional Journey

When you decided to become an educator, you entered a very special universe—one where your insights, energy, kindness, knowledge, and skills can be used to change the world. Change the world? Yes, that is what educators do. Just think of what a career in education means to you and to the millions of teachers who are your colleagues across the globe. Think carefully about why you want to be a teacher and carry your "why" throughout your career. Periodically revisiting your "why" will provide you with clarity and inspiration.

Teachers make all other professions possible. It's true, teaching is that important. Countless studies indicate that teachers are the most significant school-based factor influencing student achievement. It is teachers who get to know students, inspire them to become lifelong learners, and to believe in their ability to achieve their dreams.

It is teachers who build relationships with students and create engaging, inclusive learning communities. With teachers, students learn the knowledge and skills for self-expression and problem-solving. With teachers, students expand their horizons and discover their interests, learn to read, write, think mathematically, explore their questions, cooperate, and collaborate with others. It is a teacher who builds a safe, respectful culture that affirms students and protects them from bullies. It is a teacher who provides the first line of defense in the battle against ignorance, poverty, and discrimination in all its forms. It is a teacher who, in partnership with families, helps young people learn how to navigate life. To be kind. To be successful. To accomplish dreams. To be good citizens of the world.

What a weighty responsibility we face each school day. What a privilege it is to be an educator.

Few careers can claim to have such a powerful impact as a career in education. Teachers do change the world—one student, one classroom, one school at a time. Never doubt that, even on the toughest days, you make a difference in the lives of your students. What you do *matters*.

Congratulations on your choice of professions! We welcome you.

How to Handle Your New Responsibilities

If you are like most new teachers, you may already be concerned about how well you will handle the responsibilities that accompany managing a classroom filled with a diverse population of students—each one with unique needs, interests, and abilities. Just how do successful teachers keep those responsibilities from becoming overwhelming?

Teachers take it one day at a time. They work to maintain a balance between their personal and professional lives by paying careful attention to their own well-being. Teachers manage their professional challenges by realizing that they are not alone in their struggles and that it's okay to not always know the best solution to a problem. They reach out to a colleague next door or down the hall or in an online professional community to seek help. And even when they are dealing with the pressing details of each school day, effective teachers stay focused on what really matters—the success of their students.

All teachers experience professional challenges. First-year teachers, experienced teachers, and teachers at every grade level cope with complex problems, no matter how ideal their school situation. Anytime you feel overwhelmed, remember that you are not alone and it's likely that others have faced what you're going through. In fact, here are some of the most common challenges that teachers experience:

- Finding a sustainable work-life balance
- Meeting a wide range of students' academic needs
- Addressing students' social, emotional, and behavioral needs
- Planning and implementing engaging lessons
- Lacking time and resources
- Connecting with families and caregivers
- Integrating learning technology
- Completing paperwork/administrative tasks
- Keeping up with new initiatives
- Experiencing external pressures

If some of these problems seem all too familiar, remember that the hallmark of a great teacher is not the absence of problems but the ability to generate and implement innovative and effective solutions to an array of classroom challenges. With a positive attitude, a professional approach, a bit of creativity, collaboration with colleagues and plenty of practice, you will soon be able to manage your new professional responsibilities.

Develop the Mindset of a "Professional" Educator

Although many educators use the term *professionalism* when referring to teachers they respect, it can be a vague, complex, and sometimes biased term. Does it mean stand-offish and unapproachable? Absolutely not. Professional educators come from a wide-range of backgrounds and identities. Each state has its own professional code for teachers.

Make sure to read yours. They are all a bit different, so let's start with a description.

Professional educators are effective teachers who embody the knowledge, skills, and dispositions necessary to reach and teach all learners. Some of the many attributes educators use to describe professional educators include: caring, intentional, dedicated, effective, knowledgeable, inclusive, collaborative, always learning new things, organized, respectful of students and others, integrous, ethical, and taking pride in their work.

> "I do everything I can to make my students feel successful, safe, and cared for. That means arriving before the expected time so that the classroom is organized and ready for students. It means having lessons thought through and implemented effectively. It means modeling for my students good behavior, thoughtfulness, and a positive outlook."
>
> *Betsy Jones, 12 years' experience*

When you choose to develop the mindset of a professional educator, it infuses all aspects of the way you go about the business of teaching. You send the message that you care deeply, have high expectations for yourself, for others, and for what you can accomplish together.

What's Expected of Professional Teachers

So much is expected of teachers. Society often expects too much and you are not expected to know how to do everything your first year. As a teacher, you will be expected not only to maintain a well-managed classroom, but also to establish a classroom culture of mutual respect and high performance with your students. All teachers, no matter what subject matter they teach or the age and ability levels of their students, are expected to create this culture in their classes. Although this can seem difficult at first, this expectation can make your life as a teacher much more rewarding as you watch your students learn and grow. How will you know when you have created the positive learning environment that you want for your students?

- Teachers know students well and have developed authentic two-way communication with their families and caregivers.
- The classroom is student-centered, with students taking ownership of their learning and responsibility for their success.
- Students are curious and interested in learning, fully engaged in meaningful, respectful, and appropriate work.
- Teachers model taking risks in learning themselves, making students feel safe to take risks in learning, too.
- Teachers integrate technology that provides multiple ways for students to express themselves and problem solve.
- Students can explain to visitors what they are doing and why they are doing it.
- Students can self-assess the quality of their work and describe what they want to learn next.

- The teacher has routines and agreements in place so that students feel a sense of belonging and confidence about expectations for learning, social interactions, and self-regulated behaviors.
- The teacher uses current research and best practices to inform instructional decisions.
- The teacher makes instructional decisions based on genuine understanding of their students and a thoughtful analysis of available data.
- Students learn and grow, demonstrating proficiency of knowledge and skills, and have some voice and choice to pursue their questions.
- Students and teachers celebrate successes, share feedback, and learn from failures together.

Creating a positive classroom culture is not a task that can be done in a day or two, but rather requires consistent and sustained effort. It begins with building relationships, maintaining high expectations, and high levels of support for your students. Make sure that these expectations and goals are ones that students also value and perceive as achievable.

Knowledgeable teachers have found that it is impossible to create a positive classroom environment without encouraging collaboration. Students who work together learn to support one another. Successful teachers also focus on helping students understand the real world connections to their studies and the importance of practice and effort in achieving success.

Finally, where there is a positive classroom culture, the students and their teachers take the time to celebrate their successes as well as learn from their failures. The culture of this type of classroom is genuine, positive, and conducive to learning and growing.

Even though the expectation that you will create a positive classroom culture can be daunting at first, it is a worthy goal with far-reaching rewards. Start with building community. Plan carefully and with the needs and interests of your students and the greater school community in mind. Others have achieved this. You can as well.

Professional Growth: Find Your People

Expanding your Professional Learning Network (PLN) is one of the best ways to inspire your growth as a teacher. It's important not to work in isolation, but to connect with teachers near and far, in your grade level or subject areas, with whom you can explore challenges and new ideas. Find a PLN where you can share your authentic experiences, bring your full self to the work, and both get and give support. With a PLN, you will continuously improve your practice, avoid burnout, and sustain your enthusiasm for teaching. There are endless ways to connect with educators who will inspire you at school, in the region, across the country, and around the world. Consider the best way for you to connect such as:

- Grade Level/Department Professional Learning Communities (PLCs)
- Social Media
- State and National Associations and Conferences

Establish Your Own Professional Learning Network

Many teachers use social media to create a professional learning network (PLN). This is simply a way for individuals to connect with other educators to collaborate, share ideas, and explore common professional interests. Various platforms will come and go, but there will always be a group to join or content creator to follow for most grade levels and subject areas. Many educators who want to establish a PLN also engage with podcasts, websites, and blogs with content they want to explore further.

> "The most important thing you can do in your first year is find people whose approach to teaching you respect, then spend as much time as you can with them. This one decision will have greater impact than any other move you can make."
>
> *Jennifer Gonzalez, Cult of Pedagogy,*
> *www.cultofpedagogy.com*

EDUCATOR PODCASTS, WEBSITES, AND BLOGS

There are so many educators sharing inspiring and thought-provoking content. Following a few educators can help you keep up with educational trends while learning about new resources, perspectives, and strategies. The following are just a few possibilities:

BAM Radio Network (bamradionetwork.com): This site provides a hub for a wide variety of podcasts and blogs for educators to explore, including ASCD, Ed Week, ISTE, and many individual educators sharing wisdom.

Black on Black Education (BlackonBlackEducation.com): Evalaurene Jean-Charles is a high school teacher, and host of this podcast where she discusses the transformation of education in Black communities. She is also a consultant supporting schools to engage student voice and student-centered practices to enhance school and classroom culture.

Cult of Pedagogy (cultofpedagogy.com): With this site, Jennifer Gonzalez creates a vibrant community of teachers through her podcast, blogs, and EduTips, offering immediately usable strategies, discussions of theory, and explorations of the soul of education.

Culture-Centered Classroom (customteachingsolutions.com): Jocelynn Hubbard, host of The Culture-Centered Classroom podcast and founder of Custom Teaching Solutions, helps teachers spark joy with practical strategies and inspiration for creating inclusive, equitable, and welcoming learning environments.

Larry Ferlazzo (larryferlazzo.edublogs.org): A prolific contributor to national publications, Larry Ferlazzo is a teacher offering insightful blogs. He also writes a blog for *Education Week* called Classroom Q&A.

Leading Equity Podcast (leadingequitycenter.com): Dr. Sheldon L. Eakins interviews leading voices in educational equity focusing on supporting educators to ensure equity in their schools.

Mindful Math Podcast (mindfulmathcoach.com): As a former instructional coach, Chrissy Allison provides practical advice for math educators, including instructional strategies, time-saving tricks, and lessons learned.

Modern Classrooms Project Podcast (modernclassrooms.org): Each episode explores aspects of the MCP with teachers implementing this innovative model, which includes blended instruction, self-pacing, and mastery-based learning.

Reimagine Schools Podcast (reimagineschoolsnow.com): Dr. Greg Goins hosts this podcast featuring many of the nation's top educators, authors, and innovators in K–12 education.

Teach Like a Champion (teachlikeachampion.org): Author Doug Lemov provides a blog, units of study, videos, and insights based on his best-selling book and many other topics that can help you grow as an educator.

STEM4Real (stem4real.org): On this podcast, Dr. Leena Bakshi McLean interviews educators and thinkers exploring culturally relevant STEM instructional strategies so that every child can see themselves in a STEM field.

Truth for Teachers (truthforteachers.com): Angela Watson offers an incredible collection of articles, podcast episodes, online courses, books, and curriculum with valuable advice and encouragement about many of the challenges facing classroom teachers. The 40 Hour Teacher Workweek program (join.40htw.com) focuses on how to maximize your work week so you are not working endlessly on evenings and weekends.

World Language Classroom Podcast (wlclassroom.com): Joshua Cabral provides tips, tools, and resources for world language teachers to support students' proficiency and help them communicate with confidence.

Develop Your Skills and Add to Your Knowledge

Feed your intellect; as a teacher, you will become a lifelong learner just by the very nature of the profession. It is simply impossible to be an effective teacher and not learn and grow yourself. It's also important that teachers have voice, choice, and agency in selecting professional development that is relevant and meaningful.

While school and district leaders provide professional development opportunities, proactive educators determine the professional development activities that serve them best. Becoming a teacher who is actively involved in a program of self-directed, sustained professional development is one of the wisest decisions you can make as a novice educator.

Fortunately, there are many different professional development opportunities available for interested teachers. As you begin to take ownership of this important aspect of your new career, you may want to consider some of the options on the following pages. Learning to use the resources available to you is a productive step in your quest to develop into the kind of teacher you dream of becoming.

Attend Conferences

As a first-year teacher, you may not believe that attending a professional conference is a good use of your time when you have so much work to do and preparing for or even finding a sub can be a struggle. You may be right. If, however, your school district offers you an opportunity to attend a conference, consider accepting it. You'll benefit from the opportunity to learn new strategies and network with other professionals. Virtual conferences are often free and easily accessible. Recordings are commonly available for you to learn asynchronously. By following teachers and authors you respect on social media, you will learn about lots of virtual opportunities for learning and connecting with other educators. Conferences come in various formats from virtual to in-person, from edcamps to state and national conferences.

Participate in an Edcamp

An important part of proactive professional development are edcamps (often referred to as *unconferences*). They are free and open to educators, participant-driven gatherings where K–12 educators informally develop topics and determine facilitators to share ideas and concerns with other educators in an inclusive and friendly environment. You can learn more about edcamps that would benefit you most from the Edcamp Foundation (edcamp.org).

Join Professional Organizations

One of the best ways to acclimate to your new profession is to join an organization for education professionals. Joining a professional association is an excellent way to stay current with the latest developments and trends in education. Most of them also host state and national conferences. Through collaboration and networking, you learn from other teachers with shared interests.

Two of the largest and most well-established professional associations have merged. Association for Supervision and Curriculum Development (ASCD, ascd.org) and International Society for Technology in Education (ISTE, iste.org) have joined forces. They both provide robust support to educators with websites, blogs, newsletters, professional development courses, magazines, books, conferences, and certifications. Content from the newsletters and blogs is free. ASCD has a new teacher collection and Quick Reference Guides providing high-quality, easy-to-read tools and tips on topics such as differentiation, The Whole Child approach, backward design, gradual release, and more. ISTE standards and recommended

> "Teaching can feel a little lonely when you are in the walls of your own classroom every day. The ISTE PLN Community can connect you to others with similar interests and experiences to explore what is possible together, wherever they may be. It allows you to make real connections around the world with colleagues who inspire your practice and can become your lifelong friends."
>
> *Joseph South, Chief Innovation Officer, ASCD/ISTE*

practices support teachers to use technology to transform teaching and learning. ISTE's resources on artificial intelligence (AI) give much needed guidance to educators about the ways AI can empower teachers and learners.

Here is a partial list of some of the many professional organizations for teachers:

- American Council on the Teaching of Foreign Language (ACTFL) (actfl.org)
- American Federation of Teachers (AFT) (aft.org)
- Association for Career and Technical Education (ACTE) (acteonline.org)
- Association for Middle Level Education (AMLE) (amle.org)
- Center for Black Educator Development (thecenterblacked.org)
- Coalition of Essential Schools (CES) (essentialschools.org)
- Educational Theatre Association (EdTA) (schooltheatre.org)
- National Alliance of Black School Educators (NABSE) (nabse.org)
- National Art Education Association (NAEA) (arteducators.org)
- National Association for Bilingual Education (NABE) (nabe.org)
- National Association for Career & Technical Education Information (NACTEI) (nactei.org)
- National Association for the Education of Young Children (NAEYC) (naeyc.org)
- National Association for Music Education (NAfME) (nafme.org)
- National Council for the Social Studies (NCSS) (socialstudies.org)
- National Council of Teachers of English (NCTE) (ncte.org)
- National Council of Teachers of Mathematics (NCTM) (nctm.org)
- National Education Association (NEA) (nea.org)
- National Science Teachers Association (NSTA) (nsta.org)
- Teaching English to Speakers of Other Languages International Association (TESOL) (tesol.org)
- National Association of Special Education Teachers (NASET) (naset.org)

Read Professional Journals

Just as attending conferences can help you develop professional expertise, so can reading professional journals. Through such reading, you can learn a great deal about the interests you share with others in your field. Many of the preceding professional organizations have journals. Subscribing to one of these journals, websites, or newsletters will enrich your teaching experience in many ways:

Educational Leadership (EL) (ascd.org): This journal is the voice of the Association for Supervision and Curriculum Development and a useful resource for teachers at all grade levels. Here, you can find professional resources for your classroom as well as for schoolwide issues.

Education Week (edweek.com): This journal is a weekly periodical devoted to up-to-the-minute news and commentary about education-related topics.

Kappan (kappanonline.org): This professional journal produced by the international organization for teachers, Phi Delta Kappa, addresses issues of policy and serves as a forum for debates on controversial subjects.

Learning for Justice (learningforjustice .org): Formerly known as *Teaching Tolerance*, *Learning for Justice* provides articles and strategies to help teachers address current social justice issues, and promote equity and inclusion in education.

> "Being an educator is incredibly demanding and multifaceted work. It's important for new educators to appreciate the intellectual dimensions of this work and to read deeply and seek out the best resources and mentors. Curiosity can be a big difference maker in your growth."
>
> *Anthony Rebora, Chief Content Officer, ASCD/ISTE*

Investigate National Board Certification

You have a lot to do as a first-year teacher, and national board certification is a rigorous and intensive process. Teachers must complete three years of experience in order to finalize certification, but it's still good to know this exists and consider it for the future. You can learn more at the website of the National Board for Professional Teaching Standards (nbpts.org).

Twenty-Two Educational Websites to Explore

Websites offering free and paid tech tools, templates, resources, blogs, and instructional materials have expanded significantly. It's vital that teachers share their collective wisdom to inspire teachers and engage students. From elaborate and carefully curated sites to more humble offerings, online resources can save teachers time and money.

Teachers must, however, select supplemental resources with care, considering your learning purpose, knowing the needs of your students, and choosing high-quality resources. The following are 22 websites you may choose to explore. All of them have free resources and unless otherwise noted, they apply to all grades, Pre-K–12. In addition, a few have paid options and fees for available services.

Annenberg Learner (learner.org): Multimedia resources and professional development for all grades and subjects.

Audubon for Kids (audubon.org/get-outside/activities/audubon-for-kids): Bird-related lesson plans and activities.

Code.org (code.org): Resources to teach coding and computer science.

Common Lit (commonlit.org/en): More than 2,000 ELA resources, reading passages, and assessments for grades 3–12.

Education World (educationworld.com): News briefs, lesson plans, education tips, reviews, and professional development.

Edutopia (edutopia.org): Timely articles, sage advice, videos, and a wide range of materials.

EverFi (everfi.com/k-12/financial-education): Online financial education curriculum.

Facing History and Ourselves (facinghistory.org): Offers lessons and professional development to help teachers teach social studies, civics, and current events in middle and high school. This unique approach deepens students' understanding of how their choices and actions shape the future.

Kennedy Center Education (kennedy-center.org/education): Resident artist videos, lesson plans, digital resource library, and more to teach or integrate the Arts.

Khan Academy (grades 2 and up) and Khan Academy Kids (below grade 2) (khanacademy.org): (also learn.khanacademy.org/khan-academy-kids) Free instructional videos, personalized learning, and skill practice, including test prep.

Library of Congress (loc.gov/education): Free classroom materials, primary source documents, lesson plans, and presentations for grades 6–12.

MiddleWeb (middleweb.com): Resources, articles, and useful advice for middle school teachers.

NASA Science Space Place (spaceplace.nasa.gov): Online science activities, games, articles, and videos for upper-elementary grades.

National Gallery of Art (nga.gov/learn/teachers.html): Lesson ideas, teaching resources and professional development to incorporate art.

National Geographic (nationalgeographic.org/society/education-resources): Virtual, live, and recorded visits with explorers, maps, resources, and online courses.

Open Education Resources (OER) Commons (oercommons.org/curated-collections): Digital library of 50,000+ instructional resources, videos, mini-lessons, textbooks, lesson plans, and activities, all on a highly collaborative platform.

PBS Learning Media (pbslearningmedia.org): Videos, lesson plans, and more from the Public Broadcasting Service.

Read Write Think (readwritethink.org): Resources from the National Council of Teachers of English (NCTE) for reading and language arts instruction.

Share My Lesson (sharemylesson.com): More than 400,000 lesson plans, activities, and other resources shared by members of the American Federation of Teachers.

Smithsonian History Explorer (historyexplorer.si.edu): American history artifacts, lessons, activities, media, and primary source materials from the Smithsonian Museum of American History.

Teachers Pay Teachers (TPT) (teacherspayteachers.com): Over 8 million free and paid digital and printable resources for every grade level and subject area.

We Are Teachers (weareteachers.com): Through this online community for teachers, MDR Education provides teacher-teacher advice, lesson ideas, printables, giveaways, and more.

Take Learning Walks and Make Snapshot Observations

Although it is not always easy to find the time to visit other teachers' classrooms, the benefits of this practice are significant. You will witness another teacher's craft, their strategies, routines, student interactions, use of furniture and wall space, and more. Each school has a different culture. Hopefully you, your colleagues, and students welcome visitors frequently and in a way that does not disrupt learning. Observations and visits can be more or less formal depending on your goals.

A *learning walk* usually takes place when you and a colleague visit another teacher's classroom to observe a few minutes of class and then share your observations. A *snapshot observation* usually involves the same procedure but without a partner. Both techniques are excellent ways to learn new strategies and techniques from colleagues.

When you arrange either a learning walk or a snapshot observation, first ask permission of the colleague you want to observe to arrange a day and time and to discuss where you should sit. Usually, a brief ten-minute visit is sufficient to gather information about a specific aspect of the class that you are interested in. While you are in the room, be respectful of that teacher's work by sitting in an unobtrusive spot and taking notes without interacting with students. Enter and leave the classroom as quietly as possible, unless your colleague has asked you to interact with students.

Both learning walks and snapshots are especially good ways to learn more about how your colleagues create community, facilitate learning, manage the opening and ending of class, transitions, direct instruction, classroom routines, group work, and assessments. You can also learn how to improve your own practices by observing how other teachers interact with their students.

Set and Achieve Professional Goals

Setting professional goals not only provides direction and purpose as you focus on the larger issues involved in becoming an effective educator, but also will provide valuable baseline data so that you can chart a clear path for career success year after year. Goal-setting is often part of a teacher's annual evaluation cycle. If it is not, consider setting them for yourself. Goals tend to energize and motivate those who set them because they allow us to focus on what's important and thus to prioritize our efforts.

Experienced teachers also know that it's important to set SMART goals (goals that are *s*pecific, *m*easurable, *a*ttainable, *r*elevant, and *t*imely) because they are easier to achieve than vague ones. Many teachers find that writing down their professional goals makes it easier to assess their achievements throughout the school year and to track the professional skills they know they want to improve.

Teacher Template (p442) offers a checklist of suggested competencies for first-year teachers to focus your goal setting and inspire your thinking and Teacher Template (p443) will guide you as you take ownership of your professional growth as a teacher.

Other Strategies for a Successful First Year

In addition to taking ownership of your professional growth, there are several other strategies that can help you become a successful teacher in your first year: developing a reflective practice, learning from role models and mentors, seeking feedback on your performance, using the evaluation process to improve your performance, creating a professional portfolio, and finding a sustainable work-life balance.

DEVELOP A REFLECTIVE PRACTICE

Reflecting on our teaching is a vital aspect of our professional lives. Such reflection will take place in many ways, so find the purposeful system that works for you.

There are different ways to reflect on your teaching practice. Reflection can be as simple as a comment inserted on a doc or slides, a sticky note on a lesson plan, or a voice recording on your phone. Examining the information that you gather in these ways will allow you to discern trends and patterns in your teaching as you seek to improve your skills.

One very common and useful method of maintaining a reflective teaching practice can also involve recording ideas and observations in a journal on a regular basis. Whether you choose to maintain a digital, paper, or audio journal, it is important to reflect regularly. Selecting a couple of the prompts that follow may help you get the most out of the time you dedicate to reflecting on your teaching practice:

- What students do I need to check in with? Why?
- What worked well in the lesson?
- Where did I feel comfortable and at ease and where could I have prepared differently?
- What would I do differently next time?
- Were my goals for the lesson reasonable and appropriate?
- To what extent were my students engaged and challenged to do their best?
- How do I know my students are learning? Do they know what they are learning and why?
- What opportunities for reteaching or extending learning do I need to provide?
- At what points in a lesson did I monitor and adjust strategies? Why? How productive was this flexibility?
- What data do I need to collect before moving on to the next unit of study? How can I gather this information?
- Where do students need more support or scaffolding to understand concepts?
- Where can students have more choice and ownership of their learning?
- How can I elevate the quality of student collaboration and conversation in small groups?
- How can I leverage learning technology to meet students' needs and inspire them?

- What challenges did I face today? How well did I address them?

- How well do I listen to my students? What can I do to make sure that I model good listening skills?

- How did I show that I was enthusiastic about the subject matter?

- How effective were the motivational techniques I used? How can I modify them for future lessons?

- How can I foster an atmosphere of mutual respect and community among my students?

> "To this day, every time I teach something, I write on sticky notes with ideas on how to improve the lesson for next year. I am currently in the second week of the school year, and half of my desk is covered with sticky notes. I still have some on my desk left over from the end of last year. I will keep those notes adhered to my desk until I get the chance to revise those end-of-year lessons."
>
> *Vivian Jewell, 25 years' experience*

- How did I provide opportunities for students to think, act, and engage like the practitioners who use this subject in the world beyond school?

- To what extent did I encourage and support students?

Teacher Template 1.1 offers a template for professional self-reflection.

A Template for Professional Self-Reflection

Creating a template that works for you will make reflecting on your practices a manageable daily routine.

Date: _____

Celebrate successes: What went well today? How was it achieved?

_____
_____
_____
_____
_____
_____

Acknowledge challenges: What didn't go well? What contributed to that outcome?

_____
_____
_____
_____
_____
_____

Consider solutions: What can I do to better address those challenges? Who can support me in this?

_____
_____
_____
_____
_____
_____

Self Check-in: How am I doing? What self-care strategies were most helpful this week?

_____
_____
_____
_____
_____

LEARN FROM ROLE MODELS AND MENTORS

One of the most important ways to become an effective teacher is to find good role models and mentors. No matter how long you teach, you will be able to learn from colleagues who are generous with their time, energy, and knowledge.

New teachers often find themselves reluctant to ask for help for various reasons, such as embarrassment at not knowing information or feeling intimidated by the expertise of their colleagues. If you find yourself hesitating to ask for help, keep in mind that teachers in general tend to be friendly and supportive people who remember what it's like to be a new teacher. Most of them will be glad to support you.

Reach out. You are not expected to know everything about teaching during your first year. It is far better to ask for help than to be stressed because you are not sure what to do.

Tips for Finding Appropriate Role Models

Even though you will probably be assigned an official mentor, you can learn a great deal from other colleagues as well. If you look around your school, you'll find an organized teacher or two who can serve as role models when it comes to productivity. You will find someone who is skillful at communicating with upset family members or who engages students through innovative strategies. Beyond your school, there are educators throughout the district and in virtual communities. Soon you will see that role models for just about every aspect of your school life are all around you if you seek them out.

Tips for Working Well with an Official Mentor

Most school districts will assign official mentors to help new teachers during their first year, sometimes for the first three years. It's not always easy to begin a dialogue with a near stranger about your concerns at the start of a school year, but it is important to build rapport and not to hesitate to ask for help. Your mentor is invested in your success and was also a new teacher once so they have some understanding of what it's like to be in your place.

What should you ask of a mentor? Although novice teachers will have a wide range of needs, there are some common concerns that all teachers share. These usually can be divided into two levels of questions that you will discuss with your mentor. The first is the practical level: the daily concerns that are difficult to manage at first. The following are just a few of the day-to-day concerns that you can discuss with your mentor:

- How to get to know students
- How to handle planning and curriculum concerns
- How to use school technology
- How to obtain materials, equipment, and supplies
- How to communicate with families and caregivers
- How to manage paperwork
- How to arrange schedules and other school routines

The second level of questions that you should ask a mentor focuses on issues that are more complex. After you have settled into the school term and mastered the general information you need, you will be able to expand your focus to the art of teaching. Some of the complex issues your mentor can discuss with you can include topics such as these:

- How to solve common classroom problems
- How to support students with learning differences
- How to increase student motivation
- How to design differentiated instruction
- How to create an inclusive and positive learning environment
- How to assess students and help students self-assess
- How to engage students with a variety of teaching strategies

SEEK FEEDBACK ON YOUR PROFESSIONAL PERFORMANCE

Feedback is a gift and healthy systems have healthy feedback loops. One of the most useful ways to grow professionally is to proactively seek feedback from a variety of sources. Still, it can be uncomfortable and require vulnerability to give and receive feedback. You can do this formally and informally in many ways, such as observing and talking with students, surveying students and families, analyzing data, or asking colleagues, mentors, or administrators to observe and provide coaching. No matter how you choose to seek feedback about your professional performance, it is a wise idea to use a variety of instruments to gather as much information as possible about your skills.

Feedback is most useful when provided in the spirit of a coach. A coach is invested in your success and holds a higher vision for your performance. A critic does not. A coach will reflect on strengths and weaknesses and share ideas for improving. When gathering feedback from others, it may be helpful to mention the distinction between coaching and criticism. The cadence for informal feedback is daily and weekly. Timing for formal feedback from stakeholders is up to you, but recommended at least twice a year. To make sure that you have an accurate view of your strengths and the areas in which you could improve, try these methods of obtaining feedback:

- Ask your students, families, caregivers, colleagues, and administrators for feedback using Google Forms or the free surveys at SurveyMonkey (surveymonkey.com).
- Video yourself teaching and reflect on what you see.
- Ask a colleague, mentor, or administrator to observe you for part of a lesson.
- Use exit tickets or digital tools to poll students at the end of class to ask your students to comment on the day's lesson.

Make the Most of Peer Observations

Just as it is helpful for you to observe other teachers as they work with their students, it is also beneficial for you to ask colleagues to observe you as you teach. This can happen synchronously or asynchronously by sharing a pre-recorded video. One of the advantages of this type of informal observation is that the observer does not need to stay in your room long to observe. A quick snapshot observation of you at work is often enough time for a colleague to be able to discuss what happened in class.

It may also be beneficial for a colleague to take a more detailed and systematic approach to the observation. One way to ensure optimal benefit to this approach to peer observation is to use an organizer like the one in Teacher Template 1.2.

Make the Most of Peer Observations

Design a template to make peer observations as beneficial as possible.

Your feedback is a gift. Thank you for taking the time to coach me in my areas of strength and in my areas for growth.

Observed Teacher: _____ Date: _____ Observer: _____

The Lesson: What lesson is planned?

_____

_____

Special Requests: Are there specific areas of focus for the observer?

_____

_____

Concerns: Anything you want to share with the observer in advance?

_____

_____

Observer's response to the areas of concern noted above:

_____

_____

Celebrations: Observer's feedback on what went well

_____

_____

Engagement: Observer's feedback on the quality of student engagement

_____

_____

Questions for Reflection: Observer's questions for the observed teacher

_____

_____

Coaching: Suggestions for the observed teacher to consider

_____

_____

USE THE EVALUATION PROCESS TO IMPROVE YOUR TEACHING SKILLS

Formal evaluations are another form of feedback and part of continuous improvement. They can be of enormous benefit to you, or they can turn you into a nervous wreck. Developing a strong working relationship with your principal/supervisor, inviting them to walkthrough often, and embodying a growth mindset make all the difference. If you want to grow as a teacher, then adopt the attitude that your evaluators will reflect your strengths and offer advice in areas in which you need to improve.

As a teacher, you can expect to be evaluated on a variety of criteria often during your career. The evaluation process has several components.

First, you may complete a self-assessment and set goals for the year. You may be expected to collect data and other evidence throughout the year to track how well you have met your goals. There are often two or more formal observations during the year. If you do not already have a copy of your district's evaluation process and necessary forms, you should obtain these items. You can expect one of your supervisors to discuss your goals and lesson plan with you in a pre-observation conference. This is a good time to mention any problems you are having and to solicit advice.

Sometime after your pre-observation conference, your evaluator will make a planned classroom observation. They may use a document like the preceding Template 1.2. At this point, the evaluator will be observing your practice and student engagement. On occasion, scheduled observations will be rescheduled as administrators often have crises that disrupt their plans. After the observation, you will meet with your evaluator again. At this post-observation conference, the evaluator will reflect with you about the lesson you taught and highlight your strengths and areas for growth.

You can also expect other observations during the year. The number varies from school district to school district. Expect to have many informal visits from administrators over the course of your career but especially during your first few years as a probationary teacher.

Near the end of the school year, you will have a final evaluation conference. This conference will involve more than just a discussion of the formal classroom observations you have had throughout the year; it will address your overall effectiveness as an educator. If you have established a strong working relationship with your supervisor, there should be no surprises in your final evaluation. You and your supervisor should have a shared understanding of your strengths and areas for growth. This shared knowledge will then inform the professional development plan you develop.

How to Prepare for an Observation

In many ways, informal visits by evaluators are much easier than the planned, formal observations. You do not have time to worry about an unannounced visit, whereas knowing that an administrator is going to observe you in a few days may give you time to feel anxious. In addition, taking the following steps can help you feel confident both before and during the observation:

Step One: Be proactive. Develop a positive rapport with your principal or supervisor and invite them to stop by your classroom often. Make sure that you have a copy of the observation form. In fact, you should do this as early in the term as you can. Study the form so that you know what the observer will be looking for as you teach.

Step Two: Set the date for the observation when the observer will see student engagement, not a test or silent reading, for example. Observations should not disrupt the flow of learning in your class. Depending on the goals of the observation and the needs of your students, you will design a lesson plan that is simple or more complex.

Step Three: Tell your students what is going to happen. You have a routine for visitors established already. Let them know the name of the visitor and that the purpose of the visit is to observe teaching and learning in this classroom community. Let them know the visitor will be providing coaching to you to help you be a better teacher.

Step Four: Create your lesson plan and collect extra digital or printable copies of all materials needed for the lesson for the observer. Select an unobtrusive place for your visitor, and put these materials there.

Step Five: Breathe deeply. You got this. Expect to be nervous, but also expect to do well because you have prepared thoroughly and have a growth mindset.

Turn Constructive Feedback into a Positive Experience

One of the most difficult aspects of feedback is hearing constructive feedback and coaching in your areas of growth. Experienced teachers will tell you that although it is not easy to have a supervisor discuss the problems with your performance, such constructive feedback can be conducive to professional growth. With a professional attitude and a growth mindset, you will find that discussing your teaching performance during the evaluation conference can be a valuable way to improve your teaching skills. Here are some suggestions to make an evaluation conference a positive and productive experience:

- Remember that you and your supervisor share a goal to educate youth and grow you as an educator. You are collaborators in this endeavor.
- Go into your evaluation conference with a device or paper and pen, and an open mind. Be prepared to hear positive as well as constructive feedback about your performance.
- Listen objectively. If you find yourself becoming defensive, stop, take a breath, and remember we are educators. We are all learning and growing.
- Ask for advice and suggestions for improvement, then listen carefully, take notes, and reflect on them.
- Share your reflections and additional context as needed.
- After the conference, continue to invite the administrator to stop by and update them on your progress since the formal evaluation.

The Impact of Value-Added Assessments on the Evaluation Process

The term *value-added assessment* refers to the way that evaluators assess the performance of a specific teacher by comparing current standardized test scores with past test scores for that teacher's students. The intended result of these comparisons is to determine the contributions to student growth made by each teacher in a single year.

Although the intent of value-added assessment is to provide a reasonable and objective method of assessing teacher effectiveness, the practice is highly controversial. Some of the problems with the use of value-added assessments can include limiting the scope of an education to a discrete set of knowledge and skills, narrowing the curriculum by teaching to the test, and the need for multiple measures to evaluate teacher performance. Value-added assessments can be skewed by many factors.

As controversial as this method of assessment may be, some school districts use value-added assessments as a part of a teacher's evaluation process. The implications of this are significant for all teachers. There are several actions that you can take if your district engages in value-added assessment:

- Study the assessment for your grade level. Understand the knowledge, skill, and format of the assessment. Take the practice assessments yourself.

- Student growth on multiple measures is your goal already. Look at your students both as individuals and as part of the whole class.

- Assess your students' strengths and weaknesses in terms of their knowledge and skill level at the beginning of each unit of study. Use that early assessment as a guide when you differentiate instruction for the unit.

- Make sure to measure and record each student's mastery of the subject matter. This will allow you to correct gaps in knowledge or skills as necessary.

- Provide differentiated support for students with diverse learning needs in your class. Collaborate with specialists who also serve your emergent bilingual students, students who experience disabilities, poverty, or homelessness. This will enable you to intervene early to set them up for success.

- Teach the academic vocabulary and test-taking skills that are appropriate for your students. Offer practice sessions so that your students will not be intimidated by unfamiliar test procedures.

- Don't hesitate to ask early in the school term for assistance for students who may be struggling. Involve support personnel as well as adult, peer, virtual or generative AI tutors to help those students.

- Don't allow the standardized testing or value-added evaluation systems to diminish the rich community and world of ideas that creates joy for you and your students.

What to Do If Your Evaluation Is Poor

Almost every thoughtful evaluator will offer constructive feedback on how you can improve your teaching performance, but there is a difference between those recommendations and an evaluation that indicates that your classroom performance is not acceptable according to your school district's standards.

If you receive a poor evaluation, it is very likely that your first reactions will be anger, frustration, shock, and despair. Although such emotions are understandable, the best course of action for you to take is to process these feelings quickly so that you can respond in a professional manner. Next, you should strive to be as objective and proactive as possible in dealing with the situation. Ask yourself these questions:

- Do I understand my evaluator's concerns? Am I clear about what I am expected to do to address those concerns and the timeline for improvement?
- Whom can I turn to for support? Mentors? Colleagues?
- What immediate changes can I make to improve my teaching performance?
- How can I contact my local education association representative for guidance?
- How can I learn more about my district's evaluation, non-renewal, and termination policies?
- What long-term plans should I make to ensure that I have remediated the areas of poor performance indicated?

You should also keep in mind that your poor performance evaluation is confidential and not a topic that should be public knowledge at school, or even worse, among your students or their families. Do not vent indiscriminately or discuss your evaluation with anyone other than trusted family, colleagues, and friends. Keep in mind that you want to solve this problem, not spread the news. Even though your evaluation may be a poor one, employees are still expected to sign the evaluation. If you want to write a letter to rebut or explain any part of the evaluation, you should feel free to do so and to ask that it be added to your personnel file, along with the evaluation itself.

Finally, you should learn about your legal rights as an employee of your school district. Contact your local education association representative (if you have one) as well as your district's human relations office to learn as much as you can about how to manage your situation most effectively.

CREATE A PROFESSIONAL PORTFOLIO

Creating a professional portfolio serves two purposes: Career Growth and Reflection. Teachers are in high demand and teachers have opportunities across the country and internationally. A portfolio goes beyond your résumé to showcase your abilities and achievements to prospective employers. Additionally, as a new teacher, you will find that another valuable result of the portfolio is the opportunity it gives you to reflect on your teaching experiences and philosophy. It does not take long to set up and maintain a professional portfolio if you take the time to plan what you want to include in it. Although many teachers keep a paper portfolio, it is also easy to maintain a digital one or even a combination of both.

Whichever method you choose to use, the key to managing the portfolio process is simple: plan what you want to include and file that work as you encounter it. A lesson plan here, a survey there, photograph of you working with students, a copy of some of the snapshot observations you've done, and soon you will have a representative sampling of your work.

Most professional portfolios contain materials that can be grouped into two parts: evidence or artifacts from your career, and your reflections on various aspects of your teaching experiences. Here are some of the items you can include:

Artifacts

- Formal observations and evaluations
- Peer observations
- Student responses to surveys about your class
- Representative lesson plans—usually a week's worth
- A description of your classroom management plan
- A video or audio recording of a lesson
- Photographs of you and your classroom setup
- Photographs of students working
- Lists of committees you've served on
- Lists of extracurricular work and activities
- Annotated samples of student work
- Letters of recommendation
- Notes from students and families or caregivers
- Awards or honors
- Evidence from professional development workshops or courses
- An explanation of your teaching responsibilities

> "Schedule a gym class, hobby, or something else that starts one to two hours after the school day ends, at least two days a week. It will help you prioritize what needs to get done. Staying at school too long can lead to poor time management because you feel like you have forever to accomplish things. It can also lead to burnout."
>
> *Margaret R. Scheirer, 12 years' experience*

Reflections

- Sample pages from a journal recording your reflections on your teaching practice
- Responses you've made when observing other teachers
- Annotated lesson plans

MAINTAIN A WORK-LIFE BALANCE FOR LONG-TERM SUCCESS

It's important to have both a life and a career, and let's face it, work and life can both be unpredictable and often have competing priorities. Work-life balance is elusive; no one achieves balance at all times. It is deeply personal and doesn't look the same for everyone. It can change from season to season and year to year. You can, however, strive for a sustainable balance for your career and personal life so that both contribute to your sense of fulfillment in the long run.

Education is often ranked as one of the most stressful of all career choices. The chief cause of this ranking frequently lies in the unfortunate combination of too many pressing responsibilities and the incredible dedication that many teachers feel about their work. Emotionally, mentally, and physically challenging, teaching is a compelling profession where teachers find it all too easy to immerse themselves in their school duties to the detriment of their personal lives. The result is that many teachers report significant burnout due to a work-life imbalance.

Because being a teacher means that daily responsibilities begin early and seem never to end, it is not always easy to leave the demands of school at school. Because we are in the business of changing lives, we feel the weight of those responsibilities long after we have left the building. One of the occupational hazards all successful teachers face is that it is all too easy to take home not only our paperwork, but also our worries about our school days.

Successful teachers who want a long-term career in education must learn how to juggle the demands of being in a classroom all day long and still maintain a fulfilling personal life. The key? Finding a balance among three aspects of our lives: Self, Relationships, and Career. You will need to intentionally determine how you spend your time between the challenges of a new career and such personal needs as spending time with family members, maintaining friendships, and pursuing other endeavors that bring joy to life. To find a sustainable balance, consider putting some of these suggestions into practice:

- Make time for yourself. Sleep. Eat well. Exercise. Express gratitude. Plan enjoyable activities. Your students will not thrive if their teacher is exhausted and stressed. Fill your own bucket so you have energy to care for your students.

- Surround yourself with supportive and positive people who can help you. Being connected to others, including your PLN, is an important way to avoid the stress that can make every day miserable. Supportive colleagues can help you figure out the solutions you need.

- Don't lose sight of the big picture. No one can make every school day a success. What you can do, however, is realize that each school year is a marathon, not a sprint. It takes patience, determination, endurance, resilience, and a clear idea of the desired outcome for runners to complete a marathon; the same is true for teachers.

- Delegate responsibilities. Decide who can help you do a task, clearly explain how you want it accomplished, and then step back and allow that person to get busy. Depending on the task, this may be a grade-level colleague, a paraprofessional, a volunteer, a family member, or a student.

- See the opportunities in your problems. When you have a problem at school, try to think of it as an opportunity to learn and grow.

- Add structure to your life. Routines will prevent many stress-inducing problems. Putting your keys in the same place every day and prepping meals for the week, for example, will save you frustration later.

- Work efficiently while you are at school. Prioritize the tasks that you must accomplish and work steadily at them. Use your planning time and any spare moment to their fullest advantage. The more you accomplish at school, the less you will have to do at home, leaving you with the time you want to enjoy life away from school.

- Focus on the tasks at hand. Too often teachers find it easy to second-guess their decisions or to replay troublesome scenarios from the day. Instead of endlessly rehashing what went wrong, focus on productive tasks, such as designing the plans you need to create or new activities to spark your students' interest.

- Set boundaries. No one expects you to be on call twenty-four hours a day. Set your start and end times for school communication. Although there will be many after-school demands on your time, learn to gently decline those that are not a good use of your time.

- Keep your career worries in perspective. When something goes wrong, ask yourself if you will still be affected by it in a year, in a few months, or even in a week. Try to focus on the big picture instead of allowing nagging small issues to rob you of your peace of mind.

- Always have something to look forward to. Make a point of scheduling rest, planning a weekend excursion or an outing with family and friends or even setting aside time for a hobby. Looking forward to something pleasant in the future will help you maintain your equanimity in the present.

- Don't forget that your new profession is only one part of a rewarding and busy life. If you find that you are spending too much time at school or worrying about school after you have left for the day, then it's time to take steps to manage that school-induced stress.

- Stop trying to control everything. Choose your battles wisely by asking yourself if the issue that is troubling you is worth your time and energy.

- Allow yourself time to make effective transitions within your day. One way to manage this is by taking a deep breath between classes or activities. Another is having an opening routine that your students can do independently. This will free you to make the mental, emotional, and physical switch from one group of students or from one content area to another.

- Keep a flexible attitude. Get into the habit of looking for solutions instead of dwelling on your problems. If you are open to alternatives, you will be able to assess your options much more quickly.

- Stop rushing from one responsibility to the next. Slow down. Here are some ways to slow your school life down: take the time to eat lunch, allow yourself ten minutes to relax with colleagues at some point during your day, and use a journal for reflection.

- Reflect on the positive things that happen at school. When it comes time for that important self-reflection, be sure to think about the positive things that happen each day. Focusing on your strengths and your successes is just as important as improving your areas for growth.

- If you plan your responses to difficult situations, you will definitely prevent many problems. Think first and maybe consult a colleague before you respond. For example, have an experienced teacher read over your draft email to the upset parent.

- Take advantage of the assistance your district may offer its employees. Many districts offer various types of mental health assistance to their employees. Often referred to as an EAP (Employee Assistance Program), this district-wide assistance can take many forms, such as counseling referrals, wellness activities, online stress reduction classes, support groups, financial coaching, help with substance abuse, and many others.

Self-Care to Teach at Your Best

Caring for yourself is not selfish. Prioritizing what you need to reduce stress, reduce the risk of illness, and build resilience allows you to bring your best self to the challenging work of educating youth. Developing habits and routines for self-care in the same way you develop habits and routines in the classroom will fill your bucket so that you have energy to focus on the needs of others. Your students, colleagues, friends, and family will also benefit from and appreciate this investment you make in yourself as self-care practices will help you to be a more happy, healthy, and engaged person.

In addition to the personal benefits of self-care, research findings indicate that teacher burnout is correlated to real consequences for student learning. When teachers experience emotional exhaustion and overwhelm, students have less motivation and lower academic achievement. Implementing self-care practices early in your career is likely to help you remain in the profession longer with greater job satisfaction. We also know that when we are exhausted, we are less resilient, more irritable, and more likely to have negative interactions with students. The habits of self-care you develop will allow you to find sustainability in a profession that will take as much time as you allow it.

While the focus of this section is on the vital importance of individual self-care strategies, it's important to note that systemic changes are also needed to create sustainability in the profession and reduce burnout for teachers. Such organizational changes may include working with administrators on how to structure time in the school day and reducing the number of responsibilities and tasks required of teachers. In your first year, you may discuss with your mentor, colleagues, and supervisor the ways that the school could better support teachers, but it's more likely that you will have the time and energy to focus on that which you can control, your personal self-care.

> "The most significant element in a learning environment is the well-being of the teacher. Students thrive best when their teacher is thriving."
>
> *Jay Schroder, author of* Teach from Your Best Self: A Teacher's Guide to Thriving in the Classroom.
> *teachfromyourbestself.org*

Who knows, the commitments you make to yourself may even start to shift your school culture as you model healthy habits for your students, colleagues, and administrators. Some school and district administrators intentionally and purposefully care for the physical, emotional, and mental well-being of teachers and create a culture where self-care is the norm. Regardless of your school culture, committing to self-care is important so that you have the clarity, the joy, and the resilience that will sustain you as a teacher across a long career.

Accomplishing this takes practice and discipline. Three realities of the first year of teaching that can become barriers to self-care include:

Demands on Time: During the school year, teachers start early and end late, offering extra help after school, sponsoring extracurricular activities and athletics, or working additional jobs. Some teachers have caregiving responsibilities for children or parents who need attention outside of the school day. Sometimes a teacher's interruptions get interrupted with a steady stream of others' needs. Time is a teacher's most rare and valuable resource.

Inexperience: This is your first year teaching. Everything is new and every decision takes longer at the start of your career. So, it is common for first-year teachers to work many hours as you gain proficiency with all your many responsibilities.

Unspoken Expectations: Children are cherished. Teaching helps to determine each child's future so there are many unspoken expectations about this vitally important role. Teachers want to do everything they can to meet the needs of students; prioritizing students' needs is absolutely part of the job. This leads to an expectation that sacrifice is also required to be a teacher and guilt can ensue if teachers prioritize their own needs.

These are real obstacles strewn along the path to self-care, but there are several strategies you can use to overcome these barriers, meet the needs of students, and care for your own health and happiness. Teachers are incredible planners so plan for your self-care just as you plan for your students. Each person is unique and has preferences for how you think about and organize your time. Choose the strategies that work for you and are effective in achieving the goal: your health and well-being. Here are a few strategies that may work for you:

Set and Maintain Boundaries on Your Time

There are several ways to set and maintain time boundaries for your personal and professional commitments. You will need to find one that works for you to identify your priorities and provide adequate time for activities to avoid overcommitting. Some teachers prefer to reflect on their personal and professional priorities and think about their day in chunks of time. Some teachers write down their priorities as time blocks on a calendar so that they see it visually. Often, that which gets on the calendar has a good chance of getting done in the highly scheduled lives of teachers. Whatever strategy you use, communicate your time boundaries to others so they can respect your time and you can respect theirs.

Whether you choose to put it on your calendar or hold it in your mind, consider allocating time for your morning routine, your arrival at school, lunch, a ten-minute break midday or when students have left for the day. Determine each day what time you will leave school. During the evening and weekends, block out time for your preferred activities, those experiences that nurture your well-being. That may be time with family or friends, hobbies, or rest periods. Create intentional, reasonable limits on the time you will work on evenings and weekends.

Give yourself permission to disconnect from emails, social media, Slack, or app messages. Set an out-of-office reply on evenings and weekends to let students, families, caregivers, and colleagues know that their message is important to you, and you will respond on the next school day.

Collaborate with Colleagues

Developing structures around collaborating with teachers in your school and your wider PLN and (as the technology advances) your generative AI assistants can reduce your workload. Share the responsibilities of planning, grading, and problem-solving so that you gain the benefit of their wisdom and expertise, save time, and don't feel isolated making all the decisions. (See Section Three for more strategies on effectively collaborating with colleagues and Section Two on the use of generative AI assistants.)

Practice Saying No

Be clear on your priorities and careful about the commitments you make. Get comfortable saying no, politely. You will need to protect your boundaries so that your teaching priorities and your self-care commitments get accomplished. No one will rescue you from over-committing. This is something you must do for yourself.

Say Yes to Rest

Protecting your peace and letting yourself rest is not a waste of time. It allows you to be at your best when you are at school. Establish your bedtime and waking time. Block out time on evenings, weekends, and school breaks to disconnect, rest, and recharge in whatever way makes sense for you.

Find What Works for You

Each teacher is unique, and self-care can look different for everyone, so find what works for you. What brings you joy? What will give you a sense of satisfaction and meaningful relief from your stress? Protect time for those things and infuse them into your school day. Once you commit to prioritizing your self-care, it can take two months for a habit to form, so build your self-care habits by making consistent, daily choices. These habits may relate to your mental/emotional, physical, or social needs, so find the habits that work best for you and put one or two on the calendar to get started. Pick a couple of ideas that resonate with you. This is not a to-do list, but rather a few of the possibilities in each category:

Mental/Emotional Self-Care

- Me Time in the Morning

    Preserve five to fifteen minutes for yourself to just be, drink coffee or tea, read a book, listen to music, play an instrument, breathe, stretch, take a bath, knit, draw, write your morning pages, whatever is peaceful for you.

- Breaks during the Day

    Schedule breaks during the workday. Create space from two to ten minutes throughout the day for breathing, mindfulness, and quiet. This may be in the car, in your classroom, on the way back from dropping off elementary students at P.E., during lunch, or on a quick walk to change your state of mind. It may occur alone, with a colleague, or with your students.

- Gratitude Journal

    Create a written or spoken gratitude journal and record three things you are grateful for each day.

- Set a Closing Time for Devices

    Establish a limit for social media and use of devices so that you are not scrolling up to the moment you put your head on the pillow.

- Take Two Minutes

    In the car, in your classroom, during your bus or train commute, set a two-minute timer and do nothing but breathe in and out.

- Dance It Out

    Have a one- to two-minute dance party with your favorite music in your personal space or in the classroom. Your students might enjoy this, too.

- Connect with Nature/Greenspace
    Spend some time in the greenspace near you and notice the sounds, the sun, wind, flora, and fauna, along with the changing seasons.

Physical Self-Care

- Meal Prep

    Plan your meals and snacks each week. If you bring your lunch and snacks to school, consider preparing five lunches on the weekend so something delicious is easy to grab and go in the morning.

- Hydration

    Invest in the water bottle that works best for you. Keep it full and near you throughout the day so that it's easier to remain hydrated.

- Use the Restroom

    Some schools don't provide adequate time to take care of basic biological needs. So, you may need to develop a tag in/tag out text network to message available colleagues who can supervise your students when you need to use the restroom.

- Move Your Body

    Find your favorite form of movement such as walking, dance, running, tennis, or yoga, and set a goal of moving your body for twenty minutes, five days a week. Add it to your calendar and invite a friend or family member to join you if you wish.

- Walking Meetings

    If you have regular meetings with one or two other people and you don't need a computer for the conversation, take your meeting for a walk around the block or on the school track.

- Sleep Hygiene

    Create a nighttime routine that helps you get adequate sleep to have energy for the day ahead. Your body will appreciate going to bed and waking up on a predictable schedule.

- Power Naps

    If you are always tired, set an alarm and take a fifteen-minute power nap after school to reenergize you for your evening activities.

- Pajama Day

    They are not just for spirit days at school. Declare a weekend pajama day or a pajama morning on occasion so that you (and anyone in your home who wants to participate) remain in your PJs engaging in home-based activities that are restorative and restful for you.

- Spa Services

    While this requires additional resources, and cannot occur daily, for some people, self-care is synonymous with massages, pedicures, and spa services. Book your appointments at intervals that make sense for you. Consider getting a foam roller or neck massage device for home use so that you can have a daily spa moment.

Social Self-Care

- Connect with Family and Friends

    Call, text, and spend time with friends and family who affirm you, support you, and bring you joy. Make sure your primary relationships continue to be nurtured even with the demands of your job.

- Connect with Colleagues

    Find a mentor and colleagues in your PLN whom you trust and with whom you can be vulnerable. Discuss challenges and ask them to help you brainstorm new approaches. This reduces feelings of isolation and allows you to benefit from their wisdom and expertise.

Self-Care Hobbies

- Connect with Hobbies

   Your outside interests before you started teaching are still important. Connect with whatever restores and revitalizes you.

- Connect with Creativity

   Some hobbies may include creative pursuits that energize and delight you. Whether you prefer to create solo or with other people, don't abandon your creative hobbies such as art, reading, music, writing, journaling, poetry, quilting, cooking, photography, and more.

Include Self-Care Activities in Lesson Plans

Self-care is not just something you do alone, outside of the school day. Consider what a gift you would give yourself and your students if you purposefully included self-care life skills and strategies in your lesson plans. Self-care and self-regulation life skills align with health standards, social-emotional learning (SEL), and the Whole Child approach. Could you infuse lessons with self-regulation and self-care activities like gratitude journals, mindful breathing, physical movement, hydration, or moments in nature? Students would benefit tremendously from learning these strategies early in their lives. (See Section Seven for more details on SEL, mindfulness, and the Whole Child approach.)

   A career in education is a marathon, not a sprint, requiring deep wells of resilience and energy. Teachers cannot engage in this complex and important work if they are ill, overwhelmed, and perpetually stressed. Committing to your own self-care is one way to invest in your health, your students, your relationships, and your ability to continue teaching for many years.

Twenty-Five Strategies Specifically Geared for an Educator's Tough Times at School

Having a bad day at school? Try the following strategies to shake it off and reduce the stress that comes with a bad day at school:

1. Go to your school's library media center and escape into a good book or read a newspaper for a few minutes.
2. Talk things over with a trusted colleague or mentor.
3. Take a brisk walk around the track or the perimeter of your building.
4. Refuse to take it personally when students are rude or disruptive.
5. If you have too much to do, divide each task into manageable amounts and get busy.
6. There are several free apps for mindfulness or meditation. If you would like to try one, a good place to start is with Calm (calm.com) or Headspace (headspace.com).

7. Take a break. Change activities. Do something you enjoy instead of dealing with drudgery.

8. Close your classroom door. Set a timer for five minutes. Allow yourself to just rest and be quiet.

9. Grab a sheet of paper and a pencil. Brainstorm solutions to the cause of your stress.

10. Listen to relaxing (or energizing) music for a few minutes.

11. Eat a healthful snack. Junk food will cheer you up, but only for a few minutes.

12. Even though using mindfulness activities in class for students is now a widespread practice, there are plenty of benefits for teachers as well. A useful site for teachers is Mindful Teachers (mindfulteachers.org).

13. Acknowledge when you are genuinely upset. Denial doesn't solve problems.

14. Plan a fun activity that you can anticipate with pleasure.

15. Ask your students for their advice if the problem is one where they can help.

16. Clear up some clutter. Tidy your desk or your classroom.

17. Shift your activity. Move to another location, if possible.

18. Ask for help. Doing this can allow you to move closer to a positive resolution to a problem.

19. Post a funny cartoon, meme, or photo where you can see it when you need a laugh during the school day.

20. Tackle busywork: grade quiz papers, answer e-mail, anything to be productive instead of paralyzed in negative emotions.

21. Deal systematically with the problems that cause stress. Don't procrastinate. Cope.

22. When you find yourself dwelling on negative things that can happen at school, make a conscious effort to reframe those thoughts in a positive manner. For example, instead of thinking, "My students are always out of control after lunch," try "What can I do to give my students ways to channel their energy after lunch?"

23. Remind yourself once again that today's problems likely won't be important a year—or maybe even a week—from now.

24. Choose your battles. Is what you are stressed about worth your time and energy?

25. Take a deep breath. Hold to the count of three. Exhale slowly. Repeat until you feel calmer.

Questions to Discuss with Colleagues

Sharing ideas with colleagues is a helpful way to devise solutions to some of the problems that you must manage successfully at school. Here you will find several topics to open discussions with colleagues about successful instructional practices:

1. You have had a stressful day at school in which nothing seemed to go as you had planned. What can you do to remain confident while learning from the events of this tough day?

2. You just received an email from your principal telling you that they will visit your classroom later in the day. Your lesson is not a very exciting one, nor is it particularly well structured. What should you do? Who can offer advice?

3. You feel overwhelmed and have not been able to prioritize self-care. How can you find the time for self-care?

4. Although you are sure that you want to create a supportive network of colleagues to share ideas with, you are not sure about how to begin. How can you and your colleagues expand on and learn from your professional learning network?

5. What problems can you anticipate having as a first-year teacher? Where can you find help for them?

Topics to Discuss with a Mentor

Although the topics that new teachers need to discuss with a mentor vary from teacher to teacher and from school to school, there are some that most first-year teachers should be comfortable discussing with a mentor or a trusted colleague. You should ask your mentor about these topics from this section:

- How to learn about professional development opportunities in your school district
- Tips for making sure your evaluation process goes well
- How to set appropriate goals for your first year
- Which teachers at your school would be interested in visiting each other's classes
- How to manage school-induced stress and find a sustainable work-life balance

Reflection Questions to Guide Your Thinking

1. What are your personal strengths as a teacher at this point in your career? How can you use these strengths to overcome some of the problems that you will face this year?

2. What, if anything, makes you nervous about the evaluation process? How can you make sure that you know what to expect and how to prepare for it?

3. What are reasonable expectations around a professional development plan in your first year so that you can focus on your classroom responsibilities?

4. What part of your school life has been stressful so far? How have you managed this stress? Are you comfortable with your work-life balance so far? If not, how can you improve it?

5. What can you do to stay connected to your "why" and maintain your fresh idealism as you go through the ups and downs of your first year as a teacher?

SECTION TWO

Develop Professional Productivity Skills

When you were dreaming of becoming an educator, many of your imaginings probably centered on images of yourself engaged with students, actively exploring the world of ideas. Although that pleasant image is certainly a crucial aspect of an education career, it just can't happen without a great deal of behind-the-scenes effort and systems that work for you. Developing professional productivity skills and a reliable workflow are key components in the life of a teacher with a sustainable work-life balance.

You already have strategies and workflow systems for productivity. Some may continue to work for you, and some may not. The many competing demands teachers face require next-level productivity skills in order to be responsive and flexible to the needs of your students.

As you work through the information in this section, you'll learn additional practical skills that can help you become a more efficient teacher. The most important takeaways will include how to harness artificial intelligence (AI) to improve your efficiency and student learning, how to arrange your workspace, manage your time, prioritize tasks, stay organized, and follow through on commitments.

Artificial Intelligence (AI)

AI is transforming teaching and learning and evolving quickly. It is at once, both transformational and disruptive. Let's start with a definition. What is AI? *Artificial intelligence* is an umbrella term for applications that complete processes that we used to think required human intelligence. Some examples include self-driving cars, chatbots, music and movie recommendation systems, facial recognition, Siri, Alexa, ChatGPT, Dall-E, MusicGen, C.L.AI.RA, and a whole host of generative AI apps.

Generative AI is a hot topic in education because it is multi-modal, allowing anyone to input written or spoken prompts or images that will instantly generate written language, spoken language, images, art, or music. When ChatGPT was released on November 30,

2022, educators greeted it with excitement or horror or both. For some, it represented a leap forward in the tools available to teachers and students for self-expression and problem-solving. It put an end to the blank page problem. They reasoned that an AI co-pilot could provide meaningful support to teachers and students alike. Students may be able to gain knowledge and skills at a faster rate and apply what they learn to solving more complex problems. Companies quickly harnessed the power of GPT-4 to create digital tutors, such as Khanmigo, programmed with guardrails to coach and guide students on their learning journey, without giving them the answers.

Some districts banned ChatGPT due to concerns about safety, privacy, misinformation, academic integrity, or the existential threat it may pose to human voice and thought. When technology advances, there are often concerns about accuracy, bias, privacy, and the loss of jobs. In the case of AI, we are additionally confronted with a profound question about the vital and unique value that human beings bring to creating and decision-making.

One concern for teachers focuses on writing in an age of generative AI. We know that writing is a crucial skill; it is vital to humanity in order to organize our thinking, develop arguments, and create and share insights, poems, scripts, and stories informed by uniquely human, lived-experiences. So, what is a first-year teacher to do?

Generative AI and Implications for Your Classroom

Educators and their students already live in an AI-enabled world. Teachers must have a voice in the development of AI and teach students and themselves how AI works and how to use AI as a tool for both learning and productivity. Teachers are vital in empowering students who will both use AI and become the architects who build it ethically and responsibly.

Combining AI and human ingenuity in the field of education has the potential to create powerful opportunities for both educators and students. AI can provide educators with productivity tools, design lesson plans, materials, and assessments as well as offering diagnostic and coaching support to inform instructional strategies. AI can provide students with tutoring support to personalize and accelerate learning. It offers access to efficient tools to solve increasingly complex problems, as well as, for self-expression.

Where AI Already Enhances Learning

While there are many types of AI using machine learning and natural language processing, some that were already widely used in education before ChatGPT include:

- Online curriculum and assessment programs that personalize learning based on students' responses
- Book recommendations based on reading levels, ratings, and interests
- Predictive text and embedded editors in word processing

- Tutoring software and chatbots
- Auto-grading programs
- Interactive games
- Text to speech and speech to text technology
- Language learning apps
- Text to image
- AI photo editing
- AI-generated lesson planning

> "Many teachers express fear when asked to describe their feelings about AI. Once you learn about the transformative power of AI tools, you will be excited to try something new. Embracing the fear is part of the AI journey."
>
> *Nneka McGee, Chief Academic Officer, 16 years' experience, nnekamcgee.com and teachersintheloop.com*

And many more. . . .

What Skills and Abilities Do Students Need to Thrive in an AI-Enabled World?

As a teacher, you need to prepare students for their present and future. They will need to know how AI works, how to use it for learning, and how to build AI ethically and responsibly. The world of work is changing quickly. Students will work in many settings, across many industries, on hybrid teams that include human as well as AI team members. Learning to collaborate effectively with people and AI will be a vital skill.

Here are some universal skills that students will need to thrive in an AI-enabled world:

Critical Thinking: How to understand a problem, analyze data, reason, consider multiple perspectives, fact-check, and select an answer or approach. How to generate prompts to solicit quality responses.

Discernment: How to determine the right tools to use for any given task. When does it make sense to employ AI and when should the task be done by a human? What is reliable information and what is inaccurate or misinformation?

Foundational Knowledge: How does AI work? How to utilize AI tools and generate accurate, high-quality, useful content.

Ethical Use of AI Tools: How to cite the use of AI in work. What are AI's strengths, limitations, biases, and potential dangers? What impact does the use of AI have in the world on issues such as privacy, unemployment, and discrimination?

Human Value Proposition: What are qualities that are uniquely human? How to identify attributes of the head, heart, and hands that have unparalleled value and contribute to creating vital content. How to infuse content with insights based on experiences in the real world, and our five senses. How to enhance AI-produced content with human empathy, social interaction, emotion, humor, and creativity. It's important to keep humans in the loop.

How to Include Generative AI in the Classroom

Generative AI is a subset of AI that creates new content, including text, speech, images, and music by learning from large data sources. New teachers will need to consider how to leverage AI to support student success, ignite students' interests, and expand STEM education.

To teach students to use generative AI ethically, and responsibly, you will need to gain clarity about the acceptable uses of generative AI in your classroom. You will need to be clear about learning objectives and teach students to use the right tools based on those learning goals. Students with access, particularly middle and high school students, are often early adopters of digital tools. They are a great source of information and will teach you many important lessons.

Here are some steps to establish your approach to teaching and learning using generative AI tools. Keep in mind that it's not linear. It's an iterative and evolving process.

- Educate yourself on how AI works and how it can support or disrupt your teaching and learning objectives.
- Consider your learning goals for the year.
- Follow the acceptable use policies in your school or district.
- Scan the landscape for generative AI tools that support your goals while protecting student privacy and safety.
- Explore AI tools yourself and see what they can do.
- Confirm that the terms of use apply to the age of students in your classroom.
- Consider equity issues that may arise as a result of using AI.
- Clearly communicate expectations to students.
- Engage in conversations with your students, colleagues, families and caregivers about the benefits and limitations of generative AI.
- Develop creative assessments for when you don't want students to utilize generative AI in their workflow. For example, demonstrations of learning, in-class essays, and science-fair-style exhibitions in which students explain their learning.

Remember that you don't have to know everything to take the first steps. AI is rapidly changing so these are just a few ideas for incorporating generative AI tools into your lessons. The possibilities are endless.

Writing: Have students create an AI draft and then analyze it to make it better. Paste student writing into an AI and ask it for ways to improve the writing.

Brainstorming: Ask an AI to brainstorm a large number of ideas on any topic.

Deeper Learning: Have students select a topic, issue, question, or problem they want to pursue and begin discussion and research with an AI to extend their inquiry.

Summarizing Text: Copy and paste articles and ask for a summary at a specific reading level.

Debating: Discuss or debate issues with an AI.

Researching: Through a voice or image prompt, research flora, fauna, monuments, and more.

Changing Reading Levels: Have an AI rewrite a passage at a lower or higher reading level.

Interviewing: Interview an AI as a fictional character or as a person from a specific period in history, background, or perspective.

Addressing More Complex Problems: With an AI co-pilot, students may be able take on larger, more complex problems to solve.

Illustrating: Create illustrations in 2-D or 3-D, whether for a story, poem, film, game, song, architecture, or manufacturing design.

Presenting: Transform documents or basic prompts into designed presentation slides.

Feedback: Ask the AI for feedback on text, images, graphics, and more to improve the quality of work.

Incorporating new tools can be overwhelming. You have many resources to support you from your Professional Learning Network (PLN) to the internet to products such as Adobe, Canva, or Curipod that all have generative AI features. Generative AI is developing an interface that will be as natural for teachers as speaking to another person (who can assist with almost any task). As the machine learning continues to improve, there are also detailed "prompt books or guides" to help users input prompts to get the most accurate and high-quality results from generative AIs.

> "There will always be a new technology that is talked about nonstop. That technology will likely have some great potential for classrooms as well as some pitfalls. Use the ISTE Standards to evaluate the newest techno buzzword. They will help you ask questions about whether the technology is going to empower learners or lead to passive uses, whether it is going to support students in becoming active, engaged digital citizens, or isolate them in the digital world."
>
> *Joseph South, Chief Innovation Officer, ASCD/ISTE*

Use Generative AI for Teacher Productivity

Properly using generative AI can save teachers time. Consider any teacher task and what role generative AI can play in completing that task. Saving teachers time reduces stress, creates a better work-life balance, and frees up more time to focus on students' needs. Improper use, however, can potentially lead to serious issues. Consider ethical standards, privacy, and integrity, for example. Consider citing uses of generative AI as you would expect students to and avoid inputting confidential student information into a generative AI.

Notice that all the following suggestions are prefaced with the words *draft*, *review*, and *revise* because the AI is a co-pilot. You can have AI create a draft and prompt it to revise it based on your review. It may get you started, but you always need to review and potentially revise the work to insure accuracy, usefulness, voice, and alignment with your goals and the needs of your intended audience.

Possible Generative AI Dos: draft, review, and revise. . .

- Emails or Slack messages
- Newsletters
- Syllabi
- Presentation slides
- Field-trip permission forms
- Letters of recommendation
- Grant proposals
- Translate texts and passages from or into various world languages
- Discussion questions
- Rubrics/Scoring Guides
- Anchor/Exemplar Responses
- Lesson plans
- Learning activities, especially the most engaging and time-consuming, such as project-based learning or STEM challenges
- A list of real-life applications of the subject matter to increase the relevance of your lessons
- Simplified explanations of complex concepts
- Images/Illustrations
- Goals and objectives
- Feedback and grading for student work
- Summarizing professional articles you've been meaning to read

Possible Generative AI Don'ts:

- Pass off AI-generated work as your own
- Upload confidential information to generate IEPs, 504 Plans, and so on
- Upload confidential evaluation information

Generative AI is developing rapidly. It is changing society in ways large and small. It can be challenging to stay current and know when it is best to use the tools and when not to. By educating yourself, gaining experience with the tools, talking authentically with your colleagues and students, and considering safety, accuracy, equity, and the social impact, you will make good use of generative AI for your own productivity and for expanding educational opportunities for students.

Resources for Further Study

Given the rapid changes in this technology, it is important to continue professional learning about AI. Here are a few resources that may help you.

Websites

- International Society for Technology in Education (ISTE) (iste.org/ai)
- US Department of Education Office of Educational Technology (tech.ed.gov/ai)

Books

- *AI for Educators* by Matt Miller
- *The AI Classroom* by Dan Fitzpatrick
- *The AI-Infused Classroom* by Holly Clark
- *AI and the Future of Education* by Priten Shah

Podcast

- Digital Learning Podcast with Matt Miller and Holly Clark (digitallearningpodcast.com)

Questions to Discuss with Colleagues

Sharing ideas with colleagues is a helpful way to devise solutions to some of the problems that you must manage successfully at school. Here you will find several topics to open discussions with colleagues about successful instructional practices:

1. You want to set expectations around the use of generative AI in your classroom. What are some of the ways you can use generative AI effectively? What are some of the pitfalls, safety, and privacy concerns to consider?

2. You want to learn more about how AI works. What are some of the resources you can explore to deepen your own understanding?

3. You want to develop assessments that do not involve generative AI. What are some formative and summative assessment strategies you can implement? How can you create the assessments and give students feedback most efficiently?

4. You want to use generative AI to support students with diverse learning needs. What can you do with generative AI to better support students with disabilities, emergent bilingual students, talented and gifted students? How can you use generative AI to personalize learning?

5. You are overwhelmed by the number of tasks you must do that don't focus on teaching and learning. How can you use generative AI to improve your workflow and more effectively and efficiently complete time-consuming tasks?

Topics to Discuss with a Mentor

Although the topics that new teachers need to discuss with a mentor vary from teacher to teacher and from school to school, there are some that most first-year teachers should be comfortable discussing with a mentor or a trusted colleague. You should ask your mentor about these topics from this section:

- Where to learn more about school and district policies around generative AI
- Advice about setting and enforcing expectations with students
- How to find professional development opportunities about AI
- Suggestions for getting access to additional generative AI tools
- Discovering teachers in your school who already use generative AI effectively

Reflection Questions to Guide Your Thinking

1. What knowledge and skills do you currently possess with respect to artificial intelligence? How can you learn more and fill in the gaps in your knowledge?
2. What types of procedures and policies would be helpful to your students? How can you move forward with them?
3. What learning experiences can AI support and what learning should not involve AI? What have you observed in other classrooms that you'd like to try in your own class?
4. How well do you know your students' interests, skills, and abilities? How can you use this information in combination with AI tools to accelerate and personalize learning opportunities?
5. How can AI help you to be more productive? What teacher tasks can AI support and what teacher tasks are best accomplished without AI?

Arrange Your Workspace for Maximum Productivity

Your personal work area may determine whether you will be comfortable in your classroom or not. Because you will be spending so many of your daylight hours in your classroom, your personal workstation should be comfortable and well organized with easy access to all your frequently used materials. The area you designate as your workspace will include a place to put your computer, laptop, or device; and a place to sit, unless you prefer a standing or adjustable computer station. You will want a place to safely store your personal items, backpack or teacher bag, coat, purse, office supplies, and a locking file drawer for confidential documents.

Your workspace may or may not include a teacher desk. Some teachers want a classic desk area to work when students are not in the room. Some teachers want a workspace with a smaller footprint to free up additional spaces for instruction. Here are some suggestions for making sure that whatever you choose functions well for you:

- Consider what types of learning you want to occur in your classroom and what a warm, welcoming classroom looks like and arrange your furniture to support that first.
- Consider the tasks you will be doing in your workspace and the systems and workflows that will best facilitate completing those tasks.
- Bring yourself to work and reflect your personality in some small ways, making sure not to overdo it in a way that creates distractions or clutter.

Here are some of the items you may want to have within easy reach:

- You will be issued a computer, laptop, or other device. Be sure to consider if it needs to be connected to the projector for sharing your screen with the class. Leave room in your workspace for it and arrange the cords and chargers so that they are unobtrusive.
- Consider what items and supplies are for your personal use, what items you will share with students, and where to locate items exclusively for student use.
- You will need a safe place to store (perhaps to lock) your personal belongings, such as your cell phone, purse, or teacher bag.
- Keep your keys in a safe place. Due to school safety protocols, typically teachers carry them at all times, on a lanyard, in a pocket, or fanny pack.
- When choosing the location for your workspace, consider these needs: to maintain a line of sight to see the whole class, to confer with a student quietly, and to not block students' views of boards and screens.
- If possible, your filing cabinet and other personal storage areas should be set up near your workspace for quick access.
- It is always a good idea to leave your workspace clean at the end of each school day.

> "If I had a chance to do my first year over, I would be more organized. I would not hide my fear of failure behind bravado but ask for help from fellow teachers instead."
>
> *Deborah McManaway, 23 years' experience*

School Supplies You Will Need

You will need many supplies to provide dynamic and engaging instruction. Schools should provide teachers with the necessary supplies or a discretionary budget to purchase them. Unfortunately, some schools do not and that harsh reality is written into U.S. tax code. Teaching is one of the few professions with a unique tax break; the Educator Expense Deduction allows teachers a $300 tax deduction for out-of-pocket classroom expenses. Submit requests for school supplies to the appropriate person in your school office before assuming you need to make purchases out of pocket.

If, however, you still need to find funding, teachers everywhere are resourceful and have learned how to get what they need by reusing supplies, asking families or businesses for help, and making good use of the supplies they have. Many teachers have been able to obtain classroom supplies by asking for donations or creating wish lists on such sites as:

- Donors Choose (donorschoose.org)
- Amazon (amazon.com) *Select "add to list" instead of "add to cart"*
- Target Wish List Registry (target.com)
- Craigslist (craigslist.org)
- Freecycle (freecycle.org)

Another way that many teachers can obtain classroom furniture and supplies is by searching for freebies online. This is a great job to delegate to one of your volunteers. Explore the plentiful freebie or buy-nothing websites and social media groups to find what works for you.

The following are lists of some of the classroom supplies you may find useful throughout the school year. If your district can't supply these items for you, start with the basics and add items as you can. Many of these can be purchased at discount stores during back-to-school sales. You can also ask your mentor or colleagues for assistance in obtaining classroom supplies.

Basic Items You'll Need

- Trays or other storage container for folders and papers
- File folders and labels
- Calendar (Even if you rely on electronic calendars, a paper version for your desk or wall is often helpful.)
- Office supplies, such as pens, permanent markers, and pencils, dry erase markers, scissors, pencil sharpeners, stapler, staples, staple remover, stickers, post-its, binder rings, highlighters, sticky ticktack, binder clips, tape, paperclips, glue sticks, glue, rubber bands, push pins, hole punch, index cards, and so on

- Notepads
- Trash/recycling bins
- Tissues
- Disinfectant wipes
- Chargers for your devices
- Water bottle
- Healthy quick snacks
- Breath mints
- Utensils for lunch
- Personal items, such as hand lotion, Band-Aids, over-the-counter medicines, deodorant, hairbrush, feminine products, safety pins, and so on
- Blank greeting cards

The Dos and Don'ts of Your School Computer

After years of working on personally owned computers, you will now use a computer purchased by your employer. In public schools, that means a device purchased with public funds. Responsible use of your school computer is critical. To make sure that use of your school computer is as professional as possible, be guided by the following lists of dos and don'ts:

School Computer Dos

- Remember that the computer is the property of your school district.
- Have no expectations of privacy with respect to your use of a school computer.
- Read and understand the acceptable use document that you sign.
- Be cautious and professional when using your school computer.
- Protect your computer when you transport it.
- Create an electronic filing and organization system.
- Back up your work.
- Use your computer for school business only.
- Create strong passwords to log into the computer as well as for apps and programs you use.
- Keep your computer and virus protection updates current.
- Report any problems with your computer right away.

School Computer Don'ts

- Don't download software programs without permission.
- Don't spill food or drinks on your computer. Spills can be costly.
- Don't forget that district personnel may monitor your computer usage, including email and search history.
- Don't upload personal photos to the computer accidentally while charging your phone.
- Don't leave your computer screen unlocked and unattended.
- Don't allow students to use your computer.
- Don't accept follow requests from students and don't follow your students on their social media accounts.
- Don't visit sites with inappropriate or illegal content such as pornography or gambling.
- Don't decorate your computer with stickers unless approved by your school district.
- Don't knowingly open attachments or visit sites that could infect your computer.
- Don't share your passwords with others.

Tips for Managing Email

While some schools have started using Slack or other apps for some communications, the vast majority use email. Most teachers will admit to having mixed feelings about school email. On the positive side, it is an efficient and quick way to communicate with families, caregivers, students, colleagues, and your PLN. On the negative side, there are few barriers to sending teachers emails at any time of day or night, so the quantity, content, and timing of emails can often be overwhelming and somewhat complicated to manage.

Responding to emails often consumes far too much of a busy teacher's time. Also, an email cannot always convey the sender's tone, and so it's easy to send and receive confusing messages with the potential to create or exacerbate unpleasant situations. To make the best use of email as a tool for building relationships, achieving your goals, and avoiding unpleasantness, try these tips.

- Set specific times on your calendar each day to read and respond to emails so your inbox doesn't distract from your focus on teaching and learning.
- Typically teachers have a goal of responding to emails within twenty-four hours. What is the expectation at your school?
- Consider the best communication tool for the situation. When is it effective and efficient to send an email? When is it better to make a phone call or visit with someone in person? Choose the strategy most likely to get the best result.

- If you are considering sending an email to families or caregivers about a student discipline incident, consider making a phone call instead.
- Be very careful about forwarding email messages without the sender's permission.
- Always include a clear, concise subject line, so that the receiver can prioritize the email and respond as quickly as possible.
- Protect the privacy of your students by not mentioning them by name in emails to colleagues about sensitive issues.
- Before you send an email, take the time to proofread it carefully.
- "Reply all" for all staff emails is rarely a good idea. It just clogs up everyone's inbox.
- Avoid being too casual with your greetings or jargon, and be aware that attempts at humor can often be misread.
- Develop a systematic process for managing email folders. What process will allow you to retrieve emails quickly when needed?
- Consider your email signature and what to include. It goes to everyone you send a work email to. How should it be similar or different from your personal email signature? Does it make a welcoming, inclusive, and professional statement?
- Think about the "front page test." If your emails were subpoenaed, or published on the front page of the newspaper, how would you feel?
- If you utilize AI to draft emails for you, remember not to input confidential information and to review and revise the email for voice, accuracy, content, and audience.

Time Management for Teachers

Time management strategies are a game changer. As an adult, you have time management strategies that work for you, and as a teacher, they will be tested and you may need new, next-level strategies. Teachers have so much to do and so little free time to accomplish it that many of us often feel overwhelmed and stressed. With forethought and attention to detail, however, you can develop the time-management strategies that will make it easier for you to focus on student needs, manage your workload, and create a sustainable work-life balance. Effective time management begins with intentionality and making deliberate choices about prioritizing your professional tasks.

It's not always possible to confine tasks into the time you have, especially as a first-year teacher for whom everything is new. During some periods of the year, like the beginning of the year, teachers may work longer hours to get it all done. Having systems to fall back on will allow those periods to be the exceptions and not the rule. Think of your time-management system as the basso continuo or base line in jazz music over which musicians can improvise, but without it, the song may fall apart. The strategies in this section support you to make plans and create a frame that allows you to be nimble, flexible, and responsive to student needs.

HOW TO PRIORITIZE YOUR PROFESSIONAL TASKS

With the workplace pressure that most teachers experience, it is crucial to prioritize your tasks so that you can accomplish everything you need to do, move forward in meeting your goals, and reduce your stress level so that you can have the work-life balance that you need to succeed. Here is a simple six-step process to help you prioritize your work:

Step One: Brainstorm a list of the tasks that you need to do. Have a consistent place to write your to-do list. Jotting them down in a list electronically or on paper will make it easier for you to visualize the work that must be done. Having an electronic task list may make it easier to prioritize and add tasks to a calendar.

Step Two: After you have made a task list, go over it carefully to determine the urgency of each task. Highlight or move the tasks that should be completed before you leave school for the day to the top of the list. Some examples of an urgent school task could include:

- Whatever is creating a knot in your stomach, address it today
- Responding to an email from a family member or caregiver
- Responding to an email from a colleague or supervisor
- Making a phone call to a family member or caregiver about a problem
- Addressing a student behavior issue
- Updating your learning management system
- Making copies of the handouts you will need for the next day's lesson
- Writing a brief reflection on the day's instruction
- Making sure that the equipment and materials for the next day are ready

Step Three: After you have determined the urgent tasks, look at the list again to determine the ones that can be accomplished with a brief delay of a day or two. Highlight them in another color or move them to the next tier of your list. It is always a good idea to get the more troublesome ones out of the way first. Examples of this type of task could include:

- Recording or posting grades
- Sending home positive notes for students
- Giving feedback on assignments (Be sure to stagger due dates so that the feedback is timely and meaningful.)
- Making copies of next week's handouts
- Creating an assessment to be given next week
- Designing lesson plans for the next week and beyond
- Making sure you have enough supplies for next week's instruction

Step Four: A fourth step in prioritizing the tasks in your workflow involves determining the ones that could be postponed for several days or could even be optional. Examples of this type of task could include:

- Creating a new bulletin board
- Adjusting an alternative assessment for a current unit of study
- Browsing for creative lesson plans online
- Planning a field trip for next semester
- Updating your documents or cleaning out a file drawer
- Sharing resources with a colleague for a new unit of study

Step Five: After you have jotted down your tasks and identified their urgency level, sort them in the order that you intend to accomplish them and estimate how long each task will take.

Step Six: Add tasks requiring thirty minutes or more to your calendar during a time when you can reasonably accomplish them. That which gets on your calendar usually gets done.

To help prioritize your professional tasks, you can also adapt Teacher Template 2.1 to meet your needs.

Prioritize Your Tasks

After you have brainstormed the tasks that you need to accomplish, you can use this template to list them in the proper category so that you can add them to your calendar and manage your workload efficiently.

Do Right Away/ Time Needed	Delay Briefly/ Time Needed	This Can Wait/ Time Needed
1. _____ _____ _____	1. _____ _____ _____	1. _____ _____ _____
2. _____ _____ _____	2. _____ _____ _____	2. _____ _____ _____
3. _____ _____ _____	3. _____ _____ _____	3. _____ _____ _____
4. _____ _____ _____	4. _____ _____ _____	4. _____ _____ _____
5. _____ _____ _____	5. _____ _____ _____	5. _____ _____ _____
6. _____ _____ _____	6. _____ _____ _____	6. _____ _____ _____
7. _____ _____ _____	7. _____ _____ _____	7. _____ _____ _____
8. _____ _____ _____	8. _____ _____ _____	8. _____ _____ _____
9. _____ _____ _____	9. _____ _____ _____	9. _____ _____ _____
10. _____ _____ _____	10. _____ _____ _____	10. _____ _____ _____

A Teacher's To-Do List

Many teachers also like to use a more structured daily to-do list to manage all the tasks that they need to complete each day. Whether you choose to keep it on paper or electronically, keep it in an easy-to-access location. Having a consistent and predictable way to gather your task list is vital to successful time management. Find one that works for you. Examples include:

- Documents
- Google Keep
- Sticky notes
- Lesson Planner
- Notepad
- Dry-erase board
- To-Do List Apps: MS To Do, Trello, Hive, ToDoist, Remember the Milk

From that starting point, prioritize tasks and find time on your calendar to accomplish them. The best way to use a to-do list effectively is to determine your top priorities the day before—preferably before you leave school for the day. If you do this, when you arrive at school the next morning, you will be able to start your day with a quick review of the things that need to be accomplished. Of course, there are days when circumstances arise that take priority over the tasks on your list; however, you will have a clarity on how to prioritize and shift the items as needed.

Quick Tips for Maximizing the Time You Have at School

Learning to use the time that you have available to you while you are at school will make your school day easier and enhance your personal life by reducing the amount of work that you have to accomplish at home. Here are some quick tips to help you maximize the time that you have at school:

- Respect your time and other educators' time as a precious resource.
- Create boundaries on the amount of time you engage with your personal phone. Set your phone to do not disturb and create a system for those closest to you to break through in an emergency. Check your phone a couple of times a day when students are not present.
- Set work hours for arriving and leaving school.
- When you have complicated tasks to do, divide them into smaller pieces with specific deadlines for each one.
- Set reminders. Teachers have too much to do to keep everything straight without reminders. Set reminders on your phone or calendar when you have important deadlines.
- If a task will take less than three minutes, do it right away.
- Use either a computer or paper calendar as a planner. Record tasks, appointments, and other information you'll need to remember as you plan your workdays. Don't just plan for the day, but also for the week, for the month, for the semester, and for the year.
- Politely decline when someone asks you to give time you cannot spare.
- Keep your keys and your badge (if your district has issued you one) in the same location each day.
- Deal efficiently with mail. Act immediately on items that require a written response. Throw away or recycle junk mail.
- Set up equipment early in case there are problems.
- Arrive on time to meetings and duty assignments.
- Delegate as much as you can to students and volunteers. Even very young students can accomplish many routine tasks.
- Have emergency lesson plans ready for substitutes—just in case.

Further, you will learn to use even small blocks of time to accomplish your goals. You will be surprised at how much you can accomplish in a short amount of time if you stay focused. In fifteen minutes, you can:

- Take a walk to lower stress and restore your attention
- Grade a portion of an assessment
- Update your learning management system or web page

- Create a review sheet
- Answer a few emails
- Create warm-up exercises for the entire week

In ten minutes, you can:

- Call a student's family or caregiver
- Write a lesson plan
- Grade some essay questions
- Post grades
- Check homework papers

In five minutes, you can:

- Create a dynamic closing exercise
- Send a positive note to a student's home or to a colleague
- Use the hole punch on a set of papers
- Write a positive comment on at least five papers
- Review key points in a lesson

In three minutes, you can:

- Record grades
- Put stickers on a set of papers
- Praise a class for good behavior
- Have students write an evaluation of the day's lesson
- Tidy the room

In one minute, you can:

- Erase the board
- Display an image related to the day's lesson
- Write an inspirational message on the board

> I think what surprised me the most as a new teacher was trying to manage my time. I am very good at time management and thought it would be a piece of cake. I was wrong. I felt prepared to teach my subject, but once the real work began to happen, I had to figure out a way to still go on walks, watch TV, and hang out with friends. It took time, but I was able to prioritize life and work.
>
> *Jessica Statz, 19 years' experience*

Time Management Pitfalls

The world (and schools in particular) are distracting places. There are many stakeholders placing demands on a teacher's time. There are also plenty of pitfalls trying to derail teachers and their best-laid plans. Although there are far more tasks to be done than any teacher can ever manage to complete in a school day, look around your building for teachers who radiate a less frazzled, more calm energy. Study what they are doing to avoid time management pitfalls. Here is a quick list of some of the many things that get in the way of teachers managing their time:

- Self-interrupting cycles that shift your attention from the task you started to another task before it's completed
- Giving in to distractions when online for any reason
- Falling behind in grading, planning, and other predictable routine paperwork chores
- Trying to do everything yourself instead of asking for help or delegating tasks
- Neglecting to plan and prioritize your work
- Spending most of your planning period socializing with colleagues instead of accomplishing necessary tasks
- Disregarding the importance of using a planner, a calendar, or other scheduling strategies
- Ignoring small problems until they become more difficult to resolve
- Checking email all day long instead of at planned times
- Giving too freely of your own time to the needs of others to the point that you are not attending to your priorities

How to Minimize the Time You Spend Working at Home

In addition to the general increase in productivity that can result from sound time management strategies, there are four actions that you can take right away to reduce the amount of time that you spend doing schoolwork at home:

Action One: Focus at school. Think of every minute at school as usable work time. Even five-minute blocks of time while you are waiting for a meeting to begin, for example, can be productive if you choose. Try your best to do schoolwork at school instead of at home.

Action Two: Don't take all your work and student papers home each day. If everything is on a work laptop, just plan to address what you can accomplish in an hour or two. At home, set a timer and stop when the time you have planned for working is over. Dragging home so much work that you can't possibly complete it all will only distress you.

Action Three: When you do take work home, try to work on it as soon after you arrive home as possible. It's not always possible, but waiting until after dinner to begin working means that you will be exhausted after a long day instead of at your peak of productivity.

Action Four: Set aside time for relaxation, no matter how much schoolwork you need to do. There is no virtue in allowing schoolwork to consume an entire evening or weekend. Plan when you are going to work and plan when you are going to claim personal time.

Planning Period Productivity

Planning periods are precious to teachers and a productive planning period does not happen by accident. Setting routines for your planning period will create consistency and allow you to take control of your time at school. You can set aside specific days for certain tasks, such as grading, planning, or other routine work, for example. The key to a productive planning period is to deliberately decide how you will use the time instead of just letting it happen.

In addition to a lack of planning, another planning period time-robber is making several trips away from your classroom or planning area. It's tempting to wander around getting a snack, checking your mailbox, or chatting with colleagues. If you plan the trips you need to make during your planning period—to confer with an administrator, to the copy room, and to return a library book, for example—you will find that making one trip with several quick stops is much more efficient than if you were to make several trips.

As needed, don't forget to build in some moments of mindful relaxation. Taking the time to breathe deeply, decompress, and focus on peaceful thoughts instead of a stressful school day will refresh your spirit and make it easier to be productive the rest of the day.

A final strategy for using every minute of your planning period productively is to have the materials you need handy. Having everything ready at the start of your planning period will save you valuable time and allow you to use the time effectively.

> "During my first year, I wish I had planned ahead more. It's amazing how many times you feel a little overwhelmed when you think you've carved out time in the school day but then a million little things (parent email, administrator wants to touch base, fellow teacher has a question, the copier calls it a day on you when you need that reading for the kids) pop up, and suddenly you're scrambling when you thought you had it all under control. I've got so many memories of having that 'I got this' feeling turning to "I could have lined this up in twenty minutes yesterday!"
>
> *Kevin Healy, 11 years' experience*

Create Instructional Resources Quickly

One of the most exciting, and labor-intensive responsibilities that any teacher has is the creation of instructional materials. Although this is often one of the most pleasant teacher tasks, it can also be time-consuming, especially for novice teachers. When you create instructional materials, focus on the big picture of what you are trying to accomplish instead of getting bogged down in the details. To save valuable time while you work on this task, try some of these quick tips:

- Follow the advice you have probably heard already: don't reinvent the wheel. Adapt handouts and other materials prepared by others: colleagues in your building, in your district, or online.

- Use generative AI to brainstorm lesson ideas and draft instructional materials for you to review and revise for accuracy and your purpose.

- Although you want instructional materials to be as user-friendly and error-free as possible, you will soon find that you will tweak most of the materials you create before using them again. With that in mind, try not to be a perfectionist.

- Many teachers find it especially tempting to spend too much time designing presentations in Google Slides, PowerPoint, Canva, or Prezi to name a few. It's hard to resist searching too long for the perfect graphic or font. However, the time spent designing a presentation that is already serviceable may not be time well spent. Be conscious of when perfect is the enemy of good enough.

- As with all other facets of time management, it's important to be aware of how you are spending your time when you create instructional materials. Set a timer and try to stick to your plan or make a conscious choice to change the plan.

Stay on Top of the Paperwork

One of the best ways to stay on top of paperwork is to generate as little actual paper as possible. Of course, depending on the developmental needs of students, their access to devices, and your instructional goals, you will determine when paper is necessary and how much of it. When possible, explore paperless options.

One of the most stressful aspects of a teaching career is the pressure caused by a heavy paperwork load. Like many other professionals, teachers must successfully manage an ever-growing quantity of documents—both electronic and paper. In the last few decades, the amount of paperwork for all educators has multiplied because of changing initiatives, legal responsibilities, and the ease of electronic communication.

From student papers to the proliferation of texts, emails, notifications, directives, purchase orders, letters, forms, and publications, a teacher receives an overwhelming amount of digital and paper communication daily. You can learn to stay ahead of paperwork by creating your own systems for managing those documents, whether they are in digital or paper format.

Each teacher's organizational scheme is as unique as that teacher, but successful schemes are those that are easy to set up, simple to maintain, and logical enough to make it easy to find the documents that you need quickly. An organized document management plan will allow you to store materials that you do not need quick access to as well as to easily find the ones that you do need. Spending the time to create a commonsense system of managing your professional documents is well worth the effort because it will prevent the frustration of time wasted searching for a misplaced document.

In the information that follows, you will learn about the various documents you will have to manage, how to organize both paper and electronic files, how to organize documents related to student information, and how to grade student work efficiently.

Professional Documents You Need to Manage

Although each teacher will have specific paperwork responsibilities, there are some important documents that all teachers have in common. To create a system for organizing them for quick access, it is important to start with an idea of the documents that you will have to work with all year. Here, in brief, are some of the documents that you will have to manage efficiently:

Grading

- Your grade book
- Student assignments to be graded
- Graded student assignments
- Sample student work to assess long-term progress

Professional Business

- Your teaching portfolio items
- Your faculty handbook
- Your families or caregivers conference notes and log
- Teachers' meeting notes
- Peer observations of you and the observations you make of others
- Your evaluation
- Your reflections
- Complimentary notes from families, caregivers, students, or colleagues

Instructional Materials

- State and district curriculum guidelines
- Unit plans
- Daily plans
- Syllabi for each grading period
- Professional Learning Community (PLC) notes
- Collaborative team meeting notes
- Community contacts for guest speakers and field experiences

- Reference materials for future lessons
- Strategies and activities to incorporate into lessons
- Ideas for motivating students
- Extra handouts for students
- Makeup work for students
- Tests, quizzes, and other assessments
- Handouts for the current unit of study
- Exit or entrance slips and topics

Classroom Routines and Management

- Seating charts
- Student rosters
- Information related to class agreements, restorative practices, and logical consequences
- Information about behavior issues, such as incident reports or anecdotal notes
- Templates for routine business, such as hall passes, lunch counts, or notes home
- Reward or certificate templates
- Bulletin board ideas or materials

Student Information

- Student contact information
- Student inventories
- Student assessment data
- Attendance data
- Contact logs for meetings and phone calls
- Important emails from families and caregivers

Confidential Documents to Be Kept in a Secure Location

- Individual Education Plan (IEP) documents and notes
- 504 Plan documents and notes
- Individual Learning Plans (ILP) documents and notes for English Language Learners
- Personal Education Plans (PEP) documents
- Behavior Plans
- Mandatory reporting forms and notes
- All documents related to student health issues
- Student mental health and discipline referral notes
- Student Study Team/Child Study Team notes

What to Keep and What to Discard

Although most records are stored electronically, some of these documents will be in paper format. The types of documents and records teachers need to manage will vary depending on the grades they teach, but you can adapt these lists to help you make decisions about the materials you keep.

RECORDS TO KEEP UNTIL THE START OF THE NEXT SCHOOL YEAR

These records, whether electronic or paper, are the ones that you should store for future reference. Some teachers have even been asked to produce such documents as student work, attendance records, and family or caregiver contact logs to justify an end-of-course grade.

- Community contacts for guest speakers and field experiences
- Grades for each grading period as well as the end of the year
- Attendance records
- Family or caregiver contact logs
- Artifacts: exemplars and scoring guides to serve as anchors and inspire students
- Accident reports
- Student behavior contracts and discipline referrals
- Signed documents from families or caregivers such as progress reports, if you send notes hope for home adults to sign
- Curriculum guidelines in your state and local districts
- Course calendars and syllabi
- Teacher created resources, assessments, and answer keys
- Lesson plans (Annotated unit plans will be particularly useful when you begin to plan new units in the future.)
- Formal evaluation records, including observation notes and annual evaluations
- Personal reflections
- Teaching portfolio (see Section One) and the items to be included in it
- Positive notes from students, families, caregivers, or colleagues
- Documents or communication about students who require special consideration such as students who experience disabilities

DOCUMENTS YOU CAN SAFELY DISCARD AT THE END OF EACH SEMESTER

These records, whether electronic or paper, are generally ones that you will not need in the future. Although they may have served a valuable purpose during the semester, saving too many documents will only add clutter to your workspace and computer, making them difficult to manage.

- Meeting notes or reminders that you have already acted on.
- Routine emails about school business or daily tasks.
- Files that you no longer find relevant for lesson planning.
- Student classwork or assignments, except an anchor example or two.

Organizing Document Storage

You will need to set up an electronic and paper filing system for the paperwork you must work with each day. If you have a system in place before the term begins, you will save yourself much frustration and time later. Setting up paper document storage is not a difficult task, but it does require planning and effort.

Step One: Request Supplies
- Filing cabinet, preferably locking
- Wire file frames (if necessary)
- Hanging files
- File folders
- Labels
- Markers

Step Two: Select Categories for Each Drawer
- Confidential Files
- General Business
- Instructional Materials

Step Three: Label Everything Clearly
- Outside of the drawers
- Each file folder

Stagger the tabbed labels on hanging files and the file folders within them so that you can see what is in the file drawer at a glance.

Managing Digital File Storage

Similar to organizing paper files, creating an intentional system for managing your electronic files can save you hours of frustration searching for misplaced, mislabeled, or lost documents. With just a bit of planning, you can design a scheme for managing your electronic files so that they are quick and easy to find. Here's how:

- Use a consistent method for naming files that will make it easy to search for and easy to understand what each file contains without having to open it. Many teachers find that it is helpful also to include a date in the file name. For example, "Ch 2 Quiz 2018" is an excellent title, whereas "Ch 2" is not. Be sure that the names you give files are professional—just in case you need to share them with a colleague.

- Group like things together in folders. For example, place all links related to a unit of study in a folder labeled in such a way that you can quickly find the resources you need. Try to be as specific as possible when you name a folder.

- Create subfolders inside the bigger folders that you have for documents. For example, for a unit on *Rainforests,* the main folder could be labeled *Rainforests.* The subfolders would have such topics as "Plants & Animals," "Indigenous Communities," "Importance of Rainforests," "Threats and Solutions," "Formative Assessments," "Enrichment Activities," "Reading Questions," and so on. Try not to have layers of subfolders. A main folder with several subfolders inside is much easier to search than subfolders stored in subfolders inside a main folder.

- Place documents in folders as you work on them. If you create folders for each unit at the start of that unit and file things promptly, you will find it easy to avoid having to sort through unorganized files.

- Be selective about what you save electronically, just as you would be with paper copies. Periodically purge your folders of files that you no longer find useful. Clutter just makes it difficult to find files when you need them.

RESOURCES FOR STORING DIGITAL DOCUMENTS

Because it's important not to lose your work, you should back up your files either on an external hard drive or on a cloud backup service. Your school district will probably have a solution for this but be sure to ask for the details. You can also use portable memory storage devices, such as flash drives, or explore keeping digital files stored in the cloud as well. There are several options for securely saving digital work in the cloud. Here are some of the most common ones:

- Dropbox (dropbox.com)
- Evernote (evernote.com)
- Google Drive (google.com/drive)
- BackBlaze (backblaze.com)
- Microsoft One Drive (microsoft.com/en-us/microsoft-365/onedrive/online-cloud-storage)

How to Organize and Manage Student Information

In addition to the many other documents you will store, the information about your students that comes to you from a variety of sources throughout the term is also something you must organize. Although there are numerous ways to manage this information, many teachers have found that the following simple approach works well because it is easy to maintain:

Paper Documents

Step One: Set aside space in a lockable desk or file drawer.

Step Two: Create a folder for each student and arrange the folders alphabetically.

Step Three: Promptly file every piece of information you receive about a student. Date each item. Place new papers behind other items in a file folder so you don't have to shuffle through all of them to find one. If you don't have a dedicated folder ready, avoid putting papers into messy piles and use an in-box instead.

Electronic Documents

Follow the same general procedure for electronic documents as for paper ones. Create an electronic folder for each student as well. Store all documents relating to each student in the appropriate folder.

Develop a Consistent Workflow for Student Assignments

Depending on your class size or total student load in middle and high school, when students turn in their work, the sheer number of assignments can make it difficult to keep them organized. To streamline the way you manage student assignments, establish a consistent work flow for them (see Figure 2.1). Here is one that works for many teachers:

Paper System

Step One: Have students place papers in a designated area, such as a bin or a tray. If you provide a highlighter near where students are to turn in their work, they can

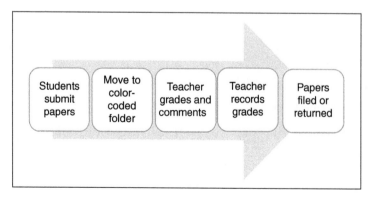

Figure 2.1 Consistent workflow.

highlight their names before submitting them. This will eliminate the problem of no-name papers.

Step Two: Move them to a color-coded folder for each subject or class period to be graded. Color coding will make it easier to keep them organized.

Step Three: Grade them.

Step Four: Record the grades.

Step Five: Return them to students.

Electronic System

This will vary depending on the learning management system and online portal you use for students submitting work. Regardless of the applications you use, make sure there is a streamlined system for naming files, submitting assignments, providing timely feedback, and recording grades.

Grading Student Work

Providing timely feedback is vital to student success. It can also be very time-consuming and stressful. Always keep in mind that your goal in grading papers is to improve student learning. As you grade, ask yourself, "What can I do to help this student?" This will help you work toward a solution to the lack of understanding that caused the errors.

Successfully learning to grade student work quickly and efficiently so that they receive timely feedback that accelerates learning and you can have the work-life balance that you need takes time, planning, and practice. In the list that follows, you will find several suggestions that you can adjust to meet the needs of your grade level and teaching practice. Although not all of them may work for your classroom, try to adapt as many as you can so that you do not have to spend hours and hours grading student work.

> "Maintain a state of calm and strive for excellence, acknowledging that perfection is an unattainable ideal."
>
> *Marsha Benjamin Moyer, CEO MBM ImPAC,*
> *30+ years' experience*

How to Grade Papers Quickly and Well

Learning to manage your responsibilities regarding grading papers efficiently will allow you to give your students the productive and timely feedback that they need to learn. The strategies will vary based on your grade level, learning goals, and whether the student work is in paper or digital format. Here are some tips:

- Determine how many graded assignments are necessary for students to demonstrate their learning and where feedback from you is required versus self-assessment or peer feedback.

- Use digital tools with auto-grading features for quick checks for understanding and objective summative assessments.

- If you have a teaching partner, consider assessing student work together as you will calibrate expectations and have more fun in the process.

- Stagger due dates if you teach more than one class or have lots of papers coming in from various assignments. If possible, try to consider student learning and your own work schedule before setting a final due date for longer assignments, such as projects and essays.

- When you make assignments with more than one part, consider grading each part separately. For example, instead of grading all the parts of an essay at once, have students turn in their outlines to be graded first. Then evaluate each student's rough draft and offer suggestions before grading the final essay.

- Be prepared when you have papers to grade: have a quiet workplace, charge your devices, have marking pens, rubrics, and answer keys ready.

- Remove as many distractions as possible when you begin grading. Turn off social media notifications and other distractions. Close your classroom door or move to a quiet place to work.

- Do not try to grade stacks and stacks of papers in one sitting. Divide the work into smaller batches and tackle these in a systematic manner. Grading in focused bursts of concentrated effort with breaks in between is an efficient way to grade quickly.

- If you are grading at home, try to use your biological clock to grade when you are most alert.

- Reward yourself when you have finished grading a set of papers. This will encourage you to stay focused.

- Make sure that the directions for each assignment are very clear. (See Section Four for help with this.) Explicit directions will eliminate many student errors.

- Before students submit their assignments, ask them to trade papers and review one another's work. A quick edit from a classmate could eliminate many of the less significant errors, such as typos.

- Create very specific checklists or rubrics that guide students as they complete assignments. This allows students to know what they must do to succeed.

- If you are not sure that your grading policies and techniques are as useful as you would like them to be, ask a mentor to review a paper or two with you before you grade an entire set.

- Don't grade everything your students produce. Some teachers find it easier to grade only part of an assignment—spot-checking for patterns of strengths and errors. Still others ask students to submit an example of their best work in a series of assignments. Formative assessments should not be graded at all.

- It is far better to focus on a few skills in each assignment rather than on every mistake that students make. Focused grading will allow you to concentrate on what's important and to determine the areas of strengths and weaknesses in student mastery.

- Don't cover papers with comments—one of the easiest mistakes to make. Instead, focus on a blend of positive comments and comments about what needs improvement. Limit yourself to three or four comments, if possible. If you need to make more comments, consider holding a conference with the student instead.

- Don't focus only on the errors that your students have made. Use a highlighter to point out the parts of their assignments that they did particularly well. Students not only appreciate the kindness in this action, but also learn a great deal from your positive comments.

- Create a method of correcting student work that is simple for your students to understand and then use it consistently. Using the same proofreading marks on every assignment, for example, will make it easy for students to understand their mistakes. Post these marks online and on the board and make sure each student has a copy.

- If using paper quizzes, grade the same page on every quiz or test in the stack before moving on to the next page.

- Make the answer sheets that your students use for quizzes and tests easy to grade. Allow plenty of room for students to write so that you can read their responses quickly.

- It's often productive to review several papers before starting the grading process to get a basic idea of the general strengths and weaknesses of the work. This could save you time later as you decide what you will need to reteach.

Grading Electronic Work

Many teachers find that it is easier, more efficient, and quicker to grade electronic work than paper submissions. Many digital tools have auto-grading features and it is easier to make meaningful comments electronically instead of having to rewrite them by hand over and over.

Another advantage of grading electronically is that you do not have to carry stacks of work home. Instead, you can grade anywhere you have a device. Another advantage is that you can grade student work in collaboration with a colleague, such as a co-teacher, with ease. Although you will want to follow the same general policies for grading electronic work as you do for paper submissions, there are some specific differences to consider. When grading electronic work, take care to:

- Teach students the file-labeling protocol that they should use to label their work. It is crucial for students to make sure that their names appear on the files so that you do not have to search for them.

- Arrange to work with a teacher buddy or two, especially at first, to share tips and techniques for maximum ease of grading and efficiency.

- Be explicit about the directions for submission deadlines. Because the work can be submitted outside school hours, make sure that students know exactly when it is due. Be clear about what constitutes late work.

● Spend plenty of time making sure students know how to submit their work. Arrange for a few practice submissions in advance of the first assignment due date. This will make it easier for students to submit their work with confidence.

Frequently Used Documents: Folder or Binder

One of the most useful professional tools that you can have is a simple collection of the documents that you use most often. Putting these documents in a single folder on your computer desktop or in a sturdy three-ring binder makes them immediately accessible.

When you set up your frequently used documents folder or binder, your purpose is to have the documents that you use every day in a convenient place. Although every teacher will have unique needs based on their teaching situation, there are some items that are indispensable to all teachers. Here is a list of some of those frequently used documents:

● Class rosters

● Seating charts

● Your professional goals

● Your daily to-do lists

● Meeting notes

● A school year calendar

● An outline of the instructional plan for the year, semester, or grading period

● Unit plans

● Daily lesson plans

● A list of frequently used comments and proofreading marks

● Grading reminders, such as due dates or grading scales

● A copy of Bloom's Taxonomy or Webb's Depth of Knowledge Framework

● Lists of instructional activities that energize lessons

● Lists of activities to use at the start and end of class as well as during transitions

● A list of ideas for integrating technology into instruction

● A list of formative assessment ideas

● A list of classroom chores for students to manage

Questions to Discuss with Colleagues

Sharing ideas with colleagues is a helpful way to devise solutions to some of the problems that you must manage successfully at school. Here you will find several topics to open discussions with colleagues about successful instructional practices:

1. In order to maximize how efficiently you use your planning period each day. What can you do to ensure that you don't waste valuable time?

2. You are spending long hours each weekend trying to get caught up on grading student work. How can you become more efficient at how you manage grading?

3. A teacher's organization systems and productivity strategies also support students in the learning process. To what extent are your systems and strategies supporting student learning? In what ways are they creating barriers to student learning?

4. What helps teachers to be productive at school? How can you identify these practices and implement them yourself?

5. What are your five most important daily tasks at school? Are you managing them as efficiently as possible? If not, what can you do to improve the way that you manage them?

Topics to Discuss with a Mentor

Although the topics that new teachers need to discuss with a mentor vary from teacher to teacher and from school to school, there are some that most first-year teachers should be comfortable discussing with a mentor or a trusted colleague. You should ask your mentor about these topics from this section:

- Suggestions for creating instructional materials quickly and efficiently
- How to obtain the basic supplies you need
- Suggestions for obtaining the extra materials and supplies that you would like for your classroom
- Suggestions for how to be as productive and well organized as possible
- Suggestions for managing the flow of documents that you are responsible for

Reflection Questions to Guide Your Thinking

1. What skills do you currently possess when it comes to being an efficient teacher? How can you capitalize on your strengths, and how can you overcome your weaknesses?

2. What supplies do you and your students still need for the rest of the term? What can you do to make sure that you will have everything? Who can help you with this?

3. How organized is your classroom at this point in the school term? What do you still need to accomplish? How can your colleagues help you?

4. Organizing your file cabinet and your electronic files is a necessary chore that you will benefit from all year. What techniques have you employed to make sure your system is efficient and easy to use?

5. What are you most confident about regarding your document management? Are you confident that you will be able to successfully manage the documents that you will need to maintain all year? What do you need to adjust to be as efficient as possible?

SECTION THREE

Collaborate with Colleagues

Collaborating with colleagues in your school community and in your broader professional network is vital for your students' learning, your success as a teacher, and your longevity in the profession. Schools, even small ones, are complex organizations with an ever-changing mixture of administrative assistants, custodians, nurses, counselors, coaches, paraprofessionals, administrators, social workers, counselors, as well as teachers, students, and students' families. Because of this complexity and the enormous power of collaboration, teachers are expected to work effectively with all members of their school community, whether that collaboration is something as simple as an informal sharing of ideas in the hallway or working together on structured teams.

Just what does it take to collaborate well with others? In general, teachers who collaborate effectively treat others with respect, behave as professionals, focus on what is good for the students, and have a positive and approachable demeanor. They view themselves as belonging to a network of other supportive professionals who comprise the larger school and education community and who act intentionally with high levels of integrity.

One of the biggest challenges facing new teachers is learning how to manage the responsibilities expected of collaborative teams as well as learning how to establish themselves as respected faculty members. In this section, you will learn how you can be a well-regarded member of the wider school community as well as how to be an effective member of a collaborative team.

Establish Your Professional Reputation

Amid trying to set up a classroom, getting to know students, and figuring out how to plan engaging instruction, it's easy to overlook the importance of something as nebulous as establishing a professional reputation. Just as you plan lessons with intentionality, bring that same sense of purpose to establishing yourself in the education profession. Cultivating a reputation as a caring, effective, and capable educator will make it easier to work well with your colleagues and to become the teacher you want to be. One of the best ways to begin to establish your reputation is to consider how you want students, colleagues, administrators, and families to describe you. What do you want to be known for?

No matter where you teach, there are some universal qualities for effective educators that you can strive to meet. These qualities include characteristics of effective teammates as well as the ability to move through challenges and the inevitable conflict that arises when you form a new team. Use Teacher Template 3.1 to examine the extent to which you embody these qualities. The results can then guide your efforts to become a well-respected professional.

Qualities of Effective Team Members

Rate how often you demonstrate the qualities in this list by rating yourself on a scale of 1 to 3. 1 = rarely 2 = sometimes 3 = always

At this point in my education career, I:

1. _____ Am courteous and collaborative
2. _____ Share my ideas, knowledge, and expertise with colleagues
3. _____ Act with integrity
4. _____ Encourage and support my colleagues
5. _____ Am positive, optimistic, and approachable
6. _____ Ask for help when necessary
7. _____ Offer to help others
8. _____ Listen actively when colleagues are speaking
9. _____ Follow through on my commitments
10. _____ See problems as opportunities and take a problem-solving approach
11. _____ Respect others' time and start and end meetings on time
12. _____ Am curious; I keep an open mind, and consider new ideas
13. _____ Effectively engage in and resolve conflicts
14. _____ Am willing to do my share of extra duties
15. _____ Communicate openly and clearly
16. _____ Maintain confidentiality
17. _____ Admit when I'm not sure of something
18. _____ Have a sense of humor and am fun to be around
19. _____ Am open to giving and receiving positive and constructive feedback
20. _____ Keep improving my teaching skills

Finding Your Way in Your New School Community

As a new teacher, it's important that you collect your fresh impressions of the school. Soon you will be an integral part of the school community and may not remember those things that make the school special or those things that could make the school better. As you gain experience and engage in school improvement efforts, your perspective and voice will be important. Establishing your reputation as an effective and inspiring educator will allow your ideas to be heard and taken seriously.

As a teacher, you are often expected to uphold the values of your community. It's important in the interview process to learn about the school community's values to make sure they align with your own. In a healthy work environment, you can bring your whole self to work and engage in the bold mission of educating youth. This way you are set up to succeed and collaboration with your colleagues as well as with the families and caregivers of your students will be much easier. You will find yourself working in a supportive environment with others who value your contributions and who trust your judgment.

It's also important to keep your commitments at school. Because this is so important, be very careful not to make commitments you cannot keep, and communicate early if you need additional support to accomplish them. You may find that it is so tempting to agree to sponsor a club or chaperone a field trip or take on other extra duties that you find yourself overcommitted. Take your time. Say no when necessary and ease into your new responsibilities.

Finally, do not share confidential information about students when you are away from school. When you do this, you violate their privacy and your professional ethics. Take special care not to talk about school matters in public spaces, like the checkout line in the grocery store. You never know who may overhear you.

Fifteen Quick Tips for Making a Good Impression at School

In addition to the more general things that you can do to establish a strong reputation at your new school, there are some very specific things that you can do immediately that will make a good impression on your colleagues:

1. Be visible. Be in the hall between classes. Stay after school. Be a recognizable figure around school.

2. Be dependable. Show up on time for meetings and be prepared to take notes. Pick up trash you find in the hall. Clean up after yourself.

3. Listen actively. Ask questions and be genuinely curious about the answers. You will not only will make a good impression, but also will learn a great deal.

4. Be courteous to all. Smile. Have a friendly greeting for everyone you meet.

5. Ask for help. No one expects anyone, especially a new teacher, to know everything. Take advantage of that goodwill and ask questions.

6. Dress the part. Come to school dressed with the same degree of formality as everyone else. Your appearance should signify that you are a professional with a serious approach to your responsibilities.

7. Be on time. Especially don't be late to class or to a duty assignment where someone will have to give up personal time to cover for you. Be respectful of your colleagues' time.

8. Keep your classroom tidy. Although it does not have to be Pinterest perfect, your classroom should reflect your concern for making a safe and productive learning environment for your students.

9. Follow school rules and procedures. Few things will frustrate your colleagues more quickly than if you decide not to abide by the same rules or procedures that govern everyone else in the building.

10. Be positive, without being toxically so. Celebrate what's going well and acknowledge the challenges. A positive, authentic, and approachable attitude will help you and your colleagues connect.

11. Be serious about your work. Teaching is serious business. Even though you want to have fun with students and enjoy the school day, be sure to let others know that you take the responsibilities of your work seriously.

12. Help out. As a new teacher, you have skills that your more experienced colleagues may not. Use your strengths to make a positive difference for your colleagues.

13. Project confidence. Stay calm. Act as if you can succeed and soon you will.

14. Put in the time and effort to plan engaging instruction. When it becomes evident that your students are learning and growing, and that you are prepared for every class, your colleagues will respect your work.

> "A simple suggestion: don't stay in your room during lunch. Eat in a common area so that you get to know your colleagues. They are your greatest resource."
>
> *Michael A. Barrs, 32 years' experience*

15. Do your best to maintain an orderly classroom. When your colleagues pass your classroom, they will be impressed if they see students engaged in learning.

When Personal and Professional Lives Collide: Social Media

Few things can ruin a teacher's professional reputation and affect the way your colleagues regard you more quickly than inappropriate content on a social media site. Teachers have lost their jobs for inappropriate posts, photos, comments, or even tags that followed them into their professional lives. Teachers absolutely have a right to free speech and a right to a private life. However, the nature of social media tends to blur the lines between private and public life. Because of this, it is worthwhile to intentionally set boundaries to protect your professional reputation from damaging personal online content. Here are some tips for making sure that your social media presence will not cause problems:

- You cannot be too cautious about your social media activity and the regulations that govern it. Familiarize yourself with your school district's guidelines for social media and take care to follow them carefully.

- Keep the distinction between your personal accounts and your professional ones very clear. Do not allow students or their families and caregivers to friend or follow you on a personal account.

- Many teachers have social media accounts for professional use only. Use this type of account for your professional posts instead of a personal one.

- Maintain healthy boundaries with students. If you do communicate with students online, be sure to use school accounts instead of personal ones and communicate about school business.

- Be careful about what you say to students online, and be clear about the tone and subjects of communication that you find acceptable from them in return. Use this as a quick guide: if content would be inappropriate in a classroom setting, it is also inappropriate online.

- Avoid browsing students' accounts, even when you have access to them. For example, if students are expected to comment on a school-based social media post for homework, don't scrutinize your students' other posts or follow links that they may have posted.

- If you have a website or blog or other shared sites yourself, be aware that you are personally responsible for the content you produce.

- Be careful to check the privacy settings on all your social media sites periodically to make sure that they are truly private.

- Protect student privacy. Learn your school/district's policy about posting photos of students or student work, captioning photos, and so on.

- Be very careful about the groups that you join. Make sure that each one is appropriate for an education professional to join.

- Avoid complaining about your job, your school, or your colleagues online. If you feel the need to complain, talk to a trusted friend, mentor, or colleague in person.

- Protect your reputation and avoid posts, references, and photos that could present you in an unfavorable way, such as: intoxication, profanity, drug use, gang activity, gambling, or any illegal activity. Even private posts may not remain private online.

- Consider on which profiles it's appropriate to identify your place of employment. You may not want to give specifics about your school. If you must, give general information such as "middle school math teacher."

- Never use your school's location in a geo tag.

- Monitor your own online presence carefully. Be aware when someone posts content about you by setting up a Google Alert (google.com/alerts) for references to your name online.

- Ask your friends to be mindful of any unflattering or inappropriate photo in which you may be tagged. Remove any that you can find yourself.

The Surprising Importance of Good Attendance

Life happens and it's not always possible to be at work. It's vital that educators have paid time away. It's also true that while substitutes work hard to implement lessons, learning is diminished when teachers are absent. You matter and your absences may negatively affect your students and your colleagues.

Your colleagues may have to give up a planning period to cover for you or help the substitute teacher manage your students' behavior. To work well with everyone in your school, enhance your professional reputation, and reduce the negative impacts of your absence, maintain strong attendance and be prepared for a time when you may have to miss school.

What to Do When You Have to Miss School

Although you should not attend school if you are ill, there are plenty of times when you may be tempted to miss a day of school when you are not really sick, just as when you were a student yourself. Be careful not to abuse your district's leave policy. If nothing else, you can never be sure when you will need to use the sick days you should have saved. A serious illness or an accident can erode years of banked leave time. Try to save those days for when you really need them.

There are several actions that you can take to mitigate the negative effects of your absence: inform the right people, leave good lesson plans, and provide essential information for your substitute.

INFORM THE RIGHT PEOPLE

- Follow your school/district's protocol for reporting an absence and arranging a substitute.
- Contact the people who are responsible for finding a substitute teacher for you. Try to do this as quickly as you can so that they can hire the most competent sub for you.
- Contact a colleague and ask for assistance. Ask that person to look in on your class during the day and to make sure the substitute knows what to do.
- Contact an administrator. Ask the administrator to look in on your classes from time to time throughout the day.
- If you think your students will not take advantage of the situation, you should tell them when you are going to be out. Ask for their cooperation and discuss your expectations of how they welcome a guest teacher. Stress the importance of maintaining the daily routine, even when you are not there.
- Developing relationships with substitute teachers you respect may allow you to request them to cover your absences.

LEAVE GOOD LESSON PLANS

- You should not ask a substitute teacher to interpret lesson plans from your plan book. Instead, give a class-by-class description of what you want your students to do.

- Let your students know that they are not just doing busywork, but that it has an instructional purpose. Make sure they know that the sub will collect the work at the end of class.

- If the work involves handouts, photocopy them in advance and label them so that the substitute can find them quickly.

- A common complaint that substitute teachers have is that teachers do not leave enough work for students to do. You should plan more work for your students than you would expect them to do if you were there. In addition, it would be helpful to provide a list of five to ten activities that students can choose from if they finish their work early.

PROVIDE ESSENTIAL INFORMATION FOR YOUR SUBSTITUTE

Learn your school/district's protocol for substitutes to log into student information systems and learning management systems. If they cannot access critical systems, then in addition to lesson plans, you should leave a well-organized, three-ring binder of information for your sub. Because most of this information is not as apt to change as your daily plans, you can make up this folder early in the year and update it as often as necessary. Your sub binder should include the following items:

- Detailed lesson plans specifically designed for a substitute teacher to follow
- An updated seating chart (preferably with photos) for each class
- An up-to-date class roster
- Attendance procedures that you want your sub to follow
- Your daily schedule
- The names of dependable student helpers
- The names and room numbers of helpful colleagues
- A notepad and pen for notes to you about the day
- Class agreements, routines, and procedures
- Where to find supplies
- A map of the school
- Your email address or phone number
- Fire drill and other emergency information
- Information about students with learning differences or medical issues
- Blank referral forms just in case the substitute encounters a serious student issue
- Extra work for students to do if they finish everything else

Collaborate Successfully with the Support Staff

As a new teacher, you will have to learn many new faces and names as quickly as possible. A school community is often hierarchical in its structure and is composed of many different people in many different roles. Each of them deserves your cooperation and respect. Here is a brief list of just some of the actions that you can take right away to treat all staff members as colleagues:

- Develop professional relationships with other staff members. Learn the roles that various people play in your school and how they contribute to the overall mission. By doing this, you will be able to be supportive when they need your help.

"You will find some of your best allies and closest friends at school. Surround yourself with positive people, but don't write off anyone. If you are open to it, you can learn something helpful from every single colleague to add to your teacher toolbox. And become friends with the custodians and the secretaries. My mom taught for thirty years, and this was her best advice to me. Give them gifts. Say thank you. Mean it. They work hard to make the school a better place and are often underappreciated. And they can be wonderful allies."

Jennifer Burns, 13 years' experience

- Learn the names of the support personnel in your school as quickly as possible. Greet each by name when you meet. Treat each person in the building with the same courtesy that you would like to receive.

- Encourage your students to respect the work of support personnel by modeling that respect yourself. Speak courteously to the paraprofessionals, cafeteria, clerical, and custodial workers as well as to other staff. Make sure that your students leave their work areas clean. Let them see you picking up trash in the hall.

- Respect your colleagues' time, equipment, and other resources. For example, if the school office manager asks you for information by a particular date, make sure you meet their deadline.

Follow the Chain of Command

To work well with your supervisors and other staff members, you must know and follow the chain of command at your school. Few things annoy other employees as much as a person who does not have enough respect for others to follow the chain of command when things are not going well.

For example, if you have requested certain repairs to your classroom and these repairs have not been made, you may be tempted to speak to the principal about this problem. If you do this instead of speaking with the custodian in charge of your classroom, you may have been unfair to that person. There may be a good reason for the incomplete repairs. As a rule of thumb, if you need additional assistance in solving a problem, it is a good idea to talk with a mentor instead of ignoring the chain of command.

Collaborate Successfully with Administrators

The supervisory staff in your school district and in your school building depend on all employees to make things run smoothly. Although it is only natural that there will be problems, it is up to you to work well with your supervisors. Having a positive relationship with the administrators at your school means that you will be less stressed, more productive, and supported at work.

There is a specific hierarchy of supervision at any school. It is likely that you report to a department head, lead teacher, or grade-level leader who serves as a liaison between staff members and administrators. Assistant principals make up the next level. At the top of the hierarchy in your school is the principal, who is the instructional leader of your building. At the district level, your supervisors may differ in their titles, but will include curriculum coordinators and assistant superintendents who report to their supervisor, the superintendent of schools. The hierarchy does not end there. The school board supervises all employees, including the superintendent.

If you want to establish productive relationships with your supervisors, you should take positive action. Don't hope that no one will notice you because you are a first-year teacher. In fact, you are particularly noticeable just because you are a first-year teacher. Here are some suggestions to establish a positive working relationship with your supervisors:

- Administrators used to be teachers; they are educators committed to the success of students, faculty, and support staff. Get to know about their career path and areas of expertise.

- Behave in a professional manner. In addition, if you maintain a solid reputation, it is easier for them to support you when you make mistakes.

- Take the time to familiarize yourself with the information in your faculty manual or handbook. This will help you avoid mistakes that may lead to negative interactions with your supervisors.

- Develop empathy for administrators. Remember that administrators are responsible for the entire school.

- Think before you voice public criticism. Accept the fact that although you are not always going to agree with the decisions and actions of the administrators with whom you work, public criticism of their actions might seriously damage your professional reputation.

- Don't threaten to send your students to the office instead of resolving the problem through other more successful methods of discipline. Maintain control of your classroom so that when you send a student out of class, the action will have meaning for students as well as for administrators.

- Remember to be professional in your dealings with administrators. Always present a calm and competent image.

- When you make a mistake, be truthful in discussing it with your supervisors. If you can do this before they find out the bad news from someone else, you should do so. Don't ever try to hide problems. Ask for help instead.

- Be positive. Sharing good news or taking a positive stance when problems occur will make it easier for an administrator to help you when you really need it. Constant complaints eventually fall on deaf ears.

- Share your successes with your supervisors. Help them create positive public relations for your school by letting them know about noteworthy news pertaining to your students.

Learn How to Collaborate as a Member of a Team

Even at the very start of your career, you can expect to belong to several different types of collaborative teams, such as vertical teams, grade-level teams, department committees, and procedure or policymaking groups—each one with its own purpose. This purpose can cover a wide range of activities—from solving problems or determining best practices to something as broad as sharing new information.

In the pages that follow, you can learn some of the skills, attitudes, and qualities that you need to develop to become a good team member as well as the behaviors that will help you get the most out of meetings and work through potential conflicts with team members.

Professional Behavior during Meetings

Meetings are important for creating community, sharing information, gathering input, and making decisions. Since time is a precious resource, it's important to have norms about how meetings are conducted. This will make the most of the time spent in meetings and ensure it strengthens school culture rather than eroding it.

Seldom will you have a week without at least one meeting. At particularly busy times of the term, you will find daily conferences are the norm. With so much of your time spent in various types of meetings, it is only sensible to make sure that your behavior is such that you will not only present yourself as a competent member of the team, but also that your collaboration skills are productive and professional. Here is a list of the behaviors that will make it easier for you to work well with your colleagues:

- Refrain from side talking. Although it is tempting to chat with someone sitting nearby, doing so will make it harder for you (and the people around you) to listen to the person leading the meeting.

- Focus on the business at hand during meetings. You will probably see colleagues grading papers, checking email, or focusing on something other than the agenda. Try not to be one of them. Instead, pay attention. Take notes. Spend the time listening and learning and not being distracted.

- Pay attention. Unless the meeting is one that requires you to work on a device, it is courteous to silence your phone, put the lid down on a laptop, and stop using a tablet. If you are taking notes on a device, make it clear that's what you're doing.

- Be on time. Set reminders to make sure that you know when and where a meeting is so that you arrive on time.

- Be prepared. If you were directed to complete a reading or prepare a document before the meeting, do so. Being unprepared for a meeting is a waste of everyone's time.

- Take notes. Although you should not be so intent on capturing every word that you miss the big ideas in a meeting, taking notes will help you stay focused and allow you to take in the content under discussion.

- Be respectful of a group leader or speaker. Be engaged. Be courteous. Be especially careful to allow speakers to finish before you respond.

- Be an active listener as you consider others' viewpoints.

- Seek clarification during meetings if you are not sure of what has been said. Ask clarifying questions to avoid misunderstanding.

- Be aware of your body language. Make it a point to appear calm and engaged when others are speaking.

- Be a dependable team member. Honor your commitments, and be honest about your abilities, time constraints, and skills.

- Be positive. Negativity makes any undertaking harder to accomplish. Begin by focusing on the accomplishments and strengths of your colleagues.

- Pick your battles. Save your time and energy for the important issues at school instead of worrying about the less important ones.

- Be straightforward (but tactful) with what you say. Talking in generalities or around a subject will confuse and irritate others.

- When you are assigned follow-up activities, complete them in a timely manner.

How to Handle Professional Disagreements

Professional disagreements are part of any school environment where many people are working diligently to help students. Because of the need for productive collaboration, it is important to learn how to handle disagreements well. If you find yourself in a conflict, try these suggestions to resolve it:

- Take the mail to the right mailbox. When you have a conflict with a colleague, set up time to talk with them directly. If you discuss the conflict with others, it should be to get coaching on how to have the conversation directly with the person involved. Email and text can be helpful tools in resolving a conflict to acknowledge a conflict and invite a colleague to a conversation and to follow up a conversation with clear next steps.

- Curriculum issues constitute a frequent area of disagreement. If you are involved in a curriculum dispute, refer to your state's guidelines and standards, and the needs and interests of your students. Be open to new ideas and share your own ideas as well.

- Instead of just reacting to a problem, respond by taking a problem-solving approach and focus on finding a solution. Deciding to resolve a problem, instead of ignoring it or lashing out in anger, is a productive and professional approach.

- Engage with empathy and self-reflection. Consider the issue from your colleague's perspective and consider how you may have contributed to the problem.

- "Disagree and commit" is a business principle that can be more helpful than agreeing to disagree. You might agree to disagree with a colleague over something superficial like the best superhero. When the topic has higher stakes, like the choice of curriculum, you are better served with a "disagree and commit" protocol. Once input is offered and a decision is made, acknowledge it is a "disagree and commit" situation. Rephrase what you are agreeing to and ask for anything you need to move forward without undermining the decision.

- Resist the urge to vent about a conflict with many colleagues. Limit its negative impact by involving as few people as possible.

When the Root of Conflict Is Bias or Discriminatory Behavior

Sometimes the source of conflict is bias or discriminatory behavior by a colleague, student, or community member. Resolving this type of conflict is layered, complex, and vitally important. It's important to interrupt and address bias or discriminatory actions based on characteristics of identity such as: race, religion, national origin, sex (including sexual orientation and gender identity), age, disability, or citizenship.

There are times when bias and discrimination are intentional or systemic and those must be addressed, often with an administrator present. In this brief section we will explore options for responding to unconscious bias and resources where you can delve deeper into the topic. It can be difficult to know how to respond so plan ahead. Here are a few strategies that can help.

If the Behavior Is Directed Toward You

Depending on the circumstances, you will consider many factors, including personal safety, when determining if or how to respond. There are many options for responding in ways that will address the behavior, repair the harm that occurred, educate the offending person, and create a more inclusive workplace. Focusing your response on the behavior and not the person can help.

Based on the circumstances, it may be appropriate to point it out in the moment it happens. "Ouch" is a powerful one-syllable word that can help teachers find their voice in the moment to express hurt and interrupt the behavior. If you are the target of a harmful action, you might choose to say "Ouch," and ask the person what they meant by that. This will give the person an opportunity to reflect and perhaps self-correct.

You may decide not to respond in the moment and instead choose to contact them after the incident saying, "Something you said earlier didn't sit well with me." Extend grace to them and ask them to explain what they meant. If they respond that it was not their intention to hurt you, you may need to explain the difference between intent and impact. "I know you may have meant X but the way I heard it was Y." Hopefully, they will take accountability and apologize, and you will have expressed your truth.

You will determine the right time and place to respond or even if you want to act at all. Practice self-care and reach out to others for support if that is helpful to you.

If You Are a Bystander

Bystanders have a powerful role in disrupting unconscious bias and creating inclusive workplaces. If you witness something, say something. Don't expect the person who is a member of the marginalized group to do the emotional labor to respond. Become an ally and intervene. Plan ahead and think about what you will say and how you would tailor your response to different situations. Similar to the preceding guidance, use *I* statements. Don't speak for anyone else in the space. For example, "Ouch, that made me uncomfortable. What did you mean by that?"

Sometimes an immediate or public response may not be possible. Similar to the guidance above, circle back to the person who made the harmful remarks and talk with them in private, saying, "Something you said earlier didn't sit well with me." Extend grace to them and ask them to explain what they meant. If they respond that it was not their intention to be offensive, you may need to explain the difference between intent and impact. "I know you may have meant X but the way I heard it was Y." Hopefully they will take accountability and apologize to those they harmed. You may also offer educational resources to them so they can raise their own awareness.

Also, it is important to loop back to the person harmed by the incident and check in. Ask them if they are okay and let them know the action you took.

If You Say or Do Something Biased

There is another powerful one syllable word to say if you make a biased or discriminatory comment and need to self-correct. Say, "Oops," take accountability for your error, apologize, and correct it.

If you are the person who said something biased or offensive and someone brings it to your attention, take a breath, try not to be defensive, and ask your colleague to tell you more about how your action affected them. Listen and believe them. Take responsibility and offer a sincere apology. Educate yourself on bias and microaggressions so that you don't repeat the behavior. Make time in the next day or two to follow up and thank them for bringing it to your attention. The goal is to take accountability, learn from the mistake, and create a more inclusive workplace.

Resources for Further Exploration

New York Times, "How to Respond to Microaggressions"

American Psychological Association, "How Bystanders Can Shut Down Microaggressions"

Forbes, "How Do You Intervene When You Witness Racism, Bias, and Bigotry in the Workplace?"

Be Guided by These Helpful Attitudes about Collaboration

Successful collaboration is a crucial part of any school setting. Here are some useful suggestions for being the best team member you can be:

- Establish group norms for the meetings you have regularly. This will help make the best use of everyone's time and expertise.
- Be patient. Feeling frustrated about meetings does not make them go away. Work to make them a better use of your time.
- Everyone on a team has a responsibility to make it an effective team.
- Even though the details are necessary in solving problems collaboratively, it's important to keep the big picture of what you are trying to accomplish in mind.
- Sharing ideas works best when everyone's ideas are considered respectfully.
- An inclusive and encouraging approach is not only pleasant, but also a productive way to work with others.
- Asking respectful and thoughtful questions is a positive way to refine ideas and to stay on track.
- Remember that issues are what's important in a meeting and not petty differences with people.

Questions to Discuss with Colleagues

Sharing ideas with colleagues is a helpful way to devise solutions to some of the problems that you must manage successfully at school. Here, you will find several topics to open discussions with colleagues about successful instructional practices:

1. A parent sent you a request to follow your personal account on social media. You don't want to upset the parent, but want to maintain some professional boundaries. What should you do?

2. A supervisor assigns you an extracurricular task that you can't possibly do well. You want to be regarded as a team player at your new school, but you know you can't adequately fulfill this responsibility. What could you do?

3. You've been assigned to work closely with a teacher whose philosophy of education is very different from yours. In fact, you are uncomfortable working with this colleague. How can you handle this situation in a productive and diplomatic way?

4. You are having such a busy day that you forget to attend your assigned afternoon bus duty. Your duty partners are clearly not pleased about this. What could you do to manage this situation successfully?

5. You find that you must miss a day of school. What can you do to make the day a productive one for the substitute teacher as well as for your students?

Topics to Discuss with a Mentor

Although the topics that new teachers need to discuss with a mentor vary from teacher to teacher and from school to school, there are some that most first-year teachers should be comfortable discussing with a mentor or a trusted colleague. You could ask your mentor about these topics from this section:

- Faculty and staff dress code policies
- District policies for staff social media use
- Procedures for obtaining substitute teachers
- The specific chain of command for your school
- The responsibilities of various administrators and other staff members

Reflection Questions to Guide Your Thinking

1. What skills do you already possess that make it easier for you to work with the various groups at your school? How can you enhance these skills to help you become a valued coworker to those around you?

2. How does learning to work well with supervisors and colleagues affect a teacher's ability to maintain a productive classroom? Identify teachers at your school who work well with their colleagues and supervisors. What can you learn from them?

3. What are your fresh impressions of your school's culture, norms, and practices? What strengths do you see? What are areas for growth? What opportunities might you have to help improve the school culture?

4. How are the various types of meetings at your school different from other meetings that you are used to? How can you make the time you spend in meetings and conferences as productive as possible?

5. Are you comfortable with the way you are currently managing your social media? What steps can you take to ensure your privacy and to maintain a professional image in your school and community?

SECTION FOUR

Become an Inspiring Classroom Leader

Many successful people will readily admit that their achievements have been shaped by an overwhelming passion, such as succeeding in business or winning athletic competitions. Education professionals are like those other successful people in that they are also passion-driven, but educators are not guided by just one passion but by three. A career in education demands that we feel passionate about supporting students as they learn and grow, about the subject matter that we teach, and about the art and science of teaching. The result? A rewarding sense of fulfillment and purpose that few other professions can equal.

As you enter the teacher profession, consider the teachers who made a difference in your life by making sure you knew they cared. Reflect on the teachers who made learning come to life because of their wonder, curiosity, and expertise in a content area. Remember those teachers who utilized creative and effective teaching techniques to inspire learning.

As you work through the material in this section, consider how you are driven by your passions. Have clarity about why you became a teacher. Hold onto your "why" and the fresh enthusiasm you have for a career in education. Staying connected to your purpose and passion for teaching will sustain you in the profession and transform the lives of your students. When you do, you will become one of those memorable educators who make a difference in the lives of students.

Inspiring Classroom Leaders Communicate Their Beliefs

In her brilliant TED Talk, "Every Kid Needs a Champion," Rita Pierson advocated for teachers caring deeply about and holding high expectations for students. She made the case that teachers' beliefs about students affect their success. She created a chant that students repeated until it became a part of them. "I am somebody. I was somebody when

I came here. I will be a better somebody when I leave. I am powerful and I am strong. I deserve the education that I get here. I have things to do, people to impress, and places to go." Check out the video online if you haven't yet seen it.

In her forty-plus years as an educator, Rita Pierson left a legacy of relationships. She was a teacher who never gave up on students. She encouraged teachers everywhere saying, "We are educators. We are born to make a difference." You have enormous power in the lives of your students. In fact, you can elevate the students in your classroom into successful scholars, or you can diminish those same students into academic failures. Your beliefs about your students and your vision for who they can become form a self-fulfilling prophecy.

The self-fulfilling prophecy begins with the expectations you have for your students. These expectations are your unconscious as well as your conscious attitudes about your students' abilities to succeed. You communicate those expectations to your students in many subtle and not so subtle ways—for example, in the language and tone you use, through your body language, by the cognitive demand of assignments you create, in showcasing heroes and leaders across content areas from diverse backgrounds, and through how much time you spend with individual students.

If you believe that the students in your class are capable of solving complex problems, engaging in pro-social behaviors, and achieving academic success, then your students are highly likely to engage deeply in learning, behave well, and strive for success. Because the power of your personal beliefs about teaching is so important, don't hesitate. Be open with your students about your beliefs in their capacity to succeed. Be explicit in your support. When you communicate openly with your students about the confidence you have in them, you will help them become the successful students you want them to be.

In her book, *Culturally Responsive Teaching and the Brain*, Zaretta Hammond identifies this teacher as a "warm demander," one who conveys care, compassion, high expectations, and high levels of support. Students develop trust in warm demanders because they know that teacher is for them, believes in them, and scaffolds support so they can succeed.

> "All learning is personal.
> The physical is the mental.
> Teaching is subordinate to learning.
> You have to love your students more than you love your content."
>
> *Elliot Washor, Ed.D.; Co-Founder,*
> *Big Picture Learning*

What Are Your Fundamental Beliefs about Teaching?

One often-asked question of teaching candidates at job interviews involves asking them to explain their philosophy of teaching. Even though there is never enough time to answer this question adequately in an interview setting, it is still an important question to consider. Although they may be aware of the latest research, effective teachers don't just thoughtlessly spin from one educational trend to another. To be effective at leading a classroom, you select the best options for your students based on your own fundamental beliefs about teaching.

As you develop your classroom leadership skills, a good place to begin is to examine your own beliefs about what is most important to you as an educator. In Teacher Template 4.1, you will be able to examine and evaluate some of the most prevalent beliefs that educators hold about teaching to enhance your own teaching practices.

TEACHER TEMPLATE 4.1

What Are Your Fundamental Beliefs about Teaching?

As you read each of the following statements about teaching, consider its importance to your classroom practice, then jot down some quick thoughts about how the belief may affect your classroom leadership. What are the implications of this belief, and what next steps are necessary to improve your classroom leadership? What's missing from this list? Add additional belief statements of your own.

Belief Statement	To what extent is this belief evident in my teaching?	Implications/ Next Steps
Relationships are foundational to learning. A class functions best when there is a sense of community and belonging among students and teachers.		
My role is to facilitate learning, not to be the sage on the stage, but the guide on the side.		
I accept responsibility for the success of my students.		
All students can learn, but not all of them learn in the same way or at the same rate.		
Student engagement is vital and active learning strategies inspire engagement.		
High expectations along with high levels of support are necessary for the success of all students.		
A diverse student population strengthens and enriches a classroom.		
There are many paths to demonstrate mastery of knowledge and skills.		
Students and their needs come first in my classroom.		
Relevance matters in learning, so students' interests must inform my teaching.		
Creating opportunities for student voice, choice, and agency in lessons increases student ownership of learning.		
Add belief statements below		

The Three Components of Classroom Leadership

The foundation of authentic classroom leadership is building genuine rapport with students and facilitating relevant and inspiring learning. (See Sections Six and Nine for more detailed information.) In the following pages, you will find information about three aspects of classroom leadership: developing your teacher persona, establishing yourself as a supportive teacher, and facilitating the flow of class time. As you work through this section, you will be able to understand the importance of a teacher who makes purposeful and intentional decisions that can have profoundly positive effects on student learning. The information you find here is designed to guide your thinking about how you show up for your students and expand your repertoire of "teacher moves" to accomplish your goals.

> "I'm consistent, I'm fair, and I'm available. Students like the fact that I'm predictable and that they can count on me."
>
> *Margaret R. Scheirer, 12 years' experience*

To begin, it's wise to reflect on your current strengths at leading a class and to build on those strengths. Teacher Template 4.2 is designed to guide your thinking about your strengths.

Assess and Use Your Strengths as a Classroom Leader

In the list here, you will be able to identify the positive teacher traits that you already have. Circle all that apply to you and add additional strengths below.

- Prepared
- Organized
- Positive
- Inclusive
- Holds high expectations
- Creative

- Fair
- Compassionate
- Creates sense of belonging
- Admits mistakes
- Humorous
- Respectful

- Forgiving
- Patient
- Curious/lifelong learner
- Adaptable/flexible
- Resilient
- Add additional strengths here:

After you have determined some of your strengths, think about their application to the three components of classroom leadership. How can you use the strengths that you circled to enhance each of the following components?

Your Teacher Persona	Your Role as a Supportive Teacher	Facilitation of Class Time

Your Leadership Persona

Teachers must establish themselves as leaders in the classroom so that learning can occur. Each teacher will bring their own personality and style to establishing themselves as an authority without being authoritarian. The way you show up for students will change slightly based on the grade level and school environments where you teach. You will develop a welcoming and inclusive classroom community based on mutual respect in which your leadership is clearly recognized. There are many aspects to consider as you intentionally develop your unique leadership persona.

The first of the three essential components of classroom leadership involves the way you show up for your students—your teacher persona. Humans act differently depending on their setting and role. We show up one way with friends at a BBQ and another way presenting at a school board meeting. So, it makes sense that the way you behave—your mannerisms, your voice, your posture—with a classroom of energetic students may be different from the way you behave in quieter settings, such as eating lunch with colleagues or hanging out with friends and family.

Effective teachers are aware that it is important to deliberately create a persona for themselves if they are to be the classroom leaders that their students need. Obviously, it would be a disservice to you and to your students if the persona you present to them is not authentic. Although you should not assume a false role, you should think about the way you want your students to view you as their teacher. Here are some of the characteristics that you may want to consider as you determine how to present yourself to your students:

Professional: From the way you greet students to the way you dress to the arrangement of the furniture in the room, you signal to your students that you are professional in your approach to your responsibilities. Your actions will indicate that you are a trained, knowledgeable, and confident educator.

Enthusiastic: You want to project energy and enthusiasm for your students, subject matter, and instructional activities. Your enthusiasm will ignite your students' enthusiasm.

Focused: Having a focused approach to the way you instruct your students will make it easier for them to concentrate on learning because you will serve as a role model. Strive to be as prepared and organized as possible before class begins so that you can focus on teaching while you are with your students.

Inclusive: When you ensure that every student is involved in the lesson and that you care about each student's success, you send a powerful message to your students. The language you use, the way you move around your classroom, your nonverbal cues, and the way you speak with all students combine to help students feel they are

> "I wish my students knew how much I focus on their learning when I am not in the classroom. I wish their parents knew that thoughts of how to make their children's learning successful consume much of my downtime."
>
> *Deborah McManaway, 23 years' experience*

part of a classroom community. Just as you should make your classroom into an inviting place for your students, so should your persona be welcoming.

Positive: Of all the traits that you should consider as you develop your teacher persona, being positive is the most important. Your hopeful and positive tone is contagious. If you want your students to be optimistic and hopeful about learning, about their class, about you, and about their ability to succeed, then you must amplify your own positive attitude. Of course there will be challenging times when positivity can be harmful, or minimize painful emotions and experiences. This type of "toxic positivity" takes a positive attitude to an extreme and can have a detrimental effect on students and colleagues.

As you read the following information, you will learn more about the various teacher moves you may want to add to your toolkit as you develop your presence as a teacher.

Use Body Language to Your Advantage

Communication is complex and nonverbal communication combines with verbal language to convey meaning. Paying attention to the nonverbal messages you send can make a significant difference in your relationships with students. In general, students are acutely tuned in to their teacher's body language. For example, when your students first enter the classroom, their initial action is to look for their teacher. Think about how reassuring and empowering it is for a student when that teacher has a courteous greeting and a welcoming smile. Smiling at students—to let them know that you are glad to see them—does not require a great deal of time or effort, but it can make a significant difference in the classroom climate right from the start of class. In fact, greeting students at the door, by name, when they arrive is one of the most powerful practices. It communicates volumes about you as a caring and welcoming teacher determined to create a community of learners.

Think of your body language as another element of your leadership—one that is silently at work every minute you are with students. It's important that your body language signals that you are at ease and confident. Your students will find it difficult to trust a teacher who sits behind a desk all class or who won't make eye contact or whose voice can barely be heard. They will also find it difficult to trust a teacher who shouts or who appears agitated.

Make sure, too, that the body language signals you send match your verbal ones. For example, if you must force yourself to hide a smile while redirecting a student, then that student will not take you seriously. If you frown while praising a class, then you will only confuse students. Avoid sending mixed signals such as these and avoid nonverbal communication that is harmful to students and undermines the learning community you are trying to create. The following are some damaging nonverbal signals you should avoid:

- Snapping fingers at a student
- Violating a student's personal space for any reason
- Throwing anything at a student

- Ignoring students who fall asleep in class
- Staying seated all class period
- Chewing gum or eating in front of students
- Speaking too rapidly, too loudly, or in a monotone
- Leaning away from students
- Avoiding eye contact with certain students
- Laughing while delivering a serious message
- Turning your back while a student is speaking to you
- Angry, aggressive behavior like throwing or slamming anything
- Rolling your eyes as if in disgust
- Sharing "knowing looks" with other students when someone is having trouble with an answer
- Talking on and on while ignoring nonverbal signals from students
- Using a sarcastic tone
- Tapping fingers to show impatience with students
- Standing with your hands on your hips, obviously impatient or angry
- Not responding to a student's answer to a question or when a student speaks to you

Use Your Teacher Voice

Many teachers intuitively use the full range of their voices during instruction, to portray characters in a read-aloud, or to sing with young students as they transition between activities. A teacher's voice is one of the most important tools in your classroom leadership toolbox. Your voice is one of the first things that students notice about you. If you are not sure of what to do, students can pick up the hesitation in your voice and lose momentum in the lesson. Conversely, a confident voice can convey information with such clarity that learning moves forward and even an unfocused class re-engages.

When you take a deliberate approach to using your voice effectively, there are several things to consider. First, think about how you can use different volumes effectively. One of the most important tips from experienced teachers is that shouting to be heard is never effective. If you want a class to listen to you, catch their attention and then slowly lower the volume of your voice. If you really want students to pay attention, a dramatic stage whisper works wonders.

Another way to make sure to use your voice effectively is to match your tone to your purpose. Teachers who do not use a serious tone when the situation warrants it can confuse students who quickly pick up on the discrepancy between the tone of voice their teacher is using and the seriousness of the moment.

You may recall teachers in your past who had unfortunate verbal mannerisms—repeating "you know," clearing their throat, or using annoying filler words. If you suspect that you may have a potentially distracting verbal mannerism, one of the best ways to be certain is to record yourself and then listen critically. You can also ask for honest feedback from colleagues or from your students.

A final way to modulate your voice to make it a more effective teaching tool is to vary the speed and the volume at which you speak. Students will have a more difficult time learning if a teacher speaks very quickly or in a slow monotone. While sometimes you will speak in a conversational tone in class, remember to engage your voice as one more tool for engaging students and helping them to understand.

How to Make a Point Students Will Remember

There are many creative techniques to help your students remember the main points of what you say to them and you will want to intentionally plan and prepare to make each technique successful. Successful teachers often experiment with a variety of approaches to ignite that spark of learning. The following techniques are some you can use, modify, or combine to inspire your students:

- Help your students make a personal connection to the lesson. They should be able to identify with the subject matter. One easy way to do this is to include the interests, hobbies, experiences, and cultures of your students when creating lesson plans.

- Invite guest speakers to talk with your students or take field trips in-person or virtually. The possibilities are endless from authors, scientists, and astronauts to museums, national parks, and landmarks. Hearing an artist discuss their creative process or a community leader talk about solving local, national, and global problems can reinforce knowledge and inspire career interests.

- Surprise students with a bit of theater. Elementary teachers may use puppets. Secondary teachers may use props or wear a costume. Carefully consider the message and impact when choosing a costume for instruction, spirit days, or Halloween. Exercise caution when dressing up as a historical figure. Be culturally responsible, have empathy, and avoid harmful, offensive, or cultural appropriative costumes.

- Include visual elements. Use media. Show film clips. Hold up objects. Do demonstrations. To make the visual elements of a lesson even more engaging, include student interaction, such as having student-made media presentations or student-led demonstrations of learning.

- Integrate digital tools such as Breakout.edu to reinforce learning in a hands-on experience that requires collaboration, problem-solving, and persistence.

- Use music and movement to reinforce learning. Songs, chants, rhythms, patterns, and physical movement can solidify knowledge and skills.

- Hide items related to the lesson in a large box. Ask students to guess what the items could be. As you open the box, have students explain or predict the significance of each item as it relates to the day's lesson.

- Play music that fits the lesson of the day and ask students to explain how it applies to the lesson.

Set the Stage

Before you begin a lesson, set the stage and develop a hook by previewing the topic in such a way that you ignite students' curiosity. If you begin in a dull way, many of your students will quickly tune out. However, if you incorporate one or more of these preview techniques, your students will be motivated to pay attention:

- Engage students' prior knowledge through a KWL (Know—Want to Know—Learned) activity or a graphic organizer.

- Activate curiosity. Start with real-world problems and real-life phenomena to surface students' questions about a topic and increase motivation.

- Post a motto, slogan, or other catchy phrase related to the lesson in a conspicuous spot and ask students to reflect on it.

- Display and talk about an unusual object related to the lesson.

- Read part of a passage to the class. Be sure to stop reading at an exciting part of the text. Finish the passage later in your presentation.

- Pass out a handout with missing parts. Your students can fill in the missing information as they listen.

- Do a demonstration and then ask students to explain what they observed.

- Take a poll of your students on some aspect of the topic. Online tools for this include: Doodle, Poll Everywhere, Survey Monkey, Slido, and Mentimeter.

How to Catch Your Students' Attention

Classrooms where students are engaged in learning are often busy, loud, energetic spaces. It's crucial that teachers develop a repertoire of attention-getting strategies to signal the class to listen. They should be fun, playful, and varied as they will be necessary throughout the course of the school day and the school year so find those that suit your style. You may want to:

- Ring a portable wireless doorbell; some have more than fifty attention-getting sounds, chimes, and tunes.

- Simply say, "May I have your attention, please?"

- Begin a series of actions that you want students to copy: touching your nose, putting your hands on your hips, and so on. Once they are copying your actions, you have their attention.

- Hold up a hand or peace sign and students will stop talking and hold up their hand or peace sign when they see yours.

- Use a class-wide countdown. Depending on the circumstances, you may be counting backward from ten or projecting a timer counting down from either thirty seconds or as much as several minutes.

- Call and Response such as "One two three, eyes on me," and students respond "One, two, eyes on you." Others are phrases from world languages, movies, songs, sports or reinforcing life lessons such as "Hakuna/Matata," "Give it, live it/Respect," "We love. . ./and care for each other."
- Spell the start of a word and students finish it. "L-I-S/T-E-N."
- Play a song that students like so that they know they must be ready to pay attention at the end of it.
- Establish a rhythmic clapping pattern that students repeat or complete.
- Use a sound such as a bell, chime, or shaker so that students can stop and listen as soon as they hear it. Outside of a gymnasium, avoid a harsh sound like a whistle.
- Flicker the lights for a visual signal.

Finally, be aware of your audience. Students do not have long attention spans. They become restless after just a few minutes. Break up activities and allow brain breaks periodically to help them focus and remain engaged.

The Right Spot at the Right Time

Teachers circulate around the classroom and select the location that best facilitates learning and supports positive student behaviors. Just moving around the classroom is not enough, however. It is important to be at the right spot at the right time during the flow of your lesson.

Before setting up furniture, teachers determine what type of instruction they want to occur and what the best traffic flow is for daily routines. Teachers will then create space for instruction to occur, including: collaborative groups, whole group instruction, flexible small groups, carpet area, lab spaces, flexible seating, or even maker spaces. Teachers generally find it helpful to position their work spaces or desks at the back or on the sides of the classroom so that all students have an unimpeded view of anything that is projected or written on the board. Not only do your students have a clear view of the board, but also when your work space is in the back or on the sides, you will be able to unobtrusively observe your students and create a quiet 1:1 conference space for students without disturbing others.

Moving around the room without the risk of tripping will be possible once you teach students where to store their backpacks and jackets properly. It is also important to choose just the right place in the room where you can deliver directions or speak to the whole group. Usually, the front of the classroom works best for this. If you move to the same spot every time you call for the attention of the group, students will soon learn to anticipate this and to focus on you when you are in that area.

Doug Lemov, author of the landmark book *Teach Like a Champion 2.0* (published by Jossey-Bass in 2015), as well as several other highly regarded authors on the topic of classroom leadership, suggest that teachers use a technique called Pastore's Perch when monitoring students. With this technique, teachers can broaden their view of the class simply by moving to a front corner of a classroom when scanning to make sure that everyone is on task. By moving just a few steps away from the center of the room to a front corner, a teacher's view of the class widens dramatically. This just-right spot makes it much easier to observe students and respond to their needs.

Finally, it's helpful to move around while deciding where to position yourself at various times during class. Can everyone see and hear you? Can you observe everyone? Can students see the board or the area where you have information projected? When you need to speak to students privately, can you do so while still facing the rest of the class?

Teach with Purpose and Relevance in Mind

One trait that effective teachers share is the ability to help students understand the purpose and relevance of their education. If you find your students questioning why they are studying a topic or completing an assignment, you have a chance to grow in the way you communicate the relevance of the subject matter to students' present and future lives. Students often do not automatically understand the connection between the education they receive in schools and the successful lives they envision for themselves when they are adults. You must help them make these connections. Preempt your students' doubts by making it clear why they need to know what you are teaching them. Here's how:

- Learn about students' interests and connect learning as often as possible with what matters to them.

- Design units of study and instructional techniques that invite student voice and choice wherever possible.

- Connect learning to current events and topics.

- Discuss the relevance of the content with students and post it either on a slide or on the board.

- Tell students how their lives will be better when they know the material you intend to teach. Focus on why students need to know the information right now as well as why they will need it in the future.

- Begin a unit by connecting it to previous learning so that students can see a progression of knowledge and skills in their schooling. Be very specific. Say, "At the end of class today, you will be able to _____" or "You need to know this because _____."

- Take the time every now and then to ask students to tell you why the unit of study is relevant to them. Make a list of their ideas and post it.

- Draw connections between what your students are doing now in your class and the work they will be doing later in the term.

Teach Your Students to Follow Directions

Effective teachers work diligently to communicate clearly and remove misunderstandings quickly. They realize the importance of making sure that students can successfully follow single and multi-step directions. Students who know how to follow directions are likely to develop strong study habits and remain engaged during class. As the leader of your classroom, it is up to you to make sure that your students receive clear directions delivered in ways that they can understand.

When students know what to do and how to do it well, confusion vanishes. Although they may still not be sure of the information in the material, at least they do know what is expected of them. The potential for failure and disruption is reduced considerably. Here are some things to keep in mind when you design and deliver directions to students:

- Make following directions well an important part of the culture of your classroom. Talk about this every day. Work on it until your students see that following directions is not only something their teacher thinks is important, but also a necessary life skill.

- Expect and command attention. When you are ready to go over written or oral directions, expect your students to stop what they are doing and to pay attention to you from the beginning of your explanation to the end.

- Provide verbal and visual directions. Leave directions on the screen or board while students are engaged in the task. Students will benefit from referencing the written or visual instructions.

- Check for understanding. Ask students to rephrase directions until you are sure everyone knows what to do.

- Consider giving directions BEFORE distributing materials to increase focus.

- Ask students to focus when you read directions and to read along with you whenever possible. They should not start the assignment, assessment, or task as you explain the directions.

Guidelines for Giving Written Directions Successfully

- Young students, emerging readers, English Language Learners, and students who experience disabilities may need more visual and verbal directions to be successful. Capable readers will need less support and generally be able to follow well-written directions.

- Check for understanding by asking students to read the directions, then restate or clarify the directions. Teachers then circulate and monitor students as they begin the working in groups or completing assignments.

- Make sure your directions align with the objectives of your lesson. This will help students understand the big picture behind the assignment.

- Express directions in the form of logical steps students should accomplish to complete the assignment. List and number the steps in the order you want students to complete them.

- Keep each statement brief. For example, try "Write your answers on your test paper" instead of "Be sure to put all that lined notebook paper you have on your desk away because I want you to write just on the test."

- Take the time to go over directions orally with students. This is especially important on multi-step activities and assessments where there may be several sections with different directions for each one.

Guidelines for Giving Verbal Directions Successfully

Before Class Begins

- Write or project the instructions where students can read them as you review them orally: on the board, on handouts for each student, on a screen, or on a large easel pad of paper.

- Word each step simply and positively. For example, "Turn to page 117" is a well-expressed direction. "Turn to page 117 and begin about halfway down the page—you don't need to read the top of the page" is not as easy to follow.

During Class Instruction

- Use an attention-getting strategy from your repertoire (see the earlier section on "How to Catch Your Students' Attention"). Something as simple as "May I have your attention, please?" is often effective.

- Work with the class to reduce the amount of time it takes to be quiet and ready to hear directions. Reducing time spent in transitions improves learning significantly.

- Don't talk over students or raise your voice. Wait until students have stopped what they are doing and can listen.

- Check for understanding by asking a student to restate the directions. If necessary, ask several students to clarify and explain until everyone is clear about what to do.

After You Have Given Instructions

- Stay on your feet to circulate and monitor students to see that they are moving forward. Give positive feedback and clear up confusion as you circulate.

- If you see that several students are having trouble, do not hesitate to stop class and clarify for everyone.

Establishing Yourself as a Supportive Teacher

The second component of capable classroom leadership, being a supportive teacher, would seem to be inherent to the task of being an educator. Being a supportive teacher, however, is far more than just saying, "Good job!" when students appear to be on the right track. Being a supportive teacher goes beyond having high expectations and providing basic encouragement. It also requires providing high levels of support.

Students need to know that you genuinely care about them in order to work hard, persist when things are difficult, and assume responsibility for their work. Supportive teachers build rapport with students, creating safe learning communities where it's okay to take risks and showing students that mistakes are just another way to learn. In the indelible words of Miss Frizzle, the act of learning requires that we "Take chances, make mistakes, and get messy."

In the following pages you can reflect on some of the many factors, strategies, and routines that contribute to establishing yourself as a supportive teacher, including:

- Developing a growth mindset
- Celebrating mistakes
- Fostering motivation
- Increasing student ownership

Develop a Growth Mindset

A growth mindset makes learning attainable for all students, while a fixed mindset limits learning. When students and teachers believe that success is achievable only by those individuals with innate capabilities, such as being intelligent or talented in some way, their mindset is said to be *fixed*. When students and teachers have the belief that success is possible through hard work, effort, and persistence, this attitude is a *growth mindset*.

First identified in 2006 by Stanford psychologist and researcher Dr. Carol Dweck, in her book *Mindset: The New Psychology of Success*, the importance of a growth mindset in students has revolutionized classroom practice. The growth mindset movement confirms what experienced teachers have recognized for years: if teachers build a supportive community and students believe in their ability to succeed, they will.

Teachers also need to embody a growth mindset for themselves. If students are to become high achievers, they need a teacher whose foundational belief is that they and their students have the capacity to learn and achieve.

Here are some of the most important concepts that compose the growth mindset movement:

- *Yet*. With this one word, students transform their thinking from a fixed mindset to a growth mindset. A negative statement such as "I don't know how to do this" becomes a positive declaration of intent when a student rephrases it to "I don't know how to do this *yet*." In a classroom where students are learning to develop a growth mindset, the word *yet* is often displayed on bulletin boards and posters and in class mottoes.

- Generic praise, although kind, is not helpful to students. Expressions such as "You are a superstar!" or "You are so smart!" do little to encourage students to persist in the face of challenges. Instead, because the praise centers on innate qualities, generic praise such as this reinforces a fixed mindset.

- Instead of generic praise, specific encouragement and feedback is a crucial tool for teachers who want to help their students seek challenges. Feedback should be specific, timely, focused on problem-solving processes, and recognize the importance of effort in increasing self-confidence. For example, "Great work on your math problem. I noticed you went back and used two different strategies to check your answer."

- The celebration of effort, hard work, and persistence is a key element of a growth mindset. Students who recognize the importance of these three traits in their academic success are more likely to welcome challenges. Teachers should arrange opportunities to celebrate these traits in addition to recognizing academic success.

- Mistakes are viewed as valuable assets to learning. Students with a growth mindset do not fear mistakes as students with a fixed mindset do. Teachers should make sure that students know that mistakes are a normal, expected, and necessary part of learning and model this when you make a mistake.

- Deliberate practice, where students focus on the parts of an assignment where they have not mastered the material and deliberately practice improving those weaknesses, is an important part of the learning process because it is specific and focused to help students gain mastery.

- Students need to be mindful of the strategies and processes that they use to arrive at answers because this awareness enables them to apply those strategies and processes in other ways.

Here are some specific strategies that you can use to promote a growth mindset among your students:

- Explicitly teach the terms *growth mindset* and *fixed mindset* so that you and your students have a common vocabulary for discussing work habits and other classroom issues.

- Ask students to discuss or review one another's work to offer specific positive as well as constructive feedback. Constructive feedback is key in helping students understand how to do their work well. This is a skill that needs to be taught so that students can share feedback in a helpful, not harmful manner.

- Have students plan their work before they begin instead of just diving in. Ask them to predict how long it will take or where they can find help if they need it.

- After students complete an assignment, hold a debriefing session where they can share their ideas about what went well as they worked and where they struggled. Sharing these ideas with classmates can build confidence.

Because of the widespread adoption of the growth mindset concept, there are countless articles and books about it. One of the most reliable sources of information for exploring the idea of the growth mindset further is Mindset Works, a website established by Dweck (mindsetworks.com).

Celebrate Mistakes in Your Classroom

One of the most positive results of the growth mindset movement is the understanding that teachers now have about how to help students (and themselves) view mistakes as an important step in the learning process. In the past, when students (or teachers) made mistakes, their attitude toward mistakes often shut down the learning process. The shift from thinking about mistakes as failure to regarding them as valuable tools in the learning process can have a positive effect on your classroom practice. Here is how to encourage this in your classroom:

- Discuss mistakes using familiar analogies such as learning to ride a bike. It's normal to need training wheels and to fall when learning how to ride a bike. We learn from those experiences and gain skills and knowledge that allows us to ride without falling.

- Share examples of inventors, athletes, and others whose mistakes led to breakthroughs. "Failing forward" is a common phrase in business, engineering, and design, where learning quickly from mistakes and failures to improve a product or solution is vital to success.

- Create high levels of trust by sharing your teacher-related mistakes, what you learn from them, and what you change as a result. Students will adopt your language and your attitude toward mistakes.

- Focus on strategies. Another way to celebrate mistakes is to ask students to discuss the strategies that they used while working on an assignment. They can share their strategies with a partner or a small group as well with the larger group or one-on-one with you. Discussing strategies allows students to see beyond the problem itself to understand the bigger picture of how to use various strategies.

- Ask students to examine *why* they made a mistake. Asking students to consider why they made the mistakes they did is also useful because it helps students understand the connection between their effort and their mistake. It's important for students to realize the difference between a mistake made because they did not fully understand a concept and one made due to a lack of focus.

- Look at the specific knowledge and skills involved in a mistake. Reframe the mistake in specific terms. Instead of saying, "I see you missed the third question" while working with a student, if you say, "The third question involves [this concept or skill]. What questions to do you have about [this concept or skill]?" When students can identify the concepts and skills that they don't yet understand, they are empowered to fill in those gaps instead of just focusing on a mistake.

- View mistakes as a public service for the rest of the class. When a student makes a mistake in front of peers, instead of making a harsh judgment, thank the student for making that mistake. Mention that it is one that other classmates probably made and that everyone will now understand the information better because of that student's mistake (and bravery in sharing with the rest of the class).

Motivation: A Daily Requirement for All Students

In addition to promoting growth mindset, teachers want to intentionally plan motivational strategies as part of every lesson plan. Teachers strive to cultivate students' intrinsic motivation by building on their curiosity and interests so that learning and growing is its own reward. However, some students may need support with extrinsic motivators as well. When students and adults approach a new task, they find motivation if they can answer yes to these three questions:

- CAN I do it?
- Do I WANT to do it?
- Are all BARRIERS that would prevent me from investing in this activity removed?

As teachers, we help students develop confidence in themselves; we expand their desire to try new and difficult things and remove barriers to their progress.

HOW TO USE EXTRINSIC MOTIVATION EFFECTIVELY

Researchers classify the various ways that we attempt to motivate students as either extrinsic motivation or intrinsic motivation. Extrinsic motivation is the type of positive reinforcement that offers external or tangible rewards to students as behavioral motivators.

Extrinsic motivation is a controversial practice because its effects do not appear to be as long-lasting as those of intrinsic motivation. Students tend to be too focused on the reward being offered rather than on the successful mastery of the material. Other problems with extrinsic motivation include some teachers' tendency to overuse it as well as the financial cost of some rewards.

Despite these negatives, however, extrinsic motivation can play a valuable role in motivating students to succeed, especially neurodiverse students. Its greatest advantage is that it makes an immediate connection between the reward being offered and the work and efforts students are expected to put forth.

If you choose to use various types of extrinsic rewards in your class, keep in mind that they work best when students know about them in advance of the work and can anticipate earning them. Take care to offer extrinsic rewards in a way that they are novel enough to be desirable and motivating to students.

TANGIBLE REWARDS STUDENTS ENJOY

You do not have to spend a fortune on rewards for your students. The most effective rewards are activities that students enjoy. Instead of shopping for stickers or other prizes, offer students some of these free rewards:

- Receiving encouraging notes on their work
- Having a positive note from you to take home
- Having you call their family or caregiver with a positive message
- Having you send a positive postcard home
- Having time to play an educational online game
- Being team captain or group leader
- Having time to work on a puzzle or other enjoyable activity
- Receiving bookmarks made by other students
- Sharing in a walk for the entire class
- Having their work displayed
- Watching video clips
- Using the library during free time
- Having a decorated desk
- Being the "Student of the Week"
- Sitting in a special desk or chair
- Borrowing a book from the classroom library
- Having time for independent reading

Make Sure Intrinsic Motivation Is a Classroom Constant

Intrinsic motivation comes from inside and it motivates students to learn and grow because they get personal satisfaction from the process and the work. It is an incentive to work that is satisfying in itself. Although extrinsic motivation can be effective in boosting students' self-confidence and their desire to do well, intrinsic motivation is a more effective way to create fundamental change in student effort and achievement.

There are countless ways to harness the power of intrinsic motivation in every lesson. For example, many students enjoy being able to use recently acquired knowledge in new ways or to engage in a community event related to the work at hand. Students are far more engaged in activities that encourage them to discover, inquire, and engage in the 4Cs: Communication, Collaboration, Critical Thinking, and Creativity.

Thoughtful teachers find ways to increase the intrinsic motivation in assignments by considering how they can incorporate at least one of the 4Cs and make assignments more engaging to their students and nurture empowered learners.

- Having a wider audience for writing beyond their teacher and classmates
- Allowing student choice in demonstrating learning: songs, skits, videos, ads, podcasts, or posters
- Gamifying lessons with: webquests, food truck or top chef style competitions, scavenger hunts, bingo, Kahoot!, Breakout.edu
- Creating their own quizzes, assignments, games, or puzzles
- Making three-dimensional graphic organizers
- Taking mini field trips within the school
- Role-playing
- Solving brain teasers
- Drawing inferences from interesting case studies
- Exploring an unusual artifact
- Racing the clock
- Racing another team in the class
- Making a movie or audio recording
- Making a slide deck for a presentation
- Defending or refuting a point in a class debate

Make Success Visible

One of the most productive ways to motivate students is to make their success visible. A classroom environment in which student engagement is valued and student success is celebrated is a positive one in which students thrive. There are different ways to make your students' success visible. Here are just a few of the methods of visually encouraging student success that you can adapt for your classroom:

- Using stickers on student papers
- Stamping student work with positive messages
- Writing positive notes to students on their papers
- Sending home positive notes or emails to parents or guardians
- Using exclamations, such as "Woo-hoo!," in unison as class shout-outs
- Using a class hand signal, such as a thumbs-up, to acknowledge success
- Displaying photographs of students with their good work as well as the work itself
- Holding brief, periodic recognition ceremonies
- Setting aside a display area for student work
- Awarding certificates for such qualities as persistence and dedication

Increasing Student Ownership

As students internalize growth mindset and gain motivation, they will also increase ownership for their learning. In a classroom with a teacher who knows their students well, holds high-expectations, and facilitates engaging lessons, students will feel an increasing sense of ownership for their own learning and for the classroom community.

To be an effective classroom leader, you must convey to your students that they can achieve success through their own effort and hard work. Here are some suggestions for how you can increase student ownership of learning:

- Teach your students how to do their work. Students should be taught the study skills they need to reach the high standards you have for them.

- Have students chart their progress to achieving skills, knowledge, and standards.

- Provide frequent opportunities for students to self-assess with prompts like these:

  - What am I good at?

  - What do I need help to do better?

  - I used to do _____ and now I _____.

  - What did I learn about this topic?

  - What do I want to learn next?

- Involve families and caregivers often to create an effective team of caring adults who want to help a child succeed.

- Create a wide variety of fair assessments. Employ many ways to assess student progress to meet the needs and abilities of your students.

- Allow no student to be invisible in your classroom. Engage each student every day.

- Provide timely feedback so that students know what they need to do to improve.

- Make sure your feedback on assignments aligns with growth mindset and helps students correct errors and improve their performance.

- When students have mastered a skill or completed a task, have the next step in learning available right away to maintain motivation.

- Maintain clear and consistent expectations. Consistently enforce class agreements, policies, and procedures.

- Provide models for high-quality student work. Give students examples to aim for.

- Use rubrics in advance of assignments. Be very specific about your criteria for success so that students have a clear idea of what is expected before they begin to work.

- When you are circulating around the room, ask your students to indicate the topics or information they understand and to highlight the key words or topics that puzzle them so that you can work together to make sure they understand their assignment.

Facilitating the Flow of Class Time

The third component of capable classroom leadership is one that teachers can direct: class time. Time and opportunity to learn are within the locus of control for teachers. You can determine how students spend the precious time they have with you as well as the opportunities they have to engage with learning.

You Direct the Time Your Students Have with You

Time is one of our most precious resources in teaching. Sometimes it will seem that interruptions such as intercom announcements, commotions in the halls, or dysregulated students disrupt your class much too often. Just as other teachers do, you will have to find ways to cope successfully with these as well as many more subtle disruptions to your planned flow of class time.

If you do not carefully direct the use of time in your classroom, what are the consequences? Consider that one of the key factors in student success is time spent learning with an effective teacher. While each state varies, students in the United States receive approximately six hours of instruction per day during 180 days in the school year. That's a little more than 1,000 hours of instruction per year. If you don't teach with a sense of urgency and purpose, then students will not have the opportunity to learn that they would have otherwise.

The results of misused instructional time can be grim. Teachers who do not use class time wisely experience far more behavioral issues than teachers who make use of every minute. Students who waste class time are less likely to succeed academically. So, what can you do to avoid the hazards of wasted class time? Start by making a commitment to yourself and to your students that time matters, and you will make the most of every minute of every day that you are together.

How Teachers Waste Classroom Time

One way to make the highest and best use of class time is to be aware of how easy it is to waste it. Some of the ways that teachers misuse class time include the following:

- Teaching lessons that are not relevant or interesting to students
- Not using the first few minutes of class effectively
- Allowing students to goof off for the last few minutes of class
- Not intervening quickly enough to keep problems manageable
- Confusing digressions from the topic with teachable moments
- Neglecting to set up equipment in advance
- Not establishing routines for daily classroom procedures
- Not double-checking links for websites students will need to use

- Calling roll instead of quickly checking attendance with a seating chart
- Not enforcing a reasonable policy for leaving the classroom
- Not providing assistance for students without materials
- Not determining students' prior knowledge of new material
- Assigning an inappropriate amount of work
- Giving confusing directions
- Making poor transitions between activities
- Giving homework that is only busywork

If you recognize these pitfalls in your practice, rest assured that it is possible to change with awareness, planning, and effort. In Teacher Template 4.3, you can reflect on your current teaching practice and how well you use class time.

How Well Do You Use Class Time?

To determine how well you use class time at this point in your teaching career, use the self-assessment that follows. Place a check mark in the column that best fits your time use for each statement. The actions listed in the first column are positive ones that all teachers should cultivate. If you mark the actions in the other two columns, you should consider how to improve your use of class time.

	I Always Do This	I Sometimes Do This	I Don't Do This
I greet students and make a quick connection with them as they arrive to class.			
I expect students to begin working on established class routines as soon as they enter the classroom.			
My students know where to get handouts and other materials they need without long wait times.			
My students follow a predictable routine for the end of class.			
I delegate as many chores as appropriate given the age and abilities of my students.			
Students know the system to access devices and log into accounts.			
When I show videos, I show only the most relevant clips.			
I test equipment before students arrive to make sure that it works.			
I give directions verbally one time while students follow along with written or posted directions.			
I have extra school supplies available for students who lack supplies.			

(continued on next page)

(*continued from previous page*)

	I Always Do This	I Sometimes Do This	I Don't Do This
I always have a backup plan in case a lesson does not work well.			
I design lessons to meet state and district objectives.			
I offer brain breaks at regular intervals so that students find it easy to remain on task.			
My students and I stop periodically during a lesson to review and recap.			
I routinely use a timer to help students focus.			
I assess my students' readiness for a unit of study.			
I teach my students how to organize their notes and other materials so they can find them quickly.			

Use the Principles of Effective Classroom Time Management

Learning to use class time wisely is a skill that will take effort, patience, and practice to acquire; however, the rewards are well worth the effort. You and your students will benefit every day from classes that run smoothly. You can eventually gather many tips from your colleagues and learn even more from your own classroom experiences; until then, you can start with these general principles for using class time wisely:

- Reduce distractions. Look around your classroom for things that might distract your students. Some obvious sources of distractions, depending on the age of your students, might be toys, smartphones, social media, windows, desks too close together, doorways, pencil sharpeners, too many posters or banners, graffiti, or—the most enticing one of all—other students.

- Raise student awareness. Your students need to learn that time is important in your class. This doesn't mean that you should rush them through their tasks, but you should discuss the importance of using class time wisely. Help them adopt an attitude of delighted urgency. Students have "places to go, people to see, things to do." Because they have so many exciting things to learn, interesting people to meet, compelling things to do, and a short time to do it all, you expect them to use time productively.

- Establish routines. If you have routines for daily activities in your class, your students will save minutes each day and hours each week instead of wasting time because they don't know what to do.

- Monitor and adjust constantly. Engaging your students (instead of sitting at your desk/work space) will allow you to clear up misconceptions and move learning forward.

- Be very organized. If your students must wait while you find your instructional materials, that is a poor use of their time.

- Take a door-to-door or bell-to-bell approach. Engage students in learning from the time they enter your classroom until the time they leave. Some teachers make the mistake of thinking that students need a few minutes of free time at the start of class and at the end of class to relax. Although students do need time at both ends of class to make effective transitions, this time should be purposeful and relate to community building or the day's lesson.

- Teach to an objective. Demystify the learning process for students by articulating the purpose of each lesson. This will also help them self-assess their progress toward gaining new knowledge and skills.

- Have great options for early finishers. Make sure that your students know the options if they finish work early. For example, writing in a journal, self-assessing their work with a rubric, silent reading, or logging into a learning app or platform.

How to Handle Interruptions

Many teachers feel frustrated when their carefully planned lesson is interrupted by either internal or external disruptions. Internally that might be disruptive student behavior or a lack of classroom routines. Externally, that might include a fire drill, a class visitor, or an internet outage. Some interruptions are beyond your control and require flexibility, but you can reduce others by building relationships with your students, delivering engaging lessons, and teaching routines and procedures to students.

If you are lucky, classroom visitors will be common because everyone will be interested in what's happening in your classroom, what they can learn from you, and how they can support you and your students. So, let's highlight one promising practice to address this type of interruption and increase student ownership for the classroom community.

At any grade level, classroom greeters are an idea worth considering. Designate a team of students who are willing and able to greet visitors. Identify the greeter and a backup greeter in your weekly class roles. Train greeters on the protocol to get up, greet the visitor near the door, ask how they can assist them, and let them know what the class is working on at that moment. Whether a student aid from the office, an administrator, mentor, caregiver, paraprofessional, or another teacher, they will be welcomed in an impressive way that causes the fewest disruptions to learning.

You can minimize the negative effects of other types of interruptions by meeting three goals:

Goal One: Prevent as many interruptions as you can. Work with your colleagues and administrators to reduce disruptions systematically where you can, such as behavior support plans, smartphones, toys, all-school announcements, special assembly schedules, phone calls to the classroom phone, monitoring students while they are using devices, or chronically absent or tardy students.

Goal Two: Minimize the disruption caused by an interruption. Although you can prevent many interruptions during your school day, some are unavoidable. For example, you cannot prevent the interruption caused by a mandatory drill, nor a message from the office requesting a student for an early dismissal. In such situations, your goal must be to respond appropriately and keep unaffected students on task. If you remind yourself that your goal is to minimize the disturbance, you are likely to create a solution to the problem.

Goal Three: Prepare for predictable interruptions. Having a plan in place for unavoidable, predictable interruptions will give you confidence. Here is a list of some of the predictable interruptions that teachers must handle successfully so that you can plan how you will manage each one:

- A student does not have school supplies or instructional materials
- A student is texting on their smartphone
- Students wander from the approved website or app while using a device
- Students ask to leave the class to use the restroom, see the nurse, or go to their lockers
- Students need to listen to intercom announcements

- A visitor asks to speak with you
- A computer or device doesn't work properly
- Students leave class early or arrive late
- Students need to sharpen pencils, staple papers, or dispose of trash
- A student from another class asks to speak with one of your students
- There is a commotion in the hallway or another classroom

How to Handle Student Requests to Leave the Classroom

Sometimes students legitimately need to leave the classroom while class is in session to use the restroom, see the nurse or counselor, or meet a caregiver for an appointment. At other times, leaving the classroom signals avoidance and can create disruptions to learning. Familiarize yourself with your school's policy on supervising students in your care and make sure your procedures align with that. It's important that you know where all students are at all times.

Making good decisions about allowing a student to leave the classroom is not always easy, no matter how much teaching experience you have. Consider the following guidelines as you begin to formulate your classroom agreements on leaving class:

- If possible, do not allow more than one or two students to leave at one time.
- Always allow students to go to the restroom or to the health clinic. Use your best judgment about other requests.
- If a student makes many requests to leave the classroom, speak privately with them to better understand what's going on and make a plan to support them and hopefully reduce the number of times they need to leave class. If this does not work, call a family member or caregiver to learn more and enlist that person's help in supporting the student.
- When you give permission for students to leave the room, make sure whenever possible that an adult will supervise them. You are responsible for your students until another adult assumes that responsibility.
- Never allow students to leave school without contacting the office or an administrator first.
- Leaving the classroom may be necessary for students to regulate their behaviors. Consult your school policies and procedures for giving students a chance to calm down. Many classrooms have a calming space in the classroom as a tool for students to regulate without leaving the room.
- When it is necessary, refuse requests in a polite but firm manner. Try one of these phrases:
  - Can you wait a few minutes?
  - Have you finished your work?
  - Let me check to see whether _____ is in the _____ office.
  - Can you do that right after class?

- By using a hall pass, such as the one in Sample 4.1, you will be able to keep track of your students. Having a hall pass procedure for leaving the classroom sends the message to your students that you take their absences seriously and care about their safety.

Keeping Track of Students Who Leave the Classroom

Teachers are responsible for supervising students in their care. School safety protocols mandate that you keep track of students who are out of your class. Depending on the age of your students and the technology used at your school, sign-out sheets and hall passes will take many forms. A few districts use smart ID badges, but most rely on low-tech solutions. You can post a sheet for students to mark as they leave, have them sign out on a computer, or maintain a class logbook. Having a sign-out sheet, such as the one in Teacher Template 4.4, will make it easier for you to keep accurate records of when your students leave your class and where they go.

Sample 4.1
Hall Pass

Student's Name: _____ Date: _____

Time out: _____ Time returned: _____

_____ Restroom

_____ Counseling

_____ Locker

_____ Library/Media center

_____ Health clinic

_____ Water fountain

_____ Principal's office

_____ Classroom

_____ Other: _____

Teacher's signature: _____

TEACHER TEMPLATE 4.4

Student Sign-Out Sheet

Student's Name	Date	Destination	Time Out	Time Returned

Use Time Wisely by Pacing Instruction Well

Purposeful lesson planning includes planning for pacing. Pacing instruction, in this context, is the art of making sure that you provide learning activities at a rate that engages students and supports their learning. Pacing instruction well is challenging because teachers work with a classroom of students who are diverse individuals with a range of interests, abilities, readiness, learning styles, and needs for support.

Although pacing instruction for maximum learning is a skill that requires experience to master, the guidelines that follow can make it easier for you to design instruction that will keep students engaged in learning for an entire class period:

- Identify the amount of instructional time available and the learning objectives.
- Know the content to avoid rambling when making an instructional point.
- Establish routines and procedures early in the year to reduce the time it takes students to transition from one activity to the next.
- Rehearse the opening hook, directions, and questions you may ask to keep the lesson moving.
- Plan how students will engage with the topic and with each other, then allocate appropriate blocks of time for those instructional strategies.
- Differentiate scaffolding and support. Provide plenty of early assistance so that those students who need help completing assignments do not fall behind other students.
- Check for understanding frequently during the lesson to make sure all students are moving in the right direction and not getting side tracked by misconceptions.
- Use a mixture of whole-group, small-group, and individual instruction to differentiate support and keep up the pace of lessons.
- Consider providing high-interest enrichment and reteaching activities for students to work on when they complete their basic assignments. Offering attractive optional assignments will engage students constructively.
- Provide directions in the form of checklists for students to follow as they engage with collaborative groups or complete an assignment to reduce confusion.
- Plan for early finishers. Post a list of activities for students who finish their work early. Suggested activities might include starting homework early, working at a learning center, playing online games for review, reading a library book, working with another student on an extra project, or organizing their notebooks.
- Monitor and adjust during the lesson based on signals from your students that indicate the pace is too fast or too slow.

> "Learning how to manage classroom time is a developed skill. The better you know the content and how you want to teach it, the better idea you'll have of how long it will take to implement. I still haven't fully mastered this, and it is now my third year of teaching, but here are some things that helped: wearing a watch, setting a timer when I was lecturing so I knew when to stop, and taking a flipped classroom approach and having students do some independent learning at home."
>
> *Jay O'Rourke, 2+ years' experience*

The First Ten Minutes of Class

Effective teachers harness the power of the opening minutes of class. It's so worthwhile that students don't want to be tardy for fear of missing the opening. You can use the first ten minutes to connect with students and get your class off to a great start. Do not waste this time. (See Section Six for Welcoming Inclusion Activities to open class.)

The first minutes set the tone for the rest of the class. If you are prepared for class and have taught your students an opening routine, they can use this brief time to make mental and emotional transitions from home or from their last class and prepare to focus on learning. You should establish a comfortable and predictable routine for the opening of class. Here is a simple opening routine that many teachers follow and that you can adapt to meet the needs of your class:

Step One: Greet each student as they enter the class. You can hand out anything you need to distribute. You can also answer questions, collect attendance notes, and check-in on the emotional state of your students. Your students will appreciate that you care enough to stand at the door to greet them.

Step Two: Elementary students may have to put backpacks in cubbies or select lunch choices, but generally, have students go immediately to their respective seats or spot on the rug. You will avoid many problems if you strictly enforce this part of the routine. Students who wander around the room while you are busy at the door can cause disruptions. Furthermore, students will often carry problems from earlier in the day into your room. By insisting that your students take a seat right away, you will help focus their energy on your class and on learning.

Step Three: Have students check the board or the screen for a predictable opening routine or exercise. The morning meeting for young students and opening exercise for older students gives them time to check in, settle down, organize their materials, and shift mental gears to what is going to happen in class. Your message on the board or screen will vary based on the grade level of students.

Step Four: Have students complete an introductory or warm-up activity. This is a great place to add a social-emotional learning (SEL) activity or check-in poll, or the activity could arouse curiosity and relate the day's new learning to previous knowledge. It should be interesting yet simple enough for students to complete with little support. The activity will thus increase their confidence so that they are even more connected as a classroom community and interested in the day's lesson.

Use your creativity and your knowledge of your students to design activities that they will enjoy as they look forward to the day's lesson. For example, ask students to do one of the following activities or modify one to suit your students' needs. Students can:

- Engage in a mindfulness or SEL activity such as breathing exercises, journaling, or check-in polls. (See Section Six for the Three Signature Practices from CASEL.org.)

- Write or share the answer to a question that requires students to make a prediction, review prior learning, or form an opinion.

- Work with classmates to combine puzzle pieces containing information about the material being studied.
- Survey classmates to gather reactions to a quotation related to the day's lesson.
- Complete a graphic organizer.
- Work with classmates to skim the day's reading and make group predictions.
- Work with a partner to solve a problem related to the lesson.
- Respond to an intriguing, open-ended question.
- List what they already know about the day's lesson.
- Solve a brain teaser.
- List three reasons to study the day's topic.
- With another student, combine information from notes.
- Watch a video clip and write about it.

As you can see, there are countless ways to open class with a predictable routine that your students will enjoy. Use Teacher Template 4.5 to make interesting and beneficial plans for the start of each class.

Plans for Starting Class Effectively

With just a bit of careful planning, you can make the opening minutes of your class a productive time that creates community and gets students ready to learn.

Lesson topic: _____ Date: _____

Materials to be distributed:

_____

_____

_____

_____

Routine procedures posted:

_____

_____

_____

_____

Day's agenda for students:

_____

_____

_____

_____

Activity to open class:

_____

_____

_____

_____

Materials needed:

_____

_____

Time needed: _____

Productive Transitions

Because your students are accustomed to the fast-paced action of modern life, they may lose interest in a lesson that seems to last too long. While there are lessons requiring sustained workshop periods, labs, or assessments, experienced teachers generally design lessons around several shorter activities. Although having several activities is sensible, it requires more transitions.

Transitions are difficult to manage well because they require students to do three things in a very brief amount of time: mentally close out one task, prepare for the next one, and refocus their mental energy in a new way. Fortunately, you can do several things to help students handle transitions effectively. Here's how:

- Design activities that flow naturally from one to the next, requiring a minimum of large-group instruction from you. Sequencing instruction in this way encourages students to manage their own learning.

- Try using a kitchen timer to set a time limit for a change in activities. When students know that they have only a minute or two to switch from one activity to another, they are more likely to move quickly.

- Teach students routines, workflows, and traffic patterns to reduce the time spent in transitions.

> "Transitions. The bell rings and I begin, as I do each class, by reading a short poem. Students turn and settle. We anchor ourselves to this space and to this time together, with words. They indulge me. This is a physics class and I welcome all students and all parts of each student. We start class with art and move seamlessly into science."
>
> *Kate Kennedy, 30 years' experience*

The Last Ten Minutes of Class

You have two goals for the end of class (for secondary teachers) or the end of an instructional block (for elementary teachers): to have students who are reluctant to leave and to have students solidify their learning through a closure activity. The last ten minutes of class are the ideal time to accomplish both goals through an optimistic closure exercise. (See Section Six for details of this signature SEL practice from CASEL.)

The routine you create for the end of class should be predictable, but also one that students can look forward to. Here is a simple two-step plan for the end of class that you can follow to make sure that the last few minutes of your class are as productive as all the rest:

- **Step One:** Do an eight-minute closing exercise. Use this brief period to help students solidify learning by reviewing what they learned and by looking ahead to what they will be learning next. Here are some activities that you can adopt or adapt to end your class on a positive note:

- Have students individually list several things that they have just learned. Have them share this list with a classmate or with the entire group.

- Ask students to predict what they will learn next.

- Ask students to predict the meaning of the key terms for the next part of the unit.

- Have students write a quick explanation of the most interesting aspect of the day's lesson.

- Hold a quick review or vocabulary practice.

- Ask students to explain the directions for their homework. Be sure to ask them to estimate how long it should take them to complete the assignment successfully.

- Reveal a final thought for the day that you have on a slide or hidden under a sheet of paper that was taped to the board earlier in the day.

- Give your students a brief passage to read and ask them to comment on it.

- Show students a relevant cartoon or illustration for a quick discussion or recap.

- Assign an exit slip activity.

- **Step Two:** Implement the two-minute dismissal. This may take longer for elementary students who will need to gather backpacks and follow protocols for meeting families and caregivers. For secondary students, after the closing exercise, allow two minutes for your students to prepare to be dismissed at your signal. During this time, they should have a routine to follow that includes the following activities:

  - Disposing of trash
  - Storing books and materials
  - Closing, storing, or charging devices
  - Checking to make sure they don't leave anything behind

During the last two minutes of class, you should move to the door so that you can speak to students as they leave. This will prevent any last-minute misbehavior and show your students that they have a teacher who cares about them. You should not allow students to congregate at the door or to jump up and bolt when the bell rings. Use Teacher Template 4.6 to create plans to help you end class effectively.

Plans for Ending Class Effectively

Lesson topic: _____ Date: _____

First Eight Minutes

Review activity:

_____

_____

_____

_____

_____

If there is homework or practice today, discuss it:

_____

_____

_____

_____

_____

Prediction activity:

_____

_____

_____

_____

Reflection on the day's learning activity:

_____

_____

_____

_____

_____

Last Two Minutes

Students clean their work areas and gather their belongings to prepare to exit. Teacher moves to the door. Students exit on a dismissal signal from you. Elementary students may line up and walk with you to their after-school pickup location.

How to Use Any Time Left at the End of Class

Sometimes, despite your best efforts, there may be a few minutes left at the end of class. Although many teachers may be tempted to allow students to just sit and wait for the bell to signal the end of class, you should consider how you and your students can benefit from these tiny gifts of free time. With just a bit of preparation and planning, you can use even these short moments to connect with your students. In addition to using any of the activities mentioned earlier in this section, here are some ideas for you to consider:

- Show a short video from an inspirational segment on TeacherTube or YouTube.
- Keep a list of school-appropriate riddles or jokes to read so that your students can leave class smiling. A good source for this is Riddles.com.
- Conduct a quick informal survey. Ask students their opinions about school events, sports, songs, or just about anything that they are interested in outside of school.
- Ask students each to state something new that they have learned during the class or the week.
- Ask students to share their favorites—favorite colors, foods, music, sports teams, and so on.
- Ask students to share their pet peeves.
- Ask students their opinions about a class problem.
- Read a biographical paragraph or story to inspire your students.
- Ask students to tell you something that surprised or confused them on the first day of school or when they were younger.

Questions to Discuss with Colleagues

Sharing ideas with colleagues is a helpful way to devise solutions to some of the problems that you must manage successfully at school. Here, you will find several topics to open discussions with colleagues about successful instructional practices:

1. Your students continue to talk while you are talking. You have asked them to quiet down several times but to no avail. What can you do to get their attention focused on you instead of on chatting with one another?

2. Your students are not as accepting of one another's mistakes as you would like for them to be. What can you do to change their relationship to mistakes and keep them from snickering when a classmate makes a mistake in front of the others?

3. You know that growth mindset is vital and want it to be part of your classroom culture, but have noticed that students still say things like, "I'm just not good at this." What can you do to help students adopt a growth mindset?

4. You have several students who are seemingly not motivated to engage in learning. What should you do to motivate these students? Who can help you with this? How can you learn more about how to motivate each student?

5. Even though you know the first ten minutes of class are crucial in setting the tone for the rest of it, your students are slow to settle down. They chat and walk around the room and are obviously not in a hurry to get to work. What can you do to make the first ten minutes of your class productive?

Topics to Discuss with a Mentor

Although the topics that new teachers need to discuss with a mentor vary from teacher to teacher and from school to school, there are some that most first-year teachers should be comfortable discussing with a mentor or a trusted colleague. You should ask your mentor about these topics from this section:

- Suggestions for the first and last few minutes of class
- How to check-in with students to support their social and emotional needs
- How to cope with some of the predictable interruptions at your school
- Suggestions for delivering effective instructions
- Suggestions for improving your classroom leadership skills

Reflection Questions to Guide Your Thinking

1. Think about the ways that you may unintentionally waste your students' time. What can you do to make the most of instructional time?

2. How effective do you think you are at being a capable classroom leader at this point in your career? What are your strengths? What are your areas for growth? How can you use your strengths to overcome your weaknesses?

3. Teachers modeling their own growth mindset is an important factor in students adopting a growth mindset. What language do you use to illustrate your own growth mindset? What do you do or say when you make mistakes? Is "yet" a common word in your vocabulary?

4. Which of the activities in this section would work well with your students? How can you organize them so that you have a quick list of activities at hand when you need it to plan instruction?

5. The beginning and end of class are times you can use to your students' advantage. What routines do you have planned to open and close class in a way that builds community and maximizes learning?

SECTION FIVE

Start the School Year Strong

The start of the school year is filled with hope, possibility, anticipation, and some nervousness. One of the most important aspects of creating the positive classroom environment that you want for your students involves getting the school year off to a great start even before the first day. Your goal for the start of school is simple: your students should look forward to the rest of the school year because they feel comfortable with you and with their classmates. To achieve this goal, you can use many different strategies.

Experienced teachers know that getting to know students and their families and caregivers before school begins can significantly reduce the first-day jitters and set everyone up for success. There are many ways to do this if your school does not host an open house before school starts. Send an email introducing yourself and inviting elementary students and families to drop off school supplies during a 30-minute window while you're setting up your class. Secondary teachers may want to host a few 15-minute Zoom meet and greets. Whatever strategy you choose, the first day will go more smoothly if you invest in creating connections early and often.

In the rest of this section, you will find some of these strategies divided into four categories: getting ready for a great year, leading the first day, establishing positive relationships, and managing the first week of school.

Get Ready for a Great School Year

Getting ready for a great school year starts before your students ever enter your classroom. In the days leading up to the first day of class, two of your most important tasks are setting up the physical space of your classroom, and starting to welcome students, families, and caregivers and preparing for open house if your school has one before school begins.

Because there are so many tasks that all teachers must complete in the few weeks before the beginning of school, and in-service days are few, it is very easy to be overwhelmed. The timeline that follows will help you prioritize your responsibilities and avoid being overwhelmed with too much to do in too little time.

A Month before School Begins

- Decide on your strategy for beginning to connect with students, families and care-givers before school begins.

- Shop the back-to-school sales for supplies.

- Make sure that your wardrobe reflects your professional status and allows you to move comfortably through your school day. For example, a kindergarten teacher may need to sit in low chairs. A physical education, art, or career technical education (CTE) teacher will need to dress for their unique classroom spaces.

- Exercise, eat well, hydrate, and get enough rest.

- Order any supplies your district has allocated money for.

- Download or bookmark your district's calendar for the school year.

- Download or bookmark your state and district curriculum guides.

- Pick up district-provided instructional materials, teachers' editions, and supplementary curriculum.

- Begin researching, reading, and studying instructional materials.

- Create your professional goals. (See Section One for help with this.)

- Plan how you will manage the stress that naturally accompanies the start of your new career. (See Section One as well as the end of this section for advice on stress management.)

Three Weeks before School Begins

- Send communication to students, families, and caregivers inviting them to connect before school begins based on the strategy you selected. Make sure to introduce yourself. (See Sample 5.1 for a letter template you can adjust to meet your needs.)

- Create a general curriculum overview for the year.

- Join at least one professional organization.

- Connect with your colleagues and professional learning network (PLN) to share how you are preparing for the school year and learn from their ideas.

- Exercise, eat well, hydrate, and get enough rest.

- Start investigating helpful websites and social media for advice and encouragement.

- Create broad unit plans for the first grading period.

Two Weeks before School Begins

- Make sure that the equipment in your room is in working order.

- Contact the IT Department if anything is out of order, or just to get to know them, prior to the first day.

- Draft your class routines and procedures. Classroom agreements will be finalized with your students. (See Section Eleven for further information.)

- Put together information for substitute teachers in case you need them.
- Exercise, eat well, hydrate, and get enough rest.
- Based on the instructional strategies you plan to use, arrange the furniture in your classroom.
- Set up your desk or workspace and filing systems.

One Week before School Begins

- Participate in school and district professional development.
- Host the in-person or virtual meet and greets you invited students, families, and caregivers to attend.
- Exercise, eat well, hydrate, and get enough rest.
- Reach out to the special education teachers to gather information about your students' needs.
- Download or bookmark the school forms you will need, such as hall passes or lunch counts.
- Work with a mentor to find answers to your procedural questions.
- Create procedures for daily routines, such as taking attendance, distributing papers, gathering on the rug, or taking a lunch count.
- Write out your first two weeks of daily lesson plans. (See Section Nine for tips on writing lesson plans.)
- Prepare a list of alternative plans to use just in case a lesson doesn't work.
- Study your class rosters to start learning your students' names.
- Create seating charts.
- Familiarize yourself with the apps and programs you will be expected to use for school business, such as attendance, grades, or your evaluation during the school year.
- Plan your personal lunch and snacks menu for the first week of school and do your meal prep.

The Day before School Begins

- Finish any last-minute tasks.
- Ask any last-minute questions.
- Exercise, eat well, hydrate, and get enough rest.
- Plan how you will manage your work-related stress.
- Lay out your first day of school outfit the night before.
- Pack your materials and water bottle so that you can start the day confidently.

Sample 5.1

Meet the Teacher Letter to Families and Caregivers

There are so many templates to choose from online. Here is a basic outline for any introductory letter. Remember to have it translated into appropriate home languages.

I.   Warm and Friendly Introduction
II. Your Teaching Background/Experience
III. Your Excitement for Teaching and the New Year
IV. Reminders of Dates or Actions Needed
V.   Your Favorite Things
VI. Contact Info

Hello Families and Caregivers,

I am so excited to meet you and look forward to having a wonderful school year. This is my first year of teaching after graduating from _____ with a degree in _____. I absolutely love teaching and this year will be an exciting time for all of us. I am delighted to be teaching _____where we will study _____.

I believe that strong partnerships between home and school are important to help your child succeed academically, socially, and emotionally. I invite you to attend Open House on __[date] at ___[time] and don't forget to email me your Tell Me about Your Student letter [link] as well.

It's important to keep open lines of communication so if you have questions, concerns, or compliments to share, please feel free to visit our class website at:_____ email me at _____ or call me at school. My number is _____.

I am looking forward to meeting you and working with you and your student to create a wonderful school year.

Best wishes,

Classroom Safety Issues

As you begin creating the classroom space you want for your students, it's important to remember that maintaining classroom safety is one of the most important tasks that we have. After all, the well-being of a classroom full of students depends on our diligence. It's a good idea for you, as a new teacher, to learn about school safety by following your district's safety procedures, talking with the custodian or maintenance personnel, observing other teachers, asking questions, and using common sense. Follow these suggestions to make your classroom secure for you and for your students:

- Check classroom windows and screens to be sure they are in good working condition.
- Check all outlets. When you do plug in equipment, make sure all electrical cords are secure.
- Keep your classroom as clean as you can to reduce the spread of contagious diseases.
- Use only cleaning supplies that meet your school's policies and are not harmful to students.
- If possible, teach with your door closed. You will maximize heating and cooling while minimizing disruptions from outside your classroom.
- Don't keep matches, sharp scissors, or other potentially harmful items where your students can access them.
- If your classroom is not in use, keep it locked. No room should be left unattended.
- Make it easy for students to move about. Space desks carefully, and don't block the exits to your classroom.
- Stabilize all bookcases and other tall pieces of equipment so that they can't tip over. Make sure all objects on them are also placed securely.
- Keep your personal belongings and confidential documents securely locked.
- Have a system in place when students leave the room. Have a sign-out sheet for time out and time returning. When students leave the room with a hall pass, be alert to when they return. You are responsible for their safety.
- Never give students keys to your classroom or car.
- Learn your school's procedures for such emergencies as fire drills, disaster drills, or intruders in the building.
- When students say that they are feeling unwell, take the matter seriously.
- Don't use hard candy as a reward or treat. It is too easy for students to choke on it.
- Never leave your students unsupervised.
- Report suspected weapons or potential acts of violence immediately.
- Be aware of the procedures you are to follow to assist your students who have a chronic illness.
- Report suspected child abuse immediately and follow school procedures. You are a mandatory reporter.

- Make your classroom as orderly as possible. Teach and enforce classroom agreements, policies, and procedures until everyone understands what is expected.
- Observe your students at all times. Be vigilant monitoring appropriate behavior, use of devices, and physical safety.
- Take a stand against bullying in your classroom. Intervene in the moment to stop the incident and make it easy for students to talk to you if they are the targets of bullies.
- Make it clear that this is an inclusive classroom, and you will not tolerate bias against anyone based on their identity. Intervene right away if you hear bias related to identity such as: race, gender, sex, sexual orientation, class, ability, religion, age, body type, language, or national origin.

Evaluate Your Classroom

When you go to your classroom for the first time, you will be able to save time if you work efficiently to plan how you want to set it up.

- You will save time if you have paper, pencil, and a tape measure (or an app that allows you to record measurements) with you on your first visit.
- Photograph the room thoroughly so that you can make plans when you are not at school.
- Measure storage areas, windows, shelves, bulletin boards, interactive boards, and dry erase boards.
- Locate the electrical outlets, internet connections, telephone jacks, and other electronic connections. Look for equipment and furniture that needs repair or that could pose safety concerns.
- Survey the room for items or areas that have the potential to distract your students.
- Count the student desks, tables, chairs, and computers to determine if you have enough for your students. Make note of any necessary repairs.
- Survey the room to make sure you have these essential classroom items:
  - Keys to the door and any lockable cabinets
  - Cables for computers and other electronic equipment
  - Extension cords
  - Emergency procedures booklet/equipment
  - Operating instructions for the heating and cooling systems
  - Windows and blinds that are clean and in good repair
  - At least one pencil sharpener
  - A clock

- Sufficient lighting
- Bookshelves
- A desk or workspace and chair for the teacher
- Empty and usable filing cabinets
- A trash container
- A recycle bin
- A computer for the teacher to use
- A classroom phone
- An intercom system

Prepare Your Classroom for Students

Your students will thrive in an environment in which you take their needs seriously and in which they feel valued. When you create a classroom that invites students to join in a learning community, you are reaching out to your students in a tangible way. An inviting classroom sends a clear message to your students that they matter.

Creating a safe and welcoming place where students can comfortably work together is worth the hard work and energy it takes to complete such tasks as moving furniture, taping down cords, and decorating bulletin boards. Preparing a classroom does take time, however. Plan to spend several hours in your room while you are setting it up. It can be fun to invite a friend or family member to assist you.

One of the best choices for a teacher who wants to create an inviting classroom is to make the classroom reflect student interests and showcase student work. Too often, teachers make the mistake of decorating their classroom beautifully, but with items that appeal to their own tastes instead of their students. With creativity and careful planning, it is possible to create a welcoming classroom without spending a great deal of money. Here are some suggestions that will help you get started:

Use the Entire Room

While you won't have any on the first day of school, leave room to decorate your classroom with student work. Students feel a sense of ownership and pride in a classroom where their work is displayed. Be sure to display everyone's work. If you hang only the best work, students might feel that you are playing favorites, which, of course, would be harmful to the class environment. You can display all sorts of student work, not just creative projects or *A* papers. Post photos, drawings, notes, sketches—anything that shows how much you value your students' efforts. Students will enjoy seeing a changing display of things they have created far more than purchased posters.

- Set aside an area for class business, where students can turn in assignments. In addition to your learning management system (LMS), you can post such items as: assignments, due dates, school announcements, and other school business.

Your students could participate in keeping this area up to date, if they are old enough to do so.

● Set aside an area for motivation. Students could illustrate words of wisdom from the internet, books they have read, or song lyrics. Consider using a giant graphic of brainstormed mottos for success to remind students how much you care about their present and their future.

Create a Calming Space

When students are dysregulated, they need a space to calm down and some strategies to self-regulate. Some schools have designated sensory rooms equipped with special equipment to help students regroup and refocus. It's also a good idea to have some of those strategies and tools immediately available. Working with counselors, social workers, or behavior and learning specialists in your school, establish a calming space in your classroom. If there is no space in your classroom, then designate a place nearby where students can go and still be supervised.

Develop a calming space where a dysregulated student can breathe and regain composure. In elementary classrooms this may be a quiet corner with plants and a cozy bean bag chair. In secondary classrooms, this might be a cozy corner of the classroom, a neighboring teacher's classroom, the counseling office, a hallway walking loop, a trip to the water fountain, or an exercise bike in the back of the room. Stock these areas with a dozen flashcards featuring various self-regulating strategies to give students some options to choose from. Include a few age-appropriate sensory tools such as fidgets, stress balls, or a pinwheel. Younger students like to watch the pinwheel spin and blowing on it requires them to take deep breaths.

Teach students how to gain access to the calming space and how to use the available tools before they become dysregulated.

Create Quick and Effective Bulletin Boards

Everything in teaching is purposeful, even your bulletin boards. Whether creating connections within the learning community or across the curriculum there are myriad ways to design bulletin boards. Many teachers also have a theme for the year or character traits they want to connect to. Perhaps you love the creativity of creating them or prefer to delegate the responsibility to a paraprofessional, volunteer, or student. Whatever you decide, you may try these simple tricks to make the bulletin boards in your classroom connection builders without taking hours of your time to maintain:

● Discover what supplies your school stocks and if they have a die-cutting machine for letters, numbers, shapes, and so on.

● If your school has a copy room, ask the staff there if they can help with bulletin boards.

- Use butcher paper or wrapping paper as a background. Staple it into place at the start of the year and you will not have to replace it the rest of the year unless it shows signs of wear.

- Borders can be store-bought or simple strips of construction paper. You could also cut out borders from old newspapers, magazines, wrapping paper, or even maps.

- Use staples to attach items to the bulletin board and adhesive-backed hooks to hang three-dimensional objects.

- The internet is full of helpful tips and design ideas for using the bulletin boards in your room to connect your students with each other and the unit of study.

TRAFFIC FLOW CONSIDERATIONS

Traffic flow in a classroom is more important than many new teachers realize when they are getting ready for the school year. It determines the ease with which students can access resources, transition between activities, or shift seating into new configurations. For example, if you place your trash can near the door, the stapler in the back of the room, and a tray to collect completed work on the side, students will wander all over your room just to throw away trash, staple their papers, and turn in their work.

Carefully consider the routine activities your students will perform before you set up your room so that you can minimize distractions and interruptions. Some of these routine activities could include:

- Entering class
- Storing backpacks and jackets
- Gathering on the rug
- Checking the calendar
- Checking the clock
- Applying hand sanitizer
- Checking the board
- Turning in assignments (digital and paper)
- Speaking with you privately
- Using a computer or device
- Picking up supplies
- Disposing of trash
- Sharpening pencils
- Using a stapler
- Engaging in a large group discussion
- Working in small groups

Seating Arrangements that Work

Arranging student chairs, tables, desks, flexible seating, and the rug area (if you have one) so that your students can pursue their work is important for their success. We know that seating can affect students' motivation, focus, relationships, and learning. The way you arrange student seating can also affect your teaching style, so make sure you choose the arrangement that supports the teaching strategies you intend to use. Your grade level and class size will also affect the seating arrangements.

During the year, you will probably move the furniture several times or even provide free or unassigned seating. Until you get to know your students and have helped them learn the routines and expectations, it is a good idea to keep your seating arrangements as predictable as possible. You may want to sketch your design or use an online classroom layout tool before you start moving the furniture. To arrange student seating for an optimum effect, keep these pointers in mind:

- Arrange seating so that you can see every student's face. Every student should also be able to see you, the board, or screen with no difficulty.
- Keep in mind that some students have "preferential seating" as an accommodation on their learning plans.
- Retain the ability to move freely around the room.
- Keep desks away from tempting graffiti spots, such as bulletin boards, window ledges, or walls.
- Avoid placing desks near distractions, such as a pencil sharpener or a computer monitor with an interesting screensaver.

FIVE STUDENT SEATING ARRANGEMENTS

Although there seem to be an endless number of ways to arrange student seating, here are five common ones that many teachers find particularly effective in helping students learn both academic and social skills. If you choose to assign seating, make sure that students know that assignments will change every month or at an interval that makes sense for your class.

Collaborative Groups or Pods: Many teachers begin the year with desks or tables arranged in collaborative groups of four to six students. If your goal is to help students develop connections, learn communication skills, and support each other's learning, then this is an effective arrangement. If possible, arrange groupings so that no one has their back to the board or screen where information will be presented. With a new class, you will not know all the students or how they interact with each other, so don't hesitate to change seat assignments once you know your students better.

Flexible Seating: Common aspects of this arrangement may include a variety of zones with low chairs, exercise balls, high-top tables, standing desks, a small couch, or an armchair. It will look different in elementary and secondary classrooms, but in both cases, students have some agency to choose the physical space that best supports their focus and learning. There are unique issues that arise from this seating arrangement. See the following "Flexible Seating" section for more details.

Whole-Group Horseshoe: In this configuration, the students on the two sides of a horseshoe face one another, while the students seated in the connecting row at the back of the horseshoe face the front of the classroom. This arrangement is suitable for full class discussions and turn and talks because it encourages students to communicate with one another.

Pairs or Triads: Seating students in pairs or triads makes it very easy for them to work together. This configuration facilitates the formation of collaborative study groups because students grow to depend on and support their group partners. It is ideal for allowing students to collaborate and engage with the large group when appropriate.

Activity Centers: Elementary classrooms and secondary science and CTE classrooms often have activity centers, lab stations, or machinery benches, respectively, where students rotate through activities. Elementary teachers may have centers for reading, writing, math, art, digital devices, or makerspaces. These are often set up along the perimeter of the classroom to allow for both a large group gathering space and small group rotations among stations.

The *Why* and *How* of Seating Charts

No matter how old your students are, seating charts are a necessary tool. Seating charts are vital when you have a substitute and can save time daily when taking attendance. If you use a seating chart, here's how you and your students will benefit:

- Teachers can create healthy and positive collaborative groups.
- Introverted students will have the same seating opportunities as extroverted students without having to compete for a seat.
- Students will not argue with one another over which desk belongs to whom.
- Struggling students may choose a more distant seat and can be moved from there to a place where you can more easily engage them in lessons or offer assistance.

"On the first day, I would have students write on an index card things that they thought I should know about them. Every year I had at least one student who let me know that they needed glasses or that they had trouble seeing the board. This helped me with finding them a good seat AND following up with Student Services for resources for glasses for families."

Allison French, 29 years' experience

- Easily distracted students can be seated in a place where it will be easier for them to stay on task.

- Students requiring accommodations can sit in a location where their needs can best be met.

Begin the school year with a preliminary seating chart that will make it easier for you to learn your students' names. In a few days, after you get to know your students, you should make up a seating chart based on other factors. Here's how:

Step One: Begin by drawing a diagram of your room in which each seat is represented by a circle or square. Many student information systems (SIS) have seating chart templates allowing teachers to drag and drop students into new seating charts.

Step Two: Using your SIS or a pencil, add the names of your students on your diagram. Begin with students who have special learning plans such as IEPs, 504 Plans, or Personal Education Plans and place them where you can best meet their needs.

Step Three: After you have considered students with learning differences, move on to the students without plans who struggle with behaviors. Place them where they can best focus on their work and practice social skills.

Step Four: Finally, place the rest of your students. Do your best to find each student a seat that will support their academic, social, emotional, and behavioral needs.

Flexible Seating

As teachers introduce more movement in the classroom and classrooms begin to reflect modern workspaces, flexible seating has become more popular. Although the idea of providing flexible seating options has customarily been more common in the younger grades than in secondary classrooms, it is a concept that is gaining in popularity in all grade levels as school districts recognize the importance of movement and student choice in promoting student achievement. In classrooms where there is a flexible seating arrangement, teachers create *student workspaces* in place of more traditional student seating.

Just a quick search of online images for classrooms with flexible seating arrangements reveals the endless possibilities and variations available to teachers interested in flexible seating. Just make sure they conform to district specifications. In a typical classroom with flexible seating, you could find arrangements that include the following:

- Soft cushions, beanbags, and chairs of all types
- Worktables for students to share
- Cubbies and bins for shared materials as well as for individual student storage
- A small work space area for the teacher
- Rugs and carpets to delineate specific work areas
- Balance balls, wobble chairs, stools, and other options for student seating

Instead of being expected to sit quietly for long periods at a desk, students in classrooms where there is flexible seating can choose to sit, kneel, stand, lean, lie on the floor, or select another option their teacher designs for them. There are several unmistakable advantages to flexible seating arrangements in classrooms. In classrooms with flexible seating, students can:

- Choose the workspace that appeals to them
- Learn to make good choices about how to work efficiently
- Move around and be more active as they work
- Be comfortable instead of restrained as they learn
- Remain on task while working because they are engaged and focused

Although the benefits of flexible seating arrangements are unmistakable, there are some important considerations, especially for first-year teachers:

- Have a clear purpose for recommending flexible seating in your classroom. What will it make possible?
- Consult your supervisor and the district's guidelines on furniture to make sure your proposal aligns with them.
- Other teachers may not have experience with flexible seating, and therefore, may not be able to offer help and suggestions based on their experience.
- Switching from a more traditional classroom arrangement where the furniture is already provided for you can create storage problems as you eliminate furniture.
- Your school district may not provide you with the funds to purchase the new equipment that you need, and the cost for many teachers (even those who are thrifty and inventive) can be significant.
- Classroom management problems may be an issue at first as you and your students adapt to new spaces and ways of thinking about how to work productively.
- Because many students with learning differences require preferential seating, it is not always easy to provide those necessary accommodations.
- Flexible seating requires experimentation, tweaking, and careful planning at a time when you are already dealing with many other classroom issues, such as instructional planning, building positive relationships, and classroom management.

Despite these negatives, the advantages of flexible seating arrangements are unmistakable. If you decide to use flexible seating, here are a few suggestions to make the process a bit easier:

- Make changes very gradually. After careful consideration, add in a shared workspace. Provide a comfortable chair or two. As students adjust to these and as you learn how to manage them well, you can then make other changes.

- Safety should be a first concern. Furniture that has been purchased by a school district has been vetted for safety issues, while furniture you purchase has not. Some districts do not allow teachers to use classroom furniture that has not been purchased by the district. Provide a proposal to your supervisor about the changes that you are planning to make to get approval before you begin.

- Expect to rethink classroom management. Different spaces require different behavior. What was unacceptable behavior in a traditional space may be acceptable in a space where there is more student movement and interaction.

- Continue to make your classroom as transparent as possible. Make sure you clearly articulate the purpose and the process to supervisors, students, families, and caregivers.

- Consider assigning spaces and rotating students through the different options at first to reduce student conflicts (they are likely to argue over seating choices), to expose students to the various work spaces, and to reduce student anxiety about having to compete with classmates for spaces.

- Help students make sound decisions about how and where they are most comfortable working. Student choice still requires teacher guidance.

- Emergent bilingual students, students with IEPs, 504 Plans, or other accommodations that require preferential seating will need options that allow for those accommodations.

- Enlist other teachers who may want to create flexible seating arrangements in their classrooms so that you can share ideas and resources.

- Don't overspend your own funds. If you are committed to flexible seating, work with your district to fund your classroom changes instead of paying for them yourself.

Welcome Your Students to a New Year

When you begin planning for the first day or the first week of a new school year, you will need to prioritize getting to know your students along with classroom management and instructional design. There is nothing more important than building supportive relationships with and among students so that all students feel welcome in your classroom. When students feel that they are valued and included, they will find it easier to cooperate, to work, and to learn. Fortunately, there are many ways to make students of all ages feel that they are welcome at school:

- Play music as they enter the room. You can use instrumental or classical music or even music with lyrics suitable for school.

- Make sure that every student is quickly seated in the right spot with as little confusion as possible.

- Smile at individuals and at the entire group.

- When students enter the room, have an interesting activity for them to do right away.

- If students do not have school supplies, lend them what they need without fuss.

> "Creating a welcoming and culturally inclusive classroom from the very beginning of the year requires intentionality around developing cultural competence, prioritizing equity, and co-creating liberatory learning spaces."
>
> *Jocelynn Hubbard, 18 years' experience, customteachingsolutions.com and The Culture-Centered Classroom Podcast*

- Make sure students know the names of several of their classmates by the end of class.

- Having students interact with classmates on the first day sends a positive message about the importance of teamwork in your class.

- If you need transitions between activities, consider playing music or showing a motivational or inspiring video clip.

- Spend time chatting with students and getting to know them as individuals.

- Talk to your students about how you are nervous and that you imagine that they are as well. Discuss your shared anxieties.

- If students will be moving between other classrooms, make sure everyone knows where to go. Passing out school maps and assigning buddies to find other classrooms are both good ideas.

- A scavenger hunt around the school is a fun way to locate important locations like the library, the gym, the cafeteria, and the office.

- Wear a name tag. If appropriate, ask students to wear name tags as well for at least part of class.

- Ask for their advice on solving a classroom problem, such as how to store materials or remember the schedule for the next day.

- Make sure you are organized and prepared for class so that you can focus on helping your students.

- Assign buddies to students. This helps students who may be new to the school or students who don't have easy social connections. Buddies can also be supportive when students miss class.

- If students have a written assignment, provide the paper. Odd shapes and colors can be more fun for students than lined paper.

- Compliment the group throughout class and especially at the end with specific and meaningful feedback on their successes.

How to Hold a Successful Open House

During an open house, families and caregivers can come to school to meet their children's teachers. In some places, this event is referred to as "Back to School Night." No matter which name your district uses, this meeting can generate goodwill, partnership, and volunteers to support you and your students all year long. It is an effective way to learn more about students' cultures and build a strong team of support for your students.

Open House is an opportunity to authentically connect with students and families. Talk with your colleagues, mentor, and supervisor about expectations for teachers at Open House. If possible, spend time getting to know parents. Have them say their name and their student's name. Ask them "What's one word that describes their Open House Experience so far?" or "What's one word that describes their student's school year so far?" or "What are you looking forward to this school year?"

In the following pages, you will find information designed to help you host an open house successfully. You will learn a few general guidelines, what to include in your presentation, ways to inspire confidence, and how to navigate tricky situations. You will also find a suggested timeline as you prepare to meet the families and caregivers who love and care for your students. It's natural to feel a little anxious about an open house, and advance preparation will ease those worries.

A Few General Guidelines

- Research the home languages of your students in advance, and make sure you have translation and interpretation services available to communicate with families that speak languages other than English.

- While your school will send a general invitation to families and caregivers, you should consider sending an additional message letting them know how excited you are to meet them. You may choose to use email or your school to home communication app. If your students have cell phones, you may also ask students to take out their phones and text the details to their home adults.

- Send the Families and Caregivers Template 5.1 as an email or Google form ahead of time asking for them to complete it by the date of open house.

- Review the schedule for open house and prepare a lesson based on the allotted time. Consider your objectives for the evening and how best to achieve them.

- Plan a brief presentation based on the allocated time and your goals. (See the next section for details of the presentation.)

- Some participants may have questions about specific students. While you won't talk about specific students at open house, invite them to set up an appointment for a call or meeting another day when you can address their question in more detail.

- Clean up your classroom to show respect for families, caregivers, and the important job of educating their children. Make the room as attractive, clean, and welcoming as possible.

- Plan and practice your presentation. This is not the time to try your skill at winging it.

- Start collecting student work on the first day of class and display it on the walls of your classroom. Families and caregivers enjoy seeing student work on display and it can help them understand the high standards and creativity you expect students to reach during the year.

- Prepare a handout with general information about the learning experiences in store for your grade level or course, your homework expectations, important dates, classroom policies, class website, snacks (any nut allergies?), volunteers, birthdays, cell phones, headphones, and your contact information. Include school resources such as meal programs, counseling, health clinic, library services and more. If you have volunteer opportunities, list these as well. This is a rare opportunity to share information and you want to make the most of it.

- Have copies of instructional materials and required reading available.

- Prepare a sign-in sheet and place it near the door. Include a column for students' names as well as one for adults' names so that you will be able to match families and caregivers to their students.

- Dress in a way that communicates confidence and professionalism without intimidating families and caregivers.

- Greet guests at the door just as you do your students.

- Place a marker, name tags, or table tent at each seat for guests to fill out.

What to Include in Your Presentation

Each school has different expectations of Open House. If teachers are expected to make a presentation, then the length of your presentation will vary based on the time allocated in your school's schedule. So select from the following list based on your goals for the open house.

- Introduce yourself, your teaching experience, and consider including a fun fact or hobby to build rapport.

- Take a minute or two for guests to voice their names and their student's name. It shows that you value knowing who is present and gives the adults a chance to start knowing each other. If it takes a village to raise a child, you can help the village start connecting.

- Share your excitement for the school year, highlights of the learning in store for their students, including an overview of the topics and skills they will study. Include any significant dates for larger projects or field trips if you have them.

- Let them know how they can support student learning at home.

- Communicate your class policies and procedures.

- Include contact information and your preferred method of communication (phone, app, or email) so they can reach you with questions, concerns, and positive feedback.

- Consider what volunteer support you need during the year and share these opportunities. It is often helpful to identify a "room parent" to help with field trips, celebrations, and more during the year.

- Leave two to three minutes for questions and prepare answers to questions you anticipate they may have.
- End on a note of gratitude for their participation and for entrusting you with their child's education.

Awkward interactions may occur at open house. Participants may ask inappropriate or challenging questions. As difficult as it may be, thank them for their question and deflect or deescalate the interaction. For example, if a participant asks a question about a specific child, let them know you want to protect their privacy and invite them to set up a private conversation later.

If someone challenges the curriculum or books being taught, thank them for the question, let them know that you teach to state standards, and suggest they reach out to the principal for more information. If you teach a topic or curriculum that might be considered controversial, you might consider having a dedicated informational evening with administrators present.

How to Inspire Confidence

- Know all of your students' names.
- Greet families and caregivers at the door. Pleasantly welcome any latecomers.
- Begin promptly. Be upbeat, enthusiastic, and positive.
- Be very careful to protect student privacy and confidentiality during open house and throughout the year.
- As families and caregivers enter your classroom, have copies of the Families and Caregivers Template 5.1 that you emailed before open house and a manila privacy envelope for collecting them.

TIMELINE FOR A SUCCESSFUL OPEN HOUSE

Advance planning will help you make the most of this opportunity to engage with families and caregivers and lay a strong foundation of trust to support student success. To ensure that you use your time wisely, you can follow the timeline provided here:

Three Weeks in Advance

- Request your school's translation and interpretation services as needed to translate communications home and interpret during open house.

One Week in Advance

- Send home open house invitations in English and the home language.
- Email home Families and Caregivers Template 5.1 in English and the home language.

- Display student work.
- Begin preparing your presentation.
- Create and copy handouts.

Three Days Before

- Finalize your presentation deck.
- Create a sign-in sheet.

Two Days Before

- Begin practicing your presentation.

One Day Before

- Practice your presentation again; you cannot be too polished.
- Begin straightening your classroom.
- Get enough rest for the long day tomorrow.
- Make a plan for your own dinner if open house is in the evening.

On the Day of the Open House

- Dress professionally.
- Adopt a positive attitude.
- Tidy the classroom one final time.
- Make sure all equipment is working.
- Put a sign-in sheet on each desk or a couple of sign-in sheets near the door with several pens or pencils nearby to reduce wait times and lines.
- Set out Template 5.1 and the manila envelope to collect completed documents that were not returned electronically.
- Place a handout, a marker, and either name tags or table tents at each seat.
- Have instructional materials and books on display and handouts ready.

"Reach out to parents and guardians at the beginning of the year. As many as you can. Not all caregivers can attend Back to School Night. But establishing a positive relationship from the start can make a huge difference. I've sent personal thank-you notes to each parent or guardian who attended Back to School Night with an observation or two about his or her child. And then followed up with those who couldn't attend with the same. If you do this early enough, there is something encouraging to say to each family."

Jennifer Burns, 13 years' experience

Tell Me about Your Student

I am looking forward to getting to know your student this year. Please share with me any information that will help me support your student's experience in my class. You should feel free to include past school experiences, medical issues, how your child learns best, or anything else that may help me be an effective teacher for your child.

Student's Name: _____

Your Name(s): _____

Relationship(s) to Student: _____

What are your student's strengths? _____
_____
_____

What are your student's interests, activities, or hobbies? _____
_____

What would help me support your student in the best way possible?
_____
_____
_____
_____
_____
_____

Do you have any concerns you would like me to know about?
_____
_____

What are your hopes for your student for this school year?
_____
_____
_____
_____

How to Lead the First Day

The first day of class can be an intimidating experience for students. They worry about many things on this day: if they will get lost trying to find the classroom, if they will have friendly classmates, whom they will eat lunch with, if they have a locker, can they open it, and if their teacher will be kind and approachable, just to name a few of their worries.

The first day of class can be intimidating for teachers, too. Not only will you meet your students, some for the first time, but also it is one of the busiest days of the year for any teacher. You must get everyone settled in comfortably while managing the first-day paperwork and all the other pressing tasks that are required of classroom teachers. By having empathy for your students and by planning and delivering engaging instructional activities, you will overcome your anxieties and make the first day of class a positive and memorable one for you and your students.

Overcome Those First-Day Jitters

There are many things you can do to handle the jitters that beginning a new school term can cause in even the most self-assured teacher. The most stressful part of your day will probably be sometime in the first half hour of class, when you realize that your students are nervous, cooperative, pleasant, and *depending on you*. To calm yourself, try an assortment of tips and techniques from this list:

- Accept the fact that you will feel nervous and excited on the first day of school. Many experienced teachers do, too. Naming your feelings will help you deal successfully with them.

- Boost your confidence by dressing well and comfortably. Teachers traditionally dress up a bit on the first day.

- Take care of yourself. Bring a water bottle to hydrate throughout the day, pack a good lunch, and try to take a break when lunchtime arrives.

- Check in with a colleague before school, if you can, to share ideas and provide mutual support.

- Pack your bag the night before and leave it by the door so that you can just grab it as you leave.

- Review your class roster(s) and say students' names aloud one last time the night before school starts. You will have students say their own names on the first day so you don't mispronounce names, but still, you will feel more confident if you rehearse them.

- Plan more activities than you believe your students can complete—and then plan some more. Avoid downtime on the very first day of school.

- Have extra supplies on hand so that every student can engage without barriers.

- Arrive early. You do not have to be so early that you help the custodians unlock the building, but you should be early enough that you do not feel rushed in finishing any last-minute tasks.

- Remind yourself that you have prepared for this moment. You got this. Then, if necessary, fake it until you make it.
- Smile and be friendly. A welcoming smile goes a long way.

What to Do on the First Day: Your Priorities

As you begin thinking about the first day of class, you should decide how to convince your students that you are the best teacher they will ever have. Your first-day jitters may be bad, but theirs are probably worse.

Because it is so important that the first day of school be an encouraging experience for your students, you must present yourself to your students in as positive a manner as possible. This will be easy for you if you focus your energy on the following six important priorities:

Priority One: Begin to Build a Classroom Community

- Plan get-to-know-you activities that allow students to engage with each other and practice social skills.
- Play name games to start learning each student's name.
- Start establishing classroom agreements to create a sense of safety and belonging while supporting learning for all.
- Even on the first day of class, your students will view themselves as members of a classroom group. (See Section Six for more information on creating positive relationships.) You can enhance this natural tendency by using inclusive words, such as *our* or *us*, when referring to the class.
- Ask for their help in such routine tasks as passing out materials, tidying the room at the end of an activity, or helping one another. These small acts help to create a sense of belonging and that the classroom is their space, too.

Priority Two: Calm Your Students' Fears

- Stand at the door of your classroom and welcome students to your class. Wear a bright name tag. Make sure to prominently display your name and room number to give students, families, and caregivers confidence that they are in the right place.
- Smile. Look glad to see every student. Greet each one pleasantly, using their name if you know them already.
- Teach your first lesson as if it is the most important lesson you will teach all year. In many ways, it is. Your students should feel that they learned something interesting and that they will continue to learn something in your class every day.

Priority Three: Introduce Yourself

- Part of building strong relationships is helping students to know you. Introduce yourself so that students can start to connect with you. Just be careful not to overshare. Here is a partial list of some information you may choose to share with students:

- What students should call you and how to pronounce and spell your name. Some schools use first names. Some use titles and last names. Some use titles paired with first names. Decide ahead of time how you want students to refer to you.

- Your name

- Where you went to college

- Where you grew up

- The positive things you have heard about them

- The positive things you have heard about the school

- What your favorite subject was in school

- A hobby you currently pursue

- Why you chose to be a teacher

- Why you are looking forward to teaching them

Priority Four: Lead Your Class

- Fake it 'til you make it. Even if you are overcome with stage fright, you must conquer your personal feelings and pretend to be confident and self-assured. Sometimes, by pretending to be confident, you can begin to convince yourself that you are.

- Have a seating chart ready so that you can show students their seats and help them get started on their opening activity at once. Have an agenda on the board or screen.

Priority Five: Engage Your Students' Minds

- Design fast-paced, interesting instruction that will appeal to students with a variety of learning styles and engage their critical thinking skills while building community. Solving puzzles, completing a challenge or scavenger hunt, quick writing assignments (if students can write), and other brief activities often work well.

- Make sure that the lesson is one that encourages them to be active and not just one that requires them to listen passively.

Priority Six: Begin to Teach the Class Routines

- It's important to explicitly teach expectations and routines in the classroom and schoolwide. Many schools organize "expectation stations" in the first week of school so that students visit various common areas like the playground, library, cafeteria, and so on, to learn expectations for those spaces.

- In younger grades, teachers will instruct and practice transitioning from the rug to seats or from the classroom to the cafeteria.

- In older grades, teachers will explain expectations and procedures around using devices or turning in assignments.

How to Get Everyone in the Right Seat on the First Day of Class

Having students sit in assigned seats on the first day of class is an excellent strategy for many reasons, but it is not always easy to bring about. Your goal should be that students feel a sense of belonging and can quickly find their seats without confusion or embarrassment. Although this seems difficult at first, with just a bit of planning and preparation, it can be done. Here's how:

Step One: Arrange the desks in your classroom in the configuration that you would like them to remain in for the first few days of class.

Step Two: Elementary teachers with self-contained classrooms generally create name plates for student desks. For secondary teachers with more than one group of students rotating into the classroom, number each desk. You can use a bright, easy-to-read label on a top corner of the desk or on the back of the chair. If you write the number on the label instead of typing it, be sure to use a pen that does not smear.

Step Three: Go through the careful process of assigning seats that was previously discussed. Review any information about accommodations or other details that you should take into consideration when assigning seats.

Step Four: After you have decided where each student will sit, put the number of the assigned desk next to the student's name on the roster.

Step Six: As students arrive in the classroom, meet them at the door. Ask them to find their names and seat numbers on the roster posted on the board or projected on the screen. They should then be able to find their desks without any hesitation.

Activities for the First Day

In addition to an overview of the day's lesson and class expectations, your first day of class can include many other activities to engage students in meaningful work. Using the planning template in Teacher Template (p444) will make it easier for you to ensure that the first day of school will be a productive and positive one for your students. Consider some of these activities when trying to decide just what you want your students to do on the first day:

- Have students create a life roadmap starting with the day they were born to today and including key moments with words and/or drawings.
- Photograph students on the first day of class to use with an "About Me" class bulletin board or slide deck.
- Distribute textbooks or instructional materials and supplies and have students skim through them, looking for items in a treasure hunt.
- Ask students to write you a brief note, telling you three things you need to know about them so that you can teach them well.

- Place a large sheet of paper on the wall. Provide old newspapers or magazines and have students tear out words and photos that describe their strengths, interests, and talents. Glue the photos and words in place to create an instant piece of art that will interest every student.

- Have older students jot down what they already know about the subject you are teaching and then share this information with the class.

- Have students fill out the student information form in Student Template 5.1.

- Have students write exit slips explaining what they learned in class on their first day.

(See the following section "Help Students Connect with One Another on the First Day" for a list of community-building activities.)

How to Establish Positive Relationships Right Away

As many experienced teachers would agree, the most important responsibility that any teacher has on the first day of school is to establish a positive relationship with students. No matter how exciting the lesson or well behaved your students are, if they leave dreading the rest of the year with you, then the first day of class was a failure.

Deliberately planning how to connect with your students and to help them connect with one another on the first day of class is a positive first step to take. In the information that follows, you will learn how to begin the process of connecting with your students. Although the information you'll find here deals with the start of school, you will find much more about building relationships in Section Six.

> "One of my professors in an education class said that years after students leave school, they will not remember what information I taught them, but they *will* remember how I treated them. That has stuck with me, and I think about it every single day that I teach."
>
> *Betsy Jones, 12 years' experience*

Connect with Your Students on the First Day

Creating a sense of belonging in your classroom is critical to student success and their overall mental and physical well-being. Effective teachers know that they can't just set aside five minutes to connect with students and then check it off their to-do lists. Instead, the activities that you use to build positive relationships with your students should be woven into the fabric of each day and the entire school year. Here are some straightforward strategies you can adapt for your classroom on the first day of school:

- Let your joy in being with your students show. Be enthusiastic, friendly, inclusive, and upbeat. If you are not glad to be there, your students will not be, either.

- Use your class rosters to learn students' names as quickly as you can. Being able to call students by name will boost your confidence as well as help you connect.

- Plan an engaging activity that showcases an aspect of the subject matter that your students will find intriguing. Allowing your enjoyment and interest to show as you facilitate the lesson will make it easier for students to connect with you.

- Make a to-do list so that the clerical work that you must submit on the first day of class is organized efficiently and will not distract your attention from your students.

- Schedule brain breaks if the class is long enough that your students grow restless. Talk to students about how you use brain breaks as a life skill to help them change their state and refocus. (See Section Twelve for more information about brain breaks.)

- Greet your students at the door as they enter, and stand at the door to say goodbye and to wish them well as they leave.

Help Students Connect with One Another on the First Day

"On the back of their name tents, students write three positive things about themselves, with caveats. I teach the word *caveat* and model the activity first. For example, one student wrote, 'I am curious and I want to learn, but I daydream.' Students share their strengths and caveats with the whole class. Not only does this set a precedent for courageous sharing, it also gives me immediate information about how kids see themselves. It's a powerful jumpstart to creating a culture that values voice and authenticity."

Nikki Darling, 15 years' experience

Although you can and should help students connect to one another all year long, it is not always easy to fit this in on the first day of school, even though it is one of your most important responsibilities. It may seem like there is not enough time for lengthy community-building activities, however, every minute invested in community-building and creating a sense of belonging in your classroom will come back to serve you and your students triplefold.

A strong sense of belonging can help prevent disruptive behaviors and generate higher engagement. You can build in various short activities that help students learn a little about one another as a foundation for the team building that will take place all year. Here are community-building activities to consider for the first day:

Getting to Know You Bingo: Give students a bingo card with statements on each square and space to write in one name. Have students move around the classroom looking for classmates who fit each descriptor. They can use a classmate's name only once on the card. Students must fill in names for each box before shouting "bingo."

Classroom or School-Wide Scavenger Hunt: Determine what you want students to discover around the classroom or around the school. Divide students into teams of four to complete the scavenger hunt. Depending on the age of your students, this can be done on paper or with an app like GooseChase.com.

About Me Table Tents: Provide blank table tents, markers, crayons, and art supplies. Ask students to write their names and symbols or pictures that represent who they are and what they love.

About Me Puzzle Pieces or Squares: Similar to the table tents, this activity creates a meaningful mosaic that can decorate the classroom for weeks to come. Distribute blank puzzle pieces, paper squares, or digital slides. Give students magazines, cards, and craft supplies to decorate the puzzle piece, squares, or slides with images and words that represent the student.

Circle within a Circle: Have students stand. Half the class forms an inner circle facing out and half the class forms an outer circle facing in. The teacher provides a prompt for students to discuss for thirty or forty-five seconds, then shift the outer circle around one person so that each prompt is discussed with a different person. Ask students to start each time by sharing their first name. Keep prompts simple like "What's your favorite food, TV show, animal, color?"

Six-Minute Walk and Talk: Each day, students talk to six different people for one minute each. The questions will change based on the age of your students. Students walk around the room and when they hear a bell, chime, or other designated sound, they pair up. The teacher gives a simple question like, "What's your favorite breakfast food?" The first student shares for thirty seconds and the teacher says "Switch" and the second student speaks. Then they move again to a new person and a new question. "What's an odd noise you do not like?" "When's the last time you cried at a film or commercial?" "What's a superpower you'd like to have?" In five days or less, they have spoken to everyone. It's a low-risk way for students to practice social skills face-to-face.

Semáforo or Traffic Light: This is not just for Spanish classes; this can be adapted to any grade or content area. Place three huge circles in three corners of the room. One green "¡Me encanta! I love it!" One yellow, "Me gusta. I like it." One red, "No me gusta. I don't like it."

Ask students to move to the corner that represents their opinion on a variety of random topics that are intended to create a variety of groupings so that students get to know each other. Once the students arrive in their chosen corners, they turn to a partner and talk about the common opinion they have on the topic. Depending on the proficiency level of the class, they would speak more or less in the target language. Sample topics may include:

- Ice cream is the best dessert
- Dogs are great pets
- Living at the beach
- Art is my favorite class
- Pineapple as a pizza topping
- 1980s music
- Tuna fish sandwich

Common Thread: Organize students into groups of four and have them find something unique that they have in common. They might discuss what they like to do, where they have been, their favorite things, how many siblings they have, and so on. At the end of three minutes, they report out the common thread that is most unique for their group. Then reshuffle the groups and do it again.

Two Truths and a Lie: Have students come up with two true statements about themselves and one lie. Older students can create a digital slide with their name and the three facts. Younger students may share them verbally or jot them down. In small groups or the full group, share the three statements and guess which one is the lie.

Timeline of Birthdays: Have students stand up and self-organize by birthday month and day January 1 to December 31. When they believe they are finished, have each person call out their month and day to see what they achieved together. For an additional challenge, try this as a silent activity.

A–Z Class Alphabet: Same as birthdays, but have students stand up and self-organize by first name or last name.

Highest Tower Challenge: Provide groups of students (three to four per group) with materials such as marshmallows and toothpicks or spaghetti and marshmallow, or paper and tape. Give them a specified amount of time and a specific challenge, such as build the tallest tower or the most creative or artistic design.

"Our favorite things say a lot about who we are and what we are passionate about. They can hold memories or connections to special people in our lives or reveal our dreams and the things we hold close to our hearts. Take a few days at the beginning of the semester to focus on students' favorite things and building relationships. Students' personalities emerge much sooner and the level of enthusiasm and excitement for what's to come is tangible. Give students an opportunity to tap into their passions and share them in a nonthreatening way; they will feel more relaxed and comfortable talking in class and get to know one another. You will love the laughter, silliness and conversations that ensue. Syllabi and rules can wait; relationships come first."

Tisha Richmond, 26 years' experience, tisharichmond.com

Cup Stacking Challenge: Divide students into groups of four. Give them four strings tied around a single rubber band and six plastic (recyclable) cups. Without touching the cups, they must work together to stack the cups into a pyramid.

Name Game: Place students in a large circle and have a soft foam or inflatable beach ball ready. Ask students to say their name and a favorite thing then toss the ball to a classmate who must say their name and favorite thing upon catching the ball. Encourage students to link something unique to their name. If everyone says their name and "pizza," or "video games," it's not as effective. Continue around the circle until everyone has had a chance to speak.

Variation on Name Game: Hand the ball around the circle in one direction. The first student says their name and their favorite thing. The next student says their name and favorite thing as well as the name and favorite thing of the person who went before them.

The last person in the circle tries to recall each person's name and favorite thing (with help from their classmates if they get stuck). Make sure to immediately correct pronunciation if a student's name is said incorrectly.

Pair Your Name with a Gesture: Each student says their name accompanied by some gesture. It can be super-simple, like swinging a bat, cradling an imaginary cat, or pointing anywhere. Learning names can be easier when associated with a movement.

Would You Rather: Come up with some options for students to declare their opinions on various light, fun topics. Such as: Would you rather team up with Wonder Woman or Captain Marvel? Would you rather have salsa or ketchup as the only condiment you could use for the rest of your life? Would you rather study math or study history? Have students declare their opinion by moving to one side of the room or the other.

How to Help Your Students Look Forward to the Rest of the Year

One of the most important tasks that you have on the first day of class is to make sure that your students leave looking forward to the rest of the year. Even if the first day does not go as smoothly as you would like, don't worry. Most students are willing to be understanding of their teacher's missteps on the first day if you have made a sincere effort to connect with them and to ensure their well-being and ease. Here are several quick ways to make sure that your students leave your classroom looking forward to an enjoyable year ahead:

- Don't promise what you can't deliver, but if you are aware of special events and other interesting activities planned for your grade level or subject matter, tell students about them. Mention such activities as the field trips that they will take, guest speakers, or various class or schoolwide celebrations throughout the year.

- Tell students about the skills they will acquire as the year progresses. Show a future difficult problem or assignment and assure students that in just a little while they will find it easy.

- Reassure students that you will help them all year. Be explicit about the ways that you intend to help them succeed.

- Show students the readings, experiments, or problems that they will do so that they have some idea of what they will be learning as the year progresses. A quick demonstration is a terrific way to generate interest.

- Talk about the types of celebrations that you like to have with your students. Even talking about something as simple as a ten-minute video clip on Fridays (Movie Day!) will build anticipation.

- Teach students an unusual fact or technique so that they have something definite to say when their families or caregivers ask, "What did you learn today?"

About Me: Student Information Sharing

While you will have a great deal of data in the student information system, giving students a chance to tell you about themselves and what they need to be successful is valuable. The questions you ask on the Student Template 5.1 will change based on the age of your students.

About Me

Your full name: _____

What do you want me to call you? _____

Your birthday: _____

If you have siblings, what are their names and ages:

_____

_____

Do you speak additional languages? ____If so, what are they?

What are your interests, hobbies, or activities?

_____

_____

Who are your adults at home and what are their relationships to you: _____

_____

_____

What are your favorite family holidays, celebrations, or traditions?

_____

_____

What do I need to know about you to teach you well?

_____

_____

What are you looking forward to learning this year?

Learn Your Students' Names Quickly

Learning how to correctly pronounce and spell your students' names is one of the most important ways you can communicate care and respect to your students. Being able to call all your students by name is an important step in getting to know them as people, creating community, and managing your class.

The depth of resentment that mispronouncing or misspelling a student's name can cause is often surprising to first-year teachers. Although teachers may think of it as a small mistake, students tend to view teachers who do not call them by the right name as uncaring and insensitive.

Set a goal to learn all your students' names in the first week of school. Sometimes class rosters change even into the first weeks of school, but don't let that get in your way. These quick tips will even make it possible for you to go home on the first day of school confident that you know the students in your class well enough to get the term off to a good start:

- Put in some preliminary work. Organize your seating charts, and study class rosters.
- Study photos of your students in the student information system and on the seating chart.
- Make sure that your students sit in their assigned seats for the first few days so that you can quickly associate names with faces.
- If you have students fill out a student information form, when you read what your students have written, mentally match their faces to the information in front of you.
- While students are working on a written assignment, walk quietly around the room, checking the roster and practicing names silently in your head.
- Ask each student to speak their name for you. Repeat it as you study the child's face.
- Use the audio recording features on Nearpod, Canva, PearDeck, or Flip so students can create a slide with their name and the correct pronunciation.
- Mark pronunciation notes on your roll sheet or seating chart.
- When you cannot recall a child's name, admit it, apologize, and ask them to remind you. When you hear it again, write it down, repeat it, and try again until you can recall it.

How to Manage the First Week

In the first week of school you will have to adjust to new routines and the uncertainties of your classroom responsibilities and help your students with their own adjustment as well. The intense paperwork load and the fast pace of each day, as well as the weighty responsibilities you must carry, all combine to make this adjustment period a tough one. It helps to know what to expect during the first week and to have a plan in place to manage the new stresses in your professional life.

What You Can Expect during the First Week

The first week of school is filled with many changes and adjustments for teachers and students. Here are some of the things that you can expect and plan for during the first week of school:

- Students will have schedule changes. Even if you teach very young students in a small school, it is prudent to anticipate that students will be added to or removed from your class during the first week.

- Some students will have trouble finding their classrooms during the first week. This is a potentially embarrassing situation for any student, which you can alleviate by standing at your classroom door and greeting students as they enter your room.

- Schools are generally required to provide the supplies students need to access an education. Many schools ask families and caregivers to purchase school supplies, creating a hardship for those who experience homelessness or poverty. Have extra school supplies available.

- Remember that students may have experienced summer slide with respect to academic and social skills. Plan to teach social skills and give students lots of practice. Plan to review some knowledge and skills from the previous year.

- Some students will struggle with behaviors. Before the first day, learn about your students' needs for behavioral supports the previous year. Create plans with the specialists in your school (special education, counselors, or social workers) to set everyone up for success.

- Your to-do list will be very long. All the tasks on it will be important ones with short deadlines.

- You will have to reach out to soothe anxious family members and caregivers who worry about their children's potential for success in your class.

- You will have to make time to hydrate, eat, rest, exercise, and take care of your personal life during the first few weeks of school.

- You will find that it is hard to pace lessons correctly during the first few weeks of school because you are not familiar with your students and the way they work and learn.

- The administrators and other staff members at your school will have to adjust to last-minute changes in enrollment and teaching positions. This may cause changes to schedules or staffing. Pay attention to the many updates that will come your way about changes affecting the entire school.

- You will notice that your students will have a wide range of learning styles and levels of readiness.

- Your students will need your patient and persistent help in learning how to relate appropriately to one another and to you as well as how to adjust themselves to the routines of the class.

- You will feel exhausted and exhilarated in the face of this demanding and worthwhile work.

Have a Plan for Start-of-School Stress

During the first week of school, you will not be alone in needing to develop stress-relief strategies for the common and predictable problems that you and your colleagues will face. In the following chart, you will find some of the problems that you can anticipate and suggested strategies for managing the stress that accompanies each one:

Problem	Suggested Stress-Relief Strategy
You are overwhelmed by the newness of everything you are required to do.	Be patient. Practice positive affirmations. Take deep breaths. You can do difficult things.
There's too much paperwork, and it is all due right away.	Make a to-do list with due dates. Put time on the calendar to complete the tasks. Work steadily and efficiently to get it done.
You can't predict how well a lesson or activity will work because you don't know your students.	This will resolve itself as you give students interest and readiness inventories and get to know them better.
You run out of lesson before you run out of class.	Have a simple extra or alternative lesson plan ready until you can learn to pace instruction correctly.
Students find it difficult to follow routines and procedures.	Talk with students. Patiently teach and reteach. If needed, calmly enact consequences until students can follow routines and procedures.
You find it difficult to attend to your personal life because you are exhausted and school preoccupies your mind.	Name this for family and friends. Do your best to be present, rest, exercise, and eat well. Soon you will have the work-life balance you need.
Students who were well-behaved on the first day of class are not as well-behaved at the end of the first week.	Talk with students. Listen to what they say. If needed, calmly enact consequences until students develop social skills. Focus on the positive behaviors in your class.
Your lesson plan was a disaster.	Remember to have a growth mindset. Be specific in your analysis. Spend time reflecting on what went well and where you could improve the lesson. Make the changes that you can right away.

Problem	Suggested Stress-Relief Strategy
You have so much to do that you worry that you will forget something important.	Make a to-do list and maintain a calendar to keep reminders of everything that you need to do right at your fingertips.
You are uncertain about what to do in situations where other teachers seem confident.	Ask for help. Don't give in to feelings of intimidation. Those confident teachers were first-year teachers once.

Questions to Discuss with Colleagues

Sharing ideas with colleagues is a helpful way to devise solutions to some of the problems that you must manage successfully at school. Here, you will find several topics to open discussions with colleagues about successful instructional practices:

1. Connecting with students is your top priority. What strategies make it easier to get to know your students? How can you find out about their interests and abilities?

2. Families and caregivers are crucial partners to support students. How do other teachers engage them at open house? To what extent can you engage them as volunteers?

3. It's all too easy to feel exhausted and overwhelmed at the start of school. How can you cope with this stress so that you can enjoy being with your students?

4. Building a learning community is vital. What community-building strategies might you use to help students get to know each other and start collaborating?

5. What seating arrangements do the other teachers at your school use that may also work well in your classroom? What do you need to consider before moving students into new seating configurations?

Topics to Discuss with a Mentor

Although the topics that new teachers need to discuss with a mentor vary from teacher to teacher and from school to school, there are some that most first-year teachers should be comfortable discussing with a mentor or a trusted colleague. You should ask your mentor about these topics from this section:

- Suggestions for student seating arrangements
- How to manage stress at the start of a new school term
- How to help students have a positive first-day-of-school experience
- Suggestions for lesson plans and activities to introduce yourself to students
- Advice about helping students adjust to your class routines and expectations

Reflection Questions to Guide Your Thinking

1. What can you do to make sure the first day of school is productive for you and your students? What small things can you do to ensure that your students are comfortable and glad to be in your class?

2. What would you like your students to say about your class at the end of the first day? What specific steps can help you achieve this goal?

3. Which seating arrangements would work best at the start of the year for your students? How can you accommodate all students? Who can help you with this?

4. How can you reach out to families and caregivers to create a successful open house and partnership to support students all year long? What barriers might exist to their participation that you can remove?

5. How can you prioritize your tasks at the start of school so that you can be sure to manage them well? How can you plan instruction and your school day successfully?

SECTION SIX

Cultivate Positive Classroom Relationships

Positive relationships with students and their adults are foundational to teaching and learning. "They won't care how much you know until they know how much you care," is a profoundly true and oft-quoted statement. Without productive relationships with your students, their families, and caregivers, no matter how well you have prepared instruction and planned classroom management, nothing will work well. These relationships are crucial to the success of your students, so build positive relationships intentionally and consistently.

As the classroom leader, you will purposefully orchestrate all these connections. You will get to know your students and let them know you care about their academic and personal growth. You will reach out to families and caregivers to give them confidence in your ability to teach their children well. As a classroom teacher, you will ensure that your students are connected to you and connected to their classmates.

In this section, you will first learn about the strategies that you can use to create that important positive relationship with the families and caregivers of your students. You will then learn how to forge the bonds that you need to work well with your students.

Engage with Families and Caregivers

Your students' primary caregivers influence how your students think, feel, and behave. If you can work well with them, not only will your students be supported in their education, but your job will be easier.

Working well with families and caregivers creates a team of allied adults working

> "Parents have worked hard to get their children to you. They want the best for their children. And you want the best for your students. Work as partners."
>
> *Anna Aslin Cohen, 40 years' experience*

together to help students succeed in school and life. Interacting professionally is vital, and many areas of this relationship may require special attention. In the pages that follow, you will learn strategies to ensure that your interactions are as productive as possible.

Earn the Positive Regard of Families and Caregivers

Whenever families and caregivers gather, they will discuss their children's school experiences and inevitably their students' teachers. Just as it is important to build a reputation for professionalism among your colleagues, it is important to earn the positive regard of families and caregivers.

Families and caregivers will have expectations of you: to care about and value their children, to inspire learning, to teach the required curriculum, to encourage achievement, and to work with them for the good of their children. Conducting yourself as a professional will allow you to build the reputation that you need to build these partnerships. Be known as a teacher who can make the world of ideas so interesting that students talk about it at home. Be known as a teacher who sincerely cares about each student's growth and development, and who is willing to partner with families and caregivers so that each student succeeds.

Although it is important to live up to expectations, it's also important to have healthy boundaries. There are three important caveats that you should consider as you work to build your reputation among your students' home adults. First, protect your privacy and your time at home and online. Don't give out your personal phone number; don't accept follow/friend requests from students, their family members, or caregivers on social media; and make sure families know your work hours. Second, be sure to respond to phone calls and emails from families and caregivers as soon as possible, but without fail, respond within twenty-four hours. Third, always treat your students with the utmost respect. Each student is someone's precious child and beloved family member.

Build Trust with a Transparent Classroom

One of the easiest ways to build trust, prevent miscommunication, and establish a positive relationship with your students' home adults is to make sure that your classroom is as transparent as possible. You can do this by providing easily accessible information about academics, student progress, volunteer opportunities, and more. If families have access to the internet and if schools invest the resources, technology makes it easier than ever to communicate from school to home through learning management systems, websites, and apps.

When you create a transparent classroom, you actively invite participation and support from everyone concerned. Digital tools make it easier than ever to update everyone about what is happening in your classroom. Your students' home adults expect to be informed about these topics:

- Students' academic and behavioral progress
- Units of study and instructional materials
- Class policies, rules, and consequences
- Beginning-of-the-year information

- Homework and major assignments
- Assessments
- Grading
- Due dates
- Field trips
- Special projects
- Resources to help students learn
- Positive things about their children
- Volunteer opportunities

One frequent complaint that families and caregivers have involves not being informed about student progress, homework assignments, and important project due dates. Take extra care to make sure families can track student progress and contact them if you have concerns. Communicate your homework expectations and policies in several different ways and make sure that all due dates are announced well in advance. The families and caregivers of your students should not have to struggle to find out if they have homework and when work is due.

Another frequent complaint is that teachers wait too long before contacting home about a problem. As you get to know students and their home lives, you will learn how to engage with their home adults. In some cases, it is beneficial to call home and have academic or behavioral skills reinforced at home. In other cases, calling home may make things worse. Always report student progress honestly and based on what you know about students, decide when to make the phone call, send an email, message in an app, or invite families or caregivers to a conference. It is usually more effective to contact home when a problem is small enough to be manageable than to wait until the situation is serious.

> "In the first two months of school, I set a goal of sending two positive emails a day to parents or guardians. Only two a day makes this achievable and more personal for each student. I found the results to be very positive, leading to much more effective communication later in the year. A great side effect was that I realized students were also very grateful. Getting a positive message from a teacher created good things for them at home. I now also integrate this into my teaching by trying, whenever possible, to send a positive email when a student achieves something. I do this especially for a student who was struggling either academically or behaviorally in my classroom. The main lesson is that positive communication with home goes a long way to improve interaction with both students and parents."
>
> *Shelly Sambiase, 8 years' experience*

Be Positive with Families and Caregivers

A positive rapport begins with you. There are many ways to make positive contacts with your students' home adults. Although it may take time to follow through on these little actions, the benefits outweigh the time you spend on them. Here are some ways you can create the positive atmosphere you want for your students:

- Communicate to students that you hold their families and caregivers in high regard.
- Make it a habit to thank families and caregivers for their support whenever you see them.
- After a family member or caregivers has helped you with a problem, take the time to call, email, send a message through your school's app, or write a thank-you note.
- Call or email families and caregivers with good news.
- Make sure the message on your school voice mail has a positive message and assurance that you will return the call within 24 hours.
- Send home positive postcards to each student in your class at least once a year. Print mailing labels and postcards, and then as you catch students doing something positive during the year, send a quick note. They will often be posted on bulletin boards and refrigerators at home for many months to come.

One of the most effective ways to be positive with the families and caregivers of students at all grade levels is to send home positive messages by email, phone, apps, or USPS, as often as you can. Even the families and caregivers of older students will appreciate the effort you take to recognize their children's hard work and successes. Technology makes this easier than ever. Consider adapting Sample 6.1 to fit your needs and the apps your school uses.

Sample 6.1
Positive Message to Families and Caregivers

Although many formats can be used to notify families and caregivers of student achievements, it is best to keep your message simple. Adapt the format of this sample message for your own students.

Hello _____.

I am writing a quick note to let you know about something wonderful that [student name] did in class recently. You will be excited to hear that _____.

I know you are as proud of this effort and achievement as I am. Thank you for your support.

All the best,

_____

Mind the Language Gap

Multilingual and multicultural classrooms are rich and wonderful places where you can invite students, families, and caregivers to share their language and culture with the classroom community. Multilingualism is a valuable and vital skill around the world, so respecting home languages and encouraging their use invites greater participation by speakers of many languages in your classroom community. Purposeful preparation will make this possible. Consider these aspects of communication with linguistically diverse families and how to build connections with them.

- Collaborate closely with the English Language Development (ELD) teacher at your school to develop communication strategies.
- How do you translate all communication from school into home languages?
- How do you access interpretation services for phone calls, conferences, open house, and so on?
- If schools fail to provide resources, temporarily using Reverso, Linguee, Babylon, Google Translate, or other apps for written and spoken translation is better than not communicating, but it does not replace the accessibility services that should be provided by schools. It may also be helpful to teach some families to use a translation app as a tool in their daily lives.

Make Phone Calls with Confidence

Contacting home with positive messages strengthens relationships and makes it easier to ask for help addressing a concern. If you initially feel uncomfortable contacting home, that's natural, but don't let it stop you; it's a necessary skill for teachers to develop. Consider what types of communication are better via email or by phone. Often when there is a concern, it's better to make a call rather than email. Your positive and problem-solving tone helps deliver the message so it can be heard. Questions can be quickly answered. There are several strategies you can adopt to make phoning families and caregivers easier:

- Remember to contact interpreting services as needed.
- Plan what you want to say and what information they need to know so that you can work together to solve the problem.
- Most classrooms have a school phone. If not, find a phone at school from which you can make the call with some privacy and in a place where you are not likely to be interrupted. Don't use your personal phone number when calling home.
- Be sure to have any notes you have made about the situation as well as something to take notes on with you.
- Don't hesitate to call families and caregivers during the work day. Typically you will call their cell phone. However, if you reach a work phone and have to communicate with one of their colleagues, protect their privacy and simply say your name without details of the purpose of the call.

> "If the email is longer than a sentence or two, call instead. If you feel that the email won't go over well, call instead. Let the parents or guardians know that you are acting in the best interests of the kids and that everybody is on the same team—student, parent, teacher, and administration."
>
> *Jared Sronce, 6 years' experience*

- Begin the conversation by asking, "Do you have a few minutes to talk right now?"

- Remember that the purpose of the phone call is to solve a problem in partnership with them. Avoid venting your frustration or increasing their vexation with the child.

- Begin with a positive statement about the student and then say that you would like to enlist help in solving a problem: "A situation came up with [student's name] today, and I wonder if you could help me."

- Be very specific about your concern using objective language about the situation or behavior.

- After detailing the concern, state what you have done to address it. Again, be very specific, and share the result of your actions.

- Pay attention while they explain what they know about the situation. Make sure to listen carefully and to clarify any points you do not understand.

- Suggest next steps for home and school. These are primarily focused on building skills and increasing a sense of belonging, not punitive in nature.

- Finish the call with a positive statement, expressing your appreciation for their partnership.

Before you go on to your next task, document the call. Complete a contact documentation form (see Teacher Template 6.1) so that you have a record of the conversation and the next steps.

Conduct Successful In-Person or Virtual Meetings

Sometimes a next step in problem-solving is meeting with the families or caregivers in person or via videoconferencing. Sometimes these meetings include the student or other teachers. Families and caregivers want to be reassured that their children can succeed in school. A strong connection with your students' home adults is achievable if you have clarity about the goals for conferences. Here are five goals you should have for every conference: Families and caregivers will. . .

Goal One: Know you are a friendly and knowledgeable teacher who sincerely cares about their child's growth and development.

Goal Two: Feel an atmosphere of cooperation and support when they are meeting with you.

Goal Three: Leave a meeting with their questions answered and all the points they wanted to discuss covered.

Goal Four: Feel respected and heard.

Goal Five: Understand the next steps and agreements developed in the meeting.

Meetings with families and caregivers are much more involved than a quick chat after school. Successful meetings require planning and attention to detail before, during, and after the meeting. Use these guidelines to guarantee that the meetings you have this year are positive and productive:

Actions to Take Before a Meeting

- Whether you or the student's family or caregiver asked for the meeting, make sure you have a clear purpose for the meeting and a clear understanding of the outcome you hope for.
- Make sure all participants know the start and end time of the meeting.
- Depending on the nature of the concern, consider if other school staff have helpful resources or skills to support the student and invite them to the meeting.
- Plan the points you want to cover. Write them down.
- Gather samples of student work or other evidence you would like to share. Include progress reports and other information related to grades or behavior.
- Review cumulative records and report card information.
- Take notes on the student's strengths and areas for growth as well as any other special information you would like to share.
- Create a seating arrangement that will be comfortable for adults. Arrange chairs around a table or desks large enough for adults in a circle. Do not sit behind your desk.
- Make sure to provide supplies for note-taking for anyone who needs them.
- Post a "Do Not Disturb" sign on your door so that you can meet without interruptions.
- Meet the attendees and escort them to your room.

Actions to Take During a Meeting

- Be prepared to begin promptly. Do not make them wait while you gather materials.
- Begin by expressing your appreciation that they have come to the meeting.
- Establish a tone of goodwill and friendly cooperation from the beginning.
- Use language that will make them comfortable. Avoid educational or classist jargon. Rephrase your message if there is any confusion.
- Begin with positive remarks about the child. Talk about the student's strengths, skills, growth, and potential. Focus on strengths, even if there is a significant concern.
- State any concerns in simple, observable, and factual terms. Express your desire to work together for a successful resolution.
- Discuss specific examples of a problem. Show examples of work or give details about the student's behavior.
- Invite families and caregivers to share their perspectives. Listen well without being defensive. After they have had the opportunity to say everything they need to say, then—and only then—can they listen to you or begin to work on a solution to a problem.

- If you want to solve a problem, give your full attention throughout the entire conference. Your nonverbal language is crucial for success. Be friendly and attentive.

- In most cases, you will listen more than you speak.

- Do not interrupt people who are speaking.

- End the conference by summarizing the main points and next steps.

- Determine what you will do to follow up or to keep in contact in the coming weeks.

- Express appreciation again for their concern and the time they have spent with you.

Actions to Take After a Meeting

- Immediately complete your notes, what was discussed, and the next steps and agreements. Spend enough time on this so that your records are complete. Should you need to refer to this material later, you may not remember details accurately if your notes are not thorough.

- Write a quick note or email thanking participants for their support now and in the future.

The Importance of Keeping Contact Records

It is a good practice to keep accurate records of the times when you have contacted home and any plans or outcomes that resulted. It's one more way to keep track of commitments and student progress. It also would be helpful to you if a student is referred for additional support services or in the unlikely event that a family or caregiver issues a complaint. Although it may be upsetting to think that this could happen, it does happen, and it's important to be transparent and accountable.

Keeping a record of home contacts does not have to be time-consuming. Keep and organize your emails sent home. Many student information systems have a log feature. Update it regularly using language that communicates to other school staff, family members, or caregivers who might read it. If a digital log is not available, use or modify Teacher Template 6.1, and keep plenty of copies on hand so that you can complete one each time you contact home.

Home Contact Form [Teacher's Name]

Student's name: _____

Family member or caregiver contacted: _____

Phone number or email address: _____

Date and time of contact: _____

Type of contact:

_____ Phone call

_____ Email

_____ USPS Mail

_____ Home visit with [name of another staff member]

_____ Informal meeting

_____ Meeting with administrator

_____ Meeting with counselor

_____ Other: _____

Person(s) initiating the contact: _____

Topics discussed:

_____

_____

_____

_____

Next steps for family members or caregivers:

_____

_____

_____

Next steps for teacher:

_____

_____

_____

Additional notes and reflections:

_____

_____

_____

_____

_____

_____

Validate the Perspectives of Families and Caregivers

In all situations, seek first to understand. In many circumstances, families and caregivers may hold different experiences and identities than you do. You may never truly be able to understand what it means to experience the world as they do. Acknowledgment of this difference is important. Some interactions with your students' home adults may be difficult or stressful. Listen to their concerns without being defensive. Name that this is a challenging situation and that you will work together to resolve it. Lead with empathy and consider what is informing the person's perspective. Here are just some of the many possibilities:

- Some adults have had unpleasant experiences or experienced harm in school themselves and bring that to this situation. You can validate the trauma of their lived experiences, while explaining what you believe to be the best course of action.
- Their child may have told them something they find objectionable about your teaching.
- One of your lessons may have contained information they find inappropriate.
- You may have allowed a problem to escalate by not contacting them as quickly as you should have.
- They may be reacting out of their own frustration with their child's behavior, particularly if the problem is one they experience at home.
- They may disagree with you about a decision you made. If you made a mistake, apologize. If you did not, then share your rationale and listen to their perspective.
- They may feel shame or embarrassment about their child's academic or behavioral progress.
- Their child may have had negative experiences with unsupportive teachers in the past.
- They may want to protect their student from a consequence.

Unreasonable Requests

Although most contact you will have with families and caregivers will be pleasant and productive, on occasion, you may have to deal with challenging requests or reactions. When this happens, the situation can be stressful. Teachers generally want to help, and yet in the face of some requests, it's important to have healthy boundaries.

When you are a new teacher, you want to help and it is not always easy to determine if requests from families and caregivers are reasonable. Here are some criteria to consider before saying yes.

- Is it related to a student's learning differences?
- Does it infringe on your time outside of work?
- Does it disrupt teaching and learning?
- Does it require you to violate your professional code of conduct?

If a request or reaction from a parent or guardian seems ineffective, inappropriate, or unreasonable to you, there are some actions you should take right away:

- Do not act alone. Delay responding until you have time to think and to consult others. As soon as you can, consult a mentor, colleague, or an administrator for advice.

- Try to be as compassionate and understanding as possible. You both want what is best for the student. That can only happen if you are all in agreement and can work together.

- When you discuss the situation with them, be clear about what is reasonable and what is not. Try to work out a compromise when you can.

- Accept that you will probably not win everyone over to your point of view. Attempt to calm the situation and offer an alternative solution.

- Learn many ways to say no, such as:
  - I would love to help, but I can't.
  - I'm sorry, I have a personal commitment.
  - I understand [summarize the issue] and I think that can best be addressed by [propose alternative to the unreasonable request].

Emotionally Charged Interactions

Families and caregivers have profound care and concern for their students and sometimes this leads to emotionally charged interactions. It's crucial that you maintain your calm and professional exterior even if you don't feel that way inside. The best way to avoid these situations is to intervene early, follow policies, procedures, and rules, maintain accurate records, present yourself as a professional, and keep families and caregivers informed about their child's progress. When you make a mistake (because you're human and you will), acknowledge it and apologize.

If you find yourself in an emotionally charged situation, it is up to you to take actions that deescalate and conclude the interaction as best you can. The following steps can help you manage meetings so that they result in productive outcomes:

- Listen carefully to what is communicated, without interrupting or correcting the narrative. Do not try to present your perspective until they have fully expressed themselves.

- Show your interest by paraphrasing what you heard and asking clarifying questions. A simple misunderstanding is often the cause of the problem.

- Make sure to restate the issue so that the other person can be reassured that you do understand. Try something like, "I hear you saying _____."

- Express your commitment to helping the student learn and grow.

- Explain the issue from your viewpoint as objectively as you can. Be specific about what was expected, what happened, and how you responded.

- Remain calm and professional. If you need a minute to compose yourself, excuse yourself to use the restroom, take a few breaths and a sip of water to gain a bit of distance.

- Engage healthy boundaries if needed. Do not accept threats or abuse from a family member or caregiver. End the conversation, letting them know you are willing to reschedule.

- If, after you have sincerely tried to resolve a problem, they remain upset, suggest calling a mediator or administrator for help.

- After any emotionally charged interaction with a family member or caregiver, notify your supervisor. Summarize what happened, and if needed, ask for assistance.

- While you may need to follow up with their student about the issue they surfaced, do not discuss the emotionally charged incident with or complain about it to your student. They are not responsible for their family member or caregiver's behavior.

Establishing Strong Student Relationships

It's up to you. Developing positive relationships with your students is crucial to student success. Your students need to feel that they matter to you, that you like them, and that you enjoy teaching them. Positive relationships are the cornerstone of teaching and learning. Based on studies of relationships, Positive Behavioral Interventions and Supports (PBIS) recommends educators use the Magic Ratio of 5:1. That means that you strive to have five positive interactions for every negative or corrective interaction with each student.

> "If you are going to teach, then you are choosing to shape the future of our country, and that is an incredible privilege. That privilege requires that you build strong relationships with your students and explore their needs so you can best serve them."
>
> *Evalaurene Jean-Charles,*
> *5 years' experience, Founder*
> *BlackonBlackEducation.com*

This builds a strong foundation of positive interactions with students so that when you need to correct behavior, a negative interaction doesn't harm the relationship.

Although positive teacher-student relationships are rewarding in countless ways, cultivating those relationships must be intentional, purposeful, and ongoing. In the rest of this section, you will explore ways to connect with students to create a learning environment based on mutual respect. In addition, you will learn how interacting with students as a *warm demander* will make it possible for you to reach every student.

Be Yourself: Use Your Unique Strengths

One of the best things about being a teacher is that you have an opportunity to share yourself—your culture, your ideas, your interests, your personality—with a group of students who look to you as a trusted adult, a role model, and guide.

Use your unique strengths as a starting point to relate to your students. Are you naturally curious? Are you enthusiastic about your content? Do you have a great sense of humor? Take a few minutes every now and then to think about the personal strengths that you bring to your classroom practice and how you can use those strengths to connect with your students. One way to think about your strengths is to use Teacher Template 6.2.

Reflect on Your Relationship-Building Strengths

Here you will find twelve statements that reflect the strengths of excellent classroom teachers who connect with their students to make learning possible. As you read each statement, think about how it relates to your teaching practice. If a statement expresses a strength that you already have, place a check mark in the blank before it. You should then be able to see your relationship-building strengths and the areas where you could grow and develop.

1. _____ I value my students' cultures.
2. _____ I create a community that is safe both physically and emotionally.
3. _____ I have high expectations for all my students and provide support for them to meet those expectations.
4. _____ I show my joy to students and smile often.
5. _____ I actively create a sense of belonging for each student in my class.
6. _____ I speak and act in a way that engenders mutual respect and trust.
7. _____ I design and facilitate high-quality educational opportunities that make learning interesting.
8. _____ I know my students' names and something about their lives beyond school.
9. _____ I don't give up on students, always seeking another strategy to help them succeed.
10. _____ I have five positive interactions for every negative or corrective interaction with each student.
11. _____ I teach social skills so that students have strategies to communicate and collaborate with each other and with me.
12. _____ My students know that I care about their academic and personal growth.

The Student-Focused Teacher

Teachers who cultivate positive relationships with their students prioritize and sustain focus on their students during each class and throughout the school year. As in all relationships, being present and giving your attention to students supports their learning and your ability to teach.

There are many potential obstacles to connecting with students. The following questions may help you gauge the types of distractions you experience. Once you are aware of any problems in this area, you may want to consider what support you need to resolve those issues to possibly increase focus on your students.

- Do you spend time on clerical or grading tasks while students are present?
- Do you engage with your cell phone while students are present?
- Do you find yourself without enough instructional materials to conduct lessons?
- Do you check email while students are present?
- Are you distracted during class by your personal responsibilities?
- Are you distracted from teaching and learning by routine clerical tasks?
- Do you focus on extracurricular responsibilities, such as clubs or sports that you coach, while students are present?
- Do conversations with other teachers disrupt class time?
- Do you conduct personal business during class time?

Maintain Healthy Boundaries with Students

Each student comes to school with their own experiences, hopes, dreams, and traumas. Teachers have the responsibility of uplifting their students, celebrating triumphs, and supporting them through challenges. Maintaining an appropriate distance to navigate these complex and sometimes painful realities is vital to create healthy relationships and reduce burnout.

As a first-year teacher, you will develop strong relationships with students to support their growth and development, and maintain healthy boundaries at the same time. There are several types of boundaries for you to establish in your first year that will serve you and your students well throughout your career. Students are neither your children, nor your peers, so you must behave accordingly with appropriate emotional, relational, communication, and physical boundaries.

Emotional Boundaries

- Be the adult in the room at all times; act in a mature manner. This does not mean that you cannot have fun with your students; however, having fun with your students should not include sarcasm, insults, or anger, playing favorites, or losing your temper. These are not only immature behaviors, but undermine the relationships that you want to build.

- Show that you care about your students. Attend school-related events and activities occasionally to show interest.
- Separate the behavior from the child. You can disapprove of the behavior while caring for the person. Treat all of your students equitably.
- Maintain a certain emotional distance from your students so that you can remain engaged without being overwhelmed by their challenges.

Relational Boundaries

- Keep relationships professional, not personal. Avoid socializing with students and their families outside of school events. One exception to this may be seeing them at larger, public, community events that you are attending to celebrate and connect with the local school community.
- Be their teacher, not their friend. They have peers for friends. You are a teacher and not a peer.

Communication Boundaries

- Maintain communication transparency. Use school-approved communication channels, not private communication channels.
- If you use social media for school business, set up a professional account. Avoid engaging with students, families, and caregivers on your personal social media.
- Write all communication to students and their homes as if it might be shared widely on social media or in the news.

Physical Boundaries

- In a caring profession, and especially with young elementary school students, it's impossible to avoid all physical contact and important to engage in appropriate touch, like fist bumps, high fives, or the occasional hug. Learn your school's policies on physical contact with students and follow it.
- Create a consent culture; always check in with a student if they would like to receive high fives, fist bumps, or hugs. Students should never be expected to have physical contact with an adult or their peers.
- Corporal punishment is against the law in many states and should be abolished. Students trust teachers to keep them safe from harm; don't hurt them.
- Teachers should never drive students in their cars or meet with them outside of school. There is always another solution to get students where they need to go.

Refer Out for Additional Services

It is easy to become too involved in helping students when it is obvious that they need more than just classroom instruction to be successful. As teachers, we are in a caring profession that values service and encourages us to help the whole child. It's impossible to just stand by when our students struggle with hunger, homelessness, or any other serious issues that make it difficult for them to learn. We want to help.

While it is essential that we help our students, it is important that we do so in a professional manner so that success is more likely and to avoid burnout from overextending ourselves. Think of yourself as a key player in getting help for your students. Once you become aware of a student's need, you should act promptly and collaborate with specialists and other service providers to offer additional services.

Remember, too, that you are part of a team of caring professionals who are all trained to assist students. Never take it upon yourself to act alone to solve student problems. Instead, involve counselors, administrators, school nurses, social workers, community agencies, and other appropriate personnel as quickly as you can.

Your colleagues in specialized fields will have access to resources and support that you do not. Their assistance and support can be more extensive and better suited to student needs than what you can offer alone. If you have students who are struggling with any of the issues in the following list, act quickly to contact other professionals to seek their help:

- Hunger
- Homelessness
- Bullying
- Neighborhood threats
- Mental health issues
- Suicidal ideation, threats, or attempts
- Abuse of any kind: physical, emotional, verbal, or sexual
- Substance abuse issues
- Pregnancy
- Serious home issues
- Gang involvement
- Attempts or threats to run away
- Chronic illness or injury
- A need for eyeglasses, a hearing aid, or other adaptive technology

Connect and Lead: Become a Warm Demander

What does it mean to be a *warm demander*? First identified by educator and researcher Judith Kleinfield, the term refers to the unique combination of a teacher's personal warmth, along with a relentless insistence on engagement, effort, and mutual respect. In her book, *Culturally Responsive Teaching and the Brain,* Zaretta Hammond defines a *warm demander* as a teacher who expresses personal warmth and simultaneously demands that students work toward high standards. In this environment, students and teachers are taken seriously. Students know the teacher is invested in their success, and cares enough to hold high expectations, give high levels of support, and never give up on them.

Sometimes new teachers hesitate to be demanding at all for fear that their students will regard them as mean. When students describe a teacher as being mean, they usually describe a teacher who is inflexible, unfair, and unduly harsh, or who singles students out for unpredictable humiliations. No one wants to be regarded as a mean teacher. After all, being mean is the antithesis of our purpose as educators.

On the other hand, teachers who are warm demanders make it clear to their students that they believe them capable of academic and personal success and that they enjoy teaching their students. They have a leadership presence with high expectations for student effort, behavior, and achievement. They are those beloved teachers with students who may be disruptive in other classes, but who engage and cooperate in their class. It is the combination of a teacher's personal warmth toward students with an unflappable approach to classroom management that makes it possible for teachers who are warm demanders to be compelling classroom leaders.

In the rest of this section, you will explore the techniques that you can use to develop your own skills as a warm demander. You will first learn about the various ways that you can project your positive concern for your students as you develop your *warm* qualities and then discover more about how to be a *demander* to create the classroom atmosphere in which all students receive unconditional positive regard and are expected to perform at their best.

The *Warm* Qualities of an Effective Teacher

Many educators find it almost effortless to develop the qualities that make up the *warm* component of being a warm demander. After all, a love of learning and educating the next generation are often the driving forces behind education as a career choice. However, it is equally important that teachers have a growth mindset regarding their students. (See more about growth mindset in Section Four.) Teachers who want to have a strong connection with their students must believe that their students are capable of school success.

With this attitude as a strong foundation, the other strategies that teachers can use to connect with their students can be successful. Here, you will find a list of some of the strategies that you can adopt as you work to improve the way that you build rapport and communicate care for your students.

- Approach students with unconditional positive regard.
- Get to know students, their interests, cultures, families, or caregivers.
- Consistently communicate your belief that they can do hard things and succeed.
- Let students know that you care enough to have high expectations for their academics and behaviors.
- Listen to and act on student input and feedback.

- Take a proactive and positive approach to classroom management.
- Offer timely and specific feedback so that students can improve quickly instead of repeating mistakes.
- Ask students to share in solving classroom problems when appropriate.
- Promote trusting relationships with and among students.
- Use positive, nonverbal communication when engaging with students.
- Scaffold instruction for student achievement.
- Model growth mindset.
- Treat all students with courtesy and respect.
- View discipline issues as an opportunity for learning.
- Create an inclusive environment where students feel a sense of belonging.
- Connect with students as individuals.
- Engage with sympathy and empathy when students experience personal problems.
- Move about the room frequently to offer assistance and engage with students.

> "Your impact as an educator is profound and enduring. While students may appreciate and hold fond memories of you, the true extent of the positive influence you have may not become apparent until years later."
>
> *Marsha Benjamin Moyer, 30+ years' experience CEO MBM ImPAC*

These strategies are ones that will allow you to project a sense of care and concern about your students. In addition, they are strategies that can improve your overall instructional practices. When students know that their teachers care about their well-being and can see them as individuals, it creates a virtuous cycle that can empower students to succeed.

How to Be a Likeable Teacher

Somewhere in your academic past, you probably had a teacher whom you liked a great deal. You looked forward to that teacher's class for lots of different reasons, but mainly because of how that teacher made you feel about yourself:

- You knew that you could ask for help without embarrassment.
- You felt intelligent and capable.
- You were confident that the teacher was your ally and watched out for you.
- You felt that you mattered to that teacher.

You can make your students feel the same about you. Becoming a likeable teacher is a worthwhile expenditure of your time when you are considering how to cultivate positive relationships with your students.

When you work to increase your likeability factor, the most important step is to first make a conscious decision to be consistent, upbeat, cheerful, and positive without being false. Here are some easy tips that will make your students glad that you are their teacher:

- Remember that the class is about your students and not about you.
- Be gentle and inclusive in your approach.
- Smile.
- Interact with your students with consistent kindness.
- At the end of class, ask students to tell you what went well or what they did right.
- Create a learning community where students can help one another. Provide opportunities for peer collaboration and support.
- When students make good choices, praise them for their effort and decision-making skills.
- Point out students' strengths. Be specific and authentic. Make it a point to compliment their effort and catch them doing the right thing whenever you can.
- Show that you have a sense of humor. Laugh often together. Having fun and laughing together will make school fun for everyone. Share a humorous story, a rhyme or saying, create a "Joke of the Week," whatever aligns with your personality.
- When you see a student trying to improve, speak privately to that student to let them know that you noticed their effort and are impressed.
- Take the time to reveal a little bit about yourself. For example, a brief story about a silly mistake you made or how you learned a lesson the hard way will make you much more accessible and approachable to your students.
- Ask questions and wait respectfully for answers. Use active listening and nonverbal cues to signal that you are interested in their responses.
- Use inclusive pronouns such as *we, our,* or *us* instead of ones that exclude students from ownership in the class.
- Use a kind voice when you speak with your students.
- Stress the things that you and your students have in common: goals, dreams, and beliefs.
- Maintain a birthday calendar for your students. Celebrate birthdays with birthday messages on the board. Remember that students from Bhutan and those who are Jehovah's Witnesses may not celebrate birthdays.
- Attend school events. If your students play a sport or perform in a concert, go and watch them to show your appreciation for their hard work.
- Be respectful in your interactions with your students and insist that they do the same. For example, saying "please" and "thank you" goes a long way.
- When students confide in you, follow up. For example, if students told you that they were worried about a test in another class, take the time to ask how it went.
- Ask about a student's family. If you know someone is ill, show your concern.

- Speak to every student each day and connect more substantively with three students a day.

- Write positive and encouraging notes to your students on their assignments. You may wish to use stickers and stamps as well.

- Pay attention to your students' health. If students need to go to the clinic, send them. When students miss several days because of illness, call to see how they are doing or send a get-well card or message.

- Use this sentence to convey your concern: "What can I do to help you?"

- Talk with students when you notice a change in their behavior. For example, if a normally serious student is neglecting their work, find out why.

- Get your students up and moving in accessible ways. It's good for learning and good for health.

- Provide opportunities for students to share their opinions and beliefs with you and with one another in an inclusive way.

- Be empathetic and sympathetic. Privately acknowledge when a student is having a bad day.

- Take advantage of as many opportunities as you can to interact with your students as people. Ask about their interests, hobbies, concerns, or families—whatever it takes to connect.

- Be fair. Few things destroy a relationship between teacher and student faster than a student's suspicion that they are being treated unfairly.

- Be honest without oversharing. Students know when they are being lied to, and those lies will destroy the relationship you want to build.

- Show respect for your students as well as for their families, neighborhoods, and cultures. You don't have to know everything; be curious and open.

- Use your students' names frequently, and pronounce them correctly and with a gentle tone of voice.

- Be relaxed. Take a few deep breaths and focus on your students. Stressed-out teachers tend to transmit that negativity to their students, who will, in turn, respond negatively.

- Make frequent eye contact with everyone when you address the whole group. While in the United States this is a norm, some cultures consider eye contact to be disrespectful. Be aware and flexible if this is the case for some of your students.

- Laugh at yourself. When you show that you have a bit of self-awareness of your own foibles, you show students how to laugh at themselves, too.

- Be the first one to admit when you have made a mistake, take accountability, and repair the mistake.

- Incorporate technology, devices, and the internet to engage students when appropriate.

- Address disruptions and disrespectful behavior immediately so that students know they can count on you to maintain a safe and respectful classroom.

- Pay attention to the emotions behind your students' words. When you know your students well enough to be sensitive to their feelings, you will find it easier to relate well to them.

Verbal Immediacy

The words you use when you speak with your students constitute one of the most important ways you have of creating a strong bond with them. Kind words spoken in a gentle voice make it much easier for your students to connect with you. If you say something unkind to a student, it will hurt even more than an insult from a peer because it is from someone the student should be able to trust.

Verbal immediacy is a communication term referring to the sum of all the verbal interactions that you have with your students that create a sense of connection. It involves friendly and open language that draws in your audience. Referring to students by name, sharing classroom jokes, greeting them at the door, and using a kind and even voice all serve to create an atmosphere in which you and your students are connected in positive ways. In this section, you will learn about communication that either promotes or harms the positive relationships with students.

Of course, all communication with students should be respectful and appropriate to their age and developmental level. Be aware that you have positional power in the classroom and want to communicate in a way that builds self-esteem and trust. Violating that trust by cursing, putting down a student, or making negative remarks about a student's identity or culture would undermine the relationship teachers are trying to develop and potentially result in disciplinary action for the teacher. If you used a term or phrase and you were unaware of its potential impact, quickly acknowledge the harm and work to repair it. Never make disparaging remarks about any student's:

- Culture
- Race
- Gender
- Sexual orientation
- Religion
- Language or accent
- Family
- Friends
- Nationality
- Clothing
- Neighborhood
- Body type
- Disability
- Age
- Appearance

"Take an interest in what's going on in your students' lives. Ask them about their weekends, their sports teams, their trips, their goals, their classes, their clubs, and their hobbies. The more you ask, the more they share, and the more comfortable everyone is with one another. These little conversations go a long way in letting students know that you care about them, and once those relationships are established, students will buy wholeheartedly into your teaching, guidance, and leadership."

Jeff Vande Sande, 2 years' experience

You should also make a point of using "I" messages whenever you can. "I" messages are statements that use such words as *I, we, us,* or *our* instead of *you.* For example, instead of the harsh "You'd better pay attention," a teacher can say, "I'd like for you to please pay attention now." "You're too noisy" becomes "We all need to be quiet so that everyone can hear," and "You're doing that all wrong!" can become "I think I can help you with that."

With these simple changes, the statements are no longer accusatory, harsh in tone, or insulting. The language points out a problem but does not put anyone on the defensive. "I" messages work because they state a problem without blaming the student. This, in turn, creates a focus on a solution and not on an error the child has made.

For more detailed coaching on communicating successfully with students, read *Connecting Through Conversation: A Playbook for Talking with Students* By Erika Bare and Tiffany Burns.

A Long-Term Process: Get to Know Your Students

Warm demanders realize that getting to know their students is vital to establishing the positive connections that they want to have with students. It builds on the foundation of how students relate to one another and engage with groups of people. While you will begin connecting with your students right away, like any relationship, it takes time to build the necessary rapport and to genuinely learn about their lives, cultures, skills, and learning needs.

Another reason that it takes time to learn about your students is that every day will bring new maturity and growth. Interests will develop and evolve, and life experiences will create change. Even though this can be challenging, learning about your students is one of the most rewarding aspects of your teaching practice. Here are just some of the ways that you can learn about your students:

- Review your students' school records. Be sure to follow the correct procedures and confidentiality regulations.

- Make a point of observing your students as they interact with one another. Who appears to be shy? Who is a peacemaker? Who is generous? You can learn a great deal about them simply by being mindful of their interactions with one another.

- When you send a positive message home, you may have an opportunity to ask questions. Likewise, when you send home an introductory letter, you can add a section asking families and caregivers to tell you about their children. (See Section Five for a sample letter for this.)

- Your students' previous teachers may be another good source of information. One drawback of this method is that you may sometimes get information that is not completely objective and that may bias your view of a student.

- One of the best ways to get to know your students and to help them get to know one another is to use ice breakers based on the social-emotional learning (SEL) Three Signature Practices from CASEL.org. As you watch students interact with one another, you will learn a great deal about them. In addition, ice breakers will give your students an opportunity to listen to and value one another's contributions to the class. Try these ice breaker strategies to learn more about your students:

  - Four Corners: The teacher designates each corner of the room with a specific interest. Students select a corner. After each selection, they turn and talk to the rest of the students in their corner about what they like within that category. Rename each corner and have students choose again. Rotate through several selections so that student groups change. Some topics may include: children's books, colors, genres of music, ice cream flavors, fruits, vegetables, and so on. Note: Choose topics that won't divide students by socio-economic status, race, gender, ability, or religion. By keeping equity in mind, this activity will create connections rather than undermine them.

  - Greeting or Closing Frenzy: If students are comfortable with this type of physical contact, teachers give students sixty to ninety seconds to greet everyone in the room by name and make some physical contact such as high five or fist bump.

  - One, Two, Three, CLAP!: Students select a partner and count to three over and over again for one minute, with students taking turns saying the next number in the sequence. Close the game and ask who made a mistake. Likely, they all will have made a mistake. In the next round, when they make a mistake, they raise their hands and say "Ta-da!" In the third round, pairs should replace the number 1 with a clap and then continue voicing 2 and 3, aloud. In the final round, replace the number 1 with a clap and the number 2 with a foot stomp and voice the number 3. When either partner makes a mistake, they both say "Ta-da!" and give a two-handed, double high-five.

- You can also learn a great deal about your students from brief writing assignments in which students write a paragraph in response to quick questions. Here are fifty suggestions for topics in the form of statements to be completed by students that you could use at any time during the year:

  1. I have a strong interest in _____.

  2. When I am an adult, I want to _____.

  3. My favorite things to do outside of school are _____.

  4. My favorite holiday is_____.

  5. My favorite things to do at school are _____.

  6. The subjects I do best in are _____.

  7. The subjects I need help in are _____.

8. If I could change anything about school, it would be _____.

9. I am looking forward to learning about _____.

10. I like it when my teachers _____.

11. A special meal I love to eat is _____.

12. I am happiest when I am _____.

13. My closest friends are _____.

14. One thing people don't know about me is _____.

15. A skill I have is _____.

16. A person I admire is _____ because _____.

17. Something I would like to learn to do better is _____.

18. My previous teachers would tell you this about me _____.

19. I am proud of myself when I _____.

20. My greatest asset is _____.

21. I am an expert on _____.

22. I have trouble dealing with _____.

23. My favorite class is _____.

24. The most influential person in my life is _____ because _____.

25. It was difficult for me to learn _____.

26. It was easy for me to learn _____.

27. Three words that describe my personality are _____.

28. One lesson I had to learn the hard way is _____.

29. I am optimistic about _____.

30. My favorite movie/TV show is _____ because_____.

31. If I could do anything right now, I would _____.

32. If I had ten dollars, I would _____.

33. When I do poorly on a test, I _____.

34. When I do well on a test, I _____.

35. I worked hard to learn _____.

36. If I were five years older, I _____.

37. I am most proud of _____.

38. The hardest thing I ever did was _____.

39. At home, I help out by _____.

40. If I were a teacher, I would _____.

41. I would like to visit _____.

42. Not many people know _____.

43. I always laugh when _____.

44. I wish teachers would _____.

45. I deserve a trophy for _____.

46. I feel needed when _____.

47. Something I value in a friend is _____.

48. The best advice I've ever received is _____.

49. My favorite day of the week is _____.

50. I worry about _____ and reduce my stress by _____.

Create a Sense of Belonging to the Whole Group

Just as it is necessary to create connections that bind students to you and to one another, it is also important for them to feel that they belong to a special community. As you work with your class to create a whole-group positive identity, encourage a sense of belonging to the entire group. Here are some suggestions to help students see themselves as part of a positive classroom community:

- Celebrate improvements that they have made as a class: demonstrating new learning, settling down quickly, leaving their work areas tidy, or performing well on assessments, for example.

- Make it easy for the group to speak with you about concerns. Have students elect class officers or ambassadors to represent them when necessary. Students may be more comfortable surfacing concerns to a peer than to the teacher.

- Set class goals for them to achieve. Although academic goals are always helpful, nonacademic ones are as well. If there is a charity drive, food collection, or class competition at your school, for example, your students can set goals for how they want to participate.

- Celebrate successes. Large and small celebrations can build a sense of unity among students.

- At the end of a unit of study, have a showcase where students can share their best work with their peers.

- Directly teach the cooperation skills necessary for a collaborative and peaceful classroom.

Hold Classroom or Community Meetings

Classroom or community meetings have several purposes. It gives students practice with social skills, an opportunity to engage in problem-solving, and a space to voice their opinions. The format and timing of class meetings will depend on what you hope to accomplish. You can hold them as often as you like, for as long as you like, with whatever rules you establish, and on almost any topic. In fact, they are so advantageous that community circles are an essential element of both the social-emotional learning and restorative justice movements. (See Sections Seven and Eleven for more information about these systems.)

For a warm demander, however, class meetings not only offer a strategic way to get to know students but also opportunities for students to interact with each other in positive ways. When you hold class meetings, you show your students that you are interested in hearing what's on their minds as individuals. Because of the inclusive nature of class meetings, students also learn to view themselves as part of a classroom community. Here are several quick tips for conducting successful class meetings:

- Keep it manageable. Establish a predictable cadence such as fifteen to twenty minutes once a week to create a predictable routine.

- Have a purpose for the meeting. Is it just a check-in? Do you need to address a behavioral issue that affects the whole class? Do students need an opportunity to express opinions about a schoolwide or community wide topic? Is it simply a chance to create community?

- Have a specific topic in mind and allow students to think about the topic by having them jot their ideas down before the meeting begins. This will build the necessary confidence students need to be comfortable speaking to the group.

- Arrange the seating so that students can all see one another, preferably in a circle on the rug for younger students, and in chairs or desks, for older students.

- Spend time before the first meeting talking about the importance of listening and respectful communication.

- Make the rules for respectful listening clear before the first meeting. This will help ensure that meetings are successful and students will be respectful and focused on the topic.

- Designate who speaks with an object, such as a talking piece that students can pass around. The only person who can speak is the person with the object. Make it possible for students to request time to communicate with the class.

- At meetings where everyone has time to speak, you will need to keep the pace of the meeting brisk. As students are learning to answer a check-in question succinctly, you may need to set a timer so that one student doesn't dominate, leaving no time for others to contribute.

- Holding a brief meeting at the end of the week is also a positive way for students to recap their learning, share a hope for the weekend, and preview what they will learn next week. Hold space for any difficult subjects students may want to voice as well.

Help Students Learn to Relate Well to One Another

To create the connections that are necessary for a productive classroom environment, warm demanders know that when students feel that they are valued members of a group, the results can be remarkable. When they do not feel this connection with their peers, dysregulation, disinterest, and disrespect can arise in the classroom.

Warm demanders know that when students are in conflict with one another, learning suffers, so they actively work to help students relate to each other as well as manage the issues that hinder relationships. They promote the values that can make it easier for students to avoid conflicts: recognize common interests, respect one another's views, celebrate one another's cultural and learning differences, and work together for the mutual good of their classmates. Warm demanders also create a sense of belonging for all their students. Teachers make time to help students work well as part of a community of learners by removing the barriers to student friendships that make it difficult for students to work together and by teaching the social skills that will serve students well in the classroom and throughout their lives.

CREATE A SENSE OF BELONGING FOR ALL

Teachers have a powerful opportunity to create a sense of belonging among students. This is vital to students' mental health and academic success. What are some of the most common barriers to peer social connection and friendships in school? A lack of communication skills, limited opportunities to get to know everyone in their class, and exclusionary or bullying behavior are the biggest barriers.

Facilitate lots of opportunities for students to experience one-on-one, small group, and whole-group collaborative communication. Provide age-appropriate scaffolding with prompts, designated roles in groups, or sentence stems to teach appropriate communication skills.

Some students could feel isolated because they do not know their classmates. Assume that students do not know one another well. Even students who have attended school together for several years may not know much about their classmates. Give them opportunities to learn about commonalities incidentally during collaborative learning and directly through activities such as Four Corners. (See the section above, A Long-Term Process: Get to Know Your Students, for details on Four Corners.)

One of the greatest barriers that you will help your students overcome is the perception that they may not have much in common with a classmate whom they do not know well. With effort and persistence, you can help students discover their commonalities so that they can create a sense of belonging for each student and build authentic friendships. Encourage appreciation for differences in interests, cultures, and abilities as well. Students do not have to be similar to one another to become friends. Create the expectation that even if all students are not friends they will treat one another with respect. Use the tips in the list that follows to guide you:

- Facilitate many opportunities for students to learn each other's names. (See Section Five for first day of school activities.)
- Orchestrate Four Corners activities.
- If a student has an unpleasant history of failure or misbehavior, make it clear that it is time for a fresh start.
- Teach your students how to interact with one another respectfully. Provide plenty of models and monitoring until they have learned to collaborate and cooperate productively.

- Let each student shine. As you get to know students' strengths, give them opportunities to exhibit their skills in class. Make sure that each student's strengths are well known to the rest of the class.

- Make it a point to recognize students who work well with others. Whenever possible, praise individual students and the entire class for inclusive and collaborative behaviors.

- Encourage students to share experiences and personal information about their interests, families, cultures, dreams, and goals while working together or in class meetings.

- Reinforce and model growth mindset. When you or a student makes a mistake, celebrate it as a learning moment to avoid embarrassment and teasing that can undermine a student's sense of belonging.

- Be careful that you model appropriate behavior, thereby encouraging your students to do the same.

TEACH SOCIAL SKILLS

Supporting a student's social and emotional learning (SEL) is as important as their academic growth. Research shows that where SEL is promoted, students have better academic performance, stronger relationships, and improved mental health. The best website to learn more about SEL is the Collaborative for Academic, Social, and Emotional Learning or CASEL (CASEL.org), which offers an interactive framework known as the "CASEL wheel" that breaks down the component parts of SEL:

> "It's important to remember that your classroom is a refuge for many students. Some can't wait to walk through your door. When you greet them with a smile, a high five, and a hello, it's like they are coming home."
>
> *Tisha Richmond, 26 years' experience,*
> *tisharichmond.com*

- Self-Awareness
- Self-Management
- Responsible Decision-Making
- Relationship Skills
- Social Awareness

CASEL's *SEL Three Signature Practices Playbook* helps teachers integrate SEL in any classroom. Those three signature practices include:

- Welcoming Inclusion Activities
- Engaging Strategies
- Optimistic Closure

The CASEL website also provides a review of SEL programs to help educators select instructional materials to teach SEL. Explicitly teaching SEL skills is vital from Pre-K through high school. In this section, we will focus on social or relationship skills.

Many teachers would like to engage students with cooperative learning, but avoid it because students don't have the skills to collaborate successfully. As a warm demander, one of the most important expectations that you can have for your students is that they treat one another with respect. You cannot assume that they have the skills to do that; in fact, teaching your students the social skills required to function well in your class will help them for the rest of their lives. The powerful CASEL framework defines relationship skills and social awareness in exquisite detail. In this section, we will focus on a few suggestions for teaching social skills in your class:

- Explicitly discuss with students the purpose of social skills
- Choose a social skill from the list below. You may want to call them Skills for Collaboration or Cooperation.
- Teach what the skill looks like by having students brainstorm examples and non-examples. You may also want to use videos, visual stories, or role playing.
- Facilitate an activity for students to practice the skill.
- Engage students in a debriefing at the end of the practice activity.

Here is a list of some of the social skills that are helpful in any classroom. All students should:

Communicate effectively

- Use an appropriate volume when speaking, while encouraging excitement, and contemplation.
- Grow their vocabulary. Refrain from using inappropriate language, such as profanity or insults.
- Say "please," "excuse me," and "thank you" when speaking with one another and the teacher.
- Raise their hands as a signal for attention and then wait to be called on.
- Address one another and the teacher by using appropriate names.
- Be curious. Consider others' perspectives and discuss ideas without making personal attack.
- Give positive feedback often.
- Take turns whether in conversation or playing a game.

Listen actively

- Listen actively for understanding.
- Do not interrupt others, unless disrupting a harmful action.

- Respond to what was said by specifically referencing the previous speaker's idea.
- Use body language that shows they're listening. Look at the speaker. Lean forward. Stay upright in their seats. Make eye contact.
- Follow directions.

Resolve conflicts well

- Take a breath or a break to self-regulate.
- Name the problem and share their concerns.
- Listen to the other person's perspective.
- Work together on a resolution.
- Take responsibility for harm.
- Repair harm caused.

Ask for and offer help when needed

- Using sentence stems to clarify what help is needed, like "I'm struggling with _____."
- Ask Three Then Me: When they get stuck, ask three classmates for help before asking the teacher or try three ways to solve the problem before asking the teacher.
- Ask permission before taking something that belongs to someone else.
- Share classroom supplies with others.

Exhibit leadership skills

- Enter the classroom with respect if late or when returning from being excused so as not to disturb others.
- Be inclusive. Respect others' identities, cultures, values, and life experiences.
- Take on a classroom job and follow through on the responsibilities of that role.
- Fulfill their specific roles in collaborative groups, such as: Facilitator, Timer, Recorder, Encourager, Spokesperson, Encourager, Questioner, Process Observer.
- Place personal belongings where they belong to avoid blocking traffic.
- Clean up their work areas.
- Speak up for others who are being disrespected.

Effective teachers model strong social skills. Each day, you have hundreds of opportunities to show your students how to be kind, caring, and inclusive. Modeling positive social skills is a powerful teaching tool.

The *Demander* Qualities of an Effective Teacher

In addition to the warm qualities of an effective classroom leader, you will need to intentionally practice the demander qualities. The three most important *demander* qualities are: being explicit about and teaching behavioral and academic expectations; maintaining a persistent focus on learning; and consistently implementing classroom policies, procedures, and agreements. These three key qualities, in combination with a warm relationship with students, make learning possible.

Explicitly teaching expectations for quality work and behavior provides clarity to students so that they can begin to self-assess progress toward academic and behavior goals. Warm demanders teach how and why students can meet high expectations for academic work to accelerate student growth. Warm demanders also teach how and why students can follow classroom procedures, routines, and policies to develop social skills that create positive learning environments and lifelong skills. You will need to persistently teach, reteach, and reinforce these skills. From one term to the next, you will see tremendous academic and behavioral growth as a result of your consistent and persistent leadership.

The second demander quality, maintaining a persistent focus on learning, sets a straightforward tone for students: they are expected to work toward mastery of knowledge and skills for success in school and in life. Warm demander teachers have extensive content knowledge, a clear idea of learning outcomes, and well-planned learning opportunities. Warm demanders also offer differentiated paths to mastery and appropriate scaffolding so that students can learn. Teachers and students in a warm demander's classroom work together. Mistakes are celebrated. There is a growth mindset. In fact, one of the chief characteristics of warm demanders is that they insist on student effort and persistence—the foundation of a growth mindset.

The third quality of a warm demander—consistently implementing classroom policies, procedures, and agreements—is possible because the teacher has taken the time to build rapport, earn students' respect, and create a positive class environment. The particulars of classroom management have been decided on with both positive reinforcement and natural consequences in place. Violations of class agreements are addressed with care to protect student dignity and to help a student, who made a choice with negative consequences, learn, grow, and repair. When a student makes a poor choice, a warm demander sees an opportunity for learning. The teacher distinguishes the behavior from the student. Depending on the frequency and severity of the violation, the warm demander will calmly use redirection strategies or enact appropriate consequences.

"R-E-S-P-E-C-T. Develop a rapport with your students and strive to be more than just the teacher who is **liked** by everyone. Strive to be both liked **and** respected. It doesn't have to be one or the other. That's the relationship you should strive to develop with your students. Get them to the point where they never want to let you down, and you'll see the results, both academically and behaviorally."

Jay O'Rourke, 2+ years' experience

Call on Students Equitably

There are many ways for students to participate in small group or 1:1 discussions. When a whole group discussion occurs, it's important that warm demanders have a range of strategies to fully engage students, prevent bias, and maintain high expectations for all students. Sometimes you will ask for a show of hands for volunteers. Sometimes you will call on students randomly. Done well, this can increase student engagement. Mishandled, it can discourage or embarrass students who don't have an idea or a correct answer to contribute.

Get to know your students. Many students will be able to participate in whole group discussions without a lot of scaffolding. Some will need a moment of independent thinking, writing, or paired discussion before contributing to a whole group discussion. Using CASEL.org SEL strategies, encourage students to say "Pass" or "Please come back to me" if that's their choice for today. Just notice if that becomes their default response and intervene to include them in the discussion.

Thoughtfully consider the types of questions you ask a whole group. Are they open-ended? Do your questions have one correct answer? Establish class norms for whole group discussions so that students know what to expect. It's a good practice, for example, to ask the whole class to think about the question before randomly calling on students. This motivates students to do some independent thinking and ensure that all minds are engaged in thinking.

There are several ways to handle this so that you can call on your students equitably. Some teachers print out a student roster or create a list of student names. As they call on students, they place a check beside their names to indicate that they have already responded.

Another technique that many teachers use is to write each student's name on a note card and then shuffle them into one stack. As students respond, the teacher creates a separate stack of note cards for those students. Once the original stack has been depleted, shuffle and begin again. A similar technique is to write each student's name on a popsicle stick. As the discussion progresses, the teacher can then separate the popsicle sticks with the names of students who have been called on with those who have not. Alternatively, recombine the cards and popsicle sticks after calling on a student so they remain engaged knowing they could be called on again.

If you want to use an online resource that students enjoy seeing in action, try using a random name generator to determine which student is called on, such as:

- Picker Wheel (pickerwheel.com)
- Wheel of Names (wheelofnames.com)
- ABCya.com (abcya.com/random_name_picker.htm)

Whichever method you use, keep in mind that if you are going to be a warm, caring teacher with high expectations, you must call on students equitably. Don't allow a couple of students to answer all the questions because that sets up a dynamic where other students disengage. Support students who don't have an idea or answer to share with additional scaffolded questions. Develop a system of calling on students that works well for you and your students and put it into action.

Questions to Discuss with Colleagues

Sharing ideas with colleagues is a helpful way to devise solutions to some of the problems that you must manage successfully at school. Here, you will find several topics to open discussions with colleagues about successful instructional practices:

1. A parent objects to a book that you have assigned for your entire class to read, even though you obtained administrative approval to use this book. How should you handle this situation?

2. In an email, the caregivers of a dysregulated student blame you for their student's disruptive behavior. Who can assist you with this issue? What should you do? What are some actions to avoid that might make it worse?

3. You are planning for conferences and want to welcome families and caregivers who speak a language that you do not speak. What resources does the school provide for translation and interpretation? What additional preparations should you make to set everyone up for success?

4. You notice that your students seem uncomfortable talking with each other and struggle to take turns in conversations. What can you do to teach social or relationship skills to improve communication and teamwork?

5. You want to facilitate a class meeting to solve a problem. Students leave the class a mess every day. What can you do to share the concern and help students brainstorm solutions so they take more responsibility?

Topics to Discuss with a Mentor

Although the topics that new teachers need to discuss with a mentor vary from teacher to teacher and from school to school, there are some that most first-year teachers should be comfortable discussing with a mentor or a trusted colleague. You should ask your mentor about these topics from this section:

• How to gather and organize information about your students
• How to engage in difficult interactions with families or caregivers

- Suggestions for helping build relationships with students
- Suggestions for having high expectations for your students
- Advice on how to find the right balance of warm and demanding for your students

Reflection Questions to Guide Your Thinking

1. You know that the ratio of 5:1 positive to negative or correctional feedback is important to maintain, but it can be difficult to do. What can you do to increase the positive interactions you have with students while still maintaining a focus on learning?

2. What are you already doing to be a teacher who is a warm demander? What aspects of how you present yourself would you like to improve?

3. How can you show that you care about students while maintaining a respectful emotional distance? Which of your students need more care and understanding at this point in the year than others?

4. What have you observed another teacher doing to forge a positive connection with their students' families and caregivers? How can you improve the way that you engage with your students' home adults?

5. What did you do to help your students be successful this week? How do you know they were successful? How did your students react to your actions? How will you celebrate these successes?

SECTION SEVEN

Equity—Meeting the Needs of All

"Be kind for everyone is fighting a great battle," the saying goes. It is a powerful adage for teachers to keep in mind in our daily work with students. Each student has unique experiences, traumas, and challenges that will require understanding, support, or intervention. Some students may experience poverty, loss, homelessness, violence, or neglect. Others may be English language learners, students with learning differences, or those who require 504 plans to remove barriers to their learning. Schools can be structured in a way that makes it difficult for students to succeed without the intervention of a dedicated teacher. Each student in your classroom has a story, and teachers must understand their needs and how to support them.

On the first day of class with your new students, the day will probably zoom past in an exciting blur of new faces and responsibilities. One of the joys of getting to know students is discovering their unique qualities. It takes a great deal of creativity, compassion, and insight to meet the needs of each student and provide personalized learning that makes the content accessible to all learners.

We now understand that, in order for students to succeed academically, we need to attend to more than simply providing instruction. We must work with home and community partners to provide more expansive supports for a student's long-term growth and development. This includes supporting students' academic, behavioral, social, emotional, and physical health. Educators now realize that having a narrow, academic-based view of their responsibilities is not meeting the needs of every student. Our approach to students must take into consideration other critical factors in their lives, such as their resources outside of school, their families, their health, their learning differences, and their overall sense of safety.

In the rest of this section, you will learn about some classroom practices and how they increase equity and help you to reach and teach *all* of your students.

The Whole Child Approach and Its Implications for Your Classroom

The Association for Supervision and Curriculum Development (ASCD), in cooperation with a host of global partners, launched the Whole Child approach to Education to support a human-centered and inclusive approach to educating all students. The Whole Child approach advocates that students will thrive in an environment where they feel safe and are treated as worthwhile individuals whose academic, social, emotional, and physical health needs are addressed.

If it was not part of your pre-service program, learn as much as you can about the Whole Child approach to education. Your district or school may make it a priority and offer in-service training. If not, explore the ASCD website and share it with other teachers in your school and professional learning network (PLN). Here are two excellent websites to help you learn more about how you can include the principles of the Whole Child approach in your own teaching practice:

Association for Supervision and Curriculum Development (ASCD) (ascd.org/whole-child): A leader in the Whole Child approach to education, at the ASCD site, you can find a great deal of useful information about the movement and about how you can incorporate the approach into your classroom.

Educate the Whole Child (educatethewholechild.org): This site offers a comprehensive view of the Whole Child approach as well as graduate courses, certification, and a wealth of links to articles and resources for educators.

As you learn more about the Whole Child approach, you will realize that it incorporates many of the best practices that you already have in place in your classroom. In classrooms where the needs of the whole child are considered, teachers:

- Create an inclusive environment where learning goals and activities are transparent to students, families, and caregivers
- Model respect for students' cultures and expect that students will also demonstrate respect for one another's cultures
- Differentiate instruction so that the learning needs of all students can be met
- Create a classroom environment where students are safe both physically and emotionally with their teachers and peers
- Provide additional instruction to address learning gaps for students to enable them to learn with their peers and not fall further behind
- Pay attention to the physical, mental, and emotional needs of their students in addition to their academic needs
- Maintain a predictable classroom environment where students work together with their teacher and classmates in a purposeful, positive way

"I wish my students knew how much I legitimately care about them. As a teacher, I *want* them to succeed in whatever way possible; it doesn't have to look like an A. For some students, success looks like improving from a D to a C, and I want them to know that that's okay and that I'm proud of them regardless. There have been countless commutes back to my home at the end of a school day when I reflect and ask, 'Did I do enough for student XYZ today?' I wish they could see that side of me as well."

Jay O'Rourke, 2+ years' experience

- Promote a growth mindset in their students so that they can rise to the challenges of school and daily life
- Connect with their students as caring adults who are concerned about the well-being and success of individual students

How to Include Social-Emotional Learning in Daily Classroom Life

Social emotional learning (SEL) is another powerful approach that focuses on the whole child instead of just on academics. Social emotional learning involves learning the knowledge, skills, and attitudes to develop the five core competencies of SEL: self-awareness, self-management, responsible decision-making, relationship skills, and social awareness. Not only does SEL increase student engagement and academic success, it contributes to a lifetime of greater health and happiness. Integrating SEL into the curriculum will also allow your classroom to run more smoothly.

SEL programs vary greatly from school to school. If your school district has adopted an SEL curriculum, you may be offered in-service training that would allow you to make decisions about content and practices in collaboration with your colleagues. Although many schools adopt a school- or district-wide program to include SEL in classrooms, yours may not. Here are two useful resources for learning more about SEL:

> **Collaborative for Academic Social Emotional Learning (CASEL) (casel.org):** At the CASEL site, you can learn the basics of SEL and how to incorporate it into your classroom. There are links to lesson plans, ready-to-use activities, research projects, articles, and practical advice for teachers.

> **Responsive Classroom (responsiveclassroom.org):** Here, you can find a great deal of useful information about morning meetings and many other strategies to integrate SEL into your classroom. At the home page, use "social emotional learning" as a search term to access the many resources Responsive Classroom offers.

If your school does not have an SEL program and practices in place, you will want to adopt some strategies for your classroom practice. Here are some to consider as you learn more about SEL and how it can improve student learning and well-being. A teacher committed to promoting students' social-emotional development will:

- Shift their mindset from finding fault with a student as a person, thinking what's wrong with the student to looking beyond the behavior and wondering what happened to the student to cause them to respond in that way
- Model emotional regulation skills in order to teach students how to deal with frustration appropriately (e.g., instead of yelling when frustrated with a student, model how to calm down)
- Implement the three signature practices from CASEL: Welcoming Inclusion Activities, Engaging Strategies, and Optimistic Closure (See Section Nine for more details on these practices.)

- Help students connect with one another through shared activities, collaborative learning, class/community meetings, team-building activities, and ice breakers
- Actively work to build a community of learners where students have positive relationships with one another and feel a sense of connection to the whole group
- Expand students' vocabularies and practice naming a wide range of emotions
- Teach students to appreciate commonalities and differences among cultures around the world and within the classroom
- Model the social skills students should learn and use
- Help students appreciate the value of giving to others by encouraging community service projects
- Celebrate mistakes and work to make the classroom a safe place for students to take risks while learning
- Help students learn to resolve conflicts in productive, positive ways
- Teach students how to set, work for, and achieve goals
- Recognize the importance of such qualities as determination and persistence
- Teach students how to work together peacefully and productively

Easy-to-Use SEL Strategies

Here are some activities that will help you integrate SEL into any grade level or content area.

- Greet students at the door as they enter the classroom
- Facilitate a morning check-in with a quick question that students can answer verbally, with an emoji, or on an app like Pear Deck, Flip, Canva, Google Forms, or Nearpod
- Use a self-awareness framework such as the Mood Meter from RULER or Zones of Regulation to help students identify emotions and learn how to shift them
- Co-create classroom agreements with your students
- Choose read aloud books with SEL themes
- Foster an attitude of gratitude with gratitude journals
- Provide reflection time for students through journaling
- Establish a calming corner in the classroom
- Engage students in writing a "Where I'm From" poem using a template modeled after the poem by George Ella Lyon
- Create a culture of kindness with Bucket Filler activities where students write positive notes to each other
- Coordinate a "Reading Buddies" classroom partnership, bringing together older and younger students to build reading skills and community
- Employ strategies for cooperative learning and project-based learning to practice problem-solving and social skills

Integrate Mindfulness to Support Students

Mindfulness practices complement SEL instruction. By increasing self-regulation and focus while reducing stress and anxiety, mindfulness improves student learning. Mindfulness is simply the act of being present in the moment without judgment, remaining calm, and increasing awareness.

In classrooms where teachers and students practice mindfulness, many students report that they are more relaxed and better able to focus and learn. Because of the deliberate slowing down required to stop and breathe deeply or to practice awareness, mindful classrooms tend to be places where students are more self-aware and have coping skills in place to manage their feelings. This increases self-regulation and reduces disruptions.

There are many ways to incorporate mindfulness into your classroom that support instruction by calming a student's state and energy level. Each of the following exercises is done individually and often with eyes closed.

- Intentional breathing exercises such as inhaling for four seconds and exhaling for four seconds. Some students like to blow on a pinwheel to make it move, which requires deep breathing.
- Breathe while tracing the outside of the hand. Inhale as you move up the side of a finger and exhale when moving down the side of a finger.
- Mindful listening, noticing what you hear around you and letting it go, or listening closely to an instrumental piece of music.
- Focus on fingers by pressing both hands together and starting with the thumbs, slowly move digit pairs apart and then back together.
- Tapping shoulders, elbows, or knees in a seated position.

There are many resources available to teachers who are interested in including mindfulness strategies into their classrooms; three excellent resources are Mindful Schools, GoNoodle, and the Mindfulness in Schools Project.

Mindful Schools (mindfulschools.org/): This site provides extensive information about mindfulness and how you can use it to help you and your students manage stress.

GoNoodle (gonoodle.com): This is a free product with quick, easy-to-use mindfulness and brain break videos for students in grades K–5.

Mindfulness in Schools Project (MindfulnessinSchool.org): This website provides courses, training, and curriculum to teachers and schools around the world. It has free downloadable resources and sample lessons under the Training & Support tab.

Establish a Safe, Risk-Taking Environment

Learning requires taking risks, and to take risks, students need to have a sense of safety and trust. No one wants to be embarrassed in front of an entire class, but your students will make mistakes, and sometimes those mistakes will be very public and result in embarrassment. Insightful teachers know that they must model and nurture a growth mindset in their students so that mistakes are opportunities for learning. Teachers also know that it is their responsibility to establish a positive, supportive classroom environment where ridicule is not acceptable.

Students who feel safe tend to have teachers who value kindness and cooperation and who make the importance of both traits part of the class expectations and culture. In short, these teachers have made it possible for students to be comfortable enough to take a risk—to try something new without fear of failure or embarrassment.

There are times when teachers may randomly call on students for an answer, idea, or opinion. In review sessions, class discussions, or any activity where students are asked to respond verbally, there is the possibility that a student will say something wrong in front of peers. To help students avoid feeling intimidated, here are a few general tips for creating a safe risk-taking environment when calling on students in class:

- Model growth mindset. Be open about the mistakes you make yourself. Model how to react appropriately when you are wrong.
- Encourage students to write out their answers before speaking. This will give them time to think as well as to engage fully with the material.
- Have students think independently, and then turn and talk to a classmate before soliciting responses.
- Make it clear that if students speak to you in advance, you will not call on them.
- When a student is struggling with an answer or response, here's how you can support them:
  - Ask if they would like to get suggestions or advice from a classmate.
  - Tell students that it is okay to say, "I am not sure, but _____."
  - Ask if they would like to opt out or take a pass on the question.
  - Tell the student to give their best guess.
  - Offer to come back to the student later.
  - Ask for clarification by saying, "I think I hear you saying _____."
  - Say, "Almost. Can you add a bit more?"
  - Ask another student to tell you what is correct about the answer and then add to it.

Create a Culturally Responsive Classroom

Developing classrooms and teaching strategies that accelerate learning for all students requires that teachers identify their own culture, learn about their students' cultures, and affirm cultures in words, actions, and lesson designs.

Teach your students to see their commonalities while valuing their differences. When you do this, you are creating a welcoming and inclusive classroom that celebrates the richness and strength found in diverse cultures. By helping students locate their own culture and identity and expanding students' appreciation of one another, you are developing skills that will serve them for a lifetime. Although the topic of a culturally responsive classroom warrants research and study, here are some general guidelines you can use to begin building a culturally responsive community:

> "Developing cultural competence is about seeing and celebrating both the beautiful and broken pieces of your own story so you can see and celebrate your students fully and connect the content to them in unique and important ways."
>
> *Jocelynn Hubbard, 18 years' experience, Customteachingsolutions.com and The Culture-Centered Teaching Podcast*

- The best place to start is with self-reflection. Consider the many characteristics of your own identity and culture, both visible and invisible. Locate your culture and consider how it influences the way you learn and the assumptions you make about others.

- Pronounce students' names correctly; apologize when you mispronounce a name. Have students record the pronunciation of their names so that you can listen to it repeatedly if needed.

- Invite students to reflect on and share their cultures. Understanding your students' cultures is critical to creating a culturally responsive classroom.

- Be aware that your attitudes are influenced by your own culture. Be conscious of your own implicit bias regarding culture, race, religion, socioeconomic status, ability, language, gender, sexual orientation, and other characteristics of identity.

- Create mirrors and windows in the curriculum for students to see themselves reflected in the curriculum and have a window into the lives of others. Representation is vitally important across content areas. Students need to learn about heroes, thinkers, and leaders from diverse backgrounds. When designing lessons ask yourself, "Do students see themselves and a range of diverse backgrounds represented in the curriculum? What are students learning about their own and other cultures?"

- Gain an understanding of learning styles from various cultural traditions. If, for example, students come from rich storytelling traditions, then create a narrative within your subject area and students will remember it.

- Get to know the community in which you teach. Engage in community events to celebrate and connect with the culture and wider community. You will, of course, greet students and families at these events, but as a general rule, avoid socializing outside of school with students and their families or caregivers.

- Add a social context for learning into lessons to bring cultural ways of knowing and learning into the classroom and help all students accelerate learning.

- Make discussing the cultures in your class and around the world an important part of what you and your students do together.

- Elevate and celebrate cultures, including languages present in your classroom. Create opportunities for students and their families and caregivers to celebrate their cultures in the classroom.

- Listen carefully to the hopes and concerns of all families and caregivers. Lead with empathy and ask questions to fully understand their goals for their children. Seeking first to understand will help you partner with them for their student's success.

- Model for students an open-minded attitude of inclusion and celebration of diverse identities and cultures. Make this very clear in all you say and do.

- Design instruction that offers a variety of cultural reference points that students can use to access the material or demonstrate their learning. You should also offer as much appropriate scaffolding as possible to all students who need it.

RESOURCES TO CREATE A CULTURALLY RESPONSIVE CLASSROOM

There are myriad resources to help you on your journey to create a culturally responsive classroom. In this list, you will find a small sample of the websites, podcasts, and books where you can further explore this vital work.

Websites

National Equity Project (nationalequityproject.org): Providing professional learning to help educators reimagine and design schools for equity. The website has free articles, tools, podcasts, webinars, videos, and blogs under the Resources tab.

Learning for Justice (LFJ) (learningforjustice.org): A project of the Southern Poverty Law Center, LFJ provides classroom resources, including social justice standards, lesson plans, standards-aligned student texts and tasks, film kits, posters, and more.

The Culture-Centered Classroom Podcast: This program by Jocelynn Hubbard inspires educators to transform teaching and learning with culturally responsive practices. Her website, CustomTeachingSolutions.com, provides many resources for teachers, including the Culture-Centered Classroom Success Kit: The Secret Sauce.

National Education Association (NEA) (nea.org/professional-excellence/ just-equitable-schools): NEA's website provides teachers with tools and professional development to create a safe, welcoming, affirming environment for all students.

International Education and Resource Network (iearn.org): Since 1988, this well-known site has connected students and teachers to collaborate with peers around the world on global projects.

Black on Black Education (BlackonBlackEducation.com): Founded by teacher Evalaurene Jean-Charles to support schools in strengthening student-centered practices, the podcast amplifies the voices and ideas of educational thinkers to transform education in the Black community. The website hosts videos of more than 90 episodes.

Books

Culturally Responsive Teaching: Theory, Research, and Practice by Dr. Geneva Gay: The term *culturally responsive teaching* was coined in the year 2000 with the publication of this book in which Dr. Geneva Gay demonstrates that students achieve more when teachers incorporate students' cultures.

Culturally Responsive Teaching and the Brain: Promoting Authentic Engagement and Rigor among Culturally and Linguistically Diverse Students by Zaretta Hammond: This brain-based approach to teaching and learning focuses on ten "key moves" to increase engagement and deepen learning.

For White Folks Who Teach in the Hood and the Rest of Y'all Too: Reality Pedagogy and Urban Education by Dr. Christopher Emdin: Dr. Emdin focuses on urban education and the power of using the 7Cs of reality pedagogy to amplify the genius of students and educators alike.

Support Vulnerable Students to Overcome Challenges

Systems get the results they are designed to achieve, so it's vital that educators create systems that result in learning for all. In fact, *equity* in education means providing differentiated supports for each student to achieve success. School failure is not inevitable for vulnerable students. With prevention, early intervention, and appropriate supports, all students can thrive.

Before we begin, a word about language. How members of groups identify and how society labels groups changes over time based on how a group understands itself, its place in society, and its hopes and dreams for the future. There are words that may be reclaimed by members of the group that would be insults if used by someone outside of that identity. The language in this book makes every effort to uplift the humanity of each student without erasing a vital part of their identity. Person-first language is not always the right choice and identity-first language is not always the right choice. There is no substitute for getting to know your students and learning what identities they hold for themselves and what language they use that allows them to walk in the world with a sense of power, pride, and possibility.

It is a tragic reality that some student groups are historically underserved and at greater risk of school failure. While it is crucial to understand that each student is an individual benefiting from unique interventions and support, to organize this section, we will consider students whose needs are often not met by traditional school structures. For purposes of arranging this section, we will place students into three categories of underserved youth. Students may, of course, fall into more than one category.

- A characteristic of identity such as race, gender, language, or sexual orientation that may result in students experiencing racism, sexism, transphobia, glottophobia, or homophobia
- Social factors such as trauma, foster placement, low socioeconomic status, homelessness, migrant or immigration status may undermine readiness, attendance, and opportunities to learn

- An identified disability, impairment, or exceptionality that qualifies a student for an Individual Education Plan (IEP), 504 Plan, or Personal Education Plan (PEP) (These plans provide specially designed instruction, accommodations, modifications, or enrichment opportunities based on students' learning differences.)

In this section, you will explore the challenges faced by vulnerable groups of students and strategies to overcome those challenges. In all three categories, the supports and interventions begin with getting to know your students; identifying their strengths to build on them; and enlisting a team of school, home, and community adults to reduce risk factors and increase protective factors that lead to student success.

> "Teaching through an equity lens is only possible once you have decided to continually develop cultural competency. This allows every educator to understand the full impact that student voice and choice have on a student's ability to thrive in a learning environment."
>
> *Jocelynn Hubbard, 18 years' experience, customteachingsolutions.com and The Culture-Centered Classroom Podcast*

One of the great joys that you will experience as a teacher will happen when, after working diligently with a student to conquer an obstacle, that student finally achieves success. At that moment, all your effort, persistence, and patience will have been worth it. Although each section is necessarily brief, it is designed to provide an overview of the challenges students may face, suggestions to provide meaningful support, and resources to learn more.

UNDERSERVED YOUTH: CHARACTERISTICS OF IDENTITY OR CULTURE

Multicultural, multilingual classrooms are rich and wonderful places that benefit all students. Exposure to a broad cross-section of students not only leads to expansive ideas and more innovative problem solving, it also gives students life skills to communicate, collaborate, and navigate in a diverse world.

Unfortunately, some students are vulnerable to poor outcomes in school because educators, school systems, and society do not yet fully affirm and support aspects of their identity. In this situation, students of color, emergent bilingual students, and LGBTQ students may experience racism, glottophobia, transphobia, or homophobia that creates barriers to learning.

High school graduation rates in the United States are lower for Native American, Black, and Latinx students than for white students. Emergent bilingual students and LGBTQ students are more likely to drop out than their English-speaking or straight classmates. It's important to be clear that culture and identity are not what makes students vulnerable. Students become vulnerable to poor outcomes if the school is not structured in ways that celebrate and support their culture and identity. Not all students who share these identities need additional support to succeed, but given the historic data, teachers must be identity-conscious and aware.

The good news is we also know what strategies improve safety, school climate, and academic outcomes. In the preceding sections on culturally responsive classrooms and the qualities of a warm-demander, we explored strategies for creating a welcoming and inclusive classroom where all students thrive. Those strategies apply here as well to create schools and classrooms that support youth who have been historically underserved due to a characteristic of their identity.

Support strategies include:

- Identify your own culture and identity on a social identity wheel. Name aspects of your identity such as: race, socioeconomic status, gender, sexual orientation, national origin, first language, (dis)abilities, age, religion, and so on, and consider how your culture and identity inform the way you navigate through the world.

- Educate yourself about the concerns and the joy experienced by people whose identities differ from your own. Learn about the richness of cultures and experiences beyond your lived experience.

> "I wish I had thought more about identity and how my own identity shaped the books I chose for my class, the questions I asked, and the projects I assigned to students. I sometimes avoided topics that felt unfamiliar to me because, frankly, I was nervous about getting it wrong. But, an identity-conscious practice helps us to examine these types of decisions and how we influence the classroom."
>
> *Liza A. Talusan, Ph.D., lizatalusan.com*

- Diversify your social media, podcast, and newsfeeds to include voices of people whose identities differ from your own.

- Pronounce students' names correctly. Insist that others do, too. Some students may use nicknames that make their names "easier" to pronounce. Even if you use this nickname, you should know how to pronounce your student's full name.

- Build trusting relationships with your students. They need to know you care.

- Maintain high expectations for students, building their knowledge, skills, and confidence.

- Assure and respect confidentiality unless you have their permission to share information, or of course, if there is a risk of harm to self or others.

- Listen to their thoughts, hopes, dreams, worries, and needs; believe them and respond accordingly.

- Engage with empathy. When a student confides in you about their life experience, or comes out to you, your initial response matters. Listen. Appreciate their courage. Offer support, school resources, or referrals. A few days later, check in with students privately. Simply ask how they're doing and if they need support.

- Identify, encourage, and cultivate students' strengths.

- Avoid tokenizing students by asking them to speak for their race, gender, country of origin, or other aspect of identity.

- Avoid using gender as a characteristic for lining up or picking teams.

- Create mirrors and windows by incorporating diverse identities in your curriculum. In this way, students will see themselves reflected in the curriculum and have a window into the lives of others. This is a vital strategy even if your class appears more homogeneous.

- Affirm diverse cultures in your words, actions, and lesson designs.

- Be a role model of acceptance and support for all your students. Use the name and pronouns that students ask you to use.

- Create classroom environments where discrimination, harassment, and bullying are unacceptable.

- If an incident happens, address it and use it as a teachable moment. Support the targeted student and hold the student who caused harm accountable.

- You are not alone. Classroom teachers should not attempt to be social workers. If a student is struggling, enlist caregivers, school staff, and community members who can provide meaningful support.

- Create a support plan that increases protective factors and reduces risk factors with the student and their team of adults.

- Monitor, adjust, and celebrate based on how the plan unfolds.

There are many resources to explore to support and affirm students' identities. Here are just a few:

Courageous Conversation on Race: A Field Guide for Achieving Equity in Schools by Glenn E. Singleton: Singleton's book provides practical tools, protocols and strategies to forge a path to progress for racial equity in schools. Explore the website (courageousconversation.com) to learn more about professional development opportunities.

Black on Black Education (blackonblackeducation.com): Evalaurene Jean-Charles is a teacher who also offers professional development on student-centered practices and a podcast on transforming education in the Black community.

Everything You Wanted to Know about Indians but Were Afraid to Ask by Anton Treuer: A professor of Ojibwe at Bemidji State University, Dr. Treuer gives candid, funny, matter-of-fact responses to 120 questions, including "What's the real story of Thanksgiving?" He provides a foundation for understanding and action.

Identity Conscious Educator: Building Habits and Skills for a More Inclusive School by Liza A. Talusan, Ph.D.: A member of the faculty at University of Massachusetts, Dr. Talusan shares practical strategies for creating inclusive school communities, providing frameworks to understand identity categories and engage in meaningful interactions with students and colleagues.

Culturally Responsive Conversations: Connecting with Your Diverse School Community by Marina Minhwa Lee and Seth Leighton: This book offers a toolkit for educators to have effective conversations with families from a wide-range of diverse backgrounds and give all students the education they deserve.

NEA Resource Library (nea.org/resource-library): NEA hosts toolkits and robust teacher resources for all identities. Insert a keyword in the library's search bar to locate the right resource for you.

Gay Lesbian Straight Educator Network (GLSEN) (GLSEN.org): This website has a robust collection of educator guides, lesson plans, and resources. Click: Work>Resources>Educator.

The Human Rights Campaign's Welcoming Schools Program (welcomingschools .org): HRC WSP hosts a professional resources library and professional development for teachers, including lesson plans, bullying prevention programs, and book lists.

Emergent Bilingual Students

Bilingualism and multilingualism are incredible assets that can lead to a Seal of Biliteracy on most high school diplomas for students and significant career opportunities for adults. Half of the planet is bilingual, but only 20% of Americans are. To acknowledge the unique potential of this student population, we use Dr. Ofelia García's term, *Emergent Bilingual (EB)*. These students are also known as *English Language Learners (ELL)* or *English as a Second Language (ESL)* students. Regardless of the descriptor, EB students have both cultural and linguistic strengths and barriers to school success in the United States.

> "Now that I have built these skills for integrating identity into my work, I see that there are holes in my own teaching and leading. I notice that there are identities that never make it into my curriculum—in our readings, books, projects, and discussions. And, now, as an identity-conscious educator, I can critically look at my own work, make improvements, and provide a more reflective classroom experience for my students."
>
> *Liza A. Talusan, Ph.D., lizatalusan.com*

Proficiency in English is generally assessed on a scale from beginner to advanced. Eligible students are assessed, and if they qualify for English Language Development (ELD) support, a plan is created. Students receive ELD instruction from a specialist, and modifications and accommodations in all classes. Here are some strategies to provide language supports in addition to the preceding cultural supports:

- Assume competence and genius in all your students. EB students are faced with twice the work, learning the content and the language. They just can't communicate that brilliance in English yet.

- Work closely with the ELD or ELL teacher to collaborate on lesson plans, learn effective strategies, and engage translation and interpreting services as required by law and best practices.

- Honor the pre-production or silent period when newcomers are taking in a new language, but speaking very little.

- Allow strategic use of the student's first language (L1) in the classroom for journaling or brainstorming or talking with other students who speak the same language.

- Look for ways to increase comprehensible input to make instruction understandable to the student. Plain language texts, total physical response, visuals, and artifacts can all increase comprehensible input.

- Visual cues can assist with language acquisition.

- Give as many directions as you can in writing as well as orally.

- Use sentence frames to support academic language development.

- Utilize the Preview–View–Review strategy to preview a lesson in the student's home language. Then teach the lesson in English and review key takeaways in the home language. Monolingual teachers can do this in collaboration with the ELD teacher or using translated anchor charts.

- Label items in your classroom to help students learn simple words.

- Facilitate student interactions through collaborative group work.

- Use graphic organizers and other helpful study devices.

- Avoid using round-robin or popcorn reading where students take turns reading a passage, one after the other. This harms fluency and comprehension. Use reciprocal or scaffolded reading instead.

- Set ambitious yet achievable goals. Modify assignments to scaffold learning.

- Don't rush to answer questions or to fill in words when students are struggling to think through their responses.

- Use translation apps like Reverso, Linguee, Babylon, or Google Translate as needed to communicate in the student's home language when school services are not available.

- Use audio books or lower-level, plain text reading passages and other technology appropriate to the age and ability levels of your students. Students benefit from both seeing and hearing the language.

Although there are many resources available to help you work well with your EB students, Larry Ferlazzo, a teacher and prolific writer from Sacramento, has a book and two websites that are particularly helpful. He offers an incredible wealth of materials—many geared to helping EB students—in his many books, syndicated columns, and blog.

The ELL/ESL Teacher's Survival Guide by **Larry Ferlazzo and Katie Hull Sypnieski:** Written by two renowned teachers of English Language Learners, this book provides powerful strategies, tools, and activities for teaching all levels of language learners.

EdWeek.org: Classroom Q&A with Larry Ferlazzo

larryferlazzo.edublogs.org: Larry's blog

UNDERSERVED YOUTH: SOCIAL FACTORS

Social factors such as low socioeconomic status, homelessness, trauma, foster placement, migrant or immigration status may undermine a student's mental and physical health, school readiness, attendance, and opportunities to learn.

Tragically, many of our students face significant challenges in childhood that can interfere with learning and school success. Low socioeconomic status has historically predicted a student's educational attainment. Teachers and school systems create the future and have the opportunity to reduce the impact of poverty and trauma and change the trajectory of students' lives.

Fortunately, we have more data, research, and strategies to support students than ever before. All of the strategies in the previous sections apply here as well, starting with building trusting relationships with your students so that they know you care. In addition these strategies support the unique needs of students facing poverty and adversity.

- Create a stable, safe, predictable environment in the classroom.
- Identify any financial costs for students to attend school, acquire supplies or textbooks, meals or participate in activities, field trips, or extracurriculars and find alternative funding sources to cover these costs for students from low-income families.
- Provide school supplies in the classroom. Learn about the resources available in the school and community to cover these expenses and share those resources (privately) with students, families, or caregivers.
- Connect with those in the school and community who provide for students' basic needs related to food, clothing, shelter, utilities, healthcare, and hygiene.
- Provide virtual and in-person field trips to expand horizons. Many students have not had opportunities to visit landmarks, museums, theaters, or natural spaces.
- Avoid questions and ice breakers that assume students had specific experiences or possessions. Instead of "Where did you go this summer?" Ask, "What was a memorable moment during last summer?"
- Teach social and emotional skills explicitly. Don't make assumptions about what students do or don't know about how to behave at school or their ability to regulate their own behavior.
- Build word wealth for students by explicitly expanding students' vocabularies.
- Provide college and career exploration opportunities.
- Create opportunities for guest speakers, internships, and job placements based on the age and interests of students to connect them to the world of work.
- Encourage future-oriented thinking. Build bridges from their current circumstances to a hopeful future.

> "I had a student visit my snack drawer every day. I found out that he was saving his school breakfast and lunch to take home to his little sister because they had very little to no food in the house. I made sure that my snack drawer was always full for him."
>
> *Deborah McManaway, 23 years' experience*

Explore these websites for more information on how to support students living in poverty:

aha!Process (ahaprocess.com): This organization was founded by Ruby Payne, a leading expert on the effects of generational poverty on students. Her book *A Framework for Understanding Poverty* explains how the silent culture clash between students and teachers in classrooms has a harmful effect on students.

National Education Association (nea.org): Resource Library. Use "children of poverty" as a search term on the home page to access dozens of helpful articles.

UNDERSERVED YOUTH: CHILDREN WHO EXPERIENCE TRAUMA

Trauma is an emotional response to a horrific experience that overwhelms a child's ability to cope. It may be an awful one-time event or an ongoing, chronic situation that harms a child's sense of safety and stability. Adverse Childhood Experiences (ACES) such as abuse, neglect, the loss of a loved one, witnessing violence, natural disasters, and more can cause a trauma response.

> "As a result of the work you do, you will be exposed to trauma, vicarious trauma, and overwhelm. When humans are exposed to suffering, hardship, crisis, and trauma there's a cumulative toll. Look for signs of vicarious trauma and overwhelm such as low morale, hypervigilance, exhaustion, avoidance, cynicism, and feeling like you can never do enough. Ask for help, talk with colleagues, friends, family, or a mental health professional. You are not alone."
>
> *Laura van Dernoot Lipsky, Founder and Director of the Trauma Stewardship Institute and author of* Trauma Stewardship: An Everyday Guide to Caring for Self While Caring for Others and The Age of Overwhelm, *Traumastewardship.com and @futuretrippingwithlaura*

Students who experience the stress of childhood trauma often see the world, including school, as perilous. They may remain in survival mode, experiencing big emotions and having difficulty with self-regulation and building relationships due to perceiving harmless stimuli as threats. Toxic stress from trauma can also cause health problems, challenges with cognition and learning or cause students to withdraw. If a teacher is not aware of a student's underlying trauma, they may just see the behavior and think it's willful.

The good news is that trauma does not have to determine a child's education or health outcomes. Teachers using trauma-informed practices and school support can help children heal by increasing their sense of safety, control, and self-worth. Many of the strategies listed under the topics of social-emotional learning and mindfulness as well as the other underserved youth categories apply here as well, starting with building trusting relationships with your students so that they know you care. In addition, these strategies support the unique needs of students experiencing trauma:

- Get to know students and lead with empathy and flexibility even if you don't know the whole story.
- Provide routine, structure, and predictability to increase a sense of safety.

- Take nothing personally when students are struggling emotionally.

- If you see a child struggling with emotions, ask what you can do to help or offer options like getting a drink of water, taking a break, listening to music, or intentional breathing.

- Build resiliency among students: set reachable goals, model learning from mistakes, recognize and encourage students to increase confidence, label emotions.

- Provide models, heroes, and leaders who overcame hardship.

- Communicate hopeful messages. Let students know that we can struggle and still be okay, that there can be hardship and beauty both in the world.

- Offer choices of activities and options for demonstrations of learning to empower students.

- Stay regulated yourself to avoid saying or doing something that will escalate a student who is in their trauma response. It is easier for students to emotionally regulate if there is an emotionally regulated adult near them.

- When confronted with disruptive student behaviors, shift your mindset from wondering what could be wrong with the student to looking beyond the behavior and wondering what happened to the child. This will allow you to be curious and see the underlying cause of the behavior.

- Have regular class meetings to create space for students to check in, feel heard, seen, and cared for.

- Collaborate with other school staff such as social workers, counselors, administrators, and nurses to create a team to support students in the healing process.

- Practice self-care and trauma stewardship to prevent the negative cumulative effects teachers can experience from second-hand trauma.

One group of students who experience trauma are those who suffer abuse or neglect. As a teacher, you are a mandatory reporter, legally obligated to act when you suspect or when a student discloses abuse or neglect. These strategies will help you respond their unique needs:

- You will have mandatory training each year. Learn your district's policy and your legal responsibilities.

- Discuss policies and procedures for reporting child abuse and neglect with the school counselor or social worker.

- When you suspect abuse or neglect or when a student confides in you, keep in mind that it is your responsibility to report this information to the appropriate authorities. You cannot promise the student confidentiality and you cannot conduct an investigation.

- Familiarize yourself with the most common signs of abuse and neglect so that you can recognize them.

- Listen carefully and nonjudgmentally to any student who discloses abuse to you. Do not allow your personal reactions to show, as it might reduce the student's willingness to talk to an adult.

- Be compassionate. Acknowledge to the student that you are aware that talking to an adult is difficult and that they are not alone.

- In the days following a disclosure and report, check in with the student privately to see how they are doing.

Here are a few resources to explore for more information on how to support students experiencing trauma:

National Child Traumatic Stress Network (nctsnet.org): Its Child Trauma Toolkit offers a great deal of useful information and links to other helpful sites.

Center for Disease Control (CDC) Adverse Childhood Experiences (ACES) (cdc .gov/violenceprevention/aces): Because ACES can have devastating consequences for lifelong health and opportunities, the CDC offers information to understand and prevent adverse childhood experiences.

Fostering Resilient Learners: Strategies for Creating a Trauma-Sensitive Classroom by **Kristin Souers and Pete Hall:** This book provides proven, reliable strategies to create a safe, strengths-based learning environment.

Trauma Stewardship Institute (TraumaStewardship.com): Through workshops, keynotes, disaster response, and its podcast "Future Tripping," the Trauma Steward-ship Institute provides practical and holistic approaches to care for ourselves while we care for others and the planet. The co-founder shares many of these practices in her books *Trauma Stewardship: An Everyday Guide to Caring for Self While Caring for Others* and *The Age of Overwhelm* by Laura van Dernoot Lipsky with Connie Burk.

UNDERSERVED YOUTH: IDENTIFIED DISABILITY, IMPAIRMENT, OR EXCEPTIONALITY

A third category of underserved youth who become vulnerable to poor outcomes if classrooms and schools are not set up for them are students with disabilities, impair-ments, and exceptionalities. These are students with a range of abilities who qualify for an Individual Education Plan (IEP), a 504 Plan, or a Talented and Gifted (TAG or GATE) Per-sonal Education Plan (PEP). These plans provide specially designed instruction, accommo-dations, modifications, or enrichment opportunities based on students' learning differences.

The United States protects the rights of all students with disabilities to access a free, appropriate public education until they graduate from high school or in some cases, reach the age of 21. Under the Individuals with Disabilities Education Act (IDEA), schools have a legal obligation to establish goals, create plans (in partnership with families or caregivers), and to monitor and report student progress toward their goals.

Special education teachers have a vital leadership role in serving students with disabili-ties. You understand the laws and best practices to reach and teach students. You provide specially designed instruction, conduct assessments, co-teach, complete documentation, and collaborate with families, caregivers, classroom teachers, and paraprofessionals to sup-port student growth. 504 coordinators provide leadership and advocacy for students to remove barriers to their educational access. TAG or GATE teachers develop PEPs to extend learning in a student's area of exceptionality.

Regular education teachers also have a crucial role in personalizing learning and a legal role in implementing plans for students with disabilities, impairments, and exceptionalities. At team meetings, you will provide information on a student's present level of performance, their strengths and areas for growth, and offer ideas about how best to support them in reaching their goals. In the classroom, you will provide instruction, modifications, and accommodations.

Neurodiversity is an asset in classrooms and society. This term encompasses many conditions and the broad range of ways that people experience and interact with the world. When these strengths are embraced in the classroom, creativity, divergent thinking, and innovative solutions can result. Focusing on a student's strengths, collaborating with your school team, mentors, families, caregivers, and your PLN will set you and your students up for success. If students engage in behaviors that disrupt learning, your patience will be tested, and you will need a wider repertoire of strategies, but never give up on them.

By the very nature of learning differences, each student is unique and each plan tailored to individual needs. In this section, we will explore some of the opportunities, challenges, and needs of students who have IEPs, 504 Plans, and PEPs.

Students with Disabilities

The Individuals with Disabilities Act (IDEA) provides protections to students with disabilities in thirteen eligibility categories. A thoughtful and proactive way to plan for and meet the needs of students with disabilities as well as everyone in your classroom is Universal Design for Learning (UDL). This powerful and effective approach to teaching and learning meets the needs of all learners by design. Teachers ask themselves these five questions:

- What is my goal?
- What barriers might interfere with student learning?
- How can I provide multiple means of representation?
- What options can I give for student actions and expression?
- How can I use differentiated engagement strategies?

To learn more about UDL, explore the resources at CAST.org. Click Resources > Tips and Free Resources, or check out their professional learning opportunities.

Many internet sites provide a great deal of information about students with disabilities. To learn more about this topic, try these websites:

Understood (Understood.org): Parents of a child with learning differences started this website to provide resources and support so that people who learn and think differently can thrive in school, at work, and throughout life. Browse its robust content library and podcasts to learn more about all topics related to learning differences.

Council for Exceptional Children (exceptionalchildren.org): This site offers resources on special education and gifted education. You will need to create a free account to access the learning library.

LD OnLine (ldonline.org): This site advertises itself as the world's largest website for students with learning disabilities and ADHD. It offers advice on instructional strategies, behavior and social skills, accommodations, modifications, and family or caregiver outreach.

Learning Disabilities Association of America (LDA) (ldaamerica.org): The LDA offers extensive resources, guides, booklets, and lesson plans for a wide range of specific learning disabilities.

You can expect to have many students with disabilities in your classes, from students who need minor accommodations to help them learn, to students with limitations to their communication, motor functioning, and more. How you approach the opportunities and challenges presented by differently abled students will depend on your attitude and the resources available at your school. Along with having a positive, welcoming, inclusive attitude, the following general strategies can guide you as you teach students with learning differences:

- Get to know your students, their strengths and struggles and help them learn, grow, and overcome their challenges.

- Be proactive and prepared when teaching students with disabilities. Make sure you understand their strengths, specific disabilities, and the requirements of their IEPs.

- Expect to work closely with the special education teachers to help you modify your instruction to meet the needs of every learner in your class.

- Accept responsibility for your students' success. Don't anticipate extensive additional training on how to help your students with disabilities. Continue to educate yourself about how to work well with students with learning differences by reading professional literature, researching relevant websites, attending workshops, and observing special education teachers as they teach.

- Be sensitive to the needs of each student and anticipate them whenever you can. For example, be sure to seat students with disabilities where they can see and hear you without distractions.

- Use the resources available to you. Study students' school files to understand the instructional strategies that have worked well in past school years. Collaborate closely with the special education teachers who are working with your students to learn the specific strategies that will help students learn successfully. Some of the other adults who can help you learn about your students are families and caregivers, the school nurse, counselors, administrators, and current or previous teachers.

- Talk with each student with disabilities about their hopes and concerns. Make it easy for these students to communicate with you. Even young children can tell you when they learn best and what activities help them learn and grow.

- Advocate for the needs of your students with the IEP team.

INSTRUCTIONAL STRATEGIES FOR STUDENTS WITH DISABILITIES

The following are some helpful ideas for teaching students with disabilities. Because students' needs vary, not all the ideas will be appropriate for each of your students, but you can adapt them to fit your students' needs.

- Support students with organization needs. Reduce the materials you ask students with executive functioning difficulties to manage at any given time.

- Consider each student's learning style when you create assignments. When you can, modify the assignment to better fit their needs.

- Be sure to provide prompt feedback when a student with disabilities completes an assignment.

- If a student struggles with writing, use assistive technology or provide smaller sheets of paper when you assign writing to scaffold success in writing. For example, start with a small Post-it and work up to a full-size piece of paper.

- Offer a variety of activities. Change the pace several times in each class so that students will find it easier to focus.

- Structure your classroom routines so that students can predict what they will be expected to do. Go over the daily objectives at the start of the class, and offer students a checklist to keep them on track all day.

- Be generous with your encouragement when your students with disabilities do something well.

- Give very clear directions. Ask students with disabilities to restate what you want them to do. On written work, use bold type or other eye-catching design elements to distinguish the directions from the rest of the text.

- Offer collaborative learning opportunities often. Working with other students often reinforces learning, gives students with disabilities a chance to interact in a positive way with classmates, and builds their confidence as learners.

- Help your students with diverse abilities understand their progress. Set small, achievable goals, and celebrate together when students reach them.

COLLABORATING WITH SPECIAL EDUCATION TEACHERS

Special education teachers and general education teachers form teams to help students who require specially designed instruction, accommodations, and modifications. One unique feature of this type of collaboration is co-teaching. Often, both teachers are present in the classroom at the same time and they take joint responsibility for the education of all students in their class. If you are fortunate enough to work with a co-teacher, consider participating in UDL workshops to make the most of your teaching partnership.

These collaborative teams of teachers face an important challenge: sharing the duties of the class so that they have common goals for delivering instruction, assessing progress, and supporting academic and behavioral growth. Successful collaboration is likely if co-teachers get to know each other and see themselves as equal partners who are actively engaged in all parts of the teaching process.

The general education teacher's responsibilities usually include the following:

- Creating activities to teach the content
- Finding and adapting resource material for all students
- Delivering effective instruction
- Meeting the curriculum requirements of all students
- Implementing behavior plans in the general education classroom

The special education teacher's responsibilities usually include the following:

- Adapting material to meet the needs of students with disabilities
- Adapting activities to match the learning styles of students with disabilities
- Modifying assessments
- Meeting the curriculum requirements of students with disabilities
- Developing behavior plans for use throughout the student's school day

What makes it possible for two teachers with different educational backgrounds to work together in a successful collaboration? The primary requirement for a positive working relationship is strong rapport and a commitment on the part of both teachers to work together for the common good of their students. Both teachers may also agree to:

- Plan lessons together
- Follow the same classroom management procedures
- Problem-solve when disagreements arise respectfully and privately
- Assume equal responsibility for what happens in class
- Present a united front to students
- Share resource materials
- Schedule time to work together on a regular basis

DISTRACTION MANAGEMENT SKILLS

It is no secret that many students (and adults) struggle with focus. Students reflect the easily distracted society around them. Few people can resist the strong pull of their phones, the internet, and social media. It is not always easy for students to resist the many temptations that can entice them away from their schoolwork. Caring teachers can help their students strengthen their ability to remain focused instead of distracted while doing schoolwork.

Here are several suggestions that you can adapt for your classes to help students learn to work with focus and to fight their tendency to be distracted:

- Talk about focus and distraction with students. Discuss the purpose of focusing attention. Brainstorm ideas, apps, and strategies that are helpful for coping with distractions and then share with the group.

- Have students share their advice about what you can do to create a classroom environment that encourages focused work. Display student-made posters or other reminders to make students mindful of the issue. When they can be part of the solution, students will have greater buy-in.

- Use a timer to create a sense of urgency and help students complete work within a specific time frame.

- When there are several tasks that students must accomplish, have students prioritize them so that they will know how to accomplish their work on time.

- Manage electronic distractions, such as cell phones, and appropriate use of devices and the internet in your classroom so they support rather than interfere with learning. (There is more information about how to manage student cell phone use in Section Fourteen.)

- As students are working on assignments, schedule brain breaks so that they can change their state and maintain energy. Discuss how this would be effective for them at home as well.

Students with ADD or ADHD

Students with attention-deficit disorder (ADD) or attention-deficit/hyperactivity disorder (ADHD) usually require intervention from supportive adults to be academically successful. If you are a general education teacher, a special education teacher or a counselor will provide information about your students with disabilities before school begins. That teacher will review strategies, modifications, or accommodations required by each student's IEP or 504 Plan with you.

ADD and ADHD can manifest differently in students, so in addition to your own research, here are some general guidelines to assist you in reaching and teaching students with ADD or ADHD:

- Enlist assistance from your colleagues and from the families and caregivers of students with ADD or ADHD. They can be an excellent source of support and advice as you work together to assist students.

- Teach school success skills. Students with ADD or ADHD have not always mastered effective school-related skills, such as taking notes or following directions. Take the time to explicitly teach these tasks and organizational strategies.

- Post schedules, directions, and routines. Clearly teach classroom procedures and provide visuals as students benefit from seeing as well as hearing directions and other information.
- Consider preferential seating to increase focus. Remove distractions.
- Give advance notice before transition times.
- Give step-by-step directions to avoid overwhelming students with large tasks. They may need guidance in planning how to accomplish their work.
- Encourage the use of guided reading strips and highlighting to focus students on important information in the text.
- Check in frequently to make sure a student is on track.
- If auditory learning is a strength, offer alternative auditory modes of learning.
- Encourage the use of assistive technology.

To learn more about how you can help students with ADD and ADHD, visit these websites that offer many practical tips, links, and articles on a variety of issues:

- Understood (understood.org)
- Attention Deficit Disorder Association (ADDA) (add.org)
- Children and Adults with Attention-Deficit/Hyperactivity Disorder (chadd.org)

Talented and Gifted Students

The assessment and identification of TAG or GATE students can be controversial, yet most states require schools to identify students as talented or gifted. Some students with exceptionalities are also at risk of poor school outcomes due to increased anxiety and depression, which is why they are included in this section.

While some gifted students may also qualify for special education under IDEA and have an IEP, most are provided support through a PEP. Each child is unique so it's difficult to characterize an entire group of students. Often, when a lesson interests a gifted child, they will take the lesson far beyond your expectations and the boundaries of the material. Gifted students can also be impatient with topics they don't perceive as interesting, and they can be especially impatient with teachers and peers whom they perceive to be less than capable. To learn more about teaching talented and gifted students, consult some of the many books and websites that other teachers have found valuable. Two helpful sites are listed here:

Center for Talented Youth at John's Hopkins University (cty.jhu.edu/resources/ educators): Johns Hopkins hosts a talent search for youth in grades 2–8 and offers resources for teachers including a reading list, blog, and YouTube channel.

National Association for Gifted Children (nagc.org): At this site, click on the Knowledge Center tab to find resources for educators: links to websites with advice, research articles, professional development opportunities and other helpful information about teaching gifted children.

When you have gifted students in your class, you may need to modify the content of the material, the learning process, or both to accommodate their needs. Use or adapt the guidelines that follow to help your gifted students be successful:

- Invite student voice, choice, and agency. Allow students to have a strong voice in how they will accomplish their goals. Gifted students are often self-directed learners. Take this characteristic into consideration when you modify the process of learning.

- Differentiate learning for the student's rate and level of learning. Set a rapid pace to compress instruction or offer extensions. Gifted students may become bored with a slower pace of undifferentiated instruction.

- Focus on having students use higher-level thinking skills throughout a unit of study; gifted students quickly master the recall and comprehension levels of assignments.

- Use technology to support research and personalized learning.

- Encourage student input in the selection of material. You may have a general unit of study, but allow students to study the details that most interest them.

- Focus on depth over breadth of content. Develop learning plans to allow deeper research into a topic of interest.

- Although allowing gifted students to serve as peer tutors is acceptable, be careful not to make this your default technique. It reinforces what they already know, but it doesn't provide enrichment of their own skills in the subject.

Students with 504 Plans

A 504 Plan is another type of legally binding learning plan that protects students who have a temporary or longer-term physical or mental impairment that does not require a teacher to provide specially designed instruction.

Students with 504 Plans might have any number of issues that require removal of barriers to succeed in school: diabetes, allergies, anxiety, depression, ADD or ADHD, temporary or chronic health issues—just to name a few. A 504 Plan removes barriers to learning by providing accommodations like safety planning for students with nut allergies, preferential seating, extra time, use of speech-to-text, access to calming spaces, or brain breaks.

When the school term begins, you will receive copies of the 504 Plans for your students. You may also meet with the 504 Plan coordinator for your school to discuss each plan and your specific responsibilities. Although each 504 Plan is unique because it is tailored to the needs of the child it protects, typical accommodations that you might see include the following:

- Training, monitoring, and care for students with diabetes
- Training and safety planning for students with allergies
- Preferential seating
- Extended time on assignments

- Extra books or materials
- Frequent contact with families and caregivers
- Access to frequent breaks or a calming space
- Written copies of notes presented orally
- Assistance with organization skills

You have a legal responsibility to both help create and implement 504 Plans to make sure students can access an education.

A useful site for learning how to successfully help students with 504 Plans is Understood (understood.org). At the site, use "504 plans" as a search term to learn more.

Questions to Discuss with Colleagues

Sharing ideas with colleagues is a helpful way to devise solutions to some of the problems that you must manage successfully at school. Here, you will find several topics to open discussions with colleagues about successful instructional practices:

1. You want to provide mirrors and windows to create a culturally responsive classroom. How do you get to know your students' cultures and where do you look for resources so that the needs of all your students can be met?

2. You observe that a student is impulsive, restless, and constantly in motion. You believe that they may have ADHD, but the family will not give permission for an evaluation. What can you do to help this student be a successful learner?

3. You have a number of students who need help learning social skills. You want to start having class meetings, but you don't know where to start. What strategies or prompts should you use? What do you do?

4. One of your students stopped turning in assignments and confided in you that their family recently lost their housing. What can you do to help this student? Who can help you support this student?

5. You have emergent bilingual students who need additional support to engage in class discussions. What strategies can you use to support their English language development?

Topics to Discuss with a Mentor

Although the topics that new teachers need to discuss with a mentor vary from teacher to teacher and from school to school, there are some that most first-year teachers should be comfortable discussing with a mentor or a trusted colleague. You should ask your mentor about these topics from this section:

- How to manage accommodations for students with 504 Plans
- Advice about how to support a student who has ADHD

- How to incorporate mindfulness practices into your classroom practice
- Advice for working well with a teaching partner
- How to support a student who experienced trauma and is now withdrawn

Reflection Questions to Guide Your Thinking

1. What do you anticipate as your biggest challenge in dealing with a specific learning disability in reading? What can you do to meet this challenge? Where can you find assistance?

2. What do you already know about your most vulnerable students who need additional support? How do your supervisors expect you to help these students? How do the students themselves expect you to help them? Who at your school can help you learn the best ways to help these students?

3. What strengths do you have that will help you meet the diverse needs of your students? How can you use your strengths to help all the students in your class reach their goals?

4. Who is struggling academically or behaviorally in your class? What school-wide programs can help the struggling students in your class? What can you do to help them be successful in your classroom?

5. How can you create the kind of culturally responsive classroom environment where all students know they are valued, affirmed, and supported? What are you already doing to create a sense of belonging? How can you improve?

SECTION EIGHT

Adapt Instruction Through Differentiation

Students are unique human beings who learn at different rates and levels and have a variety of interests and needs. "One-size-fits-all" and "teaching-to-the-middle" strategies never did work. The reality is that classrooms are complex communities with a wide span of academic and social skills. It is now typical for reading levels in a single classroom to span three to six grade levels. Differentiation is a vital teaching practice to meet the needs of an increasingly broad range of learners. Intentional differentiation motivates and engages all students.

In this section, you will learn some of the basics of differentiating instruction so that your students can create meaning, deepen understanding, and see themselves as capable learners. You will learn how to create a classroom environment conducive to differentiated instructional activities, the key strategies of differentiation, how to use formative assessments, how to provide timely feedback, how to create lesson plans for differentiated instruction, and how to lead a classroom where differentiation is built into the fabric of teaching and learning. Generative AI is making it easier than ever for teachers to differentiate for students. (See Section Two for more information on AI.)

Differentiated Instruction Supports All Learners

Teachers who intentionally differentiate instruction treat their students as individuals with varied learning characteristics instead of treating all students as if they had the same strengths, weaknesses, interests, and readiness levels. Differentiated instruction is effective because it meets students at their various rates and levels of learning and engages them with a variety of ways to interact with ideas and content.

Because instruction in a differentiated classroom takes a proactive stance toward learning differences among students, the main components of classroom instruction—content, process, and product—can all be adjusted to promote learning. Formative assessments are also a key element in helping teachers design and adjust instructional activities.

At its most basic level, differentiating instruction is being fair to all students. It means creating many paths to access learning and demonstrate mastery of knowledge and skills. Everyone has a chance to succeed when teachers differentiate.

Misperceptions about Differentiated Instruction

As a new teacher, differentiating instruction can be intimidating because there seems to be an overwhelming amount of work just to deliver a lesson. Differentiated instruction requires careful planning, but it is a manageable task and certainly worth the effort. As you learn to differentiate instruction for your students, you may hear some of these common misperceptions about differentiation:

"In the 1960s, a student was placed in my general mechanics class because he could not read. I asked him what he liked to do. He said he liked to mess with motors. He had taken his diesel tractor motor out and put it in an old pickup truck. This is what he drove to school. In the spring, the motor went back in the tractor for spring plowing. Other teachers had told me this boy was dumb."

Edward Gardner, 36 years' experience

- Differentiated instruction requires individual lesson plans for each student.
- It is impossible to cover the content because differentiation takes too long.
- All formative assessments need to be graded.
- It's okay to use differentiation for enrichment, but not for reteaching or instruction.
- It's impossible to stay organized when you differentiate instruction.

Don't give up on differentiating instruction for your students. It's doable and it's effective in supporting all students to learn. Start small and systematically develop a repertoire of ideas, strategies, and activities that can make differentiation integral to your classroom practice.

"How Can I Possibly Meet Everyone's Needs?"

It can be daunting to try to teach a roomful of students who have a wide range of background knowledge, academic and social skills. It can seem confusing at first to work out the best methods to differentiate instruction, but it is not difficult to meet the needs of the learners in your classroom.

The trick to success includes:

- Learn about your students' strengths without limiting them to learning exclusively based on that strength.
- Present content and engage students in several different ways.

- Provide a range of assessment options for students to choose from in order to demonstrate their learning.
- Lead classroom communities that offer some autonomy and student ownership of learning.

These are some other methods that will enable you to use differentiation to meet the needs of all your learners. In the list that follows, you will discover some basic guidelines to use as you offer differentiated instruction:

- Always begin with your grade level and content standards and learning objectives.
- Emphasize quality of thought rather than the size of the workload. If a student has mastered how to solve a certain type of problem, for example, don't continue to assign more of the same kind of problem. Instead, offer alternative problem types or allow the student to move ahead.
- Focus on student growth more than grades. One way to do this is to have students self-assess several times within a unit of study. Teach students to reflect and then evaluate themselves if you want them to become self-motivated learners.
- Everyone needs variety, teamwork, and hand-on activities. Offer opportunities for these whenever possible.
- Plan for student choice and autonomy. Provide a balance between teacher-assigned work and student-selected work.
- Personalize learning with the use of digital tools to allow students to work at their own rate and level of learning, to provide access to learning beyond the classroom, or to have an authentic audience for their work. You'll find a list of useful resources later in this section and in Section Nine.
- Be flexible. Always have a backup plan ready. You will need it.
- Have explicit directions for all activities. The more comfortable students are with the procedures they are to follow, the easier it will be for them to be successful.

Create a Classroom Environment that Supports Differentiation

It is necessary to create a classroom environment that supports the differentiated activities that you have designed for your students. There are two aspects to this environment: the physical space and the learning community within that space.

In a differentiated classroom, the physical space needs to be set up so that students can move around easily. Students should be able to move quickly and easily into group configurations. Supplies and materials also should be easily accessible so that students don't waste time wandering around looking for what they need. Students need to know where directions for various activities are posted so that they can refer to them as needed. In short, a comfortable physical environment allows students to focus on their inquiry or the task at hand.

A strong sense of community is also an essential part of differentiated instruction because it enables students to take the risks necessary to try new, challenging activities and to work well with their peers. In an environment that supports differentiation, classroom agreements, policies, and procedures are taught, understood, and consistently upheld. In this way, students can operate in a safe and familiar framework. Student learning differences are acknowledged and appreciated. The teacher is a warm demander who makes it clear that they appreciate students and enjoy being with them, while at the same time holding high standards and expectations for effort, behavior, and quality work.

Use Growth Mindset Principles to Support Differentiation

One of the chief characteristics inherent in the growth mindset movement is that it empowers students by encouraging them to believe in their own capabilities. Differentiated instruction has the same effect on students because it encourages them to become self-aware and to use their strengths to accelerate and deepen learning. Persistence and acceptance of mistakes are expected when differentiating instruction as well as when encouraging students to develop a growth mindset.

Because of the complementary nature of both approaches to teaching and learning, the methods that you use to encourage students to develop a growth mindset can also be used as you differentiate instruction. Specific, timely feedback, positivity, the recognition of hard work and effort, and a celebration of mistakes are just some of the components of a growth mindset culture that can make differentiation work well in your classroom.

Eleven Key Strategies for Differentiation

Successful differentiated instruction involves the use of several key strategies to design instruction. These strategies form the bedrock of the choices that teachers make when they implement differentiated instruction activities for their students. In the pages that follow, you will be able to explore these strategies as you learn how to use differentiated instruction in your teaching practice.

STRATEGY ONE: PERSONALIZE INSTRUCTION

Although differentiated instruction does not demand a separate lesson plan for each student, instruction should be tailored to meet the specific needs of individual students. Even though this may seem difficult at first, with a bit of planning and effort, personalized instruction can be managed without hassle.

To provide instruction that is customized for different students, it is first necessary to get to know those students very well. Although the techniques for getting to know your students discussed in Section Six can also be used when differentiating instruction, there are three other student qualities that you need to explore when determining how to adjust instruction: student readiness, student interests, and student learning preferences.

Student Readiness

Student readiness refers to a student's current level of knowledge or skills regarding the material in a unit of study. Having an accurate picture of student readiness is important because it is the first factor that you must consider in differentiating instruction. Prior knowledge of the material and a connection to it will influence a student's readiness to access the content, so it is helpful to determine both before planning how to differentiate instruction. Students who have a great deal of prior knowledge of the topic should be offered a different entry point to it from those students who need extra support in building background before beginning the unit. Readiness can be determined by various formative assessments, such as brainstorming what students already know, pre-tests, one-minute papers, surveys, or exit tickets.

Student Interests

The interests that students already have when they arrive in your classroom can be powerful motivators. When students have an opportunity to learn more about a topic that they are already familiar with, they deepen their knowledge and connection to upcoming related content. Students who are curious about an area of study are usually willing to persist in learning about related topics because they can see the connections among them. For example, when students are interested in fashion and studying climate change, they may be willing to learn more about related topics, such as the environmental impact of fast fashion. If a student is interested in sports and studying ratios, measuring wins and losses may help them see the value of statistics.

There are many ways for you to learn about your students' interests throughout a school term. During class meetings (see Section Six for more information about class meetings), you can pose an interesting check-in question to hear students' thoughts, ask students to share their interests, or you can have students interview one another about their interests and share that information with the class. You can also pass out note cards and ask students to write their names on one side and their interests on the other. Perhaps the most powerful way that you can learn about your students' interests, however, is to be a good listener. Students share their ideas with one another and with their teachers in every class period. Make a point of attending carefully to what they share so that you can build authentic relationships and add an extra layer of engagement to instruction.

Student Learning Preferences

It is important to note at the start of this section that there is no evidence to back the commonly held belief in education that learning styles, paired with instructional modalities aligned with that style, improve learning. Teachers may, in fact, limit student growth if they have students identify one type of intelligence and one primary learning style. With that said, self-knowledge about preferred learning methods provides students with an understanding about the ways in which they learn most effectively without confining them.

Many teachers adapt instruction based on four sensory approaches: visual, auditory, reading/writing, and kinesthetic (VARK). These learning preferences can be adapted easily to both whole-group or individual instruction. They also can be paired with other learning preferences, such as students who find studying by themselves more effective than those students who enjoy collaboration with others or students who choose hands-on activities over strictly minds-on activities.

To help students understand their learning preferences, find a survey online or create your own simple questionnaire that would be appropriate for the age and skill levels of your students. Just ask students to select statements that apply to them, such as the following:

I learn best when I:

- Work on assignments with classmates.
- Am in a quiet area where it is easier for me to focus.
- Listen to music when I study.
- Make sketches, diagrams, and graphic organizers.
- Can see a model of the information.
- Watch videos about the subjects I am learning.
- Have a buddy to study with.
- Participate in class discussions.
- Make something or build a model of what I am learning.
- Apply new knowledge and skills in the real world.

When I receive feedback on my work, I would like:

- Someone to talk me through the feedback.
- To read written comments.
- To see diagrams or graphs of my results.

You can also search for learning inventories online. Just be sure to present the activity and discuss the results in a way that expands students' understanding of the ways they learn best without limiting them. As you and your students gather data about learning preferences, keep in mind that they are not absolute choices. Students could be both kinesthetic and visual learners, for example.

Once you have determined your students' readiness, interests, and learning preferences, you will need to arrange the learning environment and adapt instructional and assessment strategies accordingly. You can use Teacher Template (p446) as a template, or you can adjust it to meet your needs.

STRATEGY TWO: FLEXIBLE GROUPING

Flexible groups are purposeful collaborative groups that allow students to be appropriately challenged. The composition of flexible groups changes frequently based on student needs in a particular area of study. Groupings should never be in permanent ability groups as this is detrimental to students. During a school term, your students should work as members of many different groups, depending on the task and content. It is important to permit movement among groups because interests and skills change as students move from one topic to another.

Flexible groupings improve classroom bonds and also have other advantages in a differentiated classroom. For emergent bilingual students, this strategy provides opportunities to practice academic and social language. It makes it easier for you to observe and assess students and allows you to assign appropriate instructional activities to meet each student's learning needs. What types of flexible groups are possible in a differentiated classroom?

- Partners, triads, or small groups up to six students
- Readiness level groups
- Homogeneous ability groups
- Heterogeneous ability groups
- Interest groups
- Learning preferences groups
- Student-led groups
- Teacher-led groups
- Impromptu study or discussion groups
- Just about any type of group that you think would benefit your students

Be mindful that students who are introverted or need time to process information independently may not thrive in a group-based setting. Make sure to give opportunities for students to engage with content independently as well.

STRATEGY THREE: TRANSPARENT LEARNING FOR STUDENTS

There should be no surprises when it comes to student learning. If students are to benefit fully from differentiated instruction, they must participate fully in the process. Unless this is an explicit expectation, students will not become the confident, self-disciplined learners that we want them to be.

Students should be involved during the process of differentiating instruction as is appropriate for their age, maturity level, and ability. Here is a quick list of some of the ways that their learning can be made transparent for students during differentiated instruction. Students should:

- Understand the relevance and purpose for learning the content
- Understand the essential knowledge and skills that they are expected to master in each unit of study
- Be aware of their learning preferences and how to implement various strategies to learn most effectively
- Use feedback to improve their work
- Understand how to demonstrate mastery
- Be aware of their progress as they work through the material
- Reflect periodically on the work and their work habits

STRATEGY FOUR: STUDENT REFLECTION

If students are to work efficiently and to learn what they are supposed to learn, then they should be encouraged to reflect systematically on their learning. When students can think about the strategies that work best for them, about how they go about their work, about their progress, and about their goals, they are more likely to remain engaged and on task because their effort is relevant and meaningful.

Reflection moves students toward being self-directed learners because it makes it possible for them to understand the purpose for their work. Reflection can also make students aware of the patterns in their work habits, see the connections between ideas, and help them develop goals and self-assess strengths and challenges. Reflection gives students a moment to find solutions to their challenges and determine what they need to do next.

Reflection may not come naturally to all students. It is up to you to set the expectation that serious thought is required when students reflect by modeling how you want their reflection to be done. It is also important that you set aside time for students to reflect frequently so that they have time to think while they are in the moment. As you begin to think about how to include student reflection in your classroom, here are some quick ways to begin. (See Section Ten for details on post-feedback reflection strategies.) To reflect on their learning, students can:

- Keep a reflection journal in a dedicated section of their student binders, notebooks, or devices. For some students, this may be an audio journal.

- Create a plan for what they would like to learn next and how they want to go about learning it.

- Color-code their work, with one color representing material that they know well, another color representing material with which they are somewhat comfortable, and a third color representing material that they need help with.

- Record problems that they experienced and how they solved them.

- Talk with peers about what worked and what did not.

- Keep a record of the highpoints of the day, the week, or the unit.

- Write an explanation of their thinking process on various questions. They can include an explanation of what guided them to answer the way that they did.

- Describe their response to feedback and the effectiveness of their response.

- Write a brief reflection of their work on a sticky note and share it with others by posting it on a designated area of the board

- Write an entrance or exit ticket about their class work.

- Predict problems that they still may have with the material and possible solutions for how they will learn it, including resources online and at school.

- Rate their day's learning on a scale of one to ten, with a brief explanation of the rating.

- Brainstorm as many ideas as possible about the day's lesson for three minutes and then look for patterns in the brainstorm.

- Explain to partners what they will do differently on the next assignment, how they prepared for this one, and what they learned from their work.

- Assess their readiness to move on to new material. If they are not ready, ask them what their next steps should be.

STRATEGY FIVE: RESPECTFUL TASKS

Respectful tasks are ones that maintain high expectations for all students while recognizing and honoring individual students' learning differences. When designing respectful tasks, teachers should pay attention to the readiness level of each student and offer all students opportunities to learn according to their own readiness levels. Teachers who design respectful tasks do so with the intention that all tasks should be equally interesting, important, and engaging. Teachers should ensure not only that each task is appropriate and fair but also that they have taken a proactive approach in determining how best to connect students' interests and accommodate students' needs. When you set about creating respectful tasks, consider these questions:

- Will the task be appropriate for students' differing readiness levels?
- Will the task include student interests so that it is intrinsically appealing?
- Will the task allow students to use their learning preferences?
- Will the task help students master the necessary knowledge and skills?
- How does this lesson connect to the world beyond school?

Although there are any number of assignment types that you can offer students, a beneficial way to stay organized and to work efficiently is to keep handy an ongoing list of the activities that appeal to your students. Here is a list of just some of the many activities that you could use to differentiate instruction for your students. The first four are among those recommended by Carol Ann Tomlinson on her website:

1. **Choice boards:** With a choice board, students are given a menu of possible tasks to accomplish. This is a structured way to allow for student choice. Choice boards can have a variety of formats including: tic-tac-toe, bingo, menus or checklists. Teachers should use Bloom's Taxonomy or Webb's DOK Framework to create a range of cognitive challenge for students.

2. **Compacting:** Based on the results of ongoing assessments, students are allowed to skip content they have already mastered and engage with more challenging work.

3. **Learning contracts:** The teacher identifies the learning targets for the contract. The student identifies how they will demonstrate their proficiency. For example, a science learning contract may specify the due dates for a student to create a model and writing a report on a specific topic.

4. **R.A.F.T.:** This is a very creative writing strategy in which students can choose the Role (who they are), Audience (to whom they are writing), Format (news article, poetry, prose, cartoon, poster, speech, ad, brochure, invitation, letter, essay), and Topic (what they are writing about). Teachers create four-column R.A.F.T. strips with tiered options in each column for students to choose from. For example, in math, an R.A.F.T. may include R: Fraction, A: Whole Numbers, F: Petition, T: To be considered part of the family, or in English, an R.A.F.T. may include R: semicolon, A: Middle Schoolers, F: diary entry, T: Please help me find where I belong.

Agendas: Students are offered individualized personal checklists of work to complete within a set time—usually a week or so. Although students may have some assignments in common, agendas allow for differentiation by offering work that is less or more challenging while appealing to diverse learning preferences.

Alphabet boxes: Students are given a grid of squares with a letter of the alphabet in each square. They then brainstorm to recall words, ideas, and concepts related to a unit. For example, in an alphabet box for a unit on climate science, a student might write "Polar bears endangered" in the *P* box, "Ozone layer" in the *O* box, and so on for every letter.

Artifact boxes: Items from a unit of study are displayed in a box for students to use to analyze and predict information. An artifact box may be used for enrichment, teaching, or reteaching.

Audio materials: Students listen to recorded materials as they read or instead of reading. Audio materials can be used to study, review, or introduce information as well as in many other ways.

Case studies: Students investigate real-life situations through reports, articles, and other observations. They complete their investigations in cooperative groups.

Chalk talks: Five students go to the board and stand so that they cannot see one another's writing. The teacher calls out a topic and has everyone in the class write about it for one minute. Students discuss the work of the five writers and compare it to the work of their classmates.

Chunking: Assignments are broken into smaller, more manageable parts, with structured directions offered for each part.

Dialectical journals: Students write two-column notes about information they read or hear about. In one column, they are given or select a topic to write about, and in the other, they write a response to the topic.

Hot Potato: Similar to the Tingo Tango game later in this list, each student has a note card with a question about the lesson on it. Students trade their cards as quickly as possible for thirty seconds. When time is called, each student will have to answer the question on their card either in writing or orally.

Interactive bookmarks: Students use premade bookmarks specific to a unit of material to record notes, answer questions, define words, and make observations as they read.

Jigsaws: Students in a group divide the material to be studied into various sections. Each group member becomes an expert on their section and teaches it to the others.

Learning circles: Students gather in small groups to discuss a reading passage in depth. The concept can be applied to reading of all sorts and to working out common problems in math or science courses.

Manipulatives: Hands-on activities can be used to help students in all disciplines learn. From science labs to word sorts and math workshop, manipulatives benefit hands-on learners so that they can associate movement and the material to be learned.

Mini-lessons: Students are given brief lessons designed to target specific areas for remediation or enrichment.

Online collaboration: Students work together to create and post blogs or to collaborate with other students on activities involving podcasts, virtual projects, or wikis.

See—Wonder—Conclude: Students look at a primary source like a cartoon or an historic photograph and describe first what they see, then what questions it raises, and finally, their conclusions about the time period depicted and what was happening in the scene. This can also be used with video clips, data sets and more.

Paper discussions: Small groups of students are seated in circles. Each group is handed a sheet of paper, and one student in each group writes a response to a question or idea pertaining to a topic. That student then passes the sheet to the next student, who adds to the response and passes it to the next student, and so on as quickly as possible within a specified time limit.

Roundtables: Students discuss their work by sitting in a circle and taking turns. This works best if they have had time to write questions, concerns, or responses to a question first.

Sticky note note-taking: Students write brief notes on sticky notes as they work or read.

Student observations: Students watch video clips or live demonstrations and then record and share their observations.

Task cards: Because of the various activities possible in one differentiated class period, task cards provide students with a discrete question or activity and explicit directions for completing that task. They can then refer to the directions as class progresses.

Tingo Tango: Students stand in a circle rapidly passing a soft foam ball or beach ball around the circle as the teacher repeatedly says, "Tingo." At random intervals, the teacher says, "Tango" instead of "Tingo." The student holding the ball at that point must answer a question or call out a fact.

Vocabulary charades: Students work in triads to act out vocabulary words and definitions. This also works well for reviewing key terms and facts in a unit of study.

Write—pair—shares: In a write—pair—share, students write a response to a question. They then share their response with a partner first and with the entire group afterward.

STRATEGY SIX: TIERED INSTRUCTION

Tiered instruction is made possible when teachers assess their students, and then use the data they collect to provide a different tier of instruction for each student. The most common types of tiers are based on proficiency and offer instruction to students on these three levels:

- Beginning students who do not know the concept or have the skill
- Proficient students who have some understand of the concept or skill
- Advanced students who have already mastered the concept or skill

Tiered instruction is an extremely flexible strategy. Every aspect of a lesson can be categorized into one of the three tiers. Teachers can differentiate process, content, and product into the three tiers, for example. In the example of one set of possible tiers that follows, you can see just how adaptable this strategy can be:

For Beginning Students

- The teacher introduces vocabulary words.
- Students read with learning buddies.
- Students use guided questions to aid comprehension.
- Students use a word bank.

For Proficient Students

- Students read a text independently.
- Students take notes on the text independently.

For Advanced Students

- Students determine the parts of the topic they would like to explore further.
- Students do independent research about the topic using several sources.

"I create groups of three to four students with a variety of strengths, whether it be organization, content knowledge, communication skills, and so on. I make sure the students know what I think they could add to the group so that they gain confidence to give advice in those areas. They get five to ten minutes of class time to work on an assigned task. It's the group's job to look out for one another if one is absent or encourage and help the other group members if they are struggling. This can be magical in some classes and mildly helpful in others, depending on class chemistry, but when it works, it can really benefit so many areas of your class."

Shelly Sambiase, 8 years' experience

If you would like to begin using tiered instruction in your classroom, the process is not complicated. Follow these steps for successful implementation of this key strategy:

Step One: Identify the standards or concepts and skills you want students to learn.

Step Two: Collect data to determine if students have the background necessary to be successful with the lesson.

Step Three: Assess students' readiness, interests, and learning preferences.

Step Four: Create an activity that is focused on the standard or concept and skills of the lesson.

Step Five: Adjust the activity to provide tiers of challenge and support that will lead all students to be successful. Think of ways to make it more accessible for struggling students and then how to provide extension activities for students who may have mastered the material quickly.

When using tiered instruction, these guidelines will assist you with wise decisions that can help your students learn:

- The knowledge and skills that students need to learn remains constant, but tiered instruction allows for different pathways to access that material.

- Although it is possible to have any number of tiers, keeping the number to three is manageable, especially when you first start using this strategy.

- Tiered instruction does not water down the material, but instead, offers a different way to learn it. The assignments in each tier should not only be respectful, but also include higher-level thinking skills.

STRATEGY SEVEN: FORMATIVE ASSESSMENT

Formative assessments are low-stakes, quick checks for understanding or snapshots of student progress toward learning goals. They are rarely graded and are powerful tools to determine what your students know and can do. Information from formative assessments helps you make informed instructional decisions about what each student needs next and helps students become more self-directed learners by tracking their own progress.

These assessments tend to be informal and brief. They can take a wide variety of forms, depending on the age and ability levels of the students as well as the subject matter being taught. Frequent formative assessments ensure that each student is making progress and a quick review of the data they yield will make it easy for you to focus your efforts on the instructional practices that will move learning forward for each student.

Frequent formative assessments can provide continual information about what your students know, what they don't know, and how you can adjust instruction to help every learner in your classroom succeed. For example, if, after instruction, you ask students to draw the water cycle for an exit ticket, you can quickly sort their drawings into those who understand completely and those who need some reteaching. You can plan flexible groups for the next day and differentiate based on that data. As you reflect on the information, you could ask yourself how you can improve the way you deliver instruction and how this can help students become more self-directed.

Types of Formative Assessments

Whether using paper or digital tools like Nearpod, Padlet, Kahoot!, Google Forms, or Pear Deck, just about any assignment or activity can serve as a formative assessment if it provides data that will inform instruction. Although formative assessments are flexible and easy to use, it is still necessary to select an assessment that will provide the targeted information that you and your students need. For example, as a quick formative assessment during a review of math strategies, you may ask students to give thumbs-up or thumbs-down signals as they rate their own knowledge. Although this will yield data, it is not as reliable as an exit ticket, because students may not be aware of the gaps in their understanding that an exit ticket could reveal. As you get to know your students and their strengths and areas for growth, selecting the most effective formative assessments will become a straightforward process.

To learn as much as you can about your students' progress and use that to adjust instruction and support students in owning their learning, try some of the suggestions for different types of formative assessments that follow. Well-crafted questions and prompts are the key to formative assessments. Consider the cognitive load required by your questions and remember to move up and down Bloom's Taxonomy or Webb's Depth of Knowledge Framework based on your learning goals. Here are some of the myriad ways you can engage students in formative assessments:

- Complete entrance and exit tickets
- Write on individual dry-erase boards and hold up their responses
- Move to one of the four corners of the classroom representing different answers or perspectives
- Take a low-stakes quiz or poll
- Think–Pair–Share
- Use ABCD cards for each student to hold up their selection when offered multiple-choice options
- Explain a key idea as if telling someone who was absent today
- Draw a visual representation of a concept
- Self-assess using a rubric
- Answer brief true-or-false questions
- Label or draw maps or diagrams
- Put items in order of importance
- Complete a brief cloze procedure
- List ten things they learned
- Match right answers to corresponding questions
- Place items in chronological order
- Create an analogy comparing new information to something they are familiar with
- Rank their knowledge about the lesson on a scale of one to five, with a reason for their ranking
- Teach a concept to a partner
- Create a "Two Truths and a Lie" activity about the lesson and get a classmate to find the lie
- Answer an open-ended question
- Brainstorm for two minutes to recall information
- Write a one-minute summary
- Use a checklist to check off the skills that they have mastered
- Make a quick sketch of three of the main ideas covered in the lesson
- Restate material in fewer than fifty words

- 3-2-1 List: three key words, two interesting ideas, and one remaining question
- Complete or make graphic organizers
- Restate definitions
- Make an entry on a dry-erase board or butcher paper "graffiti wall"
- Meet with the teacher in a mini-conference
- Meet with teammates in mini-conferences
- Predict three things that other students may find confusing
- Make a Venn diagram about the material
- Make flash cards related to the information
- Generate their own quizzes
- Determine what was the clearest point in the lesson and the muddiest point
- Write a brief outline of the main points in the material
- Classify material into categories
- Give different examples for new information
- View photographs related to the material and write captions for them

How to Gather Baseline Data before Beginning a Unit of Study

A necessary type of formative assessment that will yield valuable information is one that allows you to determine your students' level of knowledge before they begin a unit of study. Collecting baseline data will allow you not only to design differentiated instruction activities and adjust the pace of learning as the unit proceeds, but also to track student learning because you will have a clear starting point. Here are some suggested formative assessments that are particularly useful for gathering baseline data:

"Never assume that kids are coming to you with certain skills or knowledge. Students of every level are entering your classroom with deficits in writing, studying, executive functioning skills, and more. Assess them on skills that are important to their success, and if they need help, then teach them—think aloud so that they understand the process, allow them to practice these skills, and encourage them to reflect."

Jennifer Burns, 13 years' experience

- Give students a list of statements related to the unit and ask them to determine if they are true or false. Alternatively, you can ask students to agree or disagree with statements about the topic.
- Ask students to predict the meaning of the vocabulary terms they will be studying.
- Have students write a two-minute paper in which they tell you what they know about the upcoming material.
- Give students a Know—Want to Know—Learned (KWL) chart and ask them to fill it out with what they know.

- Have students share ideas and brainstorm what they know about the topic together.

- Give students a list of items pertaining to the topic and ask them to rate or rank them.

- Create a pre-test that assesses end of unit knowledge and skills.

A Useful Formative Assessment Strategy: Exit Tickets

Exit tickets have been around for a long time because of their powerful appeal to students and teachers alike. As a method of assessing student learning, exit tickets are effective for a variety of reasons. They are brief, focused on the day's learning, and easy for students to manage and for you to evaluate. Further, they can offer specific information about what students need to be successful. Another important aspect of exit tickets is that they encourage students to be reflective about their own learning and to determine their own strengths and areas in need of improvement.

One quick way to have students complete exit tickets is to ask them to complete a problem or set of problems or to answer a set of questions directly related to the day's work. Drawings, short-answers, definitions, true-or-false statements, or multiple-choice questions can all work well as exit tickets. The responses to these do not need to be graded, but rather quickly reviewed to see where changes need to be made for the next day's lesson.

Two common exit ticket activities that can yield valuable data are to ask students to relate the information in the day's lesson to the essential question for the unit by writing a quick response and to use 3-2-1 tickets, whereby students are asked to write three things they learned, two things they found particularly interesting, and one thing they are still confused about.

You can also ask your students to finish some of these sentence starters as a way for you to gather information as they leave the classroom:

- I was surprised when _____.
- I'm beginning to wonder _____.
- I think I will _____.
- I still need help with _____.
- I would have liked _____.
- Now I understand _____.
- In class tomorrow, I will _____.
- Today was valuable to me because _____.
- The easiest part of class today was _____.
- The hardest part of class today was _____.
- Because I need help with _____, I will _____.
- Today I changed the way I _____ because _____.
- Class would be more interesting if _____.
- I can be more successful in this class if I _____.

Formative Assessment Digital Tools

Because of their brief nature and because of the need for fast feedback, digital tools that help with formative assessment can be time-savers. Here is a list of some of the most efficient and easiest-to-use digital resources.

Animoto (animoto.com): Students can make quick videos to share with classmates.

Flip (flip.com): Students can make short text, audio, or video responses and more.

Google Forms (google.com/forms/): Create a new form and convert it into a quiz with an answer key and timely feedback.

Kahoot! (kahoot.com): Kahoot! allows students to give instant responses and to play various classroom games as they collaborate with one another.

Nearpod (nearpod.com): Nearpod provides many formative assessment question types from open-ended to drag and drop, polls, drawing, matching, and more.

Pear Deck (peardeck.com): Pear Deck's formative assessment templates provide students with many ways to share what they know and where they need help.

Plickers (plickers.com): Plickers is a quick and easy update to ABCD cards. Students hold up their plicker card to answer a question and teachers scan the responses with their phone app from the front of the room.

Quizlet (quizlet.com): At Quizlet, students and teachers can create flash cards and quizzes, and play study games.

Socrative (socrative.com): You can use the Socrative app for quizzes, quick questions, exit tickets and more.

STRATEGY EIGHT: EFFECTIVE FEEDBACK

According to John Hattie's *Visible Learning*, timely, quality feedback is one of the greatest supports for learning. Feedback from formative assessments provides clarity for teachers to design instruction and for students to move forward with their own learning. A test of the effectiveness of feedback is this: after receiving feedback, students should have a clear idea of what they know and what they need to do to take the next step or improve their work.

Some formative assessments are quick checks of progress and will have a correct, partially correct, or incorrect answer. Getting this feedback immediately with a digital tool or exit ticket will allow teachers to clear up misconceptions and reteach key concepts. Some formative assessments are open-ended, problem-solvers, or short essays that may require teacher or peer comments. Teach students how to provide effective feedback to each other. For peer or teacher feedback to be effective, it is:

- Written or spoken.
- Timely. The faster students understand how they are progressing on an assignment, the better. When there is a delay in feedback, there will be a delay in learning, as students waste valuable time waiting to learn how to proceed.

- Connected to specific areas of the success criteria or rubric.
- Modeling growth mindset by pointing out at least one strength as well as providing constructive feedback. Feedback should not be judgmental or harsh.
- Brief and to the point. Be concise. Be clear.
- Specific enough so that students know what to do next to learn and improve.

STRATEGY NINE: PLANNED IMPLEMENTATION OF FEEDBACK

It is not enough just to give students effective feedback; you must build in the time that they need to act on the information they receive from formative assessments. Although the time required for this will vary depending on the learning target, the student's needs, and the scope of the task, it is necessary to plan a routine for students to understand and follow through on feedback. Some things to consider as you develop the routine can include how to demonstrate that they have implemented the suggestions, when students are to do this work, how they can get the help they need, and how to take their next steps in learning and accomplish their remaining tasks with this new knowledge.

STRATEGY TEN: STUDENT CHOICE

When students have voice, choice, and agency in their learning, motivation, engagement, and learning increase. With a little autonomy and ownership, students will also likely surprise you with their creativity and by going beyond grade-level rubrics and expectations. Build in regular opportunities for student choice in what they learn (content), the resources they use to learn it (process), and how they demonstrate their learning (product).

Student-centered choice takes many forms from school-wide to individual classrooms. Some schools create learning contracts for each student in each subject, based on the questions they want to pursue and the real-world problems they want to solve. Some schools schedule a "genius hour" each week to create an opportunity for students to explore their passions. Within the classroom, there are countless ways to offer students choices when differentiating instruction; two of the easiest are choice boards and assessment options.

A choice board is usually a group of nine or more tasks that students can choose from as they work toward learning goals, although the choices may be expanded or reduced to meet the needs of different classes. To make it easy for students to complete a choice board, give a copy of the choice board to students and ask them to mark off assignments as they complete them. Leave a square blank for students to create their own option. The number of assignments that you ask students to complete will vary depending on your purpose and the amount of time available.

In the choice board shown in Sample 8.1, you can find options that will appeal to student learning preferences. Digital tools like Book Creator, Canva, and Flip can enhance student engagement with any of the choice board activities.

Sample 8.1

Choice Board for a Unit of Study on a Book

Write a summary.	Make a diagram of the plot.	Make a book jacket of the most exciting part of the book so far.
Record audio as you read the three most interesting passages aloud.	Create art inspired by the book, such as a poem, song, dance, artwork.	Sketch three of the main characters interacting with one another.
Make a video of you and some of your classmates acting out a scene from the book.	Student Choice: Add your own choice here and then do it.	Make a booklet of the words and their meanings that were new to you so far in this book.
Create a video of an alternative ending for the book.	Create a book trailer to get other students excited to read the book.	Draw a Venn diagram comparing and contrasting two characters.

STRATEGY ELEVEN: ANCHOR ACTIVITIES

Anchor activities are independent, ongoing activities that students may work on at any time when they have completed their assignments or when the teacher is busy with other students. Anchor activities maximize instructional time by reviewing or extending content. When students have meaningful go-to activities, you will also reduce distracting or disruptive behavior.

Anchor activities also promote learning because they allow students to remain focused on learning during classroom downtime. Because anchor activities are instructional, they can be used in conjunction with current or past units of study, or they can be activities of general interest, such as a cross-disciplinary project, independent research, or educational apps.

Teachers who use anchor activities often find that such activities are most successful when the expectations for academic work and behavior are explicit, when students know that their work is meaningful and will be assessed, and when students are offered choices. It is helpful to explain the purpose of anchor activities so that students understand that they are not optional and will help them learn. Be clear in modeling the routines and procedures that you expect students to follow so that they can work with confidence.

Although anchor activities can be related to the unit of study that your students are working on, they can also be broad based. Students will find anchor activities that are connected to their individual interests particularly engaging, especially if they have input into the creation of the activities. Although you will want to take your students' learning needs into consideration, here are some suggestions for engaging anchor activities that you can adapt for your classroom use:

- Reading independently
- Journal writing
- Completing creative writing projects
- Using or making flashcards
- Using educational apps and online games
- Completing puzzles
- Taking a virtual field trip to a museum or other site
- Working with classmates on a class blog, web page, or scrapbook
- Reflecting on learning
- Maintaining a binder or digital portfolio
- Completing vocabulary work
- Solving a problem of the day
- Working at a learning center
- Making multimedia presentations
- Reviewing with a partner
- Completing art projects
- Solving brain teasers and logic puzzles

> "A student touched my heart when I received a correspondence from a college adviser letting me know one of his student advisees wrote an essay about how I touched her life and made her want to go into teaching. She is now an English teacher in my same county."
>
> *Jessica Statz, 19 years' experience*

How to Plan for Differentiation

Until differentiation becomes a classroom norm for you and your students, you may feel unsure of how to plan instruction. It can be intimidating to determine how to fit all the parts of a differentiated lesson into a daily lesson plan. A productive way to manage this is to look over the following timeline of a differentiated lesson and decide how you can plan for each part. Once you have this in place, you can then determine how to include these steps into the daily flow of instruction in your classroom.

Step One: Use your state, district, and school curriculum standards to determine the objectives and essential knowledge.

Step Two: Determine how much time is needed. Will the lesson cover one day? Two days? Longer?

Step Three: Administer pre-assessments to determine student readiness.

Step Four: Use data from pre-assessments to determine tasks. You will also determine flexible groups and tiers at this point in your planning if they are to be included in the lesson.

Step Five: Deliver whole-group instruction about the material and review or reinforce the procedures and routines students should follow.

Step Six: Transition students to their flexible groups and differentiated tasks, making sure that each student has a clear idea of how to complete the work and how to signal for help when needed.

Step Seven: Provide formative assessments so that students can check their understanding. Provide quick feedback and allow time for students to implement improvements.

Step Eight: Reteach if necessary. Students who have mastered the material move to anchor activities.

Step Nine: Complete summative assessments when students are ready to demonstrate their learning.

Step Ten: Provide time for student reflection and spend time yourself reflecting on the effectiveness of the lesson. What went well? How can you improve it? What would you do next time?

TEACHER TEMPLATE 8.1

A Planning Checklist for Differentiation

You can use this checklist to think through a differentiated activity to meet the learning needs of your students. As you work through the questions in the first part of the checklist, you should be able to determine how you can effectively differentiate the activity. After you have completed this part, use Part II to guide your thinking further.

Part I: Looking at the Big Picture

After you formulate an answer for each of these questions, place a check mark in the blank beside it.

1. _____ What needs do you hope to serve by including the activity in your instruction?
2. _____ Which learning preferences will your activity appeal to?
3. _____ What materials and resources will you need?
4. _____ How much time do you anticipate will be needed?
5. _____ What preparation is necessary before you use this activity in your instruction?
6. _____ Which routines or procedures do you need to establish or reinforce?
7. _____ What problems can you anticipate? How can you prevent or solve them?
8. _____ How will you gather data before and during the activity?
9. _____ How will you provide feedback to students?
10. _____ How will students implement feedback suggestions?
11. _____ What will the products of the activity be? At what stages will these products be assessed?
12. _____ How will you know if the strategy is successful?

(continued on next page)

(continued from previous page)
Part II: A Time Line for a Differentiated Lesson Plan

As you complete each step of the process for creating a differentiated lesson plan, place a check mark in the blank.

1. _____ Use your state, district, and school curriculum standards to determine the objectives and essential knowledge.

2. _____ Estimate how much time is needed. Will the lesson cover one day? Two days? Build in a bit of flexibility just in case.

3. _____ Administer pre-assessments to determine student readiness. This may cause you to change your estimate of how much time is needed.

4. _____ Use data from pre-assessments to determine tasks. You will also determine flexible groups and tiers at this point in your planning if they are to be included in the lesson.

5. _____ Deliver whole-group instruction about the material and review or reinforce the procedures and routines students should follow.

6. _____ Move students to their differentiated tasks, making sure that each student has a clear idea of how to complete the work and how to signal for help when needed.

7. _____ Allow time for quick formative assessments so that students can check their understanding. Provide quick feedback and allow time for students to implement it.

8. _____ Reteach if necessary. Students who have mastered the material move to anchor activities.

9. _____ Complete summative assessments when students are ready to demonstrate their learning.

10. _____ Provide time for students to reflect on their learning. Spend time yourself reflecting on the effectiveness of the lesson. How can you improve it? What would you do again?

From *The First-Year Teacher's Survival Guide, 5th Edition*, by Michelle Cummings. Copyright © 2024 by John Wiley & Sons, Inc. Reproduced by permission.

More Differentiated Instruction Planning

After you have worked through the information in the timeline and in Teacher Template 8.1, you can use Teacher Template 8.2 to be precise about how you plan for differentiated instruction.

TEACHER TEMPLATE 8.2

Personalized Instruction Planning Template

To ensure that your plans for differentiated instruction are on the right track, you can use this template to design instruction that will meet the needs of all your learners.

Lesson topic: _____ Dates: _____

Concepts and essential questions:

_____

_____

_____

_____

Outcomes, objectives, and goals:

_____

_____

_____

_____

Learning style preferences (circle the preference[s] that the lesson is designed to appeal to): Visual   Auditory   Reading/Writing   Kinesthetic

Preliminary assessment activities:

_____

_____

_____

_____

Estimated time needed: _____

Direct instruction activities:

_____

_____

_____

_____

Estimated time needed: _____

(continued on next page)

From *The First-Year Teacher's Survival Guide, 5th Edition*, by Michelle Cummings. Copyright © 2024 by John Wiley & Sons, Inc. Reproduced by permission.

(continued from previous page)

Differentiation Strategies

Respectful tasks:

_____

_____

_____

_____

Flexible groups:

_____

_____

_____

_____

Tiered instruction:

_____

_____

_____

Estimated time needed for all strategies: _____

Formative assessments:

_____

_____

_____

Estimated time needed: _____

Implementing feedback:

_____

_____

_____

Estimated time needed: _____

Anchor activities:

_____

_____

Summative Assessment:

_____

_____

Reflection:

_____

_____

Classroom Leadership Strategies for Differentiation

It's reasonable to wonder just how you are going to lead a classroom in which students are engaged in many different activities. It starts with building relationships and a classroom culture, then teaching expectations and routines so that students know what to do. Some teachers wonder what the rest of the class will do when they are working with a small group of students. Once your students experience the excitement and ah-has of a differentiated class and are accustomed to the routines and expectations, they will be challenged, motivated, and engaged in learning. Here are a few tips that can help you and your students get started:

- Encourage classroom ownership and a sense of shared responsibility for the success of the entire class. Ask students to self-reflect, make informed decisions for the good of the group, articulate their learning goals, and help one another be successful.
- Appoint student experts who can help their peers.
- Have clear, written directions for all activities so that students know what to do. Many teachers find that checklists and daily agendas are effective in making assignments and expectations clear.
- Establish clear timelines for assignments so that students know that they are expected to produce work within a set time. This will create a sense of urgency and help everyone stay focused.
- Post a list of procedures for those students who finish early. Provide plenty of high interest anchor activities for these students.
- Use signals to control noise—even purposeful noise can get too loud sometimes.
- Establish class routines for turning in work, passing out materials, moving to groups, and so on.
- Keep the pace brisk and purposeful.

Multi-Tiered System of Supports

Differentiated instruction is one of the pillars of Multi-Tiered System of Supports (MTSS). MTSS is a proactive framework many schools use to support students holistically by assessing and meeting their academic, social, emotional, and behavioral needs. By identifying challenges early and quickly providing targeted, meaningful interventions, students have greater success. The MTSS model generally features three tiers of support.

Tier One supports are for the general education classroom. Teachers use effective teaching strategies and positive behavior supports to meet the needs of most students. Students who need additional support move to the next tier.

Tier Two provides small group interventions and more targeted support, sometimes in a Title One or special education classroom. This may include reading instruction or counseling groups. Students who need higher levels of support move to the next tier.

Tier Three offers intensive individualized support in addition to support in the general education classroom. Students in Tier Three may spend more time in a resource room or more supportive setting.

Differentiated instruction, Response to Intervention (RTI), Positive Behavioral Interventions and Supports (PBIS), and Universal Design for Learning (UDL) are all complementary practices under the umbrella of MTSS. Together they create a powerful, holistic, and proactive way to support all students.

For more information, visit the Center on Multi-Tiered System of Supports **(mtss 4success.org)**.

> "Nijam's struggle with inference and comprehension questions, despite her love for reading, prompted me to reevaluate my differentiation efforts. Recognizing the need to make her thinking more visible, we introduced a system of text annotation and coding. This increased Nijam's engagement and allowed her to experience success alongside her peers, inspiring the implementation of a school-wide differentiated annotation system. Through differentiation, Nijam taught us so we could teach everyone better."
>
> *Clifton Wallace, 7 years' experience*

Response to Intervention (RTI)

In the broadest sense, RTI is a form of differentiated instruction in that it offers modifications to content, process, and product to help students gain academic and behavioral skills. Although RTI is a highly successful program in many schools, it differs from classroom differentiation in a significant way: RTI is a schoolwide intervention framework instead of differentiation delivered by an individual teacher. RTI is often the process used to determine if a student is eligible for specially designed instruction and an IEP plan.

Similar to other types of differentiated instruction, RTI offers a tiered approach to interventions. In the first tier, students are instructed by a general education teacher using effective strategies, including differentiated instruction. Ongoing data collection through a variety of assessments is used to help determine the needs of all students in the class.

Students who, according to observational and performance data, are not mastering the content or acquiring the necessary skills move to the second tier of instruction. Students in the second tier continue to remain in their general education classroom and receive the same instruction as their classmates. In addition, however, students in the second tier also receive more targeted instruction to help them overcome their learning difficulties. Such instruction is usually delivered in small-group formats, often by counselors, Title One teachers, or paraprofessionals. After a specified time, if students in the second tier have mastered the material, they then move back to the first tier of instruction. If they are still experiencing difficulties, they move to the third tier.

Students in the third tier receive instruction that is more intensive and individualized than that offered in the first two tiers. Often

> "I never give up on any student, regardless of their grade, level of effort, and so on. I also make it clear to each student, over and over, that I'm not giving up, no matter what."
>
> *Margaret R. Scheirer, 12 years' experience*

a specialist or a special education teacher provides this instruction on an individual basis, although the general education teacher is still very involved. Ongoing assessments at this level continue to play an important role, as students may be referred to a team that will consider their eligibility for special education services.

Tips for Getting Started with Differentiation

Even though the process of differentiation can be exciting, it can be challenging, particularly as a beginning teacher. Here are some quick tips to help you get started:

- Take it easy at first. Start small and keep it simple. You do not have to completely revamp your lesson plans; in fact, you can begin with a strategy or two. Practice them until you are comfortable and then add to your repertoire.

- It takes time to find the resources and materials that you need to offer differentiated instruction. Use generative AI to create differentiated lessons and texts. Work with colleagues to share ideas and research online to create a bank of activities that you can draw from.

- Work out a simple system to manage the data from formative assessments and to keep track of student assignments. Find a system that is manageable for you and stick with it.

- Take the time to explain to students the purpose of differentiated instruction and how they can take ownership for their own learning and support their classmates.

- Be patient with yourself. It takes time to learn how to lead for differentiation. Just as your students are working to improve their skills levels, so are you.

Resources to Help You Learn More about Differentiation

Two of the leading models for differentiation come from Dr. Carol Ann Tomlinson and from Universal Design for Learning (UDL).

Dr. Tomlinson at the University of Virgina is the guru of differentiation. She talks about designing differentiation as a series of ongoing highways and exit ramps where students daily experience learning as part of a community, as well as learning in flexible groups, to meet them where they are to move learning forward. Dr. Tomlinson advocates that teachers can differentiate four elements of the learning process: the content (what students learn), process (the resources they use to learn), product (how they demonstrate their learning), and the learning environment (the physical space and pedagogy).

Visit DifferentiationCentral.com to see the differentiation concept map, videos, and resources.

UDL, developed by CAST, is a powerful and proactive process for differentiating learning to meet the needs of each student and help them become "expert learners." UDL acknowledges that there is a wide range of background knowledge, interests, and skills within each classroom of students. Using the UDL framework, teachers remove barriers to learning by providing multiple means of engaging in learning, presenting information, and showing what they know.

To learn more, visit UDLGuidelines.cast.org.

Because of the increasing use of differentiation, there is a great deal of helpful information available for educators who want to learn more. Here are some books and online resources to help you get started:

Books

John McCarthy, *So All Can Learn: A Practical Guide to Differentiation*

Carol Ann Tomlinson

- *The Differentiated Classroom*
- *Differentiation in Practice*
- *Leading and Managing a Differentiated Classroom*
- *How to Differentiate Instruction in Academically Diverse Classrooms*

Online Resources

Adaptive Reader (adaptivereader.com): Adaptive reader makes select novels accessible by creating leveled readers out of each book. Teachers can have students with reading levels ranging from sixth grade to twelfth grade engaging in the same text.

Differentiation Central (differentiationcentral.com): At the University of Virginia's Institutes for Academic Diversity, you can find many useful resources about differentiated instruction, including Carol Tomlinson's extensive work.

Differentiation Daily (differentiationdaily.com): Educator Paula Kluth adds fresh new tips about differentiation to this blog daily. There is an emphasis on material for younger students.

Edutopia (edutopia.org): At Edutopia, you can access dozens of well-written, practical articles about differentiated instruction. Use "differentiated instruction" as a search term.

Newsela (Newsela.com): Newsela offers real-word texts from diverse perspectives aligned with standards in English language arts, science, social studies, and social-emotional learning. Reading passages are added daily and each one is available at five reading levels.

Questions to Discuss with Colleagues

Sharing ideas with colleagues is a helpful way to devise solutions to some of the problems that you must manage successfully at school. Here, you will find several topics to open discussions with colleagues about successful instructional practices:

1. You want to provide timely and effective feedback on formative assessments. What are some of the quickest and easiest ways that you can provide feedback to your students?

2. You want to explore how generative AI can support differentiation in the classroom. How can the technology be used to differentiate content, rubrics, and formative assessments for students at various reading levels?

3. As you begin a new unit of study, you become aware that your students have various levels of background knowledge about the new content. What can you do to build the background knowledge of students who need it in your class?

4. You want students to have more voice, choice, and agency in your class. What are other strategies you can use to encourage students to pursue their interests and investigate solutions to real-world problems they want to solve?

5. Although you want to use formative assessments in your classroom, you are not always sure that the ones you have chosen are providing the most useful information. What can you do to improve the way you use formative assessments?

Topics to Discuss with a Mentor

Although the topics that new teachers need to discuss with a mentor vary from teacher to teacher and from school to school, there are some that most first-year teachers should be comfortable discussing with a mentor or a trusted colleague. You should ask your mentor about these topics from this section:

- How to obtain any additional materials and supplies you may need for differentiation
- Advice about classroom leadership specific to differentiation
- How to assess student readiness and use formative assessments
- Suggestions for instructional activities that support students in need of Tier One and Tier Two interventions
- How to create flexible groups

Reflection Questions to Guide Your Thinking

1. What are your biggest concerns about implementing differentiated instruction in your classroom? How can you overcome them? Where can you find help with this?

2. Which formative assessments do you anticipate will work well for your students at this point in the term? What do you need to know and do before administering them? Are there any accommodations or modifications needed?

3. How can you arrange your schedule so that the feedback you provide for students is timely?

4. In what ways are you creating opportunities for students to take ownership of their learning? How are you supporting them to identify and pursue their interests? What barriers need to be removed to make this possible?

5. What are your strengths regarding differentiated instruction? How can you use these strengths to your advantage when planning and implementing differentiated instruction?

SECTION NINE

Design and Facilitate Learning

Through the way you design and facilitate learning, you can either multiply or diminish critical thinking, creativity, communication, and collaboration among your students. As a teacher, you have an amazing opportunity to inspire students to become more confident, self-directed learners.

Lesson planning is one of the most important tasks you have as a first-year teacher, as a second-year teacher, as a third-year teacher. . ., and it will be just as important when you have many years of experience. Planning effective lessons is the foundation for student learning, which is the purpose of your chosen career.

When you make the commitment to carefully facilitate learning, you and your students will benefit in many ways. Here are just some of the benefits:

- You will be more likely to prepare engaging, minds-on learning experiences that leverage students' interests and learning preferences rather than relying on lackluster routines and covering content.

- You will gain confidence from having a clear plan for each day. This ease of facilitation will reduce your stress, increase student learning, and enhance your own professional credibility.

"Beginning teachers often ask me to help them think about what they should do tomorrow. I always respond with a few crucial questions:

- What are your overall purposes for teaching and student learning (and why)?
- What are your specific goals for student learning?
- What kind of learning do your goals require to ensure all students experience success?
- What do you need to remember about your students' strengths and challenges to engage them in a particular kind of learning to achieve your goals?

Only after answering these questions can you design strategies that will actively engage all students in achieving goals and demonstrating their achievement."

Vicki A. Jacobs, Former Director, Harvard's Teacher Education Program, 45+ years' experience

- You will be able to pay attention to the practices that will make your lessons powerful, such as building relationships with students, connecting learning to the world beyond the classroom and integrating technology.
- You will be able to create a coherent learning journey for students instead of just covering disjointed bits and pieces of information.
- You will be better able to personalize learning to meet each student's needs as they gain proficiency, not simply of state standards, but of the knowledge and skills they need academically, socially, and emotionally, to be healthy and successful for a lifetime.
- You will reduce your stress and enjoy your evenings and weekends more.

Have Clarity of Purpose

While generative AI tools can expedite the lesson planning process, there is a crucial role for human teachers to play, and it starts with answering the following questions. Designing and facilitating learning starts from your "why," moves on to your "how" and then arrives at the "what" you choose to teach. The big questions that follow will help you gain clarity of purpose about teaching that will inform the learning experiences you will design. You will discern what helps you achieve those purposes and the practices that do not.

START FROM YOUR "WHY?"

- What is the purpose of teaching and learning really?
- Why is it vital for students to gain an education?
- What are the success criteria you will use to know you and your students are reaching that purpose?

If at its core, the purpose of an education is to help all students create meaning, find purpose, develop academic, social, and emotional skills to improve their quality of life and career opportunities, then you will facilitate learning to that purpose. If the purpose of education is for students to identify and pursue solutions to problems and questions that matter to them, then you will facilitate learning to that purpose. Your answers to these questions will vary and likely change over time, but it's important for you to have clarity.

MOVE ON TO "HOW?"

Once you have clarity on the "why," move on to "how" you will facilitate learning. Consider the types of learning experiences, both inside and beyond the classroom, that will best help you and your students achieve the purposes you articulated when answering the preceding questions. In designing and facilitating learning, you have control over how students use their time and what opportunities they have to learn.

- How will various pedagogical approaches support student learning? Most teachers combine several methodologies to achieve learning goals.
- How do you hope to engage students in learning? Consider the role of discovery learning, direct instruction, collaborative groups, flexible groupings, learning stations, maker spaces, lab stations, whole group discussions, self-paced learning, inquiry-based and project-based learning in engaging students.
- How does the classroom configuration support or limit these experiences?
- What teaching strategies encourage students to do the thinking?
- To what extent does sitting help or harm student thinking and creativity? When is it appropriate for students to sit, and what opportunities do students have to stand and move around the classroom to enhance their learning?
- What is the role of student choice, voice, and agency in these learning experiences? In what ways can students co-create the curriculum with their teachers?
- Students can learn from anyone, anywhere in the world, at any time. How are your students engaging with virtual and in-person learning beyond the classroom? What is the role of field trips, internships, mentors, and guest educators both virtual and in-person?
- How will students apply their learning in the world beyond the classroom? To what extent could project-based learning, focused on solutions to local concerns, give students a meaningful problem to solve and an authentic audience for their ideas?

THEN DETERMINE THE "WHAT?"

With answers to the "why?" and "how?" you are ready to move onto the "what?" It's time to determine the knowledge, skills, dispositions, content, standards, units of study, and lessons that will align with the why and how of learning in your classroom.

Robert Marzano's research makes the case that students would need a K–22 school system to have time to gain mastery of all the mandated curricular standards. Teachers need to make informed choices about the most essential, power, or priority standards they will teach and assess based on three criteria: endurance, leverage, and readiness.

- Endurance means it matters well-beyond a single year or course.
- Leverage means it has value across multiple subject areas.
- Readiness means it is vital for the student to be ready for the next grade or course.

If your school or district does not provide power standards to you, then this is an important exercise to do with your grade-level or content-area team to develop consensus. Once you have identified your power standards for the year or term, unpack the standards to analyze the knowledge, skills, and level of rigor or cognitive demand required of students.

"Andrea had a horrible relationship with math and started out uncomfortable with the Thinking Classroom Problem (TCP), existing as an observer during group work. As we progressed, she began using her voice more and more and then I watched as she had the pen and was explaining her process to her group, proudly and with confidence. She enjoyed being in class and at the end of the year shared how much she felt she had grown through the TCP process, coming into her own as a mathematician."

Sarah Bestor, 5 years' experience

Here are some resources for further exploration when determining the why, how, and what of teaching and learning in your classroom:

Building Thinking Classrooms (buildingthinkingclassrooms.com): Beginning with his book, *Building Thinking Classrooms in Mathematics*, Peter Liljedahl promotes fourteen practices to amplify student thinking and deeper learning in schools. These practices aren't just for math either.

High Tech High (HTH) (hightechhigh.org): HTH is a collection of K–12 charter schools designed to be learner-centered with a focus on project-based learning. Its website (pblessentials.org) offers teacher resources for project-based learning as well as a graduate school of education.

Leaving to Learn **by Elliot Washor and Charles Mojkowski:** To increase engagement and deepen learning, Washor and Mojkowski, both of Big Picture Learning, advocate for schools to anchor learning on more real-world, experiential learning opportunities.

Modern Classrooms Project (modernclassrooms.org): Modern Classrooms Project is a nonprofit created by teachers that promotes student ownership of learning and teacher well-being through blended, self-paced, and mastery-based learning. Its website has loads of resources to explore and it offers a five- to ten-hour free online course as well at: learn.modernclassrooms.org.

Project Zero (pz.harvard.edu/thinking-routines): This website from Harvard's Graduate School of Education offers a robust, free toolbox of thinking routines each with a detailed pdf in English and Spanish to deepen learning.

The Teacher Clarity Playbook **by Douglas Fisher, Nancy Frey, Olivia Amador, and Joseph Assof:** This book offers a step-by-step process to develop coherent learning plans that lead to student mastery. It takes the big thinking of John Hattie's *Visible Learning* and embeds those ideals into the way teachers design meaningful and relevant learning experiences.

Understanding by Design **by Grant Wiggins and Jay McTighe:** Beginning with the end in mind, Wiggins and McTighe provide a valuable framework for backward planning. Teachers start with determining learning goals and the assessments that will indicate if students have reached the goals. Only once they know how students will be assessed will teachers select materials and activities for instruction. This process keeps a strong focus on student learning.

Universal Design for Learning (UDL) (cast.org/impact/universal-design-for-learning-udl): UDL provides a thoughtful and proactive way to plan for and meet the needs of students with disabilities as well as everyone in your classroom. This powerful and effective approach to teaching and learning meets the needs of all learners by design. Teachers ask themselves these five questions:

- What is my goal?
- What barriers might interfere with student learning?
- How can I provide multiple means of representation?
- What options can I give for student actions and expression?
- How can I use differentiated engagement strategies?

Backward Design

The term *backward design* was coined by Grant Wiggins and Jay McTighe in their 1998 book *Understanding by Design*. Backward design is a productive approach to instructional planning based on the idea that teachers should begin the process by determining the desired end results of instruction. With the final outcomes in mind, teachers can then design and deliver appropriate instruction tailored to help students achieve those learning goals.

Although many teachers follow the principles of backward design when planning lessons, countless others make the mistake of planning small increments of instruction instead of building a framework of carefully sequenced skills and knowledge. When you begin designing lessons to help your students gain mastery of the knowledge and skills that your curriculum requires, begin with the big picture.

Take the time to determine answers to these three questions before planning specific lessons.

Question One: What will students know and be able to do as a result of the learning experience? (This may be a single or multi-day lesson or unit of study.) Pay careful attention to the verbs you use as they determine the cognitive demand or rigor required of students. For example, the verb *understand* requires a different assessment than the verb *construct* when used in a standard.

Question Two: How will you know that students know and can do what you identified in Question One? What are the success criteria for the project or assessment?

Question Three: What learning experiences will support them to demonstrate mastery on that assessment? What are students' interests that can inform and influence the learning experiences?

Plan backward from your purpose, success criteria, learning objectives, and assessments to develop units of study and lesson plans. With the answers to these questions, you are ready to design and facilitate meaningful and effective learning experiences.

Why Strategic Steps Are the Keys to Success

As you are probably already aware, it is better to begin any project with careful planning, gathering the best possible resources, and making sure you know what to do before you begin. If these steps are important for an ordinary project, just imagine how vital careful planning is when trying to implement various instructional strategies into your classroom. Instead of taking on too much and failing to help your students, be cautious. Take your time. Be deliberate in your approach.

If you learn of a strategy that seems interesting and that you predict would work well with your students, implement it strategically. First, learn all that you can about it. Talk it over with your mentor or with others in your school communities. Next, be thoroughly prepared and have a backup plan in case your plan does not work well. Gather data as you implement the strategy so that you can assess its effectiveness. Finally, take time to reflect. What went well? What do you need to rework? How can you make sure that this strategy is as effective as possible next time?

> "Think in terms of what you want to get done in class in a week. This tends to make you plan out ahead a little farther, so in case you get through certain activities quicker than you planned, you won't find yourself in that awkward space where you now have to scramble to come up with something."
>
> *Kevin Healy, 11 years' experience*

How Prepared Should You Be?

Everything is new in your first year. It can be overwhelming. Preparation will increase your confidence, reduce your stress, and inspire student learning. Although the amount of necessary preparation varies from teacher to teacher, here are some guidelines on how prepared you should be:

At the Start of a School Year

- Get to know your students and their interests and academic and social and emotional needs.
- Be thoroughly familiar with your state's standards.
- Know the instructional material you will be expected to teach each term.
- Draft a yearlong learning plan or course overview as soon as possible.

At the Start of a Grading Period

- Design plans for each unit you intend to teach.
- Try to batch lesson plans for about two weeks in advance.

Common Planning Pitfalls

Every teacher has lessons that don't work. With a growth mindset, you reflect on and learn to improve or abandon those lessons. It's particularly challenging for beginning teachers to design lesson plans without an extensive repertoire of tried-and-true strategies and instructional materials. Every lesson plan you write in your first year is an experiment.

You can increase the likelihood of lessons being successful by avoiding some of these pitfalls:

- Ignoring state and district standards and guidelines
- Rushing to cover material instead of teaching students
- Failing to connect current learning to previous learning
- Spending a disproportionate amount of time on one unit
- Failing to include activities that engage critical thinking skills
- Not including student interests and learning preferences in the lesson
- Failing to assess students' prior knowledge before starting new instruction
- Assessing students on standards they have not adequately mastered
- Failing to use data from formative assessments before a summative assessment
- Failing to write a yearlong learning plan or course overview before deciding on unit plans and daily plans

The Practicalities of Planning

As a new teacher, learning to plan instruction efficiently takes time. Be patient as you work out the best ways to manage this important task. With practice, you will soon learn how to find instructional materials and strategies to help your students learn.

There are many tools for organizing your planning process from paper-based to digital tools. Some teachers start their thinking on dry-erase boards or sticky notes before moving it to a central location. Many student information systems also include online lesson planning features. Find the tools that work most effectively and efficiently for you. Here are just a few of the options:

- Documents, spreadsheets, or slide decks
- Paper-based planners
  - Erin Condren Teacher Lesson Planners (erincondren.com)
  - Happy Planner (thehappyplanner.com)
- Online lesson planners
  - Planbook.com
  - Planbookedu.com
  - Commoncurriculum.com

If you have a wonderful teaching partner who shares your vision and purpose for teaching and learning, then planning with a grade-level or subject area teaching partner is usually more efficient and enjoyable than planning in isolation. Generative AI tools can serve as teaching assistants in the planning process brainstorming ideas, prompts, and activities for a teacher to select from, creating rubrics, and otherwise reducing the amount of time teachers spend in the planning process. (See Section Two for more on AI in education.)

In lesson planning, teachers have two competing responsibilities that are both important:

1. To help students gain proficiency in state standards
2. To respond to the needs and interests of students

Flexibility is key. You will plan lessons to have a big picture view on the learning journey and you will iterate on that plan based on the needs and interests of your students throughout the year. To strive for a work/life balance you will want to have lesson plans a minimum of two weeks ahead and adjust them daily based on the emerging needs of students.

To understand the practical aspects of effective planning, it may help to examine the entirety of the instructional design process, as shown in Figure 9.1. Notice that culturally responsive practices, students' interests, academic, language, and social-emotional needs are considered in every aspect of the process.

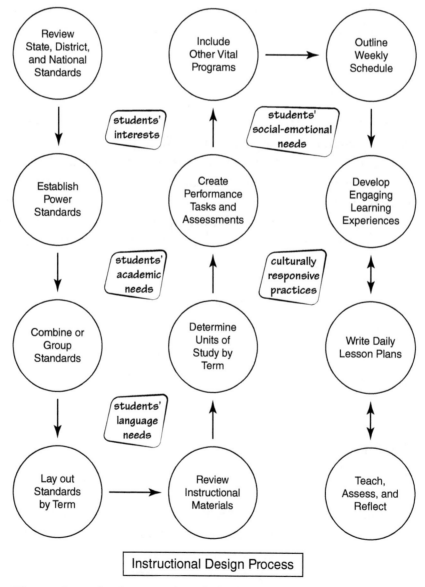

Figure 9.1 The instructional design process.

Your State's Standards

Each state's department of education has created the standards that indicate the knowledge and skills students should master by the end of each course or grade level. As you begin the process of designing a course of study for your students, you will need to know your state's standards. To learn more about the standards that apply to you and your students, try these potential resources:

- Access your state's department of education website.
- Access your local school district's website.
- Talk with other teachers at your school to share materials and lesson plans.

How to Begin Planning Instruction

In the next few pages, you will learn how to plan instruction. Teachers often describe the beginning of the process like putting together puzzle pieces or playing Tetris and the daily lesson planning as creative and exciting. The design process is similar, yet distinct for elementary and secondary teachers. Elementary teachers have multiple subjects and may be self-contained or deploy for certain subjects. Secondary teachers often have one or two subject areas, several different courses, and a larger student load.

While designing learning experiences has similar questions and sequences, depending on your purpose, the type of school you are in, the needs and interests of your students, and the structure of time in your school, your answers to the questions and your ultimate learning plan will vary. Successful planning both proceeds in an orderly sequence and has recursive and iterative moments to respond to new information and the needs of students.

> "Move from interventions to preventions by starting with the interests and choices of each and every student and build your curriculum around those interests and choices as well as their health and well-being."
>
> *Elliot Washor, Ed.D., Co-Founder*
> *Big Picture Learning*

Most importantly, teachers teach students, not simply content. Student interests, as well as their academic, social, and emotional needs, are at the center of the design process. Before school begins, teachers will begin planning without the benefit of input from their students. As you get to know students' needs, interests, and learning preferences, you will circle back to your plan, monitor, and adjust.

Figure 9.1 illustrates the instructional design process. Here's how to move through each step of the process.

Step One: Begin by reviewing the standards that apply to your grade level or content area. In most cases, your state and district will have adopted standards to guide the instructional design process. While there are many limitations to standards, they can assist teachers in creating coherence for students across grade levels and subject areas. Remember to consider what is missing from state standards as well so that you can supplement for students. Also consider additional sources of standards relevant to your work, such as ISTE's Technology Standards, Learning for Justice's

Social Justice Standards, CASEL's Social-Emotional Framework, English Language Development Standards, and Career Readiness Standards, to name a few.

Step Two: Because there are too many standards to teach in one year or term, teachers establish power or priority standards. To accomplish this, use the three-pronged criteria: endurance (meaningful beyond a year), leverage (important for more than one subject area), and readiness (vital to prepare for the next grade or course). This may be provided by districts or accomplished in Professional Learning Communities (PLC). In some cases, you may need to decide them yourself.

Step Three: Combine and group standards that make sense to teach and learn together.

Step Four: Lay out standards by term based on a learning sequence. Consider where to place foundational skills and the application of those skills in a way that creates building blocks and coherence for students.

Step Five: Review and analyze the instructional materials you are required to use. What would support students in gaining proficiency in the standards? What is missing from these instructional materials? If you don't have a required curriculum, search for instructional materials aligned to your standards and purposes.

Step Six: Determine units of study by term for the entire year. Whether you teach in quarters, semesters, trimesters, intensives, or through personalized learning plans, generally frame the units of study by term for the entire year. This will give you an idea of the scope of the knowledge and skills you expect students to master during the entire year or course. Elementary teachers may create multidisciplinary thematic units of study. Secondary teachers may use this as the building block for a syllabus. If you create essential questions for each unit, you would do that at this point in the process.

Step Seven: Backward planning begins here. Start with the end in mind. How will you know that students have proficiency in the standards? Create assessments or performance tasks for your units of study.

Step Eight: Include other vital programs or unique strategies in your design process. Again, they will vary based on your grade, school, and teaching style. Make sure you know what you will create time for over a week, month, term, or year. A few examples may include: Advisory, SMART readers, Library/Media, digital citizenship, AVID, choice reading, SEL lessons, book clubs, coding, self-paced or project-based learning, TedEd, Buddy Reading, Genius Hour, internships, virtual or in-person Field Trips, Mystery Guests or Readers.

Step Nine: Outline your weekly schedule into instructional blocks so that you clearly know the time blocks you have and where the special programs and strategies might fall. This will reflect your priorities and create some consistency and predictability for students. From this foundation you will then design learning experiences.

Step Ten: Develop engaging learning experiences for each unit of study thinking about the types of learning you want students to do. This is one of the most fun, creative, inspiring responsibilities for teachers, and will be discussed in significant detail later in the chapter.

Step Eleven: Write daily lesson plans that include differentiation strategies, formative assessments, reteaching, and extension opportunities. To reduce stress and find a sustainable work-life balance, you will want to batch daily lesson plans for at least two weeks at a time, then revise them daily based on the needs of your students.

Step Twelve: Teach, assess, and reflect. The instructional design process doesn't really have an end point. You will enact your best-laid plans, teach, assess, reteach, reassess, and reflect on how well your design supported student growth and learning, and use that to inform the way you design the next day, week, unit, term, or year of learning.

Elementary teachers have a significant challenge in creating learning blocks for all subjects. Each schedule will vary based on many unique factors at each school, but Figure 9.2 provides a sample Week-at-a-Glance for early elementary grades. It's important to note that science, social studies, and health content are often integrated into reading and writing blocks.

Time	Monday	Tuesday	Wednesday	Thursday	Friday
7:50–8:00	Morning Welcome & Attendance				
8:00–9:30	Reading				
9:30–9:45	Recess				
9:45–10:00	Snack & Calendar				
10:00–11:05	Writing	Math	Science	Math	Math
11:05–11:45	PE	Library	Math	Art and Health (alternating weeks)	PE
11:45–12:20	Lunch				
12:20–1:00	Math	Music	Social Studies	Writing	Writing
1:00–1:50	Choice Projects & Intervention Block	Choice Projects & Intervention Block	Early Release for Professional Learning Communities (PLCs)	Choice Projects & Intervention Block	Genius Hour
1:50–2:05	Recess			Recess	
2:05–2:30	Optimistic Closure Activity & Pack Up			Optimistic Closure Activity & Pack Up	
2:30	Dismissal			Dismissal	

Figure 9.2 Elementary Week-at-a-Glance.

As you begin the instructional design process, think through the knowledge and skills that your students need to master as the school year or term progresses. You may want to use Teacher Templates 9.1 and 9.2 to help prioritize your planning.

Format for a Learning Plan

Use this template as well as your state and district standards to create a brief overview of the material that will be part of your learning plan for the year or term.

Essential Units	Optional Units	Enrichment Units	Extra Practice Units

TEACHER TEMPLATE 9.2
Include Key Dates When Creating a Learning Plan

As you think through the yearlong or course learning plan, keep in mind some of the important dates that can affect instruction. Use this list and your school district's calendar to determine important dates in the school term.

1. _____ The last day of school
2. _____ The first day of school for students
3. _____ The grading periods throughout the year
4. _____ School breaks and holidays when school is not in session
5. _____ Religious holidays
6. _____ Days with an assembly schedule
7. _____ The 100th Day of school
8. _____ District meetings
9. _____ Teacher in-service days when students are not present
10. _____ Evaluation or certification deadlines
11. _____ Open house/back to school nights
12. _____ Standardized testing dates
13. _____ Benchmark assessment dates
14. _____ Deadlines for professional goals
15. _____ Professional development meetings
16. _____ Early release or late start days
17. _____ End-of-the-month emergency drills

Other dates specific to your school: _____

_____

_____

_____

_____

_____

_____

_____

_____

_____

_____

_____

_____

_____

Create Unit Plans

Once you have the yearlong or course learning plan, you, your teaching partner, and maybe even your generative AI assistant will build unit plans. Unit plans are the intermediate step between a yearlong learning plan and daily plans. When you create unit plans, you divide the topics into smaller blocks and determine roughly how you will teach them.

In the list that follows, you will find some of the features that will guide you as you plan each unit. You may also want to use Teacher Template 9.3 to guide your planning process and for your written unit plans.

- Determine essential knowledge and skills based on the endurance, leverage, and readiness criteria discussed earlier. Using state and district guidelines, as well as your instructional materials, identify the essential knowledge and skills that students must master during the unit.

- Determine your students' prior knowledge. A crucial step in preparing unit plans is to first determine what your students already know about the topic. This will dictate the activities you will include because it will provide you with information about how you should approach the various topics in the unit.

- Determine the length of the unit. To create plans for a unit of study, you must decide how long the unit will take, from the first objective to the final assessment. The length of time you plan to spend on a unit will be an important factor in determining the activities you need to plan.

- Create assessments of learning. Using backward design, determine how you will assess student proficiency on the knowledge and skills they are learning at the end of the unit. Beginning with the end in mind will inform the learning experiences that best support students to demonstrate mastery through the assessment.

- Brainstorm and research engaging and effective strategies to facilitate student learning. With the support of your teaching partner, mentor, generative AI tools, and the internet, take the time to brainstorm and conduct research to generate activities that will interest your students as you explore the material in the unit. You will need a variety of activities that will interest students, appeal to students with different learning preferences, and provide opportunities for students to engage in the four C's: critical thinking, collaboration, communication, and creativity.

- Select appropriate activities. Make a list of the activities that you believe would be most useful to your students in the sequence in which you want to facilitate them. Do they invite student voice, choice, and agency? Do they encourage students to take ownership of their learning? What differentiation strategies will you use? (See Section Eight for differentiation ideas.)

- Select materials and resources. With a timeline and prior knowledge firmly established, you can gather the instructional materials you need. What curriculum does your school provide? Are there online materials, videos, or digital tools that will enhance learning? Do your colleagues have instructional materials to recommend? Do the materials support differentiated instruction?

Format for a Unit Plan

You may want to use this as a template for creating your unit plans, customizing it as necessary to fit your needs.

Unit title: _____

Dates: _____

Objectives: _____
_____
_____

Materials and resources needed: _____
_____
_____

Essential knowledge and skills for mastery: _____
_____
_____

Activities/differentiation strategies: _____
_____
_____
_____
_____

Formative assessments: _____
_____
_____
_____
_____

Summative assessments: _____
_____
_____
_____
_____
_____

From *The First-Year Teacher's Survival Guide, 5th Edition*, by Michelle Cummings. Copyright © 2024 by John Wiley & Sons, Inc. Reproduced by permission.

CREATE DAILY LESSON PLANS

Although a yearlong learning plan or course overview and unit plans are the basis for your curriculum planning, your daily lesson plans are what will make instruction come to life for your students. Your daily lesson plans should follow a format that makes it easy for you to consult them during class.

Some teachers design their own planning templates and add information for each section. Other teachers use paper plans or online tools to develop daily lesson plans. Still others put their daily plans in a learning management system or slide deck. Choose the format that meets your school requirements and your personal organization style. Keep these pointers in mind to make sure that the lessons you plan are not only effective but also easy to manage:

- Although you will vary your lessons, routines are valuable for student learning and streamlining your planning process. Establish some discussion protocols and thinking routines (see Project Zero for more ideas: pz.harvard.edu) so that students gain competence with the structures.

- Establish consistency with your special programs so they occur on the same day each week. This creates predictability for you and the students. Some examples include: SMART readers, Library/Media, digital citizenship, AVID, or choice reading. Depending on your grade level and subject area, your routines may include: SEL check-in question on Mondays, self-paced Tuesdays, Buddy Reading on Wednesdays, Genius Hour Thursdays, or Field Studies/Field Trips on the first Friday.

- No matter what you have planned to do each day, you should include the three SEL Signature Practices from CASEL (CASEL.org):

  - First, you have a brief welcoming, inclusive opening to create community and bring the voices of all students into the room. This may be a "do now" with a share out.

  - Second, you must also include some of the myriad engagement strategies such as gallery walks or fishbowl discussions that facilitate individual and collective learning opportunities.

  - Third, end the lesson with an optimistic closure that allows students to reflect on and consolidate their learning. This practice leaves students with a sense of purpose and looking forward to the next lesson.

- Your lesson plans should be written for your own use. Even though substitute teachers, administrators, or other evaluators may ask to see your plans from time to time, you should plan for your own benefit. If you are in doubt about how much to write, begin by writing detailed plans to give yourself a needed boost of confidence.

What to Include in Your Plans

The following list will help you as you begin to write your daily lesson plans. There may be other items that you will find useful to include, such as essential questions, but the listed items will constitute a good beginning. You will also find that you do not have to cover all the items in this list in one class period or learning block. Instead, choose the items from this list that will be most effective in helping your students learn on the day for which you are creating plans.

Standards: Refer to your district or state guidelines for what students should know and be able to do at the end of a grade level. To reach a learning destination, you need to know where you are going. Having a strong understanding of these goals allows you to align instruction to help students reach them.

Learning Targets: Breaking standards into longer term objectives and then specific daily learning targets helps students take ownership of their learning. Write learning targets as "I can" statements in student-friendly language.

Materials and Tech Tools: You should determine what resources you need to teach an effective and engaging lesson.

Assessment of Prior Knowledge: You must assess your students' prior knowledge before you begin teaching a lesson to determine exactly what you need to review, introduce, or extend for students depending on their entry point.

Opening Activity: Always plan a brief welcoming, inclusive opening to create community and bring the voices of all students into the room. This may be as simple as a "do now" activity with a share out, or any of the host of CASEL SEL Signature Practices opening activities.

Anticipatory Set: Creating anticipation among your students can be part of the opening activity in your class each day. An interesting anticipatory set allows for discovery learning and gives students a chance to shift gears mentally to engage in the lesson they are about to begin. (For more information on opening and closing strategies, see Section Four.)

Mini-Lessons/Direct Instruction: Determine what direct instruction, if any, is necessary for students to be successful. Teachers sometimes deliver this instruction in person to the whole class or small groups. Some teachers pre-record a mini lesson for students to use as a resource in their learning or in a Flipped Classroom for students to watch before attending class. Carefully plan what you are going to do or say and point out where students may develop misconceptions.

Engaging Student Activities: Use a wide range of independent, collaborative, and guided practice activities that will appeal to students with a variety of learning preferences and interests. Be careful to include the 4Cs—critical thinking, creativity, collaboration, and communication.

Differentiation: Allow for differences in student abilities, readiness, and rate of learning by preparing alternative activities that provide extension or reteaching opportunities.

Optimistic Closure: Close each class with an activity designed to reflect on and reinforce learning. This practice leaves students with a sense of purpose and looking forward to the next lesson. Elementary teachers do this several times a day at the end of instructional blocks and at the end of the day.

Homework/Additional Practice: Consider the purpose of giving students work to do at home and any equity or access issues that could arise. Is additional practice needed? Are you encouraging home reading for emerging readers? Do students have the necessary internet access?

Formative Assessments: You will assess formally and informally almost every day. Be sure to include a variety of assessments in each unit of study. Be sure to include formative and summative assessments to make it easy to evaluate your students' progress.

Student Reflection: Include time for students to reflect on what they have learned during class, connections with other topics, and what they plan to learn next.

Teacher Reflection: Leave space in your daily plans to record your successes, failures, or any other information that will allow you to teach this lesson more successfully in the future.

Use Teacher Template 9.4 for creating your daily lesson plans, customizing it as necessary to fit your needs.

TEACHER TEMPLATE 9.4

Format for Daily Lesson Plans

You may want to use this format to create daily lesson plans that will be easy to follow by filling in the sections you need to cover each day. Although you may not get to all the items on this template every day, you can see at-a-glance what you have done and what you may still want to include in your instruction.

Class/Grade Level: _____ Lesson Topic: _____ Date: _____

Standards: _____

Learning Targets: _____

Materials and Tech Tools: _____

Assessment of Prior Knowledge: _____

Opening Activity/Anticipatory Set: _____

Mini Lesson or Direct Instruction: _____

Engaging Student Activities: _____

Differentiation Strategies: _____

Optimistic Closure: _____

Homework (if any): _____

Assessments: (formative and/or summative) _____

Student Reflection Activity: _____

Teacher Reflection: _____

How to Monitor and Adjust a Lesson

Monitor student responses, both verbal and nonverbal, to each part of the lesson. Students may feel frustrated or have trouble staying on task. When such behavior seems to last more than a few minutes, you must be prepared to adjust your lesson plan to meet your students' needs. Although the methods of adjusting your plan will vary from class to class, you can quickly correct most situations. The following tips will help you turn a frustrating lesson into a successful one as quickly as possible:

- Remember that often just switching to another learning modality will engage students enough that they will work to overcome any small frustrations.

- Break down tasks into smaller pieces and allow students to tackle them in pairs or small groups.

- Call a stop to the lesson and assess the situation. Check for understanding to determine what your students already know to avoid needlessly repeating information or leaving them behind by moving to a subject they are not ready to process.

- Involve your students in decisions to adjust lessons. Ask them why the lesson is not working for them and then ask for their suggestions.

ALWAYS HAVE A BACKUP PLAN

Few situations in a classroom are more dismaying than realizing that you did not plan enough to engage students throughout the learning block. In a situation like this, you must have a backup plan ready. When you write your daily plans, you should jot down ideas that would be useful as backup plans. To help you write backup plans, here are three possible ideas that you can adapt for your students.

First, you or your generative AI tools can brainstorm a list of interesting activities that are related to the general topic under study and will last anywhere from ten to thirty minutes. When you need to use a backup plan, you can quickly scan your list to select an appropriate activity.

"After a few years, you begin to feel comfortable, but it doesn't start that way. I remember looking at other teachers starting each class with ease and interacting with kids like the Pied Piper. It can be a little daunting at first. Now I walk into classes and actually find myself enjoying the little ways kids try to test you because it's an opportunity to build a relationship. That first year, anything that seems to lead a lesson astray is a travesty in your mind. It's okay to be nervous and to have those moments where you wonder how you're going to get your students to buy in; everybody has them."

Kevin Healy, 11 years' experience

Second, in a blended learning environment, you will already be engaging students with digital tools. Some students have access to personalized learning modules on a variety of online programs like Amplify, Dreambox, Edmentum, Everfi, Imagine Learning, iReady, IXL, Newsela, Panorama and more. Maybe you have created backup activities online or have chosen a quick ready-made activity on any number of digital tools, such as: BrainPop, Canva, Curipod, EdPuzzle, Flip, Flocabulary, GoNoodle, Google Apps for Education, Kahoot!, Khan Academy, Nearpod, Padlet, Pear Deck, Prodigy, Quizlet, Quizziz, SeeSaw, and many more.

Still other teachers keep an eye out for good backup plans all year long. They maintain collections of reading passages, games, and other learning activities.

DIRECT INSTRUCTION OR STUDENT-CENTERED ACTIVITIES?

> "Student voice and student-centered practice are the cornerstones of building and sustaining a strong classroom culture. If you take on the task of being an educator, you take on the task of often putting the needs of students in your classroom before your own. When you live in that spirit the more successful and joyful you will be in this work!"
>
> *Evalaurene Jean-Charles,*
> *5 years' experience, Founder,*
> *BlackonBlackEducation.com*

Should teachers be a sage on the stage or guide on the side? In general, when the purpose is to have students actively learning and thinking, teachers are guides and facilitators. When the purpose is to convey information so that students have the knowledge they need to move forward in learning, teachers take the stage for a brief time. Both strategies play a role in classrooms when used under the right circumstances and for the right purposes.

Direct instruction, on the one hand, generally involves a teacher standing in front of a classroom delivering information and is considered a more passive-learning experience for students. Student-centered instruction, on the other hand, involves a much wider range of activities where students engage in active learning such as discussions, experiments, project based learning, self-directed, and collaborative work.

Both of these categories of instruction have their place when used skillfully and appropriately as part of a well-planned lesson. Direct instruction to provide a mini lesson (no more than ten to fifteen minutes) helps students to learn. One mistake that many inexperienced teachers make is to rely too heavily on direct instruction methods.

As a rule of thumb, student-based activities should dominate the lesson. You are a more effective classroom leader while moving around the room working with groups of students and individuals who are working independently. When you plan instruction, think of yourself as that supportive guide on the side rather than as the sole source of knowledge in the room. With this mindset, it will be easy for you to select activities that engage students more fully.

HOW TO RECORD A MINI LESSON

One of the most effective ways to deliver a mini lesson is to prerecord it. It's never been easier to create a pre-recorded video of your mini lesson and post it on your learning management system. It is then available for students (and perhaps home adults) to watch and re-watch as needed, if they have access to the internet. You can show it to students, if the class is in a large group, or have them watch it independently if it's a self-paced learning day. Simply follow these five steps:

1. Determine a clear learning focus for the mini lesson.
2. Build four or five slides in a deck (slides are visual, not text heavy).
3. Select a video recording product like: Screencastify, Canva video, or Screen-cast-o-matic.
4. Create a short video (ten minutes or less).
5. Share it with students in your learning management system (LMS).
6. To increase engagement, you can upload the video to your LMS or a digital tool like Ed Puzzle or Nearpod to embed questions at various points in the video.

HOW TO USE SCAFFOLDING TO HELP STUDENTS LEARN

Scaffolding instruction is a valuable instructional strategy that can make information more accessible for students. When teachers scaffold instruction, they divide the content into small parts and provide explicit help with each part. Scaffolding differs from differentiation in that the content does not change, but rather is presented to students in small, manageable segments.

Although there are many ways to scaffold instruction, there are some strategies that tend to be more successful than others in helping students access the material once you have broken it into smaller segments. Here are some of those strategies that you can adapt for your students:

- Modeling. Model everything. Use plenty of models, examples, nonexamples, and samples to make the information as clear as possible for students.
- Provide sentence frames in a fill-in-the-blank format to create a focused starting point for student written or verbal responses.
- Build vocabulary wealth by explicitly teaching content vocabulary. Before beginning a segment of the material, teach the terms that students will encounter so that they will be familiar with them as they work.
- Discuss the specific learning strategies that students can use to unlock the material. When you share ideas about the strategies that help them learn, you empower students to make decisions about effective long-range work habits as well as how to deal with the task at hand.
- Show students videos or movie clips or provide other forms of media to help them understand the material.
- Demonstrate the process you want students to use as they work. While you do the demonstration, carefully explain each step.
- Have students brainstorm all that they know about the content to activate prior knowledge. They can share this information first with partners and then with the whole group.

- As you present information, stop frequently to review the content and check for understanding to ensure that everyone is learning.
- Have students collaborate in groups or pairs to share strategies and information that can help them unlock the content.
- Provide frequent feedback as students work on each segment to prevent student misunderstanding and to encourage mastery.
- Use visual, auditory, reading/writing, and kinesthetic modalities to appeal to student learning preferences.
- Ask students to complete graphic organizers so that they can break down the information and express it in their own words.

The 4Cs and Project Based Learning (PBL)

The 4Cs originated from a report by Partnership for 21st Century Skills (P21). This coalition developed a framework to illustrate the skills and knowledge students need for personal and professional success. The 4Cs endure as meaningful learning and innovation skills. P21 joined BattelleForKids.org, where you can download the framework. (Some thinkers have proposed a variety of 5th Cs to add to the list, including computation, connectedness, citizenship, and confidence.) This section will focus on the original 4Cs and the ways in which project-based learning (PBL) inspires all four.

Let's start with a few definitions within the context of learning:

- Communication

    Students will learn to listen well and express ideas effectively in many formats to many audiences, including multilingually.
- Collaboration

    Students will learn to work well together to achieve a goal. They will share responsibilities and value the contributions of others on diverse teams.
- Critical Thinking

    Students will use reasoning skills to pose questions, analyze information, solve problems, make decisions, and reflect on the result.
- Creativity

    Students will develop and enact new ideas, with a growth mindset, welcoming feedback, failure, and revision as worthwhile components of the creation process.

All 4Cs come together in PBL where students pose a question about a real problem and work together, over a longer period of time, to develop and enact their solution. Students often demonstrate their learning with a presentation to an authentic audience. PBL requires students to develop a driving question, investigate it using interdisciplinary skills, and develop a creative and innovative solution to the question. Because students care deeply about the topic, PBL increases engagement, deepens learning, and brings incredible ideas into the world.

Here are seven steps to get started with PBL. Planning for PBL has never been easier with generative AI support and so many free, standards-aligned lesson plans available online at PBLWorks, Teachers Pay Teachers, and SubjectToClimate to name a few. If you have concerns, start small.

Step One: Create a classroom culture that values and nurtures the 4Cs.

Step Two: Identify the unit of study and the interdisciplinary standards that students will work toward through a PBL experience.

Step Three: Brainstorm an overarching question or theme with the assistance of colleagues or generative AI tools.

Step Four: Establish the success criteria or rubric that you will use to assess students' final products, which may include videos, podcasts, campaigns, music, art, presentations, writing, models, and more.

Step Five: Download or gather resources to support student inquiry. Ask the teacher-librarian for assistance in gathering resources.

Step Six: Download or create lesson plans that facilitate the whole PBL process from brainstorming real questions, mysteries, or projects with students, to establishing collaborative groups who investigate their question and presenting a final product.

Step Seven: Reflect on the impact that PBL had on student learning.

Want to learn more about PBL? Here are a few websites and books to explore.

PBL Works (pblworks.org): This comprehensive site offers handbooks, projects, lesson plans, tools, and professional development to support teachers in implementing PBL in classrooms. It is part of the Buck Institute for Education.

SubjectToClimate (subjecttoclimate.org/lesson-plans): This website is accessible to all with ready-to-use, multidisciplinary lesson plans and resources for all grade levels. The chatbot, Climate Socrates, will answer all your questions about climate.

Teaching Channel with Learner's Edge (teachingchannel.com): This site hosts a large video library. Click "video library" and search by keyword to find videos of teaching practices and interviews about project-based learning and so much more.

Edutopia (www.edutopia.org/project-based-learning-guide-resources): This site offers lots of articles and resources to support you and your students on the PBL journey.

Project Based Teaching: How to Create Rigorous and Engaging Learning Practices by **Suzie Boss and John Larmer:** A guide for K–12 teachers on how to implement PBL with examples, tools, and tips.

Keep It Real With PBL: A Practical Guide for Planning Project-Based Learning by **Jennifer R. Pieratt:** Pieratt wrote two guidebooks, one for elementary and one for secondary teachers.

How to Teach Sustainability: Climate and Energy Education

PBL is also a powerful vehicle for students to study sustainability. Next Generation Science Standards (NGSS) require that students, starting in elementary grades, gain proficiency in core ideas around earth and space science (ESS), including sustainability, climate, energy, and weather. Providing students an education about sustainability allows them to connect personally with these complex topics. It helps students develop critical climate thinking skills and empowers them to explore innovative solutions to address climate and energy challenges. Teachers can infuse these topics across subject areas, not just limit them to the science curriculum.

"My first-graders think monarch butterflies are magical creatures. Over the last few years, the population in our school garden has dwindled. Unusually hot and dry summers turned out to be the problem affecting the butterfly's food source, milkweed. Students decided to find a solution to encourage the butterflies to return. In celebration of Earth Day, all students received milkweed seeds to grow at home! The students felt such pride knowing they could make a difference, and be part of a real solution. This was one of the most impactful moments in my classroom in the last few years. Students saw the effects in their own garden and were determined to find a solution!"

Elaine Makarevich, 30 years' experience

Yet, there are many barriers to teachers facilitating learning experiences around the vital knowledge and skills required by NGSS. Five of the most significant barriers include:

- Many teachers need more background knowledge. Few teachers in classrooms today learned about sustainability, climate change, and renewable energy in school or in teacher preparation programs.
- These subjects can surface uncomfortable emotions like grief, anger, and anxiety.
- Some educators don't see how sustainability connects to what they already teach.
- Even with the scientific background knowledge, teachers may lack standards-aligned instructional materials to teach their grade level in developmentally appropriate ways.
- Providing a local context for learning requires understanding the ways that sustainability, climate change, and energy affect your community.

There are several strategies you can use to overcome these barriers, meet the learning needs of students, and give them a sense of agency in the face of the climate crisis.

- Find others in your school, district, or online educator communities who are interested in learning more about sustainability, climate change, and energy education.
- Analyze your school's science and social studies curricula for helpful resources.
- Explore the free K–12 resources, professional development, and articles at SubjectToClimate.org.

- Watch the Climate Solutions 101 videos at ProjectDrawdown.org and discuss them with colleagues.
- You don't need to know everything before you begin. You can start small and learn with your students what the key issues are facing your community and what local leaders propose as solutions.

How to Use the Issues-Academics-Standards Framework

The topic of sustainability reaches across subject areas, not just science. In fact, Estefanía Pihen González, founder of Hahami.org and Project Director at Climate Action Pathways for Schools, developed an Issues-Academics-Standards (IAS) Framework to guide teachers in developing lessons about sustainability that are nested within a core academic topic (Figure 9.3).

To align the issue, the academic area, and the standard, teachers ask three questions before selecting activities.

Question One. Issues: What is an issue that connects to social sustainability, climate change, energy, or environmental sustainability that your students won't stop talking about? What issues are happening in your community? It is crucial to remember that, when introducing an issue, students learn not just about the causes and consequences, but also about what is being done to address that issue. This ensures that lessons are solutions-oriented rather than focused on doom and gloom.

Question Two. Academics: What academic content do you plan to teach that would be a good vehicle to explore that issue? This may be for lessons or a unit of study in any subject area. Ideally, you connect the issue through academic content in multiple subjects. For example, if one issue for fourth graders is deforestation and they are about to study adverbs in English Language Arts, then the lessons can be infused with videos and writing experiences focused on adverbs through the content of deforestation.

Question Three. Standards: Which standards in that academic content area connect to the issue? Once you have determined the academic topic(s) you will link to the issue, use your state's standards to begin shaping the activities that will be part of your lesson and/or unit. Think of teaching strategies that allow you to teach the subject matter content while also learning about the issue.

While designing lesson plans, use the principles promoted by Education for Sustainable Development (ESD). The principles include: critical thinking; systemic thinking, cooperative learning, sharing personal and community values, local and global citizenship, innovative and curious thinking, contextualized learning, fostering empathy, and envisioning better future scenarios or futures thinking.

In an example for high school, perhaps tenth graders care deeply about not being able to swim in a local lake. They are about to study civic engagement in social studies. State social studies standards often ask students to analyze how human activity has changed the

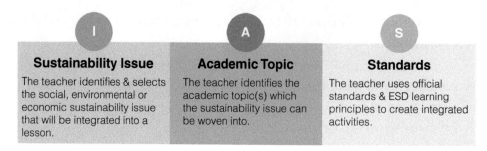

| **I**
Sustainability Issue
The teacher identifies & selects the social, environmental or economic sustainability issue that will be integrated into a lesson. | **A**
Academic Topic
The teacher identifies the academic topic(s) which the sustainability issue can be woven into. | **S**
Standards
The teacher uses official standards & ESD learning principles to create integrated activities. |

Apply I.A.S. as a design method to create an integrated lesson plan

includes learning activities that have integrated content about the issue (causes, consequences) and for the issue (actions, solutions) into the learning process of an academic topic

Figure 9.3 The Issues-Academics-Standards (IAS) Framework.

"Start with what you know or a skill you need to teach. For an ELA lesson on tone, I had my sixth graders pick three specific feelings and write three separate sentences sharing their feelings about climate change. Students first identified feelings like anxious, frustrated, worried; then used three describing words for each feeling to write their sentence. Students found safety and relief putting feelings into words, sharing them with others, and practicing a content-related skill."

Yen-Yen Chiu, 22 years' experience

physical environment. The students' interest in the lake, explored in the context of social studies and aligned with a state standard, creates an opportunity for students to pursue an independent project exploring their issue and proposing solutions to it.

Activities to Engage Students

Based on your answers to the preceding I-A-S questions, there are many ways to engage students in learning around sustainability, climate, and energy:

- Organize outdoor learning, community service, and field experiences so students can connect personally with natural spaces.
- Offer project-based learning (PBL) interdisciplinary projects in which the students pose a question about sustainability, climate change, and energy in their homes, schools, or communities and develop solutions. The Bye Bye Plastic Bags initiative came out of one such class project.
- Show a video clip or short documentary on a sustainability question relevant to student interests and have them discuss it in small groups, then write a reflection based on your prompt.
- Study current events and ask students to brainstorm what they would have done and what governments should do in response.
- Every April 22, celebrate Earth Day with resources from EarthDay.org.

Rather than focusing on the issues in the entire world, teachers may create opportunities for students to study how to improve conditions in their local communities or at their school. Some teachers and students work with their schools to implement:

- Composting
- Green schoolyards
- School gardens
- Farm-to-school cafeteria programs
- Renewable energy such as electric school buses and solar power
- Energy efficiency with Net Zero Schools

Reducing Climate Anxiety

One of the barriers teachers face to integrating sustainability, climate, and energy education is the feelings of fear, sadness, and anxiety that can surface when we contemplate such a weighty topic. Sadly, it is true that some students and teachers are grappling with climate anxiety. The good news is that psychologists recommend easing these worries by gaining a sense of agency through taking action. So, learning the facts and finding ways to take action can actually reduce climate anxiety.

Helping students to name their emotions and develop a plan of action is a social-emotional learning skill that they can use for a lifetime. Responding to age-appropriate reflection questions may help students relieve their eco-anxiety.

- What feelings does the climate crisis bring up for you?
- What could you do to help and be part of the solutions?
- What knowledge or skills could you contribute to the work?
- Are there one or more solutions that really inspire you?
- What efforts are happening in your community that you might join?
- Who among your friends and family might join you?

Professional Development and Ready-to-Use Resources

Sustainability in this context means meeting the needs of the current generation without jeopardizing the ability of future generations to do the same. Empowering students with the knowledge and skills required by the Next Generation Science Standards (NGSS) can help make that possible. Education is one of the critical strategies to stabilize Earth's climate by 2050. By integrating instruction around the climate crisis, teachers empower students to adapt and create the changes needed in their own communities. There is extensive professional development, ready-to-use resources, and videos available at these websites.

Project Drawdown (drawdown.org): Project Drawdown centers on a vast collection of climate solutions along with articles and professional development resources. The free mini-course, Climate Solutions 101, offers six fifteen-minute videos focused on the solutions to climate challenges.

SubjectToClimate (SubjectToClimate.org): SubjectToClimate has high-quality, robust professional development and an extensive catalog of teacher-created, standards-aligned lesson plans. Climate Socrates is an AI helpbot that can answer all your questions around sustainability, climate change, and energy education as well as pedagogical strategies.

Find the professional development homepage at: subjecttoclimate.org/professional-learning. Find the lesson plan homepage at: subjecttoclimate.org/lesson-plans.

Teaching Climate Change for Grades 6–12: Empowering Science Teachers to Take on the Climate Crisis Through NGSS **(Rutledge.com):** Search "teaching climate" on the homepage to find a book by Kelley T. Lê that helps secondary science teachers develop curriculum to teach to NGSS standards.

Resources for Further Exploration

Be Smart (pbs.org/show/its-okay-be-smart/episodes/): This PBS Show, *It's Okay, Be Smart*, hosted by Dr. Joe Hanson, provides fascinating ten- to fifteen-minute videos on many science topics, including sustainability, climate change, and energy.

Climate Literacy and Energy Awareness Network (CLEAN) (cleanet.org): Search through an extensive, curated collection of free, high-quality teaching materials to engage students in learning about climate and energy. CLEAN also offers professional development and a newsletter.

Earth Day (Earthday.org): Earth Day has dynamic fact sheets and toolkits on twenty-plus subjects connected to environmental science as well as strategies for engaging in Earth Day.

The National Aeronautics and Space Administration (NASA) (climate.nasa.gov/for-educators): NASA offers an extensive library of videos, lessons, and K–12 resources to engage students in a study of climate change, STEM, and more. NASA also provides additional links to sites such as: Climate Kids, Jet Propulsion Lab (JPL) Education, NASA Wavelength, NOAA, and more.

National Center for Science Education (NCSE) (ncse.ngo): Provides lesson plans to help teachers teach accurately and confidently. Select "Teaching Resources" from the main menu.

Roots and Shoots (rootsandshoots.org): Jane Goodall's program for youth focuses on service learning projects and provides teachers with tools, training, and resources to live Jane Goodall's credo: "What you do makes a difference, and you have to decide what kind of difference you want to make."

United Nations Sustainable Development Goals (sdgs.un.org/goals): Explore the UN SDGs at this site.

Maintain a Bank of Activity Ideas

Many experienced teachers maintain a bank of activity ideas to save time when planning lessons, ensure that students are engaged, and to always have fresh ideas handy when you plan instruction. In the list that follows, you will find twenty-five activity ideas to use as a base for your own activity bank. Consider how some of these activity ideas can connect students with the content and learning goals. Have students:

1. Ask and investigate a question or problem they care deeply about
2. Reflect on their growth as a "practitioner" (reader, mathematician, writer, scientist, historian, artist, musician, woodworker, chef, etc.)
3. Take a virtual fieldtrip
4. Write a journal entry
5. Make a blog post
6. Create or maintain a digital portfolio
7. Take and share photographs
8. View a video clip
9. Play a game online
10. Host a game show
11. Write a personal narrative
12. Create a bumper sticker
13. Make a video
14. Invent and play a board game
15. Write a caption
16. Complete a scavenger hunt
17. Make a collage
18. Create a wall of fame
19. Create a flowchart
20. Make a flag or banner
21. Create a greeting card
22. Teach the class
23. Draw a diagram
24. Write an exposé
25. Invent a better way

Class Discussions toward Civil Discourse

If you have fond memories of classes in which everyone seemed to be involved in discussing a topic of burning importance, you probably want to help your students have that experience, too. Remember how you left the room exhilarated, still exploring ideas, and in full possession of strong opinions that you did not hold when class began?

Class discussions are an excellent way to facilitate instruction that students will remember long after the class is over. Best of all, class discussions create active learners who are building their critical-thinking and communication skills while expanding their knowledge of a topic.

It's vitally important for teachers to be able to facilitate discussions on a wide range of current events and topics of study as you help students develop skills for civil discourse that leads to mutual understanding. The goal is to teach students how to think critically and how to communicate respectfully. Teachers have a crucial role in facilitating discussions.

1. Start with some personal reflection. Can you engage in respectful dialogue with people who have ideas different from your own? Do you appreciate how cultural backgrounds influence how people communicate? Can you listen to people with different perspectives without interrupting?

2. Build a supportive, inclusive community within the classroom with activities that help you get to know students and students get to know each other. Develop and model a culture of openness and curiosity across academic content areas with open-ended questions.

3. Create a safe and open forum for the discussion of ideas. The classroom needs to affirm human dignity, critique ideas, not individuals, and remain free from personal attacks.

4. Establish, model, teach, and enforce ground rules or norms for discussions. Teach the value of dialogue in class discussions, which is different from debate.

5. Teach students an age-appropriate Claim-Evidence-Reasoning (CER) method to support their opinions with evidence and connect the claim and evidence in their reasoning. They will use this in writing and verbal discussions across the curriculum.

6. Utilize strategies that engage all voices in the room in pairs, triads, small group, whole group, or with digital tools like Flip or Padlet.

7. Start small to practice with discussions about topics and questions related to classroom agreements, school rules, divergent strategies to solve math problems, a piece of literature, poetry, or songs. Move on to students analyzing and rewriting letters to the editor.

8. Debrief at the end of discussions to reflect on the quality of the discourse and check the temperature of the class.

Over the course of the year, controversial issues will arise connected to the curriculum, current events, and students' lived experiences in the world. Anticipate what issues may arise; prepare ahead of time and talk with colleagues, supervisors, and mentors to develop confidence in facilitating discussions and processing controversial issues in a way that helps students build critical thinking and civil discourse skills.

What role should you take in a class discussion? First, envision yourself as the facilitator of the discussion. Your job is to prepare for the discussion, maintain a safe and open forum, watch the time, and provide time to debrief at the end.

Discussions will take place in pairs, small groups, and large groups; they will span every subject area and grade level. Some will focus on analysis of a story or solutions to a math problem. Others will span the gamut of subject areas and current events. The level of facilitation needed will depend on student communication skills and the sensitivity of the issue. Think about your role in three basic components: what to do to prepare for the discussion, what to do during the discussion, and what to do after the discussion is over.

Before the Discussion

- Develop discussion procedures with students. Post procedures in a prominent place in the classroom. You should consider how you want your students to communicate with one another and with you.

- Teach students to disagree respectfully with each other or with you, using sentence stems like:

  - "I feel that…."

  - "I suggest that…."

  - "I would like to add…."

  - "I respectfully disagree with ___ because ____."

  - "I have a different idea about that…."

- Convey the purpose of the discussion. What outcomes are you hoping for? Do you want students to analyze an issue? Combine information in a new way? Brainstorm new ideas?

- Create the questions your students will discuss. Successful questions for class discussions require higher-order thinking skills. For the first discussion session, prepare ten thought-provoking questions. Use your students' reactions to gauge how to prepare for future class discussions. When appropriate, give students advance copies of questions so that they can prepare.

- Arrange the furniture to encourage student-to-student dialogue. Determine if students will sit in pairs, small groups, or the whole group. Set up chairs so that students can see one another's faces.

During the Discussion

- Follow through with procedures. As the discussion gets under way, remind students of the importance of the expectations and procedures for class discussions. Be steadfast in implementing them. It may be difficult for your students to adjust to them at first, but with persistence, you will succeed in having productive class discussions.

- Introduce the topics of discussion. Make sure the discussion questions are displayed visually, not just verbally.

- Teach your students the importance of supporting their opinions. When someone makes a point, prompt them with the CER model so that claims are supported by evidence and reasoning.

- Encourage deeper thinking. Elicit thoughtful responses by trying these techniques: invite a student to build on someone else's response or ask for elaboration.

- Make sure there is equity of voice and everyone can participate. Monitor the participation of highly verbal students. One easy way to do this is to give all students the same number of slips of paper. Each time someone speaks, he or she must give up one of the slips. When a student is out of slips, he or she is out of opportunities to speak.

- Recognize speakers. To determine who gets to speak, have an unbreakable object, such as a book or stuffed toy, for students to hand to one another as they take turns speaking.

- Encourage risk taking. Make it easy and nonthreatening for all students to risk answering. Encourage and validate answers when you can.

- Step back. Refrain from dominating the discussion. A class discussion works best when all students are prepared and when all students join in.

After the Discussion

- Have students reflect on the discussion by asking for:
  - Written or oral feedback on what went well
  - Suggestions for improvement
  - A retelling of the important points
  - A written or oral summary

Here are three websites to further explore strategies for teachers to facilitate discussions toward civil discourse.

Facing History and Ourselves (facinghistory.org): Use "civil discourse" as a search term to find the teacher's guide, "Fostering Civil Discourse: How Do We Talk about Issues that Matter."

National School Reform Faculty (NSRF) (nsrfharmony.org): NSRF offers many protocols for efficient communication and group processes in downloadable pdfs.

Explore the Five Whys for Inquiry, Probing Questions Exercise, Consultancy, Three Levels of Text, Block Party, and more.

Learning for Justice (learningforjustice.org): Use "civil discourse" as a search term on the site to find a compilation of strategies and articles about "Helping Students Engage in Civil Discourse."

Inclusive Practices for Teaching Difficult Histories

All the work you do to create an inclusive classroom community, where your students learn the critical thinking and communication skills to engage in civil discourse, will also support you when you teach difficult histories. A difficult history is characterized by oppression, violence, and trauma. In the history of humanity, there are many such periods, and these topics arise across content areas. Anxiety about teaching these topics and supporting student responses often means that teachers avoid teaching an accurate and inclusive history.

This is complex, sensitive, and important work. It's crucial that you know yourself, your students, and your community. The guidelines and requirements for teaching difficult histories will vary by state, district, and school, so make sure you know what is required in the school where you teach and follow those guidelines.

In this brief section, you will learn seven steps to help you identify difficult histories, engage students with promising practices, avoid practices that cause harm, and explore resources that offer more detailed guidance.

Step One: Create a positive and inclusive classroom community.

Co-create class norms with students about how to engage in respectful discourse. Acknowledge the sensitive nature of difficult histories.

(See Section Eleven for more details on creating agreements and norms.)

Step Two: Review your state standards.

Understand what the required knowledge and skills are for your grade level and subject area.

Step Three: Identify the difficult histories you will teach this year.

Some examples of difficult histories include: slavery, Holocaust, genocides, atrocities, colonization, American Indian Removal, Thanksgiving, Trail of Tears, Jim Crow, Civil Rights, and much more.

Step Four: Do your research.

Explore the resources at the end of this section as well as the specific content. What occurred during this historical period? What were the impacts of the harm caused? What does your school's instructional materials say about this time period? Are there perspectives missing? How will you highlight the strength, hope, resiliency, and heroes within oppressed or marginalized groups, in spite of the harm they were forced to endure? Consider what is developmentally appropriate for your students.

Step Five: Consult your Professional Learning Network (PLN).

Talk with your colleagues, mentor, supervisor, and PLN to learn more about the approaches they recommend.

Step Six: Avoid teaching strategies that cause harm to students.

Do not trivialize traumatic experiences with games, reenactments, and simulations.

Do not ask students to reenact a traumatic history.

Do not ask students to embody and represent a perspective that promoted hate, perpetrated atrocities, or violated the human rights of others.

Simulating traumatic events is not an effective method for creating empathy, and can, in fact, cause harm to students.

Step Seven: Engage students with promising practices.

- Highlight the purpose of the lesson or unit.
- Review class norms and expectations for engaging in the unit of study.
- Leverage primary sources to help students understand the impact of this historical period.
- *Instead of* asking students to embody an historical figure in the first person, *have them* become an expert or biographer of that historical figure.
- *Instead of* asking students to write a first-person diary entry of a victim of an atrocity, *have them* write in the third person about the people who were harmed.
- Include positive messages about the resilience and contributions of oppressed groups and historical figures within marginalized communities.

Resources for Further Study

Websites

Facing History and Ourselves (FHAO) (facinghistory.org): FHAO has free classroom resources for grades 6–12 ELA and social studies to support teaching complex moments in history. FHAO uses lessons of difficult historical periods to encourage students to stand up to bigotry and hate.

Learning for Justice (learningforjustice.org): Use "hard history" as a search term on the site to find magazines, study guides, lesson plans, and webinars on how to teach difficult histories.

National Museum of the American Indian (NMAI) (americanindian.si.edu): The Smithsonian NMAI has many high-quality resources for teachers. The NMAI Native Knowledge 360 site provides lessons, resources, virtual student programs, workshops and more to incorporate indigenous narratives and accurate information to provide new understandings about American Indians in the past and present. From the homepage, click "Education" then "Native Knowledge 360."

US Holocaust Memorial Museum (USHMM) (ushmm.org): USHMM provides valuable lesson plans, videos, posters, lectures, virtual field trips, interviews with survivors, and training materials to explore the Holocaust, antisemitism, Nazism, propaganda, other genocides and more. From the homepage, click "Teach" to discover high-quality printable and online resources.

Books

Courageous Conversation on Race: A Field Guide for Achieving Equity in Schools **by Glenn E. Singleton:** Singleton's book provides practical tools, protocols, and strategies to forge a path to progress for racial equity in schools. Explore the website to learn more about professional development opportunities (courageousconversation .com).

Everything You Wanted to Know about Indians but Were Afraid to Ask **by Anton Treuer:** A professor of Ojibwe at Bemidji State University, Dr. Treuer gives candid, funny, matter-of-fact responses to one hundred and twenty questions, including "What's the real story of Thanksgiving?" He provides a foundation for understanding and action.

Use Graphic Organizers to Engage Students

Can you imagine how hard it would be to make up a seating chart without the chart? You would have to write sentence after sentence explaining who would sit where. Instead of writing it out, you save time by using a graphic organizer. Graphic organizers are useful ways for students to organize information so that they can learn it.

Graphic organizers can help students decode, process, understand, and retain information. Further, graphic organizers can help students solve problems and comprehend material quickly. When students create graphic organizers, they can see the relationships among the important elements in the assignment. Moreover, students of all ages and ability levels can use them successfully for a variety of purposes:

- To take notes on mini lessons and readings
- To describe people, places, events, ideas, or objects

- To compare and contrast
- To determine the validity of assumptions
- To classify and categorize information
- To determine relevant details
- To see how parts make up a whole
- To solve problems
- To predict outcomes
- To plan reading and writing activities
- To understand cause and effect
- To support arguments
- To organize concepts into key components
- To analyze vocabulary words
- To organize textual material
- To identify patterns
- To create models

Online resources abound to access graphic organizers that are already designed for you and your students; try these websites:

Canva (canva.com/graphic-organizers/templates): Canva is free for teachers and students and has more than five hundred graphic organizer templates or you can design your own.

Education Oasis (educationoasis.com): At Education Oasis, you will find more than sixty downloadable or printable graphic organizers.

TPT (teacherspayteachers.com): Has over 400,000 graphic organizers, in both printable and digital formats.

Providing Models, Examples, and Samples

Unless your students are engaged in discovery learning where models would stifle their exploration, model everything from classroom procedures to anchor papers. Providing models, examples, and samples of the kinds of work that you expect from your students is key to ensuring that they know what to do and how to do it well. Many experienced teachers find that offering multiple models, examples, or samples makes it easier for students to avoid copying and to examine the excellent qualities of each instead.

As a new teacher, you may not have very many exemplars on hand to show your students. To overcome this, create one or two yourself and ask other teachers at your school for help. As soon as high-quality student exemplars are turned in, display them for others to see. These three ways of obtaining good models, examples, and samples are well worth the effort because these items will build your students' confidence and knowledge.

To make sure that you will have plenty of excellent models, examples, and samples for future use, save documents, slide decks, videos, and photographs of projects and presentations. Imagine how convenient and fun it will be next year to show a quick slideshow of some of this year's student work when you begin a new unit.

Tech Resources to Support Blended Learning

Blended learning combines digital learning experiences and face-to-face strategies to enhance student learning. Fortunately for teachers today, there are generative AI assistants and countless resources to support blended learning on the internet. Common Sense Media (CommonSense.org) is a tremendous resource that provides thorough reviews of websites and tech tools to give educators greater confidence when adopting them.

With just a bit of searching, you can discover the latest information about the content that you want to teach, lesson plans, videos, primary sources, and more to support lesson design. In addition to the lesson plans available online, you also have many technology resources and digital tools to augment and accelerate learning.

With this wealth of information and resources at your fingertips, you will find it easy to design and facilitate instruction geared to help your students succeed. In the following pages, you will explore some of the most common technology resources, digital tools, websites, and apps to engage students and enrich your instruction.

In your first year of teaching, to avoid feeling overwhelmed, streamline your digital ecosystem and select a handful of digital tools and a few trusted websites to enhance your instruction. Bookmark and organize them for ease of use.

Devices, Digital Tools, and Internet Resources to Enhance Learning

Technology integrated instruction isn't about chasing the next shiny object. It's about selecting the best tool to accomplish your and your students' goals. To guide you, consider the S.A.M.R. Model created by Dr. Ruben R. Puentedura that lays out four levels of

"Use technology in active, transformational ways—to do things with it that were impossible before, not that simply imitate paper-based practices. Swim with the sharks using VR. Control an electron microscope at a university lab far away. Collect water samples with other classrooms across the country and compare contaminants to track regional pollutants. Let students use powerful digital creation tools to express their own vision and values for the present and the future they envision."

Joseph South, Chief Innovation Officer,
ASCD/ISTE

tech integration so that you can see the range of possibilities and intentionally select the digital tools and teaching methods that can transform teaching and learning.

Substitution: Digital tools are a substitute for analog methods. For example, substituting a word processor for a pen and paper in a writing assignment.

Augmentation: Digital tools help improve functionality. For example, text-to-speech improves the writing process.

Modification: Digital tools significantly redesign learning tasks. For example, students create a video presentation that allows them to use their voice and multimedia elements to express their ideas.

Redefinition: In this most advanced use of tech integration, digital tools allow students to create and pursue tasks that were not previously possible. For example, using virtual reality to take students on immersive field trips or exploring Google Earth's Timelapse to see how the Earth has changed over time and then interviewing people in a distant location about their experience of those changes.

As teachers select strategies and technology products to enhance learning, they should start with the International Society for Technology in Education (ISTE) Standards for Students found at ISTE.org. Understanding the standards will inform how you leverage technology to help students become:

- Empowered Learners
- Digital Citizens
- Knowledge Constructors
- Innovative Designers
- Computational Thinkers
- Creative Communicators
- Global Collaborators

Digital citizenship and media literacy go hand in hand with technology-integrated instruction. Don't assume that students know how to use technology ethically and with integrity as a tool for learning. Here are two high-quality, free resources for teaching digital citizenship. Classroom teachers may provide the instruction or collaborate with your teacher-librarian or media center staff to make sure students gain these skills.

Common Sense Media (commonsense.org/education/digital-citizenship): Common Sense Media, in partnership with Project Zero at Harvard, designed developmentally appropriate lessons to address media balance and well-being, privacy and security, digital footprint and identity, relationship and communication, cyberbullying, digital drama and hate speech, and media literacy for grades K–12.

Be Internet Awesome (beinternetawesome.withgoogle.com): Designed in partnership with Google, the Net Safety Collaboration, and the Internet Keep Safe Coalition, this site offers five lessons and an adventure game to practice online safety skills, set in Interland. Pear Deck created flashcards and presentations to support this curriculum.

No matter how comfortable you may be with a device, software, or app, integrating technology resources into your instructional practices takes careful thought and planning to ensure success. Make sure to address equity of access issues when integrating technology into instruction. Do all students have the necessary devices? If the tech resource is to be used at home, do all students have access to the internet at home? As you begin planning how to integrate these resources into your classroom, you will need to work with colleagues and supervisors to determine the best ways to overcome barriers to access.

Here are tips on how to integrate devices, digital tools, and web resources into your lesson plans.

DEVICES

Many schools and districts provide 1:1 portable electronic devices for student use at school and at home or a cart of devices for classroom use. Tablets, Chromebooks, and laptops are the most common types of mobile technology provided to students, but the device many students have easiest access to is their smartphones.

SMARTPHONES

In addition to school-provided devices, smartphones have become essential for daily living and ubiquitous among students. Even some kindergarteners arrive at school wearing the latest smartwatches. Smartphones cause many challenges and present many opportunities in a classroom.

Smartphones can create significant distractions and conflicts at school. When students are constantly texting, checking messages, scrolling social media, watching videos, recording their fellow students or teachers, or using their phones to cheat on assessments, they are not focused on learning. Beyond academics, if students only interact through screens and texts, they lose vital social and communication skills.

Sadly, in a hyper-connected world, too much screen time may leave students feeling less connected to others and more isolated, often with negative effects on their mental health and well-being. Each school district develops policies about smartphone use at schools; some policies ban them entirely. Learn the rules that govern smartphone use at your school.

If students have smartphones in your classroom and you have a purpose that smartphones will help your students achieve, then teach expectations around how they are used as a tool for learning. Here is a list of just some of the many ways in which smartphones can support learning. Students can use their smartphones to

- Look up information and how-to videos they need for a learning task
- Dictate using the voice-to-text feature to draft a piece of writing
- Check or solve problems using the calculator feature
- Time themselves or classmates with the timer or stopwatch feature
- Translate between English and a student's first language
- Create short videos to explain a concept, interview someone, or do a book talk
- Use apps for language learning, vocabulary study, surveys and many more
- Stay organized with school to home communication apps like Remind.com or ClassDojo.com
- Photograph their notes and share them with classmates
- Set reminders or calendar events for due dates or homework
- Create a private study group on a social media platform
- Stage a scene from a book, photograph it, and share the photo
- Photograph important information on the board that they do not have time to write down, for later use
- Record (with permission) a mini lesson or oral presentation
- Listen to podcasts
- Read an article
- Access school e-mail or a class website
- Access maps and other types of related information
- Read ebooks or listen to audiobooks
- Listen to music with headphones during a quiet work time
- Watch videos recorded by the teacher in a flipped classroom
- Use various apps to access dictionaries or search the internet

TABLETS, CHROMEBOOKS, AND LAPTOPS

Personalization of learning and bringing the world into your classroom has never been easier with student access to devices. In fact, students can now learn from anyone, anywhere in the world, at any time and enhancing learning through technology makes this possible. Tablets, Chromebooks, and laptops are powerful tools to increase student ownership and engagement in active learning as well as a catalyst for self-expression and problem solving. However, if students lack access to the internet, this creates a digital divide that must be bridged before expecting device use at home.

The activities that students will be able to do will depend on your learning goals, professional development in blended learning, and instructional methods as well as the software, apps, features, and internet speed available through the devices and the network.

Technology is not always the right tool to reach a learning goal. For example, hands-on drawing, painting, performing, building, sculpting, cooking, and manufacturing may require leaving the digital tools at times to create objects and art in the world. Collaborative, face-to-face discussions strengthen social-emotional skills. With generative AI available to create content for students, teachers need to facilitate some in-class, paper-and-pencil writing experiences to make sure students are building independent thinking skills. It's vitally important to know when putting away devices is the better instructional choice.

Here are just a few of the things that internet-connected devices make possible. They allow students to:

- Go paperless
- Own their learning
- Organize and consolidate learning in a central location
- Collaborate easily with classmates via videoconferencing, shared docs and decks
- Connect learning to the world beyond the classroom
- Engage with human and generative AI tutors
- Utilize Khan Academy and other online curriculum for reteaching, extensions of learning, and tutoring
- Access digital textbooks and supplemental learning materials
- Find answers to their immediate questions
- Collaborate with others around the world
- Engage in self-paced learning on online platforms
- Evaluate the reliability and credibility of websites
- Compose music
- Film and edit movies
- Study any language in the world
- Create interactive time lines
- Create and post videos of various types
- Create and share ebooks and book trailers
- Share their work and progress with their families or caregivers
- Read and edit one another's work
- Share videos from YouTube, the Teaching Channel, or TeacherTube
- Donate rice through Freerice (freerice.com) by playing learning games
- Listen to podcasts on various topics
- Take electronic notes on readings or face-to-face presentations

INTERACTIVE SMART BOARDS

If you have one in your classroom, there are many websites with information, ideas, and lesson plans for using interactive smart boards. These engaging lesson ideas and activities appeal to all students—from our youngest students to the oldest. In the list that follows, you will find just a few of the ways you can use an interactive smart board in your classroom. Teachers can use interactive smart boards to:

- Write, type, highlight, and annotate on the screen using the stylus or their fingers.
- Share multimedia content: Google Slides, PowerPoints, Prezis, videos, websites, and more.
- Have students play review games on interactive websites.
- Record, screenshot, and share lessons to their LMS.
- Engage students with interactive games including relay races, Pictionary-style games, drag and drop sorting activities and so much more.
- Check for understanding with interactive quizzes.
- Find and mark errors in math problems or written work.
- Create and annotate diagrams or other graphic organizers.
- Provide opportunities for students to take virtual field trips.
- Teach students how to analyze a passage, photograph, film clip, or work of art.
- Have students solve problems while working with classmates.
- Simulate science experiments.
- Explore interactive maps and timelines.
- Share exemplary work done by students.
- Work out solutions to puzzles with students.
- Work with students to create class poems, stories, or quotations of the day.
- Show students how to create and use spreadsheets and tables of various types.
- Highlight the key features of a text.
- Have students correct errors in sentences or problems.
- Show students how to research databases and archived information.
- Have students create graphs and other nonlinguistic representations.
- Ask students to create various types of timelines or flowcharts.

DIGITAL TOOLS

With so many great digital tools providing curriculum, engaging students and inspiring learning, it can be difficult for educators and IT professionals to choose the ones that meet their students' needs. Both Common Sense Media and ISTE evaluate digital tools and provide reviews, badges, or seals for their alignment with rigorous criteria.

If you are looking for digital tools to help learning come to life in your classroom, consult with your colleagues and supervisor, and don't forget to ask the IT department what they will support on the network. Some of them include core curriculum and some are for more specialized tasks like learning games, collaboration, presentations, student responses, quizzes, and brain breaks. Some digital tools are free and some have subscription or licensing fees. Here is a quick look at many of the most widely used digital tools.

Amplify.com: Amplify provides engaging digital and print core curriculum and assessment tools for K–12. Social-emotional learning is imbedded in its products, including: Core Knowledge Language Arts, ELA, Science, Desmos Math, early literacy in English and Spanish, Caminos Spanish Language Arts for K–5, interactive quests, digital libraries, and more.

BrainPop.com: BrainPop offers fun videos, learning activities, and quizzes to build literacy skills across subjects for grades 3–8, plus BrainPop Jr. for K–2 and BrainPop Science for middle school.

Canva.com: Canva is free for teachers and students to design presentations, posters, infographics, lesson plans, and more using thousands of educational templates.

Curipod.com: Curipod is a tool to develop slideshows, quizzes, polls, and interactive lessons. It offers a generative AI that will build a first draft of lessons for teachers to refine.

DiscoveryEducation.com: Providing a comprehensive suite of K–12 curriculum resources for virtual field trips, science, STEM, coding, Mystery Science, math, social studies, and more.

Dreambox.com: Dreambox helps teachers differentiate instruction for core math and reading instruction K–12.

Edmentum.com: Edmentum offers a host of online curriculum and assessments, including Study Island, Exact Path, Apex Tutorials, Reading Eggs, project-based learning, and courses for grades 6–12.

EdPuzzle.com: EdPuzzle has interactive video lessons that are ready-to-use, as well as the option for teachers to record and edit their own videos.

Everfi.com/k-12: Everfi has free interactive game-based lessons for K–12 students in financial education, character education, health and wellness, STEM, and career readiness.

Flip.com: This free app from Microsoft allows teachers to create safe online spaces for students to share their ideas in short video, text, and audio messages.

Flocabulary.com: Teachers can grow students' literacy skills with standards-aligned, video-based lessons and activities that leverage the power of hip-hop and storytelling.

GoNoodle.com: GoNoodle gets K–5 students (and their teachers) moving with short interactive activities, brain breaks, and mindfulness experiences from one to twenty minutes in length. Just press play. Both free and subscription options are available.

Google Apps for Education (edu.google.com): Used by a majority of educators, the G-Suite is free and streamlines teacher and student tasks. It includes Google Classroom, Gmail, Sheets, Docs, Slides, Drives, Forms, Calendar, Jamboard, Sites, Play, Meet, and they all integrate at Google Workspace for Education to streamline teacher productivity and student learning.

ImagineLearning.com: Imagine Learning creates K–12 digital-first solutions. Products include: Twig Science, Illustrative Mathematics, and EL Education. The supplemental and intervention suite equips learners with personalized instruction for English and Spanish literacy, math, coding, and more. Imagine Edgenuity is their complete courseware solution. In addition, Imagine Learning provides virtual teachers, tutors, and speech language therapists for schools. Teachers can access the blog for tips, tools, and strategies to enhance learning.

iReady (curriculumassociate.com): iReady is an online program for reading and math with an adaptive assessment tool as well as lessons to support personalized learning for grades K–8 in reading and mathematics.

IXL.com: IXL provides a diagnostic assessment and analytics for English language arts and mathematics as well as comprehensive curriculum in K–12 math, ELA, science, social studies, and Spanish.

Kahoot.com: Kahoot! Is a game-based platform that makes it easy to create, share, and play games and quizzes.

KhanAcademy.org: Khan Academy provides free online courses, lessons and practice in all subjects, plus life skills, computing, arts, and humanities. Khan Academy is a nonprofit with the mission of providing a free world-class education for anyone, anywhere. The AI tutor, Khanmigo, helps students without giving them answers.

Nearpod.com: Nearpod's interactive, slides-based lessons help teachers gather data on student learning with formative assessments, interactive videos, games, simulations, and more. Select ready-to-use lessons or create your own.

Newsela.com: Newsela offers real-word texts from diverse perspectives aligned with standards in English language arts, science, social studies, and social-emotional learning. Reading passages are added daily and each one is available at five reading levels.

Padlet.com: Teachers and students can create beautiful boards to collect, organize, and present anything, such as student responses, blogs, portfolios, maps, timelines, Q&A, video playlists, and so much more.

Panorama Education (panoramaed.com): Panorama can improve school climate with SEL check-ins, assessments, and interventions, feedback surveys, and an all-in-one platform to strengthen MTSS, RTI, and PBiS systems.

PearDeck.com: Pear Deck transforms slide presentations by adding interactive elements and formative assessments to existing presentations. It provides easy access for students, lots of ready-to-use templates and lessons for teachers.

Prodigy (prodigygame.com): Prodigy's game-based learning motivates students to practice and learn math, reading, and writing in grades 1–8.

Quizlet.com: Quizlet helps students study by repeated practice and reinforcing learning with flashcards and an AI tutor.

Quizziz.com: Quizziz offers several tools to make learning interactive, including lessons and formative assessments.

Seesaw (web.seesaw.me): Teachers in grades K–12 can create or send assignments in Seesaw. Students use a suite of tools to take pictures, draw, record videos, and more to create a digital portfolio. Families can see their student's work and even leave comments.

WEBSITES FOR LESSON PLANS AND RESOURCES

Here, you will find two lists to help you create effective lesson plans for your classes. The first is a list of online resources that are specifically for lesson plans. The second list contains sites that can help you enhance your lesson plans with interesting resources and materials. These sites allow teachers to access lesson plans that cover all grade levels and content areas.

Facing History and Ourselves (FHAO) (FacingHistory.org): FHAO has free classroom resources for grades 6–12 ELA and social studies to support teaching complex moments in history. FHAO uses lessons of difficult historical periods to encourage students to stand up to bigotry and hate.

Learning for Justice (LFJ) (learningforjustice.org): A project of the Southern Poverty Law Center, LFJ provides classroom resources from free lessons, student texts, tasks, a range of teaching strategies, film kits, posters, and more to teach reading, social-emotional skills, hard histories, and current events.

Lesson Planet (lessonplanet.com): Lesson Planet enables teachers to search more than 550,000 teacher-reviewed open education resources, lesson plans, media, and collections in an online, professional community. A free trial is available.

National Education Association (NEA) (nea.org): The NEA website offers thousands of lesson plans in its Resource Library in an easily searchable format. Teachers can find a variety of lesson planning resources as well as practical tips for classroom use.

Open Educational Resources (OER) Commons (OERCommons.org): This is a public digital library of tens of thousands of open educational resources, including curated collections on many diverse subjects such as STEAM, engineering, Shakespeare, arts, women's history, and more.

PBS Learning Media (pbslearningmedia.org): PBS has curated free curriculum-aligned videos, interactives, lesson plans, and more. This includes PBS media from

Ken Burns, U.S. History Collection, Reading Rainbow, and more. Browse by subject and grade.

Read Write Think by NCTE (readwritethink.org): NCTE offers curated collections of lesson plans, teaching materials, and professional development on topics frequently taught in classrooms. This includes primary sources, booklists, authors, assessments, media literacy, and poetry to name a few.

Share My Lesson (sharemylesson.com): Share My Lesson is maintained by the American Federation of Teachers. Developed by teachers for teachers, this free platform provides more than 500,000 teaching resources as well as an online collaborative community.

Subject to Climate (SubjectToClimate.org/lesson-plans): This robust site makes climate education accessible to all with ready-to-use, multidisciplinary lesson plans and resources for all grade levels. The chatbot, Climate Socrates, will answer all your questions about climate.

TPT (teacherspayteachers.com): TPT is the largest marketplace for Pre-K–12 resources created by teachers, with more than seven million free and paid resources in all grade levels and subject areas. Teachers can also follow teacher-authors and create wish lists.

Teaching Channel (teachingchannel.com): Learner's Edge expanded the Teaching Channel into a platform for professional development. It hosts a video library showcasing innovative and effective teaching practices as well as graduate-level courses. Teachers can watch brief videos of effective teaching ideas that they may want to implement in their own classrooms.

WEB RESOURCES FOR ADDITIONAL LESSON PLAN ENHANCEMENTS

Edublogs (edublogs.org): Edublogs is a site that offers a user-friendly way to create and post blogs.

Pinterest (pinterest.com): Pinterest is a popular way for teachers to search for ideas and inspiration, bookmark, collect, organize, and share images and links on a Pinterest board.

Poll Everywhere (polleverywhere.com): Poll Everywhere offers a free plan for educators that will allow students to take and share polls of various types.

TED (ted.com): At the TED site, you and your students can access videos delivered by great thinkers and experts covering a wide range of topics.

Timetoast (timetoast.com): Students can use this site to create and share time lines in just a few minutes.

"There's an App for That!"

Educators will find that there are apps or online tools for just about every aspect of your professional life:

- Tracking grades and data
- Accessing documents when you are not at school
- Reading books with students
- Helping students build vocabulary
- Providing study guides for students
- Having students view a fact or word of the day
- Accessing reference materials of all types
- Finding games for your students to play
- Organizing your classroom
- Ordering supplies
- Editing papers
- Creating lesson plans and sharing them
- Finding video clips to engage students
- Accessing blogs and podcasts
- Searching the web
- Collaborating with colleagues
- Sharing documents with your professional learning community or PLN members
- Creating lesson plan ideas

To learn more about the apps and online tools that can increase your knowledge and improve your teaching skills and productivity, one of the best places to begin is with the pages devoted to online tools for educators at Kathy Schrock's Guide to Everything (schrockguide.net/online-tools.html). Kathy is a former Director of Instructional Technology with all the certifications and extensive experience. Visitors can access information about hundreds of carefully selected and categorized educator-recommended online tools.

What Is the Right Quantity and Quality of Homework (aka Practice)?

Part of lesson planning involves determining whether students need additional practice beyond class time. Teachers should consider replacing the term *homework* with *practice*. Students practice instruments, sports, art, theater, and other extracurriculars. They also sometimes need math practice, reading practice, science practice, and more to gain proficiency with academic knowledge and skills.

For decades, the issue of homework and its impact on student learning, attitudes about school, stress, sleep, and home life have concerned students, families, and educators. The research studies conducted by Harris Cooper and another by John Hattie in *Visible Learning* indicate that homework (beyond daily reading) has almost no correlation to elementary student achievement, but the right amount of homework and asking students to do the right types of tasks can correlate to increased student achievement among secondary students.

Many teachers hope that the right amount of quality homework will reinforce and accelerate learning, promote responsibility and organization, and engage students in learning beyond school. Families and caregivers appreciate the connection between home and school that is created by homework where they can see their children engaged with schoolwork.

There are, however, significant concerns around homework that focus on equity, student stress, and the quantity and quality of homework. Teachers need to know their students and cannot assume they have a quiet, dedicated space to work, access to the internet, or support from adults at home to complete homework. It's important for schools to provide support for students to address these inequities as it pertains to homework. Students with disabilities may require more time with a homework task than other students. In well-resourced communities, students often receive too much homework, creating significant strain on students and families. In under-resourced communities, students may receive little homework, which may disadvantage secondary students.

Technology adds another layer of complexity to the homework question. It provides 24/7 access to learning tools and practice. It also provides a generative AI assistant that could do some homework assignments for students. So, teachers need to consider the types of assignments that encourage students to do their own independent thinking and learning as well as those that require the use of generative AI.

Some elementary schools have banned homework before grade 5, with the exception of reading every night, but most continue to have homework policies seeking the right quantity and quality of homework. Harris Cooper, who conducted the Duke University study, developed the "Ten-minute rule" for homework. First graders have ten minutes of homework per night, second graders have twenty minutes, and each year an additional ten minutes is added until, in high school, students have a maximum of two hours of homework per day.

Depending on the bell schedule, the Ten-minute Rule could be a good rule of thumb to answer the quantity question, especially for middle and high school students. When a student has more than one teacher assigning homework, those teachers should take care not to overload a student. It's important to communicate with colleagues so that a student's overall homework load is reasonable.

Beyond the amount of homework, the purpose for and quality of the homework is even more important. The right type of homework is connected to current study topics, reinforces previous instruction, can be completed independently, and it creates a positive home-to-school connection. Quality homework is not "busy work"; it is interesting, engaging, appropriately challenging, and differentiated based on students' needs.

One unique teaching approach requires an entirely different approach to homework. Teachers who structure learning around a "Flipped Classroom" provide interactive videos with new learning for students to watch as homework. Then, when students are in class with their teachers, they focus on the application of the knowledge and skills presented in the video.

There are many steps you can take to make sure that the homework you assign serves its intended instructional purposes, promotes learning, and does not cause conflict between home and school.

Step One: Learn about your school and district's homework policy. In public schools, it's likely written up as a school board policy.

Step Two: Talk with colleagues about their homework practices.

Step Three: Get to know your students, their needs, interests, families, and caregivers.

Step Four: Make reading at home an important component of homework, especially in the elementary grades, and avoid homework on weekends and holidays as much as possible.

Step Five: Consider whether the ten minutes of homework per grade level guideline works in your classroom.

Step Six: Write down your homework policy and communicate it to families and students in several different ways.

Step Seven: Hold a high standard for the homework you assign. Make sure it aligns with your learning goals, isn't busy work, and clarifies the role that a generative AI assistant should or should not have in the assignment.

Step Eight: Support students who do not complete homework assignments.

Step Nine: Check in with students periodically to understand the impact that homework has on their lives, and adjust your policy if it's not getting the results you want.

"Once, I harshly spoke to a student for not having a homework assignment done. The lack of the assignment precluded her taking part in class that day. She sat outside our work circle. At the end of class, she handed me a folded note. Inside it asked for my forgiveness but told me that, the night before, her mother's boyfriend (one of a long series) had kicked them out of his trailer. She asked her mother what to do, and her mother couldn't give her any suggestions, so she loaded everything she owned into her ragged car and drove to a Walmart one town away. That store had a snack bar and was open all night. She spent the night in the store, then dressed in the store's restroom and came to school. This was a wake-up call for me. Sometimes what we do in class is not the most important part of a student's day. Homework? Maybe not as important as I thought."

Luann West Scott, 42 years' experience

SPECIFIC STRATEGIES TO MANAGE HOMEWORK ASSIGNMENTS SUCCESSFULLY

Homework assignments need not be a headache for you or your students and their families. Instead, homework assignments can function as you intend them to: as a logical and helpful extension of learning done in the classroom. Students engage in learning in class or at home that is interesting and relevant to them. Here are several general homework strategies you can use to help your students find success:

- Incorporate generative AI into some assignments (if all students have access to devices and the internet).
- Provide homework that a generative AI assistant can't do.
  - Use digital tools and have students record videos of themselves talking about the assignment they completed, what they learned, and the process they used to complete the assignment.
  - Increase the complexity of homework, so that it includes data created in class, from surveys or science labs they conducted, or learnings from field trips (virtual or otherwise) that they experienced.
  - Wherever possible, make the learning personal to the student, their neighborhood, their culture. Students are eager to express their own opinions and eagerly share their experiences.
  - Connect homework with local issues on the school or community level.
  - In class the next day, have students explain their thinking and show their work, in all subjects, but especially in math.
- Provide students with as many choices as you can.
- Designate some nights as homework-free nights.

In addition to these general strategies, there are several different things to consider when you design and give assignments. Giving effective homework assignments can be broken into three components: before, while presenting, and after the assignment. Use the following suggestions to help make homework a successful experience for you and your students:

Before the Assignment

- Teach the academic skills that your students need to complete their work independently.
- Allow students to design their own homework assignments when appropriate. If they did not finish an assignment in class, they should have the option of completing it for homework, for example. If students are working in a group, they should have time together to plan the work they need to complete outside of class.
- Have a well-published schedule for homework so that students can anticipate assignments.

- Provide as many options as you can for assignments so that students can do work that is interesting and that encourages them to want to learn more.

While Presenting the Assignment

- Spend enough time going over the assignment and checking for understanding that students know you are serious about it and know what is expected of them.
- Give plenty of models, samples, and examples, letting students know what their final product may be.
- Don't wait until the last few minutes of class to assign homework. If you want students to take an assignment seriously, it should not be a last-minute item. Be sure to check for understanding to make sure all students know what is expected of them.
- Write the homework assignment (if any) in the same spot on the board each day. Write it on the board even if you also post it online.
- Ask students to estimate how long it will take them to do the assignment so that they can set aside the time to do it. With time, students will become adept at planning their work.

After the Assignment

- Offer help to students who may need extra assistance in doing their work. A bit of extra time with you after school will often clear up problems and give students a confidence boost.
- Be reasonable if a student requests an extension. Sometimes unforeseen events interfere with students completing homework on time.
- Have a routine to check or review homework at the start of class on the day it is due. If students had required homework, then you should connect with it in a meaningful way. This is usually done best in small groups.
- Few homework assignments need to be graded. In a proficiency, competency, or mastery-based grading system, homework is often optional and not graded.
- Determine what assignments are assessments of student learning that need to be required and graded.

Questions to Discuss with Colleagues

Sharing ideas with colleagues is a helpful way to devise solutions to some of the problems that you must manage successfully at school. Here, you will find several topics to open discussions with colleagues about successful instructional practices:

1. You want to create a homework policy that follows school guidelines and supports students and families. What is the right amount and the right type of homework for your grade level and subject area? Who can help you develop a policy?

2. You want to support students in developing the 4Cs, but they don't work well in small groups yet. What strategies can you use to help them learn to collaborate? Who can help you with this?

3. You have high expectations for students, but your school's curriculum is too advanced for many of your students. You know you should teach to the grade level standards, but you want to address students' learning needs. What should you do? To whom can you turn for help?

4. It's not always easy to facilitate class discussions. How can you decide what the right format, ground rules, and prompts are to inspire a great discussion?

5. You want to integrate digital tools into an upcoming lesson. How can you plan this so that the implementation goes smoothly and helps students learn?

Topics to Discuss with a Mentor

Although the topics that new teachers need to discuss with a mentor vary from teacher to teacher and from school to school, there are some that most first-year teachers should be comfortable discussing with a mentor or a trusted colleague. You should ask your mentor about these topics from this section:

- How to obtain instructional materials and resources
- Which colleagues can share lesson plan ideas with you
- What restrictions there are (if any) regarding devices and digital tools
- Strategies for appropriately teaching difficult histories
- Suggestions for how to adjust lessons that are not going well

Reflection Questions to Guide Your Thinking

1. How can you incorporate student interests into learning activities? Where can you learn about more collaborative activities that would work well in your classroom?

2. What can you do to make sure class discussions are valuable and help students develop civil discourse skills? What do you need to teach your students about their role in class discussions? What do you need to do to prepare for a successful class discussion?

3. What are your strengths in designing learning experiences? How can you use these strengths to design and facilitate high-quality instruction that will help your students succeed?

4. What are your views on homework and how much and what type of work should be assigned? What equity issues exist in your classroom that might create barriers to students engaging with homework?

5. To what extent do you want to use project-based learning to engage students in real-world learning? Where can you find ideas and lesson plans? Who can help you with this?

SECTION TEN

Measure Student Progress with Summative Assessments

Summative assessments measure student progress toward mastering the knowledge and skills required in the class or grade level. Students take summative assessments when formative assessments indicate they are ready to demonstrate their learning. Summative assessments give students feedback on their progress, their strengths and gaps while giving teachers feedback on how well they aligned instruction with the objectives and needs of students.

> "Understand what a student can do, not what they can't do. We tend to use deficit and not asset measuring in schools."
>
> *Elliot Washor, Ed.D., Co-Founder*
> *Big Picture Learning*

Teachers gather lots of information before giving students a summative assessment. This includes observation from daily interactions, data from formative assessments, work samples, and discussions. (See Section Eight for more information about formative assessments.) As you read through the material in this section, you will learn more about how to design and use summative assessments to measure your students' mastery.

Summative Assessments to Measure Mastery

There are myriad ways for students to demonstrate their mastery of standards, to not just recall knowledge, but apply the skills they have learned. Examples of summative assessments include: tests, quizzes, end-of-unit or end-of-term exams, projects, exhibitions, writing, speeches, performance tasks, and portfolios.

As you create various types of summative assessments, it is important to always keep in mind that those assessments must accurately measure student mastery. It's easy to be so caught up in the process of writing questions or constructing performance tasks that the instruments you create don't accurately measure mastery as they should. To help you with this, try to *avoid* assessments that:

- Don't have clear success criteria or rubrics
- Are too long to complete in the allotted time
- Don't really assess the standards you have taught
- Use a format that is difficult for students to follow
- Ignore higher-order thinking skills
- Contain poorly worded directions
- Don't align with your objectives and instruction
- Contain trick questions
- Don't match the test-taking skills of your students

Tests and Quizzes

Tests and quizzes are tools that many teachers use to measure students' progress. Both tests and quizzes can be classified as either summative or formative assessments depending on the way teachers use the data collected from them. Generally, if you give a quiz or a test and then assign a grade for that assessment, then it is a summative assessment of learning, not a formative assessment for ongoing learning.

Although tests and quizzes both offer many advantages, using these instruments has a few disadvantages. Too often, tests and quizzes focus on lower-level thinking skills, such as asking students to just recall information, or the question formats do not appeal to the learning preferences of all students. The following strategies offer ways to design tests and quizzes as one measure of mastery:

> "When thinking about technology use in the classroom, concentrate on creating assessments (whether formative or summative) which allow students to showcase their content knowledge in a creative way. Have a list of creation tools available for them to choose from, or have them present you with another tool they would like to use. From podcasts to videos to TikToks, the number of online tools are endless!"
>
> *Kathy Schrock, 44 years' experience*
>
> Take a look at the categorized list of my favorites on this page of my site (schrockguide.net/online-tools.html) and feel free to explore more of Kathy Schrock's Guide to Everything here! (schrockguide.net).

- Plan with the end in mind. Design your summative assessment at the start of unit planning, before you develop lesson plans. Then learning will align with learning goals and prepare students for success on the summative assessment.
- Update your summative assessment based on the learning that actually occurred.
- Many published and online curricula have pre-made assessments and question banks to get teachers started. Make sure that the test or quiz aligns with the standards you want to assess.
- Determine whether a print or digital format better meets your and your students' needs.

- Use a generative AI assistant or digital tool like Curipod to draft assessment questions aligned with standards and select those that work best for your students and your purpose.

- Include a variety of question types on each test or quiz. Objective questions do not always give an accurate assessment of your students' thinking. A balanced combination of brief objective questions and constructed response questions will usually provide a better assessment than either type will by itself.

- Use Bloom's Taxonomy or Webb's Depth of Knowledge Framework to write questions that go beyond recall to more complex levels of learning. Offer a reading passage or problem followed by questions that require students to apply their knowledge or use another higher-level thinking skill.

- In the planning process, develop assessments with your colleagues. If you and other teachers teach the same grade or content area, you can save time by using the best questions from one another's assessments. As a new teacher, this will also offer an opportunity for you to learn more about assessment construction from reviewing your colleagues' work.

- Reduce potential confusion by grouping similar question types together.

- Begin any test or quiz with questions that your students will find easier. This will help them gain confidence.

- Make sure to give explicit directions that are easy to follow. When you change question types, you must give new directions, even if the procedure seems obvious.

- Number each page on a paper-based test so that students can keep track of where they are in the assessment.

- Build confidence with encouragement, clarifications, and advice. Suggest how long a section should take to complete, underline key words, or even remind students to double-check their work.

- Accessibility. Be sure to use a plain font that is large enough for students to read easily and include any other supports and accommodations students may need.

- It's not always easy to judge how long it will take students to complete an assessment. To judge the length of your test or quiz, take it yourself and then allow two or three times that amount of time for your students to complete it.

- Experienced teachers maintain banks of questions or question ideas that they can use again in a different format or on future tests and quizzes.

Create Useful Objective Questions

Objective questions are limited in what they can measure and may allow students to guess correctly without explaining their thinking. Still, they can be useful when used well in assessments. In some cases, your curriculum will provide tests and quizzes you can modify. In some instances, you will create your own. With the help of a generative AI assistant, developing objective questions aligned to standards does not take much time and digital tools will often auto-grade them. Use the following tips to create different types of objective questions that allow you to assess your students' knowledge and understanding accurately.

True-or-False Statements

- This type of question is less useful than others because students have a good chance of guessing the answer. Use it sparingly if at all.
- Make sure that the answers don't follow a pattern.
- Take care to write statements that are similar in length. Often the true statements tend to be longer than the false ones.
- If you would like to increase the thinking skills required on a test with true-or-false statements, ask students to explain their reasoning as part of the assessment.

Matching Questions

- Involve higher-level thinking skills by asking students to do more than just recall information when creating questions that require students to match information. For example, instead of just asking students to match a famous person to an event in history, have students read a brief passage about the event, determine the cause, and then match the cause to the event.
- Take the assessment yourself first to make sure that the answers don't follow a pattern or inadvertently spell out words when the answers are selected.
- Encourage students to cross out answer choices as they use them.
- Offer more answer choices than questions.
- Limit matching lists to ten or fifteen items rather than a longer list that students will find difficult to follow.
- If using a print format, arrange matching questions to fit on the same page so that students will not be confused by having to flip the page back and forth.

Short-Answer/Constructed Response Questions

- Design short-answer or constructed response questions to yield responses that can be a word, a phrase, or even a paragraph in length.
- Keep in mind that although it does not take long to create short-answer questions, it does take longer to read them and provide feedback.
- Short-answer questions are especially good for encouraging higher-level thinking skills because answers are not predetermined, so students must think of their own responses.
- Use a generative AI assistant to brainstorm assessment questions aligned with standards and select those that work best for your students and your purpose.

- If you are typing the assessment, make all the blanks in short-answer questions the same length; otherwise, many students will interpret the length of the line as a clue to the answer.

- Short-answer questions take students longer to answer, so you should factor in the extra time when you develop the assessment.

Multiple-Choice Questions

- Use multiple-choice questions to measure your students' mastery of both simple and complex concepts.

- Make each answer choice significantly different from the others to reduce confusion.

- Avoid overusing one letter. You can do this by making up the answer pattern in advance and arranging the questions so that the answers conform to that pattern.

- Provide answer choices that are all roughly the same length to avoid giving away the answer.

- Make every answer choice a possibility by not including options that students can immediately eliminate as likely answers. For example, if your science test includes a question about who discovered DNA, don't give "Superman" as one of the answer choices.

What if Your Students Don't Reach Proficiency on a Test or Quiz?

Few things are as discouraging as having several students do poorly on a test or quiz. When this happens, there are three possible causes: the test or quiz itself is flawed, students did not prepare adequately, or you did not sufficiently help students understand the material before giving the assessment. Here are some suggestions on how to handle each problem:

- The assessment is flawed: Look at the assessment. Is the format easy for students to follow? Are the point values logical? Do the questions match the way you taught the material? You can correct this situation by designing another test or quiz and using the first one as a pretest and study guide.

"Lani, a high-achieving student, developed crippling test anxiety that rendered her unresponsive if unsure of the answer to a test question. Inspired by Rita Pierson's TED Talk, which celebrated even minor triumphs, our team recognized the need to foster a growth mindset and provide mindful feedback so Lani could develop positive associations with summative assessments. With the support of a dedicated team and family over the course of four years, Lani developed tools to manage her test anxiety and learned the importance of embracing errors as part of the learning process."

Clifton Wallace, 7 years' experience

- Students did not prepare for the test or quiz: Determine the reasons why your students did not prepare. Ask them to describe how they studied and why they did not study more. Take the time to teach students how you expect them to review and prepare for tests. You can also correct this problem by designing a new test or quiz and by using the one that students failed as a pretest and study guide.

- You did not sufficiently help students understand the material: Sometimes teachers overestimate their students' readiness to take a test or quiz. When this happens, learn from your mistake and help students master the material before the next assessment. You should also consider the types of formative assessments that you used because the data they provided were not a good predictor of student success. You can correct this problem by using the first test or quiz as a review guide to help students determine what they do and don't know. Remedy the situation by reteaching and then reassessing.

How to Use Alternative Summative Assessments

Traditional tests and quizzes are limited in the ways they can motivate students to demonstrate learning. Test questions need to be high-quality to measure higher order thinking skills. So, using alternative summative assessments is important to measure students' strengths and how well students can apply their learning.

One subset of alternative assessments is Performance Tasks or Performance Assessments that present a situation and require students to apply knowledge and either perform a task or create a final product to demonstrate their learning. They can be completed individually, in pairs, or small groups, depending on your purpose.

Just as the course content and instructional process can be differentiated, so can the way you assess student mastery. One way to do this is to use alternative assessments: methods of determining mastery that often require students to demonstrate understanding in ways other than traditional written tests and quizzes. Students who do not read or write well may struggle with tests and quizzes, even though they may know the material as well as students with stronger skills. Traditional tests assume a certain ceiling on student knowledge and skills, whereas with alternative assessments, teachers are often surprised by what students are capable of when given the opportunity to share what they know. Recognizing the need for a variety of assessments, educators have developed a wide array of assessment instruments to measure what their students know.

As you plan the types of assessments that you will use to determine your students' mastery of the material, you should use both traditional and alternative assessments. In combination, they provide a more complete view of what students know and can do, and the combination allows students to comfortably use their preferred learning styles.

Begin slowly, choosing alternative assessments that are easy to manage. As you grow in confidence and as you get to know your students' strengths and weaknesses, you can incorporate assessments that are more extensive. When you make up your next assessments, consider using some of the following types of assessments in addition to traditional measurements:

- Project-based learning culminating projects
- Exhibitions
- Gamified competitions like The Great Bake Off or Shark Tank
- Oral reports or performances
- Research projects
- Paper bag reports
- Essays or other writing projects
- Demonstrations
- Creative projects: music, art, videos, podcasts, plays
- Panel discussions
- Multimedia projects
- Portfolios
- Diagrams, infographics, or other graphic representations
- Online assessments
- Student choice (Ask students to propose a way that they could demonstrate their proficiency in a standard. Review students' ideas and approve those that meet your requirements.)

Multi-Genre Research Projects

In an age of generative AI, students may need motivation to create their own writing that is meaningful and personal to them. Teachers may need an assessment that measures students' strengths in a variety of writing modes. One way to do that is through an alternative assessment such as the Multi-Genre Research Project. It gives students choice and creativity as they combine genres to explore an object of significance to them, an event, a text, a story about themselves or a relative, or a person of interest.

It is important that teachers avoid narrowing this to simply completing a family history; be aware that a family-focused project can be sensitive for individuals, as many students do not have access to their family's history. Creating space for individual students to write with a simple focus on a special object tucked away as a keepsake, dive fully into an event, trace a history, or offer multiple interpretations of a text can elevate the importance of engaged writing while teaching vital research skills.

In the multi-genre research project, students conduct research and then complete four writings in four different genres. This could include: a biographical sketch, letter, poem, song lyrics, cartoons, op-ed piece, top-ten list, brochure or a visual, to name a few. For example, one student was fascinated by a wedding cake topper that crowned many wedding cakes in her family. She explored the history of wedding cake toppers and the marriages that lasted (or didn't) in her family. The combination of creative writing and nonfiction on a topic that is deeply personal and interesting to students gives life to extraordinary pieces of student writing. Use "multi-genre research project" as an internet search term to find books, blogs, and articles with all the details.

How can you determine whether an alternative assessment will be successful with your students? Follow these suggestions:

- Make sure to align the assessment very closely with the material. For example, asking students to demonstrate a process is an appropriate assessment after you have taught them the steps of the process.
- Have clearly articulated success criteria on a rubric. Give scoring information to students when you make the initial assignment. No matter which method of assessment you use, your students need to know the criteria for success before they begin their work. Rubrics, models, samples, and examples are necessary for students to understand what is expected of them.

There are many different alternative assessments you can use throughout the school year. Here, however, is a brief list of some alternative assessments that you may find particularly easy to incorporate into your lessons:

Open-Ended Questions

When answering open-ended questions, students can reveal what they know about a topic without the constraints of questions requiring fixed-answer responses. Asking open-ended questions based on real-world situations will also yield meaningful responses that require students to use higher-level thinking skills to demonstrate knowledge of standards. Here are some examples of well-worded, open-ended questions:

- In the novel *Wonder*, Mr. Tushman says, "Always try to be a little kinder than necessary." Use two pieces of evidence from the text and one example from your own life of characters or people who follow this advice.
- Provide students with the text of or a passage from Dr. King's "I Have a Dream Speech" and ask them to identify references to ideas from the U.S. Constitution or Declaration of Independence, and then reflect on why Dr. King chose to include these ideas in this speech.

Variations on Traditional Tests

There are many variations on traditional tests that can help you assess your students' knowledge. Depending on the skills and abilities you want to measure, consider using one or more of the following:

> "Talk to the kids. Don't just take the grade on a test or essay. If the kids don't seem to be doing well, talk to them. Find out what they know and what might be holding them back."
>
> *Mary Landis, 22 years' experience*

- Group tests: Students work in small groups to answer questions.
- Partner tests: Students work in pairs to answer questions.
- Open-book or open-note tests: Students can refer to their books or their notes when answering questions.

Rubrics

A rubric is a tool that makes learning visible to students. It defines success criteria for assessments so that students and teachers can evaluate the quality of the work. Students use them to understand expectations and guide their thinking, whereas teachers use them to assess student mastery.

The goals for an assignment are very clear when students receive a rubric before they begin. Because students know what to do, their work is usually of higher quality than it is with traditional assessments. Rubrics often help students improve their work in process before completing it. Rubrics are also used by teachers to assess mastery after a summative assessment is completed.

There are two general types of rubrics: holistic or analytic. Analytic rubrics are used for evaluating summative assessments with criteria for the student product listed on the left, and descriptions of student performance and a rating scale (often 1–4 or 1–6) listed across the top.

There are several advantages to using rubrics as criteria for summative assessments. One is that, because they are explicit about expectations for the assignment and given to students in advance, they are fair. Students, and their families and caregivers, know the quality of work that is expected. Another advantage is that rubrics make it easier to give students helpful feedback quickly. There is no need for lengthy marginal comments when the expectations for success are expressed clearly in the rubric.

How can you use rubrics in your class? Although it takes practice and patience to learn how to develop a clearly expressed rubric that supports student thinking without being too prescriptive, you can begin with these steps:

Step One: Determine the criteria by which you will evaluate an assignment.

Step Two: Decide on the levels of mastery you want in an assignment. Begin by determining the highest and the lowest levels and then determine the levels in between.

Step Three: Create your own rubric using a generative AI tool. Develop a chart format similar to the one in Sample 10.1. Using a chart makes it easier for students to see the relationships among the various assessment items.

Step Four: Show students models of acceptable and unacceptable assignments. Demonstrate how you would evaluate each assignment using the rubric.

Step Five: Encourage students to practice using the rubric with several model assignments before they begin work on their assignment.

Step Six: Students complete their assessment or project.

Step Seven: Students self-assess using the rubric. Peers may also give feedback during this step.

Step Eight: Teachers evaluate student work using the rubric.

Step Nine: Provide time in class for students to reflect on the feedback they received, ask questions, and determine how they will implement that feedback in their learning.

Here are some questions to ask about the quality of the rubric you create.

- Does the rubric evaluate surface and deeper learning?
- Does it use an even number of performance levels, four or six, to adequately define what the continuum of learning looks like?
- Is the language student-friendly, positive, descriptive, and measurable?
- Will the use of the rubric promote growth mindset?

Many websites are devoted to the various types of rubrics. To begin refining your knowledge and to access free models, try these sites:

Quick Rubric (quickrubric.com): This is a free and easy way to create rubrics with editable templates. A subscription will get teachers more features.

Rubric Maker (rubric-maker.com): It is a free and an intuitive way to create, save, print, and export rubrics as pdf files. Teachers will need a subscription to access the library of rubric templates and other features.

PBLWorks.org: Has several project-based learning rubrics to use as models.

Kathy Schrock's Guide to Everything (schrockguide.net): Along with one hundred rubrics, this extensive site hosts dozens of informative articles about rubrics, plus examples and instructions for specific types. You can learn how to create or modify rubrics, how to use rubrics in your classroom, or even how to guide students in creating their own rubrics.

Sample 10.1
Analytic Rubric

This sample rubric is one that teachers and students could use for an individual presentation in grades 3–5.

Criteria	Emerging (1)	Approaching (2)	Proficient (3)	Advanced (4)
Ideas and Information	No accurate information yet. Attempts to state the main idea or subject of the presentation and other information.	Some accurate information. States the main idea or subject but does not yet use supporting evidence.	Accurate information. Presents the main idea and some supporting evidence clearly.	Demonstrates deep understanding by presenting accurate information, the main ideas, and robust, pertinent supporting evidence.
Organization	Presentation does not yet have a clear beginning, middle, and end.	Presentation has a clear beginning, but does not yet have a structure beyond that.	Presentation has a clear beginning, middle, and end with ideas connecting to each other.	Presentation has a strong beginning hook, middle, and ending conclusion.
Public-Speaking Skills	Is not yet comfortable with the topic. Voice, posture, and eye contact do not yet engage the audience.	Is not yet comfortable with the topic. Voice, posture, and eye contact sometimes engage the audience.	Is comfortable with the topic. Voice, posture, and eye contact engage the audience.	Demonstrates strong enthusiasm for the topic. Voice, posture, and eye contact engage the audience during the entire presentation.
Presentation Visuals	Does not yet include visuals.	Includes few visuals or visuals that do not support the audience's understanding of the topic.	Includes visuals that support the audience's understanding of the topic.	Includes visuals that support and extend the audience's understanding of the topic.
Response to Q&A	Not yet able to answer questions about the topic.	Able to answer some basic questions.	At ease with answers to all questions.	Demonstrates full understanding, and able to answer all questions with some elaboration.

GRADING

The results of summative assessments form a student's grade and report card. The central purpose of grading is to provide feedback to students (and those who support them) on a student's progress toward meeting learning goals, their strengths, and where they need support. Grading at the high-school level also communicates to post–high-school college and career audiences. Grading systems have the power to create a more equitable, dynamic school culture that supports learning for all, or undermine it.

As a first-year teacher, you will learn about the grading policies and practices at your school. In some cases, schools will have a minimum requirement for the number of assignments that earn a grade each term. As you gain experience, you will undoubtedly revisit your grading practices and determine if they meet the needs of your students. You may want to explore the resources at the end of this section to learn more from a range of educators and researchers working to improve this core component of education.

The results of summative assessments are recorded in a school's student information system, and ultimately, used to generate report cards. These systems are transparent to students, their families, and caregivers who can access the student information system to check student progress at any time. There are two main grading systems in use in the United States.

Traditional Grading

A traditional grading system generally has an *A, B, C, D, F* grading scale or numbers from 1–10 or 1–100. It is often the grading system that teachers experienced when they were students. Scores are averaged over time with larger summative assessments having a higher number value, and thus, having greater weight in a final grade. Participation points, homework, and extra credit may be factored into the grade. There may also be penalties for late work.

If a student earns an 85% in a class or subject area, they will generally earn a *B*, but what does that communicate? Did the student understand 85% of the content? Did they complete 75% of the tasks and get 10% of the extra credit? Does 85% in one teacher's classroom calibrate with grades from another teacher in the same grade level or subject area?

If you are required to use a traditional grading system, ask yourself these questions to make sure that students are set up for success:

1. Do student grades reflect their content knowledge and skills?
2. How can you help students grow career readiness skills like responsibility, organization, study skills, and integrity? To what extent can you report progress on these skills separately without including behaviors in the student's academic grade?

3. All students don't learn at the same rate. How can your grading weight learning that occurs later in the term more than learning assessed early in the term?

4. What equity issues exist for students and how does your grading policy create greater equity?

5. Do zeros reflect behavior or knowledge? In a traditional system, some teachers use an "Incomplete" or a 55% as a placeholder for missing work, instead of zeros.

6. Have students internalized what a grade means in your class? Ask students to explain what their grades mean in terms of their progress on their learning journey and what they need to work on to improve.

7. What are several ways that you communicate about the grading system with students and families?

Standards-Based Grading (SBG)

Also known as competency-based, proficiency, or mastery grading, SBG measures student progress toward mastering specific knowledge and skills. Students receive grades based on proficiency levels from 1–4 or 1–5 such as: Emerging, Approaching, Proficient, and Advanced. Students only receive grades on summative assessments of learning and summative assessments are aligned to specific standards.

The grades are based on the most recent evidence of learning so that if a student does not demonstrate proficiency the first time the standard is assessed, they can improve their grade by demonstrating mastery on a subsequent assessment of that standard.

If a student earns an 85% in a class or subject area in an SBG system, they will generally earn a B, but what does that communicate? It lets students, families, and others who support students know that they demonstrated proficiency in 85% of the content. If there were fifteen summative assessments in a term and a student earned ten 4s and three 3s and two 1s, then they earned 51/60 (85%) possible points. This student demonstrated proficiency in thirteen of the fifteen standards, and there are two standards that specifically indicate what they still need to learn. If the student later demonstrates proficiency in those two standards, their grade can improve.

If you are required to use an SBG system, ask yourself these questions to make sure that students are set up for success:

1. Do student grades reflect their content knowledge and skills?

2. How can you help students grow career readiness skills like responsibility, organization, study skills, and integrity? To what extent can you report progress on these skills separately?

3. What equity issues exist for students and how does your grading policy create greater equity?

4. What opportunities do students have to get feedback, revise, and resubmit work? To what extent are there opportunities to retake summative assessments resulting in improved student learning?

5. Have students internalized what a grade means in your class? Ask students to explain what their grades mean in terms of their progress on their learning journey and what they need to work on to improve.

6. What are several ways that you communicate about the grading system with students and families?

THE IMPORTANCE OF POST-FEEDBACK REFLECTION

It is an awful feeling when a teacher has spent time providing feedback on students' work and there's no time set aside to review and implement that feedback. This work may linger in a learning management system, get stuffed in a notebook, or be recycled without students spending time with that feedback. If student work is important enough to provide feedback, then it's important enough to carve out time for reflection and teach students how to do that well.

Creating a classroom culture of feedback and reflection is vital to instilling a growth mindset in students. It's important at all grade levels for both students and teachers. Here are some steps to establish your reflection process:

Step One: Set up a central location for all student reflection to occur so that, ultimately, reflections for an entire semester or entire year are gathered in the same place. Young students may even use emojis or reflect verbally.

You may want to use a template that has four columns with developmentally appropriate headings:

Title of the Summative Assessment	Reflect on the Feedback I Received	Reflect on the Effort I Put into the Assessment	Explain How I Will Implement the Feedback

Step Two: Prioritize time (20 minutes) for reflection after students receive feedback on summative assessments. Write it into your lesson plans.

Step Three: Before sharing individual student feedback, share a couple of positive observations about the class's work as a whole and a couple of areas for growth.

Step Four: Have students review your feedback online or on paper, and complete their reflection.

Step Five: As students develop a stronger growth mindset and gain comfort and confidence with the feedback process, have them talk in pairs about the feedback to add coaching from their peers to the process. Note: Remember to reflect on your own effort, results, and student feedback about the unit of study as well.

ADDITIONAL GRADING CONSIDERATIONS

In both grading systems, you will need to develop an assessment plan. It is best if you develop this with your grade-level or subject-area colleagues for consistency, and then adjust it based on the needs of your students.

- As a rule, formative assessments are not graded since they reflect progress and not mastery.

- Students generally will not take summative assessments to check for mastery until they have demonstrated proficiency on formative assessments.

- While there is some flexibility, students can't remain on the first unit all year. When it is time for the classroom community to move ahead to the next unit of study, a student who has not yet gained proficiency in a standard will have future opportunities to demonstrate proficiency on the missing skills.

- Teachers rarely assign grades for homework because that is practice and not a summative assessment. It is likely that there is already a policy in place for homework grades in your school and district. You should consult a mentor or your colleagues for your district's or school's policies regarding homework grades.

- In order to maintain clear communication with students, families, and caregivers, it's important to update your grade book weekly.

- Students' grades are confidential; the Family Educational Rights and Privacy Act (first enacted in 1974) protects them. By law, you should never announce grades, tell a student's grade to a classmate, or allow students to look at your grade book.

How to Manage Student Grades

As summative assessments occur throughout a grading period, it is necessary to manage them seamlessly to communicate student progress to students, families, and caregivers. Accurately and promptly recording student grades is a necessary part of any teacher's daily responsibilities. Having a well-organized approach to how you will manage the assignments that you must grade, record, and return promptly will save you time and stress.

As you devise a plan to manage student grades throughout the term, you can talk with your colleagues to learn what works for them. With their advice, and with time and practice, you will soon find the methods that will work for you. As you begin formulating your plan to manage student grades, keep in mind that there are several things that are necessary for a plan to work well. Any grade management plan should:

- Be in line with your district's and school's policies and procedures. If you are fortunate, many of the decisions that you will have to make will already be in place in those policies and procedures. As you gain experience, if those policies and procedures are not meeting the needs of your students, then recommend changes.

> "I catch myself always thinking about what I could do in class to make something better, but it's in a good way. When it comes to paperwork, I try to do my best to leave it all at school. That way, when I'm home, I'm home."
>
> *Jared Sronce, 6 years' experience*

- Be transparent. Student information systems make transparency easy. Students, families, and caregivers have access to their own portals.

- Be easy for you to use. Keeping up with your grading responsibilities takes time. As you figure out how to manage grades, try to keep the process as simple and streamlined as possible so that you can manage the task quickly and efficiently.

Here are some books and websites for further study about standards-based grading practices:

GreatSchoolsPartnership.org: This nonprofit has resources and exemplar grading practices and policies. Use "grading" as a search term on their website.

ModernClassrooms.org: This nonprofit's website and its podcast have a great deal of support for teachers to learn about blended instruction, self-paced learning, and mastery-based grading

A Teacher's Guide to Standards Based Grading by Robert Marzano (marzanorsources .com): Find this book as well as *Formative Assessment and Standards Based Grading* and many other professional development resources here.

A Repair Kit for Grading: 15 Fixes for Broken Grades by Ken O'Connor (oconnorgrading .com): Find this book as well as *How to Grade for Learning* and other resources here.

The Standards-Based Classroom: Make Learning the Goal by Emily Rinkema and Stan Williams (makelearningthegoal.com): Find this book and an immense library of learning targets and grading scales here.

Fair Isn't Always Equal 2nd Edition, by Rick Wormeli (rickwormeli.com): Discover this book and many articles, podcasts, videos, presentations, and professional learning opportunities here.

Success with Standardized Tests

Neither teachers nor students like standardized tests, but they are often a fixture on school calendars each spring. They are also often gatekeepers for college admission, graduate school, and professional licensure. It is highly likely that your students will have to take at least one standardized test this year. School districts rely on standardized tests to assess the performance of schools and how well teachers are achieving the goals of the school district. Because standardized tests have serious implications for everyone involved, the test administrators in your district will probably give teachers a great deal of information about the specific tests that students will take. Standardized tests do not have to be a headache for you and your students if you take care to do three important things: prepare all year long, teach test-taking skills, and assume your professional responsibilities.

YEARLONG PREPARATION

All of the great work you do to build rapport with students and teach them to think critically, read, write, and solve problems is the best preparation for success on standardized tests. There are a few additional steps you can take to set students up for success. Here are some suggestions to follow all year long:

- Provide solid instruction that is aligned with your school district's and state's curriculum guidelines.
- Talk about the test as an interesting challenge they get to undertake. Make students aware of the test.
- Offer a variety of testing formats and instructional activities all year long so that students can naturally develop skills as test takers.
- Use the materials offered by your state's department of education and your local school district as a planning guide. Often there will be course blueprints and ancillary materials that will help your students to learn the necessary content.
- Offer your students practice tests in the same format as the actual test. When they are informed about what to expect, they can take the test with confidence.
- When students practice for the test, gather data and use this information to offer differentiated reteaching activities.

TEST-TAKING SKILLS

Prepare your students by making sure they are test wise. They should not feel intimidated by the format or process of a standardized test if you take the time to teach test-taking skills. The tips that follow can help you teach important test-taking skills:

- Teach students to take the time to listen as the test examiner reads the instructions, even if they believe that they are familiar with the directions. They should also re-read the instructions for themselves as they work through the test.
- When your students take practice tests, show them how to pace themselves.
- Young children taking assessments may need to learn how to use the computer keyboard, headphones, or other features to take standardized tests.
- Practice reading test items together and analyzing what information the answers require. Many mistakes happen because students do not read the questions carefully.
- Be aware that students often become bogged down in a difficult reading passage and just skim the questions. Teach them to read the questions carefully first and then skim the passage, looking for the answers.

- When students have passages to read, teach them to underline or highlight the parts of the passage that are covered in the questions.

- Teach the process of elimination regarding answer choices. Students should practice eliminating the answers that are obviously not correct until they arrive at a reasonable answer.

- Encourage students to go back and check their work. If the test is a very long one, or if it is timed, teach students to check the questions they are unsure of first and then check others as time permits.

YOUR PROFESSIONAL RESPONSIBILITIES REGARDING TESTING

As a classroom teacher, if yours is a benchmark grade level, you will have test administration responsibilities. It is important that you follow the test protocols when you administer them. It may be helpful to keep in mind that standardized tests are just that—standardized—so that the same testing conditions can be in place for every student. In the list that follows, you will find some suggestions for making sure that you manage test administration in a professional and competent manner:

- Be aware that you will probably be asked to attend training sessions to prepare for test administration. Take the training seriously and don't hesitate to ask questions.

- Allow yourself enough time in advance of the date of the test to carefully read the procedures and directions for testing. If you are not clear about what you are supposed to do, ask the staff member in charge of testing at your school.

- Familiarize yourself with the directions that you are supposed to read aloud, if any, to students during testing. Do not deviate from the script that you will be given.

- Make sure that you have a reliable way to time tests if they are supposed to be timed.

- Do your best to prevent violations of test security. Here are some specific suggestions for this:
    - Monitor students carefully during testing. Don't check email or grade papers during the test, for example. Take care not to look at the tests as you administer them.
    - Don't give in to the temptation to quiz your students afterward about what was on the test.
    - Take care that all students turn cell phones or other electronic devices off and place them in a secure place during the testing period.

- Be aware that teachers are often asked to sign an acknowledgment that they have received information about the test that their students will be taking. When you sign such an acknowledgment, you are indicating that you understand the kind of help you can offer your students before and during the test.

- Gently refuse requests for help from anxious students during testing. If you are not sure how to do this in an appropriate manner, ask the testing coordinator at your school for advice before the day of the test.

- If students are supposed to receive testing accommodations, be scrupulous in providing those accommodations.

- If you encounter problems during testing, report them to the testing coordinator as soon as you can. Some of the problems that you may have to report could include a fire drill, loud noises, a ringing cell phone, a student racing through the test, or a disruptive student.

A final word about success with standardized tests: some of the biggest complaints about standardized tests center on bias inherent in testing and the way they pressure teachers to teach to the test. Some opponents of standardized testing claim that the flaws inherent in standardized tests require teachers who want to have successful students to teach only the material that will be covered on the test. Although it is inevitable that there will be flaws in systems of standardized testing, teachers who want their students to be successful certainly do not teach to the test. In fact, teachers whose students are successful test-takers make a point of teaching the most important concepts in the curriculum instead of dwelling on what may or may not be tested. They may prepare their students by strengthening the test-taking skills specific to their subjects or grade levels, but teachers should not limit their students by teaching to the test.

Questions to Discuss with Colleagues

Sharing ideas with colleagues is a helpful way to devise solutions to some of the problems that you must manage successfully at school. Here, you will find several topics to open discussions with colleagues about successful instructional practices:

1. You want to create a grading system that accurately communicates what students know and can do. What grading system do they use? How does it measure student progress?

2. You want students to reflect on the feedback they receive. What types of reflection tools do they use to help students reflect on their progress?

3. One of your students has an accommodation allowing him to have extra time on tests and quizzes. How should you provide this accommodation? Who can help you with this?

4. You are developing an assessment plan for the semester. You would like to collaborate with your colleagues to share the workload, have a similar number of summative assessments, and create some common assessments for the grade level or subject area. Would this be possible? If so, how might you proceed?

5. You want to offer alternative assessments and some choice to students but are not sure what would be most appropriate and manageable. How should you proceed? Who at your school can help you expand the types of summative assessments you offer?

Topics to Discuss with a Mentor

Although the topics that new teachers need to discuss with a mentor vary from teacher to teacher and from school to school, there are some that most first-year teachers should be

comfortable discussing with a mentor or a trusted colleague. You should ask your mentor about these topics from this section:

- How to learn about your school's grading policies, including homework, participation, and extra credit
- Advice about how to provide fair and equitable grades for students with disabilities who have accommodations and modifications on their IEPs
- How to create high-quality tests and quizzes
- How to quickly and efficiently provide feedback on summative assessments
- How to find advice and information about the standardized tests that your students will be expected to take this term

Reflection Questions to Guide Your Thinking

1. Is your current grading policy providing accurate information about students' academic progress? Are you keeping students, families, and caregivers as informed as they should be?

2. When students receive feedback on a summative assessment, can they talk about what they know and what they need to learn next in your class? How can you help them take more ownership of their learning? Who among your colleagues might help you with this?

3. What can you do to help students understand rubrics and use them for self-assessment? What strengths do they already have that you can capitalize on? How will you know you have been successful at helping them with this?

4. What do I know about how my students learn and what inspires them? Am I measuring their strengths? What amazing learning experience can I provide for them connected to our unit of study? What's the best summative assessment strategy to assess their learning?

5. How have you created time and structure for student reflection? How have you created the same for your own reflection? Are there any patterns in your reflections about which you want to take action?

SECTION ELEVEN

Classroom Management and Restorative Practices

Creating and maintaining a classroom environment where all students can learn the academic and behavioral skills that they will need for a lifetime is no easy task. It involves building relationships of mutual respect with students, co-creating classroom agreements, teaching and reteaching acceptable behaviors, and responding consistently when someone or something is harmed. This is vital to developing a community of learners who care for each other and can safely learn and grow together.

The increased social-emotional needs of students and the harmful effects of punishment and exclusionary discipline are well documented. Fortunately, when we know better, we can do better. Teachers and schools now create comprehensive, classroom management strategies infused with research from social-emotional learning (SEL), trauma-informed practices, Positive Behavior Interventions and Supports (PBIS), Positive Discipline, and Restorative Practices.

In this section, you will explore how to develop and teach community agreements, logical consequences, and restorative practices with the goal of developing an enduring social contract that sets up you and your students for success.

TAKE NOTHING PERSONALLY

Your leadership, upholding community norms and following through on agreements, gives students a sense of safety and confidence. Students need your consistency and predictability so that they feel safe and confident. While you will inevitably experience frustration with student behaviors, leading your classroom well requires that you take nothing personally. This can be very difficult to do, yet is foundational to developing the same growth mindset toward student behaviors as you have toward their academics. It is never okay to yell at students and detrimental to get into power struggles with students. Maintaining a professional distance from disruptive behaviors allows you to remain calm, think clearly, respond appropriately, and model the behaviors you want students to learn. Even a hurricane has a calm eye at the center of its swirling winds. Hopefully, your classroom will not resemble a hurricane, but if at times a storm blows through, be the calm eye.

"In my first year of teaching high school, Jack would regularly derail the sports medicine class with negative and sarcastic remarks. One day after class, I asked Jack if he had a minute to check in. I shared how it felt to be on the receiving end of his comments. Jack took a pause and apologized for making me feel that way. He also shared the physical and mental health challenges he was facing. This gave me a new perspective when interacting with Jack. From that class period on, Jack and I had great communication with only the occasional sarcastic remark that I was now able to appreciate."

Becca Laroi, 9 years' experience

Create Relationships of Mutual Respect

All learning and success as a teacher begins from a foundation of knowing your students and developing relationships of mutual respect. This happens by interacting with each student every day and communicating through your words, lessons, and actions that you care. This relationship is the greatest leverage teachers have to help students learn and grow with their behaviors as well as academics. Students want teachers to approve of, affirm, and validate them. They will care about you and want to follow directions and take risks to learn new things if they know you care about them.

See Sections Four and Six for detailed strategies on how to create a firm foundation with relationships of mutual respect.

Develop Classroom or Community Agreements

All communities have agreements or norms governing acceptable behavior that all members of the group are expected to follow; classrooms are no exception. Providing guidelines for acceptable behavior protects all students' rights to learn. Students of all ages benefit from this guidance to establish a tone of mutual respect, trust, and cooperation.

Positive Behavior Interventions and Supports (PBIS) recommend three school-wide agreements to create positive, predictable, equitable, and safe learning spaces in grades K–12.

The 3Bs are: Be safe. Be respectful. Be responsible.

From these 3Bs teachers work with students to define and teach what it looks like to be safe, respectful, and responsible in the classroom by developing a behavior matrix. The matrix is a basic table describing appropriate behaviors that embody the 3Bs during morning meetings, at centers, during mini lessons, in small group discussion, on devices, and more.

Across the school, teachers and support staff develop and teach shared expectations for what the 3Bs look like in shared spaces like the cafeteria, hallways, library, playground, restrooms, assemblies, on the bus, and online. These expectations are written in student-friendly language based on the grade level.

THINK THROUGH YOUR EXPECTATIONS

When creating agreements for your classroom, you should follow these guidelines to ensure their success. Class agreements should be:

- Stated in positive terms
- General enough to cover a broad range of activities
- Easy for students to remember
- As few as possible to create the learning environment you want
- Appropriate for the age and ability levels of your students

While you will want to engage your students in developing class agreements, you will want to think through the whole process ahead of time. You may want to start class with three general expectations: be safe, be respectful, be responsible and consider what each of those means more specifically in your classroom. For example, in an elementary classroom, to be safe, students need to keep their hands and feet to themselves. In a high school classroom, to be responsible may mean that students need to bring their devices to class every day.

Whether you start with the 3Bs and create a behavior matrix or develop a few expectations of your own, begin thinking about your expectations by following these four steps:

Step One: Determine what areas your expectations need to cover. Begin by asking yourself these questions:

What are some behaviors that make it possible for students to succeed?

What are some behaviors that make it difficult for students to succeed?

What limits should I set to guarantee that all students can exercise their right to learn?

Step Two: Write a rough draft of expectations. Remember to word them as positive behaviors. Share them with your colleagues to make sure they are in line with school rules and appropriate for your students.

Step Three: Less is more. Establish three to five expectations so that they are easy to remember. Can you combine a few to cover a general range of student behavior? For example, you could combine "Bring your textbook every day" and "You will need paper and pens in this class" to read: "Bring the materials you will need for class."

Step Four: Now that you've thought it through, set aside your rough draft and engage students in creating class agreements as a community.

Engage Students in the Process

Mutual respect means welcoming student voice into the development of class agreements. It also allows you to better understand how each student's personality and culture informs their needs and behaviors. There are many strategies you can use to increase student ownership and buy-in for class agreements. You may want to start individually or in pairs before moving to a larger group format. For younger students, you may need to first introduce vocabulary around behaviors and feelings. Here are a few ways to engage students in developing classroom agreements:

- Have students write, discuss, record, or develop a poster for a gallery walk with their responses to these questions:
  - Describe the spaces where you do your best work. Or describe your ideal classroom.
  - How do you want your teacher to treat you?
  - How do you want to treat one another?
  - How do you think your teacher wants to be treated?
  - What does it look like when you are treated with respect?
  - What should we do when a conflict arises or someone doesn't follow our agreements?

After gathering student input, the next step is to refine the lists of expectations that students develop. Here are some possible ways to accomplish that:

- Have students take home the whole list to discuss with their families and caregivers.
- Give students three dots to vote on their top three expectations.
- Create a final draft based on student input.

Publish the final draft of the classroom agreements and display them prominently in the classroom. Then determine:

- Do you want students to sign the class agreements poster?
- Do you want each student to have a copy of the agreements?
- How can you share classroom agreements with families and caregivers in a way that encourages students to talk about them at home?
- How often do you review the classroom agreements and determine if they need updating?
- How will you engage new students with the classroom agreements in a way that helps them to feel ownership as a member of the community?

There are many more places to find lesson plans to engage students in creating class agreements. Here are a few:

CapturingKidsHearts.org: Whether your school can hire the organization for professional development or you are just looking for good ideas, read the blog on this site for excellent ideas on developing classroom agreements.

Positive Behavior Interventions and Supports (PBIS) (PBIS.org): This robust website provides videos, publications, and background information on PBIS with classroom guides on how to get started and on a wide range of topics like bullying prevention and substance abuse.

SmartClassroomManagement.com: Michael Linsin provides teachers with simple and effective classroom management strategies. His website has a blog with hundreds of articles as well as books and professional development opportunities.

The Teacher Toolkit (theteachertoolkit.com): This site offers strategies and tools by teachers for teachers. Watch the welcome video to learn how to navigate the site, then click "View our Tools" to see all the categories. Click "Classroom Management" for videos, strategies, and detailed directions.

Teach and Model Classroom Expectations and Procedures

Just as you teach academic skills, you need to teach behavioral skills and procedures. You will prevent many disruptive problems and create a positive classroom environment if you take the time to teach and model classroom expectations and procedures.

- Follow the expectations yourself. Students are quick to point out if you don't.
- Take the time to teach classroom expectations and procedures to your students.
- Role-play what positive behavior looks like during a variety of class activities. You may want to take the role of a student and ask a student to take the role of a teacher. For example, sit on the rug modeling a few ways to sit safely or sit at a student's desk and raise your hand to ask a question.
- Teach students about the logical consequences that will help you and the students live by the class agreements, and repair harm when someone doesn't follow the agreements. You may want to role-play these as well.
- Practice common routines with the class like arriving to the classroom and storing backpacks, charging devices, sharpening pencils, turning in work, and more.
- Reteach expectations as students return from vacations and new students join the class.

Positive Reinforcement and Logical Consequences

Provide lots of positive reinforcement for positive behavior. It can take many forms and is personalized to students based on how much support they need. There is a great deal of research on reinforcement and the ways to provide positive feedback to students in ways that help them develop skills for self-reflection and not become overly dependent on adults for approval. Here are some general guidelines for positive reinforcement:

- Remember the 5:1 Magic Ratio for positive to negative interactions from Section Six. Build a bank of positives that reinforce growth mindset and encourage students.

- The goal is to help students develop intrinsic motivation to meet classroom expectations. Sometimes extrinsic reinforcement is necessary for some students to get there. Assess what positive reinforcement means for each student and the class as a whole.

- Use authentic encouragement that connects a student's effort to a positive outcome.

- Work with special education teachers, counselors, and social workers to develop positive reinforcements and consequences for students who have IEPs or 504 Plans and need additional support.

- Send positive feedback home through an app that connects school to home, email, or the USPS. Not only does this create goodwill with families and caregivers, if in the future, you need to call home about a disruptive behavior, they already know you care about their child.

- Develop a classroom routine that reinforces the whole group's good work. The marble jar or "warm fuzzy" jar, for example, where a teacher drops marbles or pom-poms in the jar for excellent collective work and whenever the jar is filled, there is a popcorn party, free choice period, or preferred activity that the students really care about.

Proactive, positive reinforcement will not, however, eliminate all behavior issues. You will also need to develop consequences for disruptive behaviors. Consequences are not punishment and do not induce arbitrary suffering for misbehavior. Consequences are not exclusionary; they teach students skills and result in a stronger connection to the classroom community.

Logical consequences are vital for upholding class agreements and teaching students important behavior skills. Develop clear logical consequences using Positive Discipline's "3Rs and an H." Consequences must be:

- *Related* to the behavior
- *Respectful* to the student and all involved
- *Reasonable* to the student and all involved
- *Helpful* to the student as they learn and grow

For example, if a student draws on a desk, the logical consequence may be to clean the desk, but if the teacher expanded the consequence to working with the custodian to clean the cafeteria, then the impact is no longer reasonable. Some examples of logical consequences may include students:

- Receiving a reminder to stop the behavior
- Giving students a choice to stop the behavior or experience a logical consequence

- Filling out a reflection sheet to identify their behavior, who it affected, and what they can do differently next time
- Fixing something they broke
- Losing a privilege connected to the unacceptable behavior
- Going to a calming space or taking a walk when highly emotional
- Talking privately with the teacher about the incident
- Talking with the person who was hurt and repairing the harm
- Calling home to let families and caregivers know about the behavior
- Having a conversation with a counselor or social worker
- Creating a behavior contract with a dean or administrator
- Conferencing with students, families, and caregivers

Here are a few additional guidelines to help you make the most effective and suitable decisions about consequences in your classroom:

- First and foremost, when you observe a student behaving in a way that doesn't meet your expectations, be curious. Ask them calmly, "Are you doing okay?" Leading with compassion will let them know you care and provide you with helpful information to resolve the situation.
- Model and teach the ways that students are to behave during consequences in the same way that you teach class expectations. Show the whole class the appropriate way to use the calming space or reflection center before anyone needs to use it.
- Consequences should be timely. Having a student apologize to a classmate for a disrespectful comment several days after the comment happened is not a productive consequence, for example. Instead, a quick, sincere apology in the moment would repair the situation without additional drama.
- Consequences should be appropriate in severity. If an infraction is slight, keep the consequence slight. For example, students who make a mess in class should clean it up. Students who speak disrespectfully to you should meet with you privately to discuss the behavior.
- Students learn to self-regulate their behavior more quickly if you establish and follow predictable consequences. Teach students the levels of consequences that you will use. For example:

  - Level One: Verbal reminder
  - Level Two: Meet with the teacher + Logical consequence
  - Level Three: Contact with home adults
  - Level Four: Meet with the dean or administrator

Finally, consequences should be discussed, taught, and published so that students know what is expected of them. Discussion at the start of the term, brief verbal reminders early in the term, and periodically as needed are all useful methods of making sure students know what is expected.

Classroom agreements, positive reinforcement, and logical consequences mean little by themselves. Teachers bring them to life and make them meaningful in the context of caring relationships with students and a supportive classroom community. You will need to develop, present, and teach classroom expectations and consequences in a way that strengthens your relationships. You will need to live them in a way that affirms the dignity of individual students and maintains a safe learning environment for all.

When a student violates a classroom agreement and has completed their consequence, greet them warmly and convey to them that every day is a new day full of opportunities to make fresh choices. There are many resources to support you in developing classroom agreements, positive reinforcement, and consequences. Here are a few:

> **LoveandLogic.com:** Love and Logic offers strategies to make teaching fun and less stressful with tools and techniques that provide choices, limits, and consequences in a way that nurtures decision-making skills in students.
>
> **PositiveDiscipline.com:** Positive Discipline provides professional development and teacher resources to teach students social and life skills. It centers on five criteria for positive discipline: 1) Kind and Firm, 2) Belonging and Significance, 3) Effective Long-Term, 4) Social and Life Skills, and 5) Capable Students.
>
> **ResponsiveClassroom.org:** Responsive Classroom has professional development, books, and resources to support engaging academics, positive community, and effective management. It earned the CASEL SELect Program designation for its strength in social and emotional learning.
>
> **SmartClassroomManagement.com/blog:** The blog at this site provides over seven hundred articles with practical tools and strategies for teachers to create a space where students can learn and teachers can teach. In addition, there are books and professional development opportunities.
>
> **WeAreTeachers.com:** Use "classroom management" to search for articles full of tips, strategies, and resources provided by MDR Education.

Restorative Practices

Also referred to as Restorative Justice, Restorative Practices originated from Howard Zehr's book focused on the carceral system called *Changing Lenses—A New Focus for Crime and Justice*. Implemented in schools, Restorative Practices address the school-to-prison pipeline by shifting away from a traditional, punitive approach to discipline. Implementing Restorative Practices increases empathy, accountability, and repairs harm in a way that strengthens both student skills and the learning community.

The Restorative approach combines elements of social-emotional learning (SEL), multi-tiered systems of support (MTSS), and trauma-informed practices, into a school-wide and/or classroom process to address conflict. Schools using Restorative Practices report improved attendance, fewer discipline issues, and reductions in suspensions and expulsions.

Here are a few processes that are part of a restorative model:

- Create and teach classroom agreements or norms
- Establish and teach logical consequences
- Teach accountability and repair skills such as "I statements" and authentic apologies
- Facilitate daily or weekly community circles with a check-in prompt
- When a conflict occurs, ask questions that encourage self-reflection and problem-solving; listen to understand; validate students' feelings
- Restorative conversations can be quick and informal with a teacher or a peer conversation, or in the case of a more significant conflict, it may take some time and require additional staff support
- Some restorative questions may include:

  1. Gather facts and accountability. What happened?
  2. Establish the need behind the behavior. What did you want? Is it okay to want___?
  3. Identify the concerning behavior. Did your behavior work for you?
  4. Identify replacement behavior. What could you try next time that would work for you?
  5. See the ripple effect. Who was affected by what happened?
  6. Develop empathy. In what ways were they affected?
  7. Agree on a repair plan. What do you think you need to do to make things right?
  8. If appropriate, the person harmed will share what impact the incident had on them. (There are times when the harm is severe and it is inappropriate to require the victim of the behavior to confront the person who harmed them.)
  9. Facilitators check to make sure the repair occurred.
  10. In circumstances where the whole class is affected by student behavior, a conversation may be facilitated in the whole group, if it can occur in a way that creates healing and empathy.

Schools that utilize Restorative Practices often teach families how to use these strategies at home. Restorative Practices are not a program. It's a process, and here are some resources to learn more.

International Institute for Restorative Practices (iirp.edu): The publishers of Restorative Works! Podcast and magazine also offer professional development on restorative practices in schools.

Restorative Justice Partnership (RJP) (rjpartnership.org/resources): Based in Denver, RJP provides an implementation guide and teacher resources.

Restorative Practices: Fostering Healthy Relationships & Promoting Positive Discipline in Schools (schottfoundation.org/restorative-practices): Developed by the Schott Foundation, Advancement Project, AFT, and NEA, the guide for educators provides details on why and how to implement restorative practices in your classroom or school.

Teaching Channel (teachingchannel.com): Click on the K–12 Hub for videos, blogs, downloadables, lesson plans, and presentations. Again, use keywords such as "restorative justice" as a search term to find dozens of videos and resources to help you.

Better than Carrots or Sticks: Restorative Practices for Positive Classroom Management **by Dominique Smith, Douglas Fisher, and Nancy Frey:** This is an excellent book about restorative practices.

Develop Policies for Your Classroom

Policies are those general principles that teachers use to consistently, fairly, and equitably respond to a range of student needs and behaviors that may fall beyond the classroom agreements. Before you can develop a set of policies for your own classroom, you should first consult your school district's policies, your school's policies, and those policies that the other members of your grade-level or content area team already have in place.

For example, your team may do standards-based grading and have a policy that allows students who do not yet show mastery on a summative assessment to retake it. Your classroom policy could complement that broader one if your policy were that students could retake assessments during a free period or after school. Some of the areas for which you may need to design policies include these:

- Office hours for students who need extra help
- Classroom cell phone use
- Backpacks in class
- Food in the classroom
- Reteaching/missing assignments after an absence
- Cheating and plagiarism
- Tardiness
- Appropriate language
- Late or missing graded assignments
- Appropriate homework help
- Conflicts with classmates
- Technology use
- Listening to music in class

- Grading
- Forgotten materials
- Use of generative AI

When developing policies, lead with empathy, have a clear purpose for the policy, and make sure you can consistently follow the policy. To make it easier to take a systematic approach to establishing your classroom policies, consider using Teacher Template 11.1 to work through the process.

Establish Procedures for Your Classroom

"Just this week I had the occasion to encounter a brand-new teacher in the hallway. She was teary-eyed. I asked her what was wrong, and she said her class had fallen into disarray when she asked a student to put away her phone. I asked if she had a procedure for that, and she didn't yet. She was crying, she said, because she thought they wouldn't like her anymore. I asked if she had friends, and she replied 'of course.' Then I told her she didn't need students for friends; they needed her for structure. I told her they would like her if they respected her, but they never would if she tried to be their friend. Kind, yes. Fair, yes. Friend, no. Good and fair procedures eliminate tears."

Luann West Scott, 42 years' experience

From energetic kindergartners to sophisticated seniors, students and teachers need routines and recurring procedures in their school day and week to keep learning on track. As you begin establishing the procedures for your classroom, it is sensible to think of them as the steps that you want students to follow when performing tasks. The particulars of these procedures will vary from teacher to teacher and from grade level to grade level, but adhering to specific procedures for various tasks and activities will help the classroom community run smoothly.

Planning Classroom Policies

Use this template to jot down your ideas about some areas for which a formal policy is necessary, what you want to accomplish with your policy, and what you might include in that policy. As you complete this document, consider the policies of your district or school as well as those of your teaching teams when planning for your own classroom policies.

Students who need extra help:

_____
_____
_____

Classroom cell phone use:

_____
_____
_____

Backpacks in class:

_____
_____
_____

Food in the classroom:

_____
_____
_____

Reteaching/missing assignments after an absence:

_____
_____
_____

Cheating and Plagiarism:

_____
_____
_____

Tardiness:

_____
_____
_____

(continued on next page)

From *The First-Year Teacher's Survival Guide, 5th Edition*, by Michelle Cummings. Copyright © 2024 by John Wiley & Sons, Inc. Reproduced by permission.

(continued from previous page)

Appropriate language:

_____

_____

_____

Late or missing graded assignments:

_____

_____

_____

Appropriate homework help:

_____

_____

_____

Conflicts with classmates:

_____

_____

_____

Technology use:

_____

_____

_____

Listening to music in class:

_____

_____

_____

Grading:

_____

_____

_____

Forgotten materials:

_____

_____

_____

Use of generative AI:

_____

_____

_____

"Spending time on routines and procedures will save you time in the long run. Teach them. Model them. Reteach them and return to them often. Use visuals as reminders. Take a picture of what a desk should look like at the beginning of class and then show it before the bell rings. You might not even have to say a word. And if you decide you don't like your procedures, change them. Ask other teachers for ideas, or ask the students themselves what works for them."

Jennifer Burns, 13 years' experience

Before school begins, you should decide what classroom routines and procedures you want to teach your students to follow. It's important to have these in place before the first day of class, as they will inform the way you set up your classroom. It is also vital to creating a positive classroom environment and successful students. Use Teacher Template 11.2 to help you begin to formulate your class procedures.

TEACHER TEMPLATE 11.2

Planning Classroom Procedures

The following are some of the essential classroom areas that require carefully planned procedures. To determine the best course of action to take for each item, first consult your colleagues or mentor to make sure that the procedures you establish are in line with or an improvement to the procedures that other teachers in your building use.

Beginning class: _____

Ending class: _____

Being tardy to class: _____

Making up learning after an absence: _____

Handing in work: _____

Using cell phones: _____

Keeping the work area clean: _____

Formatting written work: _____

Using the classroom library: _____

Finishing work early: _____

Listening to intercom announcements: _____

Being a classroom helper: _____

Lining up: _____

Going to the health clinic: _____

Using a device (iPad, laptop, Chromebook): _____

Asking questions: _____

Handling emergencies: _____

Going to the restroom: _____

Having materials needed for class: _____

Making up missing or late graded assignments: _____

Sharpening pencils: _____

Water bottles or hydration: _____

Assigning homework: _____

Turning in money: _____

Taking attendance: _____

Taking lunch counts: _____

Getting students' attention back to the teacher: _____

Taking summative assessments: _____

Conducting emergency drills: _____

Other procedures specific to your class: _____

_____

_____

How to Say No Courteously

Teachers spend their days bombarded by a steady stream of requests from students who want to go to the restroom, the office, a locker, the clinic, or to call home, open a window, shut a window, sharpen pencils, and hear the directions just one more time. Fielding these entreaties tactfully requires quick decisions not only about whether the request is a sound one, but also about how the response will affect the entire class as well as the student making it.

Saying yes and being flexible to respond to students' needs is important for teachers, and so is the ability to discern when the correct answer is no so that students persist and disruptions to learning are few. No is not a popular answer, and you should think through your rationale and be prepared to share it.

One of the most useful skills that a teacher can develop is the ability to refuse a student's request without causing offense. Although it may seem impossible, this is not as difficult as it sounds. Instead of abruptly refusing, try one of the statements or questions that follow. Each one is designed to say no in a pleasant, nonconfrontational way that preserves the student's dignity. Remember to keep your tone neutral and pleasant.

- Let me think about that for a little while.
- Let's talk about that after class.
- Let's finish this first.
- I don't think that is the best decision because _____.
- Are you sure that's a wise choice?
- What do you think?
- Could you give me a moment?
- Can this wait?
- What are the pros and cons involved in your request?

- How are you planning to do that?
- How will you accomplish that?
- Can you tell me why that might not work?
- Would you ask me again in a moment?
- Have you finished your assignment?
- How will that help you achieve your goal?
- Why don't you give that some more thought?

Empower Your Class with Student Ownership

Many ways of encouraging students to follow class policies, procedures, and agreements will be more effective than imposing your authority as a teacher on students. Spending time in the first days of a term listening to student input and developing thoughtful agreements, routines, policies, and procedures will result in a more productive classroom environment all year long. Follow these strategies to solicit your students' support:

- Involve students early. The more involved your students are with class expectations early in the year, the more likely those expectations are to be successful. This success will be generated by the sense of ownership your students will gain through their involvement.
- Ask students to tell you the reasons behind a behavior expectation.
- Have students role-play scenarios illustrating various aspects of the class behavior expectations.
- Occasionally quiz your students orally about the rules in rapid-fire bursts of questions at the start or end of class. Make it an enjoyable competition to engage everyone.
- Have students make up songs, chants, gestures, or mottoes for various agreements.
- Make movement a regular part of every work period to help students remain in a positive, learning frame of mind.
- Encourage self-discipline and redirect student energy whenever you can.

Promoting Self-Discipline

The ultimate purpose of the careful thought and effort that we pour into classroom leadership is not to create mindlessly compliant students, but to encourage students to be self-disciplined. When students assume control of their own behavior choices, a positive shift occurs in the classroom. Self-directed students are confident, productive, and on-task far more often than not.

Despite the impossibility of ever knowing for certain just how successful your attempts to help students assume responsibility for their actions will be, you must work toward that goal. You should not only maintain boundaries and guide your students so that they understand what they should do but also help them internalize that doing the right thing at the right time benefits their learning and relationships.

Fortunately, you have countless chances to help students in their efforts to become self-disciplined. Here are two that are essential for creating the positive environment that you want for your students:

- Maintain high expectations for all students. You don't have to expect perfect behavior all the time, but too often our students are much more capable than we give them credit for being. It is especially important to maintain these high standards when students seem to struggle. It is a disservice to lower standards instead of helping students rise to meet them.

- Be encouraging and positive with students. Students whose teachers make it abundantly clear that they have confidence in their ability to succeed are students who are more apt to become self-disciplined than those whose teachers doubt their students' abilities. If you want positive actions from your students, then you must show your own positive side.

Resources for Further Exploration

To learn more about the practical aspects of a well-managed classroom, you can explore some of these resources:

National Education Association (NEA) (nea.org): Use "classroom management" as a search term to access helpful articles about how to manage a classroom successfully.

Smart Classroom Management (smartclassroommanagement.com): Use "class rules" as a search term to access helpful articles about how to establish rules successfully.

TeacherVision (teachervision.com): Use "classroom management" as a search term to find dozens of articles and other useful resources.

Teaching Channel (teachingchannel.com): Click on the K–12 Hub for videos, blogs, downloadables, lesson plans, and presentations. Again, use keywords such as "classroom management" as a search term to find dozens of videos and resources to help you learn and grow.

Questions to Discuss with Colleagues

Sharing ideas with colleagues is a helpful way to devise solutions to some of the problems that you must manage successfully at school. Here, you will find several topics to open discussions with colleagues about successful instructional practices:

1. You have carefully thought through and engaged students in developing class agreements and you want to maintain them, yet you are not sure when to be flexible and when to be strict. How can you determine the best course of action to take when upholding class agreements?

2. A couple of teachers at your school seem to abide by their own rules instead of the ones for the entire school. This inconsistency has created problems for you and your students as you ask them to follow school rules. How can you handle this tactfully and effectively?

3. One of your students repeatedly disrupts class. The consequences that you have in place are not effective in changing her behavior. What should you do?

4. Some of the policies around student discipline at your school are outdated and not effective any longer. How can you change these policies and explore a more restorative approach?

5. What routines and procedures do your colleagues have in place that you think would be effective in your classroom? How can you share ideas about these procedures and how to implement them?

Topics to Discuss with a Mentor

Although the topics that new teachers need to discuss with a mentor vary from teacher to teacher and from school to school, there are some that most first-year teachers should be comfortable discussing with a mentor or a trusted colleague. You should ask your mentor about these topics from this section:

- Suggestions for class agreements that would be appropriate for your class
- Advice about how to create different classroom routines and procedures
- How to create appropriate, logical consequences for your students
- Where to learn more about district and school policies that affect you and your students
- How to create student ownership of their own behavior and the classroom agreements

Reflection Questions to Guide Your Thinking

1. What policies do you anticipate needing for your class that are not on the list given earlier in this section? How can you plan for them?

2. What other types of procedures besides the ones in this section would be beneficial to your students? How can you plan for them?

3. What can you do to improve the quality of restorative conversations and reduce the time it takes to have them? How can you help students to learn and genuinely change their behavior?

4. What classroom management systems do you currently have in place that are effective? What makes them effective? What can you add to your other policies and procedures to increase their effectiveness?

5. What techniques to support student behavior have you observed in other classrooms that you would like to try in your own class? How easily could they be adapted to meet the needs of your students?

SECTION TWELVE

Prevent and Minimize Disruptive Behavior

Keep calm and carry on learning. This is the goal of a positive classroom environment and it is the result of many factors. Instead of only reacting to disruptions, you will need to believe that students do well when they can; intentionally teach pro-social behavior; build supportive relationships; and establish classroom agreements, policies, and procedures to help prevent and minimize disruptive behavior.

Researchers have learned a lot about what's happening when student behaviors are challenging and even appear disrespectful. According to William Glasser's Choice Theory, we know that behavior is driven by a need; it is an attempt to satisfy one of the five basic needs to:

- love and belong
- be powerful
- be free
- have fun
- survive

So it's important to observe behavior and ask yourself what's beneath that behavior? What unmet need is the behavior trying to satisfy? Dr. Dan Siegel, in his book *Brainstorm: The Power and Purpose of the Teenage Brain*, talks about how the brain is wired to keep us safe. Students, especially those with a history of trauma, scan the landscape for threats and go into fight-or-flight mode quickly. He offers a powerful hand model of the brain and explains what happens when students become dysregulated and "flip their lids" and what happens when students learn to integrate the parts of their brains.

Visit drdansiegel.com/resources/, where you can explore many resources and watch a video of Dr. Siegl demonstrating the hand model of the brain and explaining the way that the parts of the brain work together.

The number of social interactions teachers have every day is significant, and while you will make mistakes, strive to bring more empathy and humanity into each of those interactions. With a proactive approach to disruptive behavior, you will be able to create the culture and climate that you want for your students. You will feel more confident about how to lead your classroom so that the real business of your class—student learning—can take place.

Before you begin learning about how to prevent or minimize the discipline problems in your classroom, you can use Teacher Template 12.1 to reflect on how well you are already managing this part of your teaching practice and to make informed decisions about the plans you want to create to have a healthy climate in your classroom.

TEACHER TEMPLATE 12.1

How Proactive Are You Currently?

As you consider how you can minimize the negative impacts of disruptive behavior in your classroom, reflect on your current approach. Are you doing everything you can to be the proactive teacher you need to be?

Read each of these beliefs or practices and self-assess on each one. Use a 1–4 scale: 4 = excellent, 3 = very good, 2 = average, 1 = area for growth. If you do not have a 3 or 4, then that practice is something that you may want to add.

1. _____ I see the good in students and believe students do well when they can.
2. _____ I have a set of positively stated norms or agreements posted in my classroom.
3. _____ I use a friendly and firm voice when I ask students to do something.
4. _____ I teach students affective skills like self-control, empathy, responsibility, and cooperation.
5. _____ I have established my calm presence as a classroom leader and convey an expectation of cooperation.
6. _____ I have established reasonable and logical consequences for a range of disruptive behaviors.
7. _____ I have taught students the agreements, routines, procedures, and consequences that will create a healthy learning community.
8. _____ I make sure to build relevance and engage students' interest in every lesson.
9. _____ I consistently maintain classroom agreements.
10. _____ I lead with empathy when intervening with a behavior issue. I ask students calmly, "Are you doing okay?" to make sure students know I care.
11. _____ My students perceive that my actions are fair.
12. _____ I get to know my students and their interests, needs, and cultures.
13. _____ I contact family members and caregivers to support student behaviors.
14. _____ I follow the 5:1 ratio, giving my students five encouragements before one correction.
15. _____ I monitor my students consistently during class.
16. _____ I am intentionally proactive in my approach to behavior issues.
17. _____ I respect the dignity of all my students and treat them with respect.
18. _____ I cultivate a sense of community and leverage the positive community to prevent and minimize disruptive behavior.
19. _____ I use nonverbal interventions to address minor behaviors.
20. _____ I accept responsibility for what happens in my class.
21. _____ With elementary students, I get on their eye level to intervene in behavior, rather than towering over them.

It's Up to You

Yes, it "takes a village to raise a child," and yes, you have a team at school and home to support students. Still it's also true that you are their best hope for success. Teachers see the good in students and hold a vision for their growth and ultimate success. Teachers determine how much time students have to learn and what those opportunities to learn look like. So it is also true that it's up to you. You can do this. You can create positive learning communities and prevent and minimize the disruptive behaviors that will arise in your classroom.

As a classroom teacher, being proactive and preventative is an easier task than having to cope with serious issues once they have occurred. It's likely that even with proactive steps in place, you will need to respond to disruptive behaviors. After all, students are young people who are learning academic and behavioral skills they need for a lifetime. With a growth mindset, we know that mistakes and misbehavior are part of the process of learning. Teachers can make a difference in the lives of their students and need to thoughtfully set about doing so.

> "Classroom culture and climate starts with you. Your manner, your poise, your assurance. Your voice is calm, well moderated, evenly paced, and easily heard. Nothing shakes your calm. You know what is acceptable in your classroom, and you communicate that to your students."
>
> *Anna Aslin Cohen, 40 years' experience*

Your Goal: Keep Calm and Carry on Learning

Because it's easy be anxious about how you will successfully create the climate that you want for your students, the true goal of those efforts can be obscured. As you work to create an orderly environment by preventing or minimizing disruptive behaviors, keep in mind that in addition to teaching students pro-social skills, one of your goals is for students to continue learning without interruption. Although cooperative behavior is necessary, try to keep in mind that it is only a means to achieve a much bigger purpose: student learning.

Your Calm Assumption of Cooperation

It's natural to be nervous. You are responsible to lead a classroom of young people for the first time. You want to project confidence even when you lack it. A teacher's anxiety and uncertainty transmit themselves in many subtle and not so subtle ways—none of them conducive to creating a positive classroom climate. Even if you are so anxious that you can feel your knees knocking together, your students still need you to lead them. In this case, "Fake it 'til you make it" is good advice.

Adopt and then project the proactive stance that you are certain that your students will cooperate. Calmly relay this expectation through body language and tone of voice. Assume a general air of confidence in their willingness to follow your guidance, and your students will respond in a positive way. If you allow your apprehension to be obvious, then your students will not feel confident, and may lose focus and engage in inappropriate behaviors.

A firm voice. A friendly smile. A confident posture. A lot of encouragement. A matter-of-fact tone. These will allow you to deliberately project that calm expectation of cooperation—and ultimately, of success—that can minimize or prevent disruptive behaviors.

Be Aware of the Causes of Most Disruptive Behavior

If you are to create a healthy culture and climate, then it is important to look at the big picture to understand what may cause disruptive behavior. Humans are complicated beings with complex reasons for acting the way they do. Your students' behaviors can become easier to support once you are aware of the underlying causes and can address those causes instead of just reacting to the behavior itself. See Section Seven on trauma-informed practices for more strategies. Here are some of the reasons why students may make poor choices in class:

- Their work is too difficult, too easy, or just not an appropriate match for their learning preferences.
- They perceive their teacher as uncaring or having said something that made the student feel "less than."
- They perceive their classmates as uncaring and don't feel a sense of belonging.
- They are distracted or bullied by someone in the class.
- They see no connection between the lesson and their goals for the future.
- Their culture is not affirmed and celebrated by you or the school.
- They have not had an opportunity to learn vital communication and social skills.
- They lack the resources they need, such as a computer, internet connectivity, or school supplies.
- They have not yet mastered the academic skills needed to do their work and need additional scaffolding or help.
- They don't yet have the organizational skills needed to manage their time, materials, or assignments.
- They may lack basic needs such as food, clothing, shelter, or a supportive home adult.
- They may not have slept the night before due to homelessness or a difficult situation at home.

Avoid These Mistakes

To prevent or minimize disruptive behaviors in your class, it's important to avoid these mistakes that may cause harm or undermine trust. First-year teachers are not always sure about the best course of action to take when confronted with a behavior issue. While you are not expected to know everything about how to manage a class, there are some mistakes that no teacher should make:

- Raising your voice
- Being sarcastic
- Embarrassing students
- Accepting too many excuses or being a pushover
- Making bargains with students to coerce them into obedience
- Making fun of students, especially any aspect of their identity or culture
- Allowing students to bully or harass one another
- Blaming the entire class for misbehavior
- Holding grudges
- Allowing small problems to become large ones
- Being a poor role model
- Assigning work as punishment
- Nagging students
- Being confrontational
- Ignoring serious misbehavior
- Losing your temper

Three Crucial Teacher Traits that Make a Difference

Positivity. Consistency. Fairness. These are three traits of teachers with healthy classroom communities. Without all three of them working in unison, you will find it difficult to prevent or minimize disruptive behaviors. Once students begin to perceive that you are positive, consistent, and fair, however, you will notice that they will no longer test the limits of what is acceptable (and your patience) to work cooperatively with you.

These crucial traits will make it easier for students to trust you and to be confident that you are the kind of teacher they need. If you focus on manifesting these three teacher traits in all you do, you will see the positive results in your classroom.

BE POSITIVE: BUILD ON STUDENTS' STRENGTHS

Although it is very easy to have a positive relationship with students who already have strong academic and behavioral skills, it is not always easy to have the same positive relationship with those students who struggle with academic and behavioral skills. It is even more important that you work to have a positive relationship with every student—especially those who need you most. Students who find school difficult need even more positive interactions with their teachers than the students for whom school seems to come easily.

Most students can recite mistakes they have made, what they should not do, and what they are not good at. If those same students are asked to share their five greatest strengths, however, they may be at a loss. As teachers, we need to spend significant time focusing on our students' strengths and successes. When students have clarity about their strengths, learning success can become a self-fulfilling prophecy.

On the one hand, when our students believe they are capable, they are going to be brave enough to take that extra risk that will generate even more success. Critical comments, on the other hand, can destroy even the bravest student's confidence. There are many ways to bring a positive focus on your students' strengths in your lessons. Here is a quick list of just some of the ways you can engage in a strengths-based, positive manner with your students:

- Give your students genuine and specific encouragement throughout the day. Along with growth mindset, this is a teacher's default way of being.

- Use positive body language to convey your respect and sincerity when you listen to and talk with students.

- Create opportunities in writing and community meetings to share hidden talents and skills.

- Be generous with sincere positive feedback. Students who are aware of what they are doing correctly tend to repeat it.

- Ask students to tell others in their small groups what they did right on a difficult assignment so that everyone can benefit.

- When students go over feedback on their work, have them reflect on the things they did well as well as correct their errors.

- During class discussions, ask students for their advice or opinions on topics of study and challenges facing the class. Students often have important insights and solutions to problems that surprise many adults, even those who know them well.

- Classes seem to take on a personality of their own. Use this to your advantage when you can. For example, if a class is very talkative, turn this into a strong point by giving them lots of opportunity for debate and discussion.

- Be specific and sincere in your feedback so that students know what they did well.

- Connect positive behaviors to what those behaviors make possible or outcomes for the whole class. This is a way for students to learn the purpose of behavior and cause-and-effect relationships.

- Use exit slips to periodically ask your students what they did well during class. How did it make them feel? What did they gain from this behavior? How did everyone benefit?

BE CONSISTENT: BUILD TRUST AND CONFIDENCE

As a teacher, you will make hundreds of decisions every day. Not only will you have to make many of these decisions quickly, but you will also have to make them in front of a crowd of students—all of whom have a range of needs and often, cell phones with cameras. You will never have enough time to think through many of the decisions, so you will have to think fast.

The number of quick decisions required of you may sometimes make it difficult to be consistent. However, consistency is one of the most important tools you have in reducing disruptive behaviors because predictability builds trust and gives your students well-defined boundaries for their behavior. Consistent empathetic leadership in partnership with shared agreements and logical consequences provides a predictable environment. Being consistent will make your students comfortable and confident in class.

If you want to become more consistent in the way you respond to student behaviors, there are some easy techniques that can help you get started. Here are several suggestions to create the consistent environment you want for your students:

- Consistently lead with empathy and curiosity about student behaviors.
- Consistently take nothing personally.
- Flexibility goes hand in hand with consistency, otherwise teachers become rigid and unable to accommodate students' needs.
- Maintain classroom agreements with each student, every day.
- Be prepared and organized so that you will be able to focus on your interactions with students and find it easier to make effective, quick decisions each day.
- In behaviors, just as in academics, you will need to consistently differentiate instruction and practice. A child with ADHD may need more frequent breaks than the class to meet the same high expectations for behavior.
- Intervene early when students are struggling so that issues remain manageable.
- Teach and reteach class agreements and procedures as often as needed, including when you return from school vacations.

BE FAIR: BUILD MUTUAL RESPECT

One of the surest ways for teachers to cause disruptive behaviors is to treat your students unfairly. Even very young students are quick to notice actions that they perceive as unjust and to react accordingly. Students will be more cooperative with you and with one another if they feel that you regard them with respect. Here are some tips on how to make sure that your students will regard you as a teacher who is fair to everyone in the class:

- Listen and be curious when students are speaking. Teachers who take the time to listen carefully get to know their students well. Once that vital connection is made, students will find it easier to behave in an acceptable manner because they will feel connected to you and to the class.
- When intervening with a minor disruptive behavior, consider asking, "Are you doing okay?" to convey your care and concern.
- With elementary students, whenever possible, get on their eye level to intervene in behavior, rather than towering over them. This body language builds trust and communicates your interest in what they have to say.

- Allow students to explain their perspective whenever possible. Make it easy for students to talk to you when they experience problems.

- Keep in mind that *fair* does not mean *equal*. *Fair* is "equitable." Teachers provide the instruction and supports based on students' unique needs. An emergent bilingual student or a student with disabilities will need supports that will not necessarily be needed by others in the class.

- Don't play favorites. This is one of the fastest ways to ruin relationships with students. View each student with positive regard.

- Don't give your students unpleasant surprises. Announce tests and quizzes in advance. Publish assignments and due dates in various ways so that all students know what is expected of them.

> "Consistency is really important; you cannot have students wondering what the expectations in class are. Having said that, life isn't just absolutes; there's an awful lot of gray out there. Some students may need a little more time, some students are going to have to see that note sheet you had everyone fill out with some answers already filled in. We can bend our rules and expectations in a lot of situations to allow students to get what they need. If a student struggles with writing, the wheels won't come off if we ask him or her for two really strong paragraphs instead of the four we assigned. The hope is to build them to the full assignment down the road. Don't be too rigid."
>
> *Kevin Healy, 11 years' experience*

- Make your high expectations clear and make success attainable. Give students examples, models, and samples so that they know what to do to be successful.

- Make sure that the amount of practice outside of class that you assign is reasonable.

- Expect your students to observe the same norms as the rest of the students in your school in addition to the classroom agreements that you have established.

- Have the same high expectations and high levels of support for academic and behavioral success.

- When you make a mistake, admit it, and model a genuine apology. Be honest with your students.

R-E-S-P-E-C-T: FIND OUT WHAT IT MEANS TO ME

Respect can be a noun or a verb meaning "admiration or having regard for the feelings and rights of others." In classrooms, *respect* means being taken seriously, and both teachers and students want to feel respected. Building a classroom culture founded on mutual respect means a commitment by students and teachers to behave in ways that both earn and extend respect.

Students will describe classrooms where mutual respect is present as places where they feel heard and cared about. They feel a sense of belonging in a community where their voice matters in learning, and in making the classroom and school better places.

No matter how interesting the subject, how dynamic the instruction, or how well planned the procedures, if we do not have a culture of mutual respect with our students, learning is unlikely to happen. Respect is one of those vital intangibles that is difficult to define. It's the constant delicate balance among the many roles we assume in our workday: educator, motivator, humorist, listener, adviser, evaluator, entertainer, guide, comforter, and role model.

Having your students' respect is one of the biggest assets any teacher can bring to school each day. When you have earned your students' respect, you will be able to prevent or minimize almost all the disruptive behaviors that come your way.

How do teachers lose the respect of their students? There are lots of ways a teacher can be disrespectful and cause students to lose faith. Here is a brief list:

- Being inconsistent and unpredictable
- Not keeping your word
- Not getting to know your students
- Losing your temper
- Refusing to admit when you make a mistake
- Treating students unfairly
- Assigning work that is inappropriate, too challenging, or not challenging enough
- Treating students harshly
- Not being prepared or not knowing the material
- Being insensitive to students' needs
- Being emotionally unstable
- Not being a good adult role model

If these are the ways teachers can lose respect, how then can you earn your students' respect? The best way to ensure that you have earned your students' respect is to fulfill your responsibilities as a teacher. You earn respect throughout the school day in the many large and small decisions that you make, such as providing feedback promptly, being prepared for class, and treating all students with dignity.

There is no better way to improve how you teach than to be a reflective practitioner. When teachers examine how they fulfill their responsibilities—assessing their own strengths and areas for growth—then they can work systematically to improve the areas where they are not as strong as they would like to be. This attitude will yield countless rewards for a long time. You treat students with respect when you take these actions:

- Listen to students and cultivate student voice, choice, and agency in all you do
- Create a welcoming and inclusive classroom; affirm students' humanity and cultures
- Behave consistently and predictably
- Keep your word
- Get to know your students
- Maintain a calm demeanor

- Protect students from bullying and harassment by creating a healthy classroom climate and by addressing any incidents immediately
- Have high expectations and high levels of support for all students' academic and behavioral success
- Avoid backing students into corners; always allow them a way to avoid embarrassment
- Help students develop effective work habits
- Acknowledge concerns and allow students to voice their concerns
- Make teaching social skills part of the daily fabric of your class
- Use calming spaces and other interventions that can help students compose themselves when they experience heightened emotions
- Provide predictable routines and procedures so that students can go about their work confident that they know what to do
- Avoid power struggles
- Encourage, encourage, encourage

Withitness: An Attitude, a Skill, and a Necessity

Building a culture of mutual respect helps students to do the right thing, even when you are not watching. Yet, monitoring student behavior is a necessary skill for teachers. Almost everyone has had at least one teacher who was able to write notes on the board and ask students in the back of the room to stop texting at the same time. Such teachers' expertise is an inspiration for us all. Educational researcher Jacob Kounin first coined the term *withitness* in his 1977 book, *Discipline and Group Management in Classrooms*. What is *withitness*?

Dr. Robert Marzano defines *withitness* as "the ability of teachers to monitor and be aware of what is happening in the classroom at all times." Teachers with highly refined withitness skills can identify and prevent problematic behaviors and intervene appropriately when disruptive behavior occurs.

Teachers with withitness are said to have eyes in the back of their head. As amazing and inspiring as it may be, however, no one is born with the trait of *withitness*. As a method of preventing classroom disruptive behaviors, withitness is crucial. Teachers who are alert to what is happening in their classrooms are far more likely to be able to prevent or minimize problems; they are tuned in to all their students rather than checking email or conferencing with just one student while ignoring nearby students who may also be off task.

They are also the teachers who have positive relationships with their students. Although positive relationships are valuable for a variety of reasons, these connections often allow a teacher to predict student behavior. Knowledge of students, constant vigilance, and the ability to imagine what could go wrong in classroom situations combine to proactively prevent or minimize misbehavior.

Teachers who have honed their withitness skills know that it's not enough just to actively supervise their students. What is important is that they make their vigilance obvious to their students in many subtle ways—a nod, a friendly smile, a puzzled frown, proximity. Letting students know that you are aware of their behavior often convinces them to make good choices and that misbehavior is just not worth the trouble.

Withitness is easy to master with just a bit of care and effort. Here are some simple tips for cultivating your own classroom withitness:

- Don't *ever* turn your back completely on a class. Not even once.
- Be alert to stealthy signs and signals among your students.
- Greet students at the door. Use student arrival time to pay attention to students' emotions. This will allow you to check in with students, predict, and diffuse conflict.
- Use quiet reminders throughout instruction so that students know what is expected of them and will not misbehave because they are frustrated or bored.
- Be prepared for the day's lesson so that you can stay attuned to student behavior as you deliver instruction.
- As quickly as you can, try to learn your students' strengths and areas of growth. This knowledge will make it easier for you to predict their behavior.
- Develop your ability to switch rapidly between tasks. Teachers with the ability to overlap their attention find it easier to monitor classes. For example, teachers can take attendance with a quick glance around the room at the start of class while students are working on independent warm-up activities.
- Pace lessons so that the workflow can help you keep students engaged. For example, have assignments ready for the early finishers instead of expecting them to just sit quietly with nothing to do while others finish.
- Arrange your classroom furniture so that you can see every student and be seen from every desk in the room.
- It's easy to be too optimistic about the success of an activity when planning instruction. Be aware of this tendency and predict the times in a lesson when more watchfulness could be necessary.
- Be sure to explain the expectations and procedures for each activity that may be new or unfamiliar to your students. This will make it easier to monitor behavior because it encourages more students to stay on task.
- Stay on your feet and monitor your students. Move around the room instead of sitting at your desk or standing in one spot for too long.

Use Teacher Template 12.2 to assess your current level of withitness.

TEACHER TEMPLATE 12.2

Assess Your Current Level of Withitness

Take a few minutes to reflect on your current level of withitness and to determine where you could improve. Rank yourself on a scale of 1 through 3 regarding how successful you are in practicing the following strategies, with 3 being as successful as possible. Any strategy for which you can't rank yourself as a 3 may be one that you continue to work to improve.

1. _____ I develop mutual respect with students so they learn to behave well even when I'm not watching.

2. _____ I take a proactive stance toward preventing or minimizing disruptive behavior.

3. _____ I trust my intuition. If something seems amiss among my students during class, it probably is.

4. _____ When conducting 1:1 student conferences, I arrange myself so that I can continue to see the rest of the class.

5. _____ I know my students very well. I am familiar with their strengths and areas for growth.

6. _____ I greet students at the door at the start of class to connect with students and address any potential concerns.

7. _____ I am prepared for class so that I can focus on my interactions with students.

8. _____ I can switch between tasks so that I can overlap my attention, doing one task and monitoring the class.

9. _____ I circulate well in the classroom, connecting with each student, and minimizing the time I spend sitting at my workspace.

10. _____ I have arranged my classroom so that I can see all my students and be seen by all of them.

11. _____ When I need to talk privately with a student in the hallway, I keep the door open so that I can monitor the rest of the class.

12. _____ Students do not congregate around my workspace. I go to them instead.

13. _____ I make a point of spreading out my attention instead of spending too much time with one or two students.

14. _____ I pace lessons so that they flow in a quick and thoughtful tempo to keep every student engaged.

15. _____ As I work with one small group of students, I make a point to remain aware of what the rest of the class is doing.

How to Help the Whole Group Stay on Task While You Work with Small Groups

One of the most difficult classroom withitness skills to develop involves keeping the rest of the class on task while you work with an individual student or small group. Developing student ownership and self-direction takes time and at those times when your attention is elsewhere, students can lose focus and engage in disruptive behaviors.

However, with diligence and a bit of planning, even this difficult skill is one that you can develop. To begin, try some of these easy suggestions:

- Take care to make your expectations for behavior during small group and 1:1 conference time explicit. Spend time at the start of an activity explaining the procedures and model the self-direction skills that you want all students to use as they continue their learning. Be sure to include information to help the students who finish their work earlier than the others.

- As you design your lesson plans, the work students engage in as you hold conferences should be work they can complete without your support.

- Depending on the age and access available to students, provide videos, information, and helpful resources for students in your learning management system.

- Arrange for student experts to be available to help those students who need assistance or assurance that they are on the right track as they work. Consciously planning this will make it easier than if you try to include it on the spur of the moment.

- For questions that can't be answered by their peers, designate a place for students to post their questions to be answered after the small group conference concludes.

- Furniture arrangement is key. Set up your classroom so that you have a small group or conference area that allows you to face the class: a kidney-shaped table or group of desks in a corner of the room is ideal. Be sure that your chair faces the class and that the students you are conferring with face you.

- Do not linger with the small group. Have a plan for the conference and stick to it.

- As you work with the small group, scan the room to monitor the other students. Gentle verbal reminders or encouragement for on-task behavior addressed to the entire group are often enough to keep everyone moving forward.

Observing to Develop Self-Directed Learners

As a teacher, one of the most important skills for you to develop is observing—actively monitoring your students from the moment they enter the room until they leave. Although there are many different activities that you could observe in class, to increase students' skills as self-directed learners, it is crucial that you focus on your students' work habits. By paying careful attention to students as they work, you will help them stay on task and be successful. Furthermore, any problems that might arise will stay small if you are actively working to facilitate instruction through continual attention to their progress and needs.

There are several more benefits that you and your students receive when you know what students are doing at any given moment. When you successfully observe your students, you

- Create a positive class atmosphere
- Respond quickly to students, needs to keep learning moving forward
- Keep problems small
- Reinforce productive behavior
- Keep students focused on learning
- Help students develop strong work habits
- Maintain a strong connection with each and every student

Although monitoring student work habits while they are in class is not complicated, it requires effort to become a habit. These suggestions will help you get started:

When You Present an Assignment

- When you present an assignment, take the time to model how you want students to complete it. Show examples of proficient work and examples of work that doesn't yet meet standards.
- Have students estimate how long it might take to complete the assignment so that they have an idea of how to pace themselves.
- Ask students to share shortcuts or other bits of helpful advice about completing the assignment.
- If it's a longer project or collaborative work, have small groups create a project plan for the assignment.

While Students Are Working

- After your students settle in to work, wait about two minutes before you start walking around to see what they are doing. Allow time for students to get started on the assignment and for questions to arise.
- Model for students what level of collaboration is appropriate for the assignment. If they are working in pairs or small groups, perhaps you review roles for each member of their team.
- If students become distracted, ask if they have a question and stand near them for a moment.
- Give all students a share of your attention. Some teachers tend to focus on only a few students. To determine how evenly you spread your attention, carry a copy of your class roster. When you speak with a student, place a mark next to the student's name. After doing this for a day or two, you will be aware of any unconscious patterns you follow and will be able to adjust your behavior.

> "Do your best to get to know your students. Even if you have a tough kid, find *one* thing that you can discuss with the student about their life. Find it. It will make a difference in all aspects of your class."
>
> *Jessica Statz, 19 years' experience*

- Ask students who have a question that others may also have to write it on the board so that you can address it for everyone.

- Create a checklist for your students to follow as they work. If they use the checklist, you will be able to determine their progress as you come by their desks. You can also ask students to show you each item on their checklists as they work through it.

- Ask students to write their names on the board when they have finished. This not only lets you know who is finished but also lets other students know which classmates can help them if you are busy.

- Be supportive by using one of these statements:
  - At this moment, what skills are helping you?
  - How may I help you?
  - When I come by your desk, please show me _____.

Be Proactive: Three Helpful Activities while Monitoring

There are three specific activities to use while monitoring students that can make a difference in how well they stay on task: how to arrange for students to get help quickly, how to use your "teacher look" to its fullest advantage, and how to use brain breaks to keep students energized and on task. All three activities will allow you to use the time with your students productively and to be proactive in preventing or minimizing disruptive behaviors.

HOW STUDENTS CAN GET HELP QUICKLY

How much help is the right amount of help? Productive struggle is helpful for learning, but frustration is a potential cause of disruptive behaviors. Students signal frustration in many ways, such as putting heads down on their desks, distracting classmates or even engaging in disrespectful behavior or work refusal. Savvy teachers make it easy for students to self-monitor the types of help they need and reduce frustration.

If you establish classroom routines for students to have access to key resources, peer support, as well as teacher assistance, they will be able to persist through frustration and accelerate their learning. Effective systems for getting help reduce the time between students finding an obstacle to learning and having the answers they need to move forward. Help-seeking is also a vital life skill and a crucial aspect of problem-solving and self-regulation. It can also be socially risky for students to acknowledge not knowing something in front of their peers.

In your classroom community, normalize supporting each other on the journey of learning new things. Provide several systems for students to get the help they need from materials, each other, and from you. Here are a few possibilities:

- Link helpful videos and other resources in your learning management system for students to access.

- Provide students with safe websites where they can get appropriate help.

- Teach students to use Khanmigo or other safe AI tutorbots that coach students toward an answer, without giving them the answer.

- Teach students how to help each other without doing the thinking for a classmate.

- Have students work together in collaborative groups so they can naturally support each other and clarify questions as they go.

- If students have proficiency and complete an assignment early, one of their early finisher tasks may be to assist others in the class.

- Use a "Three Before Me" strategy where students try to help themselves with available resources and consult two peers before asking the teacher: (1) review available resources (materials, links, tutorbots), (2) ask a peer, and (3) consult another peer.

- Have a "Genius Bar" on your dry erase board where students can write their names when they need teacher support. You can see from across the room who needs assistance, and they know how many students are in front of them. Students erase their names when their question is answered.

There may be times when you want students to rely on your support. If you arrange signals to enable your students to indicate when they need help, you can prevent or minimize much of the off-task behavior that can happen when students do not know how to proceed. Signals can be as simple as colored strips of paper on a desk to something as elaborate as a small, preprinted flag. To make it easier for your students to communicate with you and to get help quickly, consider these ideas:

- For each student, tape three note cards together to form a triangle or tent that can stand on a desk. On each side, place a signal that will let you know how a student is doing. A question mark could indicate that the student has a question, a smiling face could mean that the student has no questions, and a frowning face could mean that there is a serious problem.

- Have a supply of red, yellow, and green recyclable cups or other similarly colored tokens available for students to place on their desks when they need assistance.

HOW TO USE THE "TEACHER LOOK"

Do you have vivid memories of a teacher who was able to redirect students with a single glance or refocus an energetic class with a calm, yet insistent gaze? Paired with a positive relationship with students, the "teacher look" is an effective strategy for preventing or minimizing disruptive behaviors without interrupting the flow of learning for all students. Here are three variations:

Teacher Look One: For slight misbehavior or misbehavior that is just starting, try this variation: Look directly at the offending student and arrange your expression into a look of mild surprise. Your expression should convey your disbelief that they would even consider the behavior.

Teacher Look Two: For more blatant, but still mild, misbehavior: Look directly at the offender and slightly frown. Add a subtle headshake and move closer to the misbehaving student at the same time if you need to increase proximity to change behavior.

Teacher Look Three: For flagrant misbehavior that can still be redirected nonverbally: Stand next to the student while continuing to speak to the rest of the class. Pause in midsentence and look directly at the offending student. Hold the pause just briefly. At this point, you should have eye contact with the student. If the student's demeanor indicates cooperation, resume teaching. If not, another intervention may be required. (You'll find more about this later in this section.)

HOW TO USE BRAIN BREAKS TO INCREASE FOCUS

Not only do brain breaks restore students to an optimal state for learning, it's also one of the quickest and most effective ways to prevent or minimize disruptive behaviors. Brain breaks are brief activities that allow students to move around, shift focus to something light and entertaining, or engage with classmates, and ultimately, return to learning refreshed, energized, and better able to focus. Students of all ages should have periodic brain breaks during class.

Because brain breaks allow students to work off excess energy and to focus on their work, they also serve to prevent or minimize behaviors that can disrupt a classroom when students are distracted and restless. As a bonus, brain breaks can also be a fun time for you and your students. You will find that laughing together and sharing the silliness of a brain break can improve your relationship with students. Here are some things to consider as you plan the brain breaks in your classroom:

- Most experts agree that a brain break every hour is appropriate for students, no matter their grade levels.

- Many teachers keep a list of brain breaks handy so that the novelty of the break can add to the fun. To start your own list of brain break activities, just use "brain break" as a search term in a web browser. Many educational websites and bloggers have extensive lists of possible activities.

- Another good source of brain break ideas is to ask students to suggest ones that they would enjoy.

- A brain break should be brief—no more than five minutes. Most experienced teachers would recommend breaks that are two to three minutes in duration so that students do not lose the momentum of their learning flow.

- You may also consider having students lead the brain breaks in your class. This could be a rotating classroom job for students.

- You will soon find that your students will have favorite brain breaks. These can also be useful ways to connect with students.

- Older students may want to use the time to check messages or otherwise be on their cell phones. Although this is a pleasant activity, it does not encourage social and communication skills and it is difficult to get students settled back on task quickly; so it is not a suitable activity to use as a brain break.

Here are some of the more common brain breaks that could appeal to students of all ages:

- Use transition times for mindfulness checks. As students line up to go to PE, have them name their emotions or take a few deep breaths.

- Pose or stretch of the day. Teach students a stretch or a yoga pose for the day or week, then periodically, set a timer and have students simply stand and stretch for thirty to sixty seconds.

- Toss out a soft ball or stuffed toy and have students toss it to one another. You can add depth to this by having students call out review facts as they toss.

- Shake it out. Play an up-tempo song. You can ask students to give you the name of a favorite early in the term to help you generate a school-appropriate playlist. Older students can give their arms and legs a shake. Younger students may even dance.

- Focus on a sound. Have students close their eyes and simply listen to a ring, gong, wind, ocean, river, chime, or other calming sound.

- Watch a funny or inspiring movie clip together.

- Have students walk around the room talking with classmates about three things they like and three things they dislike.

- Have students write their names or draw pictures in the air.

- Start a rhythmic clapping pattern for students to follow along.

- Project the lyrics to a favorite song and ask students to chant them together.

- Have students play the Rock, Paper, Scissors game.

- Students can practice deep-breathing exercises.

- Create the sound of a rainstorm as a class with just fingers tapping on a desk. All students start tapping with one finger, then two all the way up to all five fingers, then moving from five fingers down to one as the storm ends.

- For grades K–5, play a brain-break video from the free site GoNoodle (gonoodle .com). Use the duration filter to select a brain break of the right length.

- WeAreTeachers.com has lists of and links for brain breaks for all grade levels. Use "brain breaks" as a search term on their homepage.

Intervene Appropriately to Minimize Misbehavior

Proactive and preventative measures don't always work. There will be times that you have to intervene to address inappropriate behavior. Like many other teachers, you may sometimes feel unsure about when you should intervene to prevent or cut short a possible problem. When and how you should act depends on the type of problem and its potential for disruption. Classroom behavioral issues can usually be divided into two categories: nondisruptive behaviors and disruptive behaviors. Disruptive behaviors require direct interventions and redirection. (Suggestions for dealing with this type of behavior can be found in Section Thirteen.)

Nondisruptive behavior problems affect only the student with the issue and are much easier to manage. Students may struggle with focus, organization, or study habits. Sometimes, these challenges can escalate into disruptive behaviors as students become frustrated or assume that they don't need to listen, pay attention, or complete a task.

Although it's not always possible to catch a misbehavior early enough to keep it in the nondisruptive stage, teachers who monitor their students carefully and who intervene while a problem is still contained to one student will find that it's not difficult to keep problems small enough to be easily managed. Try these twenty interventions to prevent or end a nondisruptive behavior problem as soon as you see it starting:

1. Move closer to the student.
2. Remind the entire class to stay on task.
3. Encourage the entire class for their focus and study skills.
4. Maintain eye contact.
5. Check in with the student, quietly asking "How are you feeling today?" or "How can I support you today?"
6. Ask the student to explain the directions to you.
7. Reassure the student that they are on track.
8. Help the student estimate how much longer a task will take.
9. Offer a high five or fist bump with a smile.
10. Point out the correct parts of the work that the student has completed.
11. Send the student to get a drink of water or to take a quick walk.
12. Have the student set a goal to have the work completed by an agreed-upon time.
13. Ask the student to tell you their plan for finishing the work.
14. Try the mildest form of the Teacher Look.
15. If appropriate, have the student work with a partner.
16. Point out the strong work the student has already completed.
17. Offer your help.
18. Gently remind the student of the class agreement that they are breaking.
19. Explain the directions in a different way.
20. Glance or smile at the student.

An Invaluable Tool: The Power of Community and Positive Peer Pressure

One of the greatest tools to prevent or minimize disruptive behaviors is the power of a healthy classroom community and the positive peer pressure that can be applied to uphold class agreements. Teachers can harness the human desire to belong and perform well in the presence of peers by making each student feel that they are a valuable member of the class. To increase the sense of belonging that you want for your students and to reduce the occurrence of misbehavior, it's important to build a sense of trust among your students through supportive peer relationships. Once you have established the inclusive environment where students feel that they are part of a classroom community, they will be more inclined to behave well so that they can continue to belong.

Questions to Discuss with Colleagues

Sharing ideas with colleagues is a helpful way to devise solutions to some of the problems that you must manage successfully at school. Here, you will find several topics to open discussions with colleagues about successful instructional practices:

1. You observe a pattern of disruptive behavior between two students day after day. How can you discover the reasons for your students' behaviors? What can you do to prevent or minimize this behavior? How can you replace it with more positive behaviors?

2. Respect means being taken seriously, and both teachers and students want to feel respected. What do your colleagues do to create an environment of mutual respect? What have you already done to convey respect for your students?

3. Which teachers in your school seem to have a highly developed sense of withitness? What can you learn from them to improve your own teaching practice?

4. Sometimes when students are working through an assignment, you notice that they don't ask for help when they need it. What solutions can you generate to support students in asking for and receiving the help they need to move learning forward?

5. What suggestions do your colleagues have for interventions that can prevent or minimize disruptive behaviors? Which techniques have already been successful for you and your students?

Topics to Discuss with a Mentor

Although the topics that new teachers need to discuss with a mentor vary from teacher to teacher and from school to school, there are some that most first-year teachers should be

comfortable discussing with a mentor or a trusted colleague. You should ask your mentor about these topics from this section:

- Advice on how to monitor students as they engage in learning
- Suggestions about how to teach self-regulation skills
- How to improve the way you give encouragement
- Suggestions for brain break ideas appropriate for your students
- How to achieve the 5:1 ratio for positive interactions you have with students

Reflection Questions to Guide Your Thinking

1. When do you find it difficult to be consistent with students? What has made you aware of this? How can you become more consistent in how you lead the class?

2. How can you convey the expectation that your students will uphold classroom agreements and cooperate with your requests and policies? What are you already doing to communicate this expectation? How can you improve?

3. Engage with empathy. What do you think it's like to be a student in your class? Consider students from a range of identities. Does each student feel a sense of belonging? How do you think your students view you—do they feel respected by you?

4. Do your students respect you? How can you determine this? What are your strengths in this area? How can you improve?

5. Take nothing personally and maintain calm in the face of challenging behaviors. How are you doing in this area? When have you been successful in not taking a student's behavior personally? When have you noticed yourself taking things personally? What can you learn from this to continue growing this skill?

SECTION THIRTEEN

Engage in Responsive Discipline

Bullying, harassment, disrespect, aggression, defiance—the array of behavior issues that teachers face can be overwhelming. One of the most significant challenges that teachers face is knowing the right course of action to take when confronted with such a wide range of challenges. Well-constructed responsive discipline practices can help and are necessary for a safe, healthy, and inclusive classroom.

The word *discipline* comes from the Latin root word *discere* meaning "to learn." Responsive discipline is another opportunity for students to learn. It builds skills, personal accountability, and connections to community. This is in sharp contrast to harmful, punitive discipline practices that exclude students from learning and disproportionately affect students of color and students with disabilities. Responsive discipline policies and practices are tools that will help you create a positive climate and culture. They align with the Restorative Practices detailed in Section Eleven.

One aspect of the discipline dilemma that you will have to navigate is your inexperience and the ways in which it may contribute to the behavior issues in your classroom. You may behave in ways that are inconsistent or lack a repertoire of responses to use in the face of disruptive behaviors. The good news is that exploring this section and preparing ahead of time can help you avoid teacher moves that may escalate disruptive behaviors.

As a first-year teacher, however, you have an advantage that your more experienced colleagues may not. You can take a fresh approach to leading your classroom because the newness of each challenge will necessitate conscious and careful decisions. Every challenge you encounter is an opportunity for you to develop the skills you need to engage in responsive discipline in ways that improve student behavioral skills and create a strong sense of community in your classroom.

> "Be discreet and talk with students privately when there's a problem. When I am frustrated, I give us both time apart before I work through the situation. I need to be clearheaded and to focus on the behavior—the student's action—not the person."
>
> *Laura Moore, 18 years' experience*

The Big Picture: Be Positive and Not Punitive

Although attitudes and practices are changing, punishment is still used far too often in classrooms by frustrated teachers who feel overwhelmed by discipline issues and who are continuing the practices they were accustomed to in their own school experiences. Students must feel supported by their teachers. They need teachers who value and affirm them as individuals and as members of a classroom community. They need teachers who view them as capable of success—who see their possibilities beyond their mistakes.

What Is Expected of You as a First-Year Teacher?

Although it is not always easy to determine just how flexible or firm you should be, it's particularly difficult during your first year. Many new teachers make mistakes as they work to become skilled at leading their classes because they have not learned what their school community expects from them. Although expectations for student behavior can vary greatly, there are some common discipline practices that you will be expected to implement. As you work to create a safe and productive classroom climate, keep the following expectations in mind. All teachers are expected to:

- Maintain an orderly learning environment where students feel a sense of safety and community as they work toward academic goals.
- Be proactive in preventing or minimizing as many behavior issues as possible to help students stay focused on learning.
- Make thoughtful, informed decisions geared to help students move toward self-discipline.
- Work with students to resolve classroom problems and conflicts.
- Establish, teach, and enforce reasonable class agreements, including logical consequences for breaking them.
- Make student safety a priority. Never allow any activity that could endanger students.
- Handle most disruptive behaviors on their own, but refer a student to a counselor, social worker, or administrator when needed.
- Use the least intrusive and most appropriate interventions and redirections when necessary.
- Respect the dignity of all students.
- Be familiar with the basic laws pertaining to schools, especially regarding your responsibilities, due process, and students' rights.
- Be proactive in seeking the most appropriate help in handling a discipline situation, whether that help is from a mentor, a colleague, the student's last teacher, family or caregivers, an administrator, or another source.
- Maintain accurate discipline records and documentation throughout the year.

Understand Your Legal Responsibilities

As a new teacher, you may feel particularly vulnerable to becoming embroiled in legal problems at school because you are unsure of your responsibilities under the law. Almost all the legal policies involving teachers center on one tenet: teachers have a duty to take care of their students—to protect their safety and welfare at school. *In loco parentis* literally means "in the place of the parents," and defines the special relationship that legally exists between teachers and students.

Teachers should be familiar with basic school law to understand the laws, policies, and procedures governing their school conduct and duties toward students to reduce the risk of legal problems. An informative source is the sixth edition of *School Law and the Public Schools: A Practical Guide for Educational Leaders* by Nathan L. Essex, which was published in 2021. The book covers legal issues in education such as:

- Religion
- Freedom of expression
- Dress and appearance
- Search and seizure
- Use of cell phones
- Due process
- Corporal punishment
- Bullying and harassment
- Child abuse
- Individuals with Disabilities Education Act (IDEA)
- Isolation and restraint laws
- Civil rights
- Right to privacy
- Duties of supervision

What are your responsibilities? Use the guidelines in the list that follows to make sound decisions for your students and for yourself:

- Protect students from harm—both physical and emotional.
- The policies and procedures in your classroom must have a clear educational purpose and must be governed by common sense. The logical consequences of not following a class agreement must be appropriate to the behavior. You must publish class agreements and the consequences for your students and their families and caregivers.
- Teachers are obligated to make their students aware of the risks in activities. Whether the hazard is from running with scissors or operating equipment in a career technical education class, students need to be taught how to stay safe and avoid danger.

- In general, younger students need to be more closely supervised than older students.

- Teachers should never embarrass a student in front of their peers.

- If you have a student who is aggressive or hostile toward others and you ignore the problem, you have neglected to protect the students who may be assaulted. Be aware of potential problems, and if possible, seek assistance before trouble can occur.

- A student's privacy is protected by law. Do not gossip about a student, post grades publicly, or reveal confidential information. Be especially careful about what you transmit electronically or in writing. Keep confidential material in a secure area.

- A student's freedom of speech and expression is protected by law if that speech or expression does not cause significant disruption to the learning environment.

- If your students are required to submit a permission slip signed by a parent or guardian before attending a school activity, such as a field trip, that permission slip does not exonerate you from liability if a student is harmed. A permission slip is not a legal document that will protect you in court.

- You must supervise your students at all times. Special education students; young students; and those with impulsive, uncooperative, or unpredictable behavior usually require higher levels of supervision than others. The type of activity that students are engaging in also determines the level of supervision required. No matter how mature they are, never leave students unsupervised. Have someone cover your class if you need to step out for any reason.

- You should design activities with safety in mind. Consider the potential for danger to students when you design active classroom games, lab experiments, group activities, or competitive events that could quickly get out of control.

- If you suspect that a student is the victim of abuse or neglect, you are legally obligated to report it to the appropriate authorities. Make sure you learn the school's mandatory reporting process before you might need it and discuss any questions or concerns about the reporting process with a social worker, counselor, or administrator.

- You must be aware of the requirements and restrictions in a student's IEP or 504 Plan. You are bound by law to follow those requirements.

- Students have protected rights to privacy. The decision to search students' personal property involves legal constraints. Don't take it upon yourself to search student backpacks, cell phones, or lockers. Involve an administrator instead.

- Teachers are expected to know about their students' medical needs and behavior challenges as well as any other special factors that could put them in harm's way, like food allergies. Hopefully information will be easily available in your student information system or a specialist will provide information about your students. If they don't, take the time to review your students' records at the start of the term so that you have the knowledge to protect your students and yourself.

- If you have knowledge of students sexting, do not attempt to intervene yourself. Report the problem to an administrator immediately. Because underage sexting can be considered child pornography, it needs to be handled carefully.

- While teachers have a lot of flexibility to use copyrighted material with students, they are expected to observe copyright and fair use laws that can be nuanced. A local resource for information about copyright laws in almost every school district is your school library. Teacher-librarians generally have up-to-date information about the latest copyright laws and can offer guidance.

- Keep accurate records of conferences, interventions, student behaviors, and other pertinent information. Typically this is done online in the student information system. If needed, use Teacher Template 13.5 and Teacher Template 6.1 to keep a record that you can refer to if you are asked to give information at a Student Study Meeting or in court.

- Students have a right to due process. If you are not sure about what course of action to take when a problem arises, call in an administrator before you act in a way that might be in violation of a student's right to due process.

Due Process Procedures

School discipline can harm students and damage the careers of teachers who violate students' rights. Although by far most of the discipline issues that you will have to handle will be minor, some of the more serious ones, such as possession of illegal substances or fighting, will require you to act decisively. When you do, it is important to keep in mind that one of the most significant rights of students accused of misconduct is the constitutional right to due process, especially if the proposed consequence will exclude them from school. Here is a very brief explanation of the conditions for due process:

- School and classroom rules must be reasonable.
- Students must be notified of school and classroom rules and policies.
- When a student is accused of violating a school rule, they must be made aware of the specific charge, the evidence, and proposed consequence.
- Students have a right to tell their side of the story.
- There must be a full investigation.
- There must be documentation of the incident and the investigation.
- The disciplinary action must be fair and based on the published school rules and policies.
- The student usually has a right to a hearing for suspensions and expulsions.
- The student has the right to appeal the disciplinary action.

How to Handle Discipline Problems If Your School Climate Is Not Positive

Despite the best intentions of providing a positive, productive classroom environment for every student, when the schoolwide climate is negative, teachers struggle to teach and students struggle to learn.

If you teach in a school with a negative culture and climate, there is a great deal that you can do to make a positive difference in the lives of your students. An effective educator in a school where the environment is not positive directs their students toward the future. They help students establish goals and develop skills that will lead to a productive and happy life ahead.

To manage this, your attitude should be one of realistic optimism. Teachers who are effective in schools with negative climates are mindful of the daily challenges that they and their students face. They acknowledge these concerns and problems, and then find ways to solve or at least manage them so that students can be successful.

These teachers also believe that change is possible and that they are the agents of that change. With this attitude firmly in place, teachers have been known to inspire entire classes to reach unprecedented success and school communities to improve.

With a positive, problem-solving attitude, you will have a much greater chance of successfully managing your daily challenges than if you spend your days bemoaning your school's problems. In addition to these productive attitudes, there are several strategies that you can use to address the negative elements of your school's climate:

- Start small. Keep your classroom clean and organized so that students have an inviting, welcoming, orderly place for learning.
- Identify the strengths in your school and work to build on them. Become a band booster, athletic team fan, or sponsor of a student club, for example.
- Engage students in discussions of how they would like the climate and culture to change. Students help create the culture and their voices can be a powerful catalyst for change.
- Work with your colleagues, student leaders, and administrators to develop or improve school-wide expectations, policies, and procedures.
- Make sure that all students are taught school-wide expectations, policies, and procedures, along with the positive and negative consequences of behaviors.
- No matter what happens in the rest of the school, your classroom should be a place where students are expected to be safe, respectful, and responsible.
- Be realistic about what you can achieve. Although you may not be able to change the total environment of your school quickly, even small changes are worthwhile. Move forward with reasonable, achievable goals and a vision for what is possible.

Focus on These Coaching Tips

Because there are so many aspects of responsive discipline, it's helpful to consider these coaching tips that can set you and your students up for success and make it easier for you to address disruptive behaviors as they arise. Here are ten to consider:

1. Project confidence as a classroom leader. You have the right to teach and your students have the right to learn.

2. Build relationships of mutual respect with your students.

3. Teach behavior skills so that students know what's expected of them.

4. When disruptive behaviors occur, take the time to discover the underlying reasons for the behavior and take that into account when determining consequences.

5. Use timely and appropriate strategies geared to keep misbehavior as small, manageable, and contained as possible.

6. When you respond to misbehavior, do so in such a way that you protect students from harm and protect the misbehaving student's relationship to the rest of the classroom community.

7. Work with your students and support students to learn pro-social behavior in your classroom. Handle as much as you can without sending a student to the office. Don't hesitate to ask for advice, but assume responsibility for supporting student behaviors yourself.

8. Be prepared. Have a plan for how you will react when misbehavior happens. Have class agreements, policies, and procedures in place.

9. Take nothing personally with respect to student behaviors. This will allow you to remain calm in the face of challenging behavior.

10. Manage your stress regarding the discipline issues in your classroom. Once you have done the best you can to address a concern, mentally leave it at school. Keeping your work-life balance is crucial to your personal health and long-term, professional satisfaction.

Cultivate Grace under Pressure

Don't lose your temper in front of your students when you are upset. Giving in to the emotion of the moment will not only cause you stress and affect your judgment but also harm your relationship with your students. Learning the fine art of grace under pressure is not easy, but responding with grace is a powerful tool for any teacher. Here are several strategies that other teachers have found useful:

- Remember that losing control will only make the situation worse.
- Count silently to ten before you speak. While you are counting, make your face appear as calm as possible.
- Instead of shouting, lower your voice to a whisper.

- If there is a great deal of noise and commotion without a threat of violence, stand quietly and use an attention getting signal or wait for it to subside. Shouting at your students to settle them down will only add to the noise.

- Talk to your colleagues to vent your frustration and to plan ways to manage discipline issues differently.

- Remember that you determine what happens in your class. If you lose control, you are not working to solve the problem. Channel your energy toward managing the situation in a positive way.

- Ask your students for help when you are upset. This will redirect their attention toward a productive contribution.

Don't Take It Personally

You want to take the compliments and the constructive feedback to heart, but you don't want to take disruptive student behaviors personally. You are not alone if you feel personally offended by a student's comment or behavior. After a tough day, negative student attitudes and behaviors can sometimes cause teachers to wonder why they bothered to get up, get dressed, and go to school.

If you were to discuss such a day with an experienced teacher, the chances are good that you would hear, "Don't take it personally." This is excellent advice, but it is one of the hardest things for new teachers to learn to do. However, if you are to thrive in your new profession, it is an attitude that you must embrace. Recall these pointers the next time you are tempted to take it personally when your students do not uphold classroom agreements:

- Students will not always behave well or say the right thing. After all, they are still children and still learning—even the seniors.

- Part of being a teacher is setting limits and establishing boundaries for your students. Although this is necessary, it isn't always easy to determine what is acceptable behavior and what is not.

- Teaching is a complicated task. During a typical school day, you will make as many as a thousand decisions. Not all of them will be popular with your students.

- As the adult in the classroom, you must consider the needs of all students. When a student disagrees with a teacher, it is often because that student is only considering what they want instead of what would be good for the group.

- Your students do not really know you. They see only one side of you—the teacher part. They may react to the authority part, not to you as a person.

"Don't allow conflicts to escalate.

I remember a student whom I thought was lackadaisical; she deemed me unapproachable (perhaps even a jerk). However, she's the one who had the courage to see me after school. What resulted was an hour-long conversation where we actually *listened* to each other.

What did I take from this? That we don't know what is going on in a student's life outside of school and that we shouldn't expect a student to have the coping skills of an adult who has had multiple life lessons to guide them into better decision making."

Michael A. Barrs, 32 years' experience

You Could Be Creating Some of the Problems in Your Class

Your inexperience will cause you to inadvertently make many mistakes, and sometimes the mistakes you make will create behavior challenges. The good news is that you can usually prevent them from happening again. In the following list of common teacher-made mistakes, you will find some of the reasons why you may have experienced discipline problems. With each mistake listed here you will also find a more effective strategy.

Mistake One: You refuse to answer or give a poor answer when students question you about why they should learn the content and skills they are studying.

Solution: Consider student interests in developing lessons. As you begin a unit of study, create a hook that helps students understand the relevance of the subject matter. Make sure that students are aware of the real-life applications for the learning you require of them.

Mistake Two: You present yourself in too tentative a fashion—too easily sidetracked and lacking confidence.

Solution: Approach students with sincere care and confidence. Set limits and take a positive approach to all students by preparing interesting lessons and attending to the classroom concerns that will make your students more successful in school.

Mistake Three: You are too vague in giving directions to your students.

Solution: Whether giving academic directions or behavioral corrections, be specific when telling students what they need to do. Instead of saying, "Don't be rude," a better choice is to say, "Please wait until I have finished before talking."

Mistake Four: You are unclear in the limits you set for your students, resulting in a constant testing of the boundaries and of your patience.

Solution: Be as specific as possible in setting limits when you establish your class agreements and procedures. Students need to know and understand just what they should do and what will happen if they choose not to follow the directions you have for them.

Mistake Five: You give too many negative directions and don't model the respectful tone you expect from students. This sets an unpleasant tone for your students.

Solution: Replace your negatives with positives. Instead of saying, "Don't play around," you will be more positive if you say, "Please get started on your assignment now."

Mistake Six: You try to solve behavior issues without trying to determine the underlying causes.

Solution: Talk with the student. Listen to what they have to say. Spend time trying to figure out what caused the problem to begin with. If you don't determine the root of the matter, you won't be successful in preventing it from reoccurring. You may also misread the situation and provide an unfair consequence.

Mistake Seven: You react to a behavior issue by becoming angry and upset.

Solution: Instead of spending your energy in anger, take the time to examine the problem objectively before acting. Take a problem-solving approach to really deal with it.

Mistake Eight: You neglect to command attention by talking over students, even though they aren't listening.

Solution: Wait to give directions or instruction until you have your students' attention. There are many techniques you can follow for gaining students' attention. Ring a wireless portable classroom doorbell, set a timer, ask a leading question, hold up something unusual, or stand in the front of the room are just some examples. See Section Four for more attention-getting techniques.

Mistake Nine: You have lessons that are not aligned to students' needs. Students either have too much work to do and give up or they don't have enough work.

Solution: Differentiate instruction to meet students' needs and provide regular brain breaks to keep students at their peak zone for learning.

Mistake Ten: You give consequences without proof or by blaming the wrong student.

Solution: Determine who did what before you act. Unfair consequences will create long-lasting bad feelings among your students. Take your time to discover what really happened and who needs to take responsibility and repair the harm they caused. If you make this mistake, apologize profusely and repair the harm.

Are You Too Strict or Too Flexible?

It's not easy to find a balance between being too strict and too flexible when you are just beginning your career. Just how much should students get away with before intervention is needed? When is it okay to bend the rules? When is it necessary to be strict about a rule or procedure? Finding the balance in the way you interact with your students takes time, but making intentional decisions about that interaction is crucial. One of the most critical issues in earning student respect is the balance you must maintain between being too flexible and being too strict.

The best way to find a balance is to make yourself aware of the areas where you may be inclined to be overly flexible or overly strict. If you are still not sure of the best course to take, ask yourself these questions:

- Is this student behavior appropriate?
- What will happen if I choose to ignore this behavior?
- What will happen if I choose to address this behavior?
- What message about future behavior am I sending to my students in the way I respond?

Teacher Template 13.1 can help you self-assess.

Are You Too Strict or Too Flexible?

Select the letter of the response that is closest to your own approach and put it in the blank. After you have responded to all ten scenarios, check what your responses reveal about how flexible or strict you tend to be.

1. _____ Students jokingly insult one another while waiting for class to begin.
   a. Ignore the horseplay. Class hasn't started yet.
   b. Remind students of the procedure for starting class and the class agreement about showing respect for others.
   c. Tell students to stop and to get to work right away.

2. _____ A student is lost in a daydream instead of finishing an assignment.
   a. Tell the student that if they don't get to work, there will be more to do for homework.
   b. Continue teaching and wait to see how long it takes the dreamer to get back to work.
   c. Move to stand near the student.

3. _____ Students take too long to get their materials arranged for a test.
   a. Remind them to hurry.
   b. Start the test and let them catch up.
   c. Tell them they have one minute to get ready and then time them by watching the clock.

4. _____ Students ball up papers and toss them at the wastebasket while you are giving directions about an assignment.
   a. Shake your head, frown, and move near them.
   b. Stop what you are saying and reprimand them.
   c. Finish your directions. Go to the students and quietly ask them about the behavior.

5. _____ Students chat while you are explaining the small-group assignment.
   a. Ignore it.
   b. Stop, give them your teacher look, and wait for them to pay attention.
   c. Tell them to stop talking and start paying attention.

(continued on next page)

(continued from previous page)

6. _____ While sitting on the rug for read aloud, a second grader repeatedly taps the student in front of her.

   a. Pause the read aloud and remind her to keep her hands to herself.

   b. Ask her to go sit at her desk for the rest of the read aloud. This will help all students remember to keep their hands to themselves.

   c. Ignore the behavior and keep reading.

7. _____ Students turn in very sloppy or inaccurate work.

   a. Refuse to take it until they redo it.

   b. Take it but give a lecture about work habits.

   c. Talk with students about the reason for the messiness and how to correct it.

8. _____ Students are tardy to class without a good reason.

   a. Enforce your rules regarding tardiness to class.

   b. Refuse to let them in without a pass.

   c. Meet them at the door and ask why they are tardy.

9. _____ Students talk back rudely when you have corrected them.

   a. Send them to the office.

   b. Reprimand them privately.

   c. Ignore it after giving them your teacher look.

10. _____ Students ignore you when you call for the class to quiet down to work.

    a. Keep asking until they listen to you.

    b. Raise your voice until no one can ignore you.

    c. Give the signal that they recognize as a sign that they need to get quiet.

What Your Responses Reveal About You

You might be *too flexible* if you chose these answers:

1. a
2. b
3. a
4. a
5. a
6. c
7. b
8. c
9. c
10. a

You might be *too strict* if you chose these answers:

1. c
2. a
3. b
4. b
5. c
6. b
7. a
8. b
9. a
10. b

Patience Is Key: There Is No Fast Track to a Good Discipline Climate

It takes time for students to learn the social, emotional, and communication skills needed to meet your high expectations. It takes time for them to learn to trust you enough to settle into the rhythm of school. It takes time for them to develop to make the kind of progress that you hope for them.

It's especially important to be patient with students at the start of the school year. As a rule of thumb, it takes about six weeks for students to adjust to school and to your expectations. It is also important to understand that the fragile success you have at six weeks may vanish as the winter holidays draw near. You will need extra patience then to manage student excitement and anxiety as the holidays approach. This pattern will repeat itself throughout the year as holidays, school vacations, and special events come and go.

The key to maintaining your equilibrium throughout the school year is to develop patience and then more patience: patience with students, patience with your own skills, and patience with the community-building process.

Seek First to Understand

Whenever you must address a discipline issue, take care to understand the reason for the student's behavior before you act. If you make the effort to determine why your students act the way they do, you will benefit by having a clearer understanding of some of the times when your students are going to have trouble staying on task.

There are many ways to understand why your students behave the way they do. Talk with the student and listen more than you speak. Confer with teachers who taught your students in the past or family members or caregivers. To learn about students' behavior when you are facing a discipline problem, maintain an open and supportive relationship with students, listen to what they say, and solicit their input when appropriate. When you do make the effort to learn more about your students' behavior, several beneficial things will happen:

- Your students will feel less frustration because you will be inviting them to talk about their feelings.
- You will gain an understanding of what caused the problem.
- If there are causes other than what you first noticed, you will be able to act on them.
- You will gain insight into how your students think, feel, and respond.
- You and your students will have a common ground for discussing other choices they make in the future.
- You will probably have prevented this problem from recurring.
- Your bond with your students will be stronger because you will have shown them the respect of listening to and caring about what they had to say.

Project a Calm and Confident Demeanor

When addressing disruptive behavior, it's important to convey to your students that you are in control of yourself and the situation, especially during a severe incident. To do that, use your body language and your tone of voice, as well as the words you say, to project a calm and confident demeanor.

Stand tall. Hold your head up and shoulders back. Look directly at the class or the student whose behavior requires intervention and speak calmly and with authority. If necessary, move to the front of the room or closer to the problem to be heard. Give directions in simple sentences without lots of explanation. Be concise. If students sense that you are angry, upset, or uncertain, the behavior will likely escalate.

When students sense that you are calmly in control of the situation, they will stop testing boundaries and listen to you. They will look to you for guidance. They will be calmer. Be the self-assured role model they need in difficult times, as well as in the conflict-free times in your class, and you will find it easier to address challenging behavior successfully.

Behaviors that Create an Unsafe Classroom

Be safe. Be respectful. Be responsible. These are the three basic classroom expectations recommended by Positive Behavior Interventions and Supports (PBIS). When students engage in serious behaviors that create an unsafe classroom, you need to act. Classrooms with a positive culture and climate share three important characteristics:

- The students and teacher co-created, know, and understand the class agreements, policies, and procedures that guide the entire class.
- The focus is on learning both academic and behavioral skills and cooperation.
- There is a persistent tone of mutual respect among students and the teacher.

When you and your students are working toward establishing and maintaining a positive class culture, significant disruptive behaviors can undermine that culture and you will need to act quickly to stop the behavior, repair harm, and help students to feel safe. Here are some of the most difficult disruptive behaviors:

- Threats and intimidation: Students are not allowed to threaten or harass one another or you. This prohibition means that you will need to immediately address any bullying, teasing, discriminatory speech, sexual harassment, or threats of physical harm.
- Substance abuse: Be aware of the signs of substance use so that you can intervene appropriately if a student is under the influence. Remember that the school nurse or a designee should administer all medications.
- Insubordination: Despite your efforts to build respectful relationships with students, students may refuse to follow your instructions or behave in ways that

appear defiant, talking back, mocking, and so on. While it's important to avoid power struggles, it's important to intervene to restore the social contract.

- Dangerous behavior: Behaviors that could endanger a student range from explosive outbursts, dysregulated behavior, running with scissors, lighting matches, leaving the school campus, engaging in horseplay, or running in the halls to ignoring safe driving rules in a high school parking lot.

- Dishonesty: It's difficult to create emotional safety in the face of dishonesty. Students need to learn the importance of honesty. Students should not forge notes from home, cheat, commit plagiarism, or lie to others.

- Violence: School violence in the form of mass shootings is tragic and the threat of it creates an unsafe environment. Likewise, students who fight or bring weapons to school undermine your and your students' sense of safety. Know your school's lockdown and lockout protocols. Intervene to end physical altercations immediately without risking your own safety.

> "Take the student aside and ask what is going on. You might be surprised that it has nothing to do with you or the class. Ask what you can do to make it better for the student. If you put the onus on the student, the situation usually improves. If it does not, get the parents or guardians involved."
>
> *Deborah McManaway, 23 years' experience*

Develop a Repertoire of Responsive Discipline Options

Disruptive behavior is a challenge with lots of solutions. Developing a repertoire of responses to use, depending on the circumstances, is vitally important to maintaining a sense of safety in the classroom. Responding to solve the problem will move you and your students toward a solution; you have many constructive options. If you are to choose the most appropriate action to take, you will need to be aware of which options are likely to be most effective in each situation.

It may be helpful to select from this list of effective ways to respond when students engage in disruptive behavior so that you can make wise choices from among the many options you have:

- Consciously choose to ignore the behavior. This is an effective option if you plan how to use it, if the behavior is fleeting, and if other students are not seriously affected by it—for example, when a student wanders briefly or gets a slow start on an assignment.

- Delay acting. It is appropriate to delay when the action you plan to take would cause further disruption. As an example, if a student is tardy to class, instead of interrupting a class discussion, you may welcome them to class with a nod and delay speaking to that student until you can do so quietly and inquire why they were late to class.

- Use nonverbal actions. Nonverbal actions, such as proximity, moving closer to a student, making eye contact, or making inquiring facial expressions, are unobtrusive ways to provide correction. This is often an appropriate choice for supporting and reminding students who are side-talking and off task.

- Give encouragement to the entire class for excellent behaviors. Supporting positive behavior will encourage those who are engaged to stay on task and will remind those who are not, what is expected.

- Give a quiet redirection. Giving a quiet verbal correction when a student engages in disruptive behavior will usually end it. Try to be positive instead of negative. "Remember when we line up, we keep our hands to ourselves," or "Your group needs your input. Please open your book and get started," will be more effective than a more negative command, such as "Stop playing around this instant."

- Confer briefly with students. In a brief conference, you can check in and ask a student if they are okay. Remind a student of the class agreement, redefine acceptable limits of behavior, ask them what they can do differently, and encourage positive behavior.

- Hold a longer conference with students. Schedule a longer and more formal conference with a student when there are several issues to be resolved or when the behavior is chronic or serious. The emphasis should be on understanding the causes of misbehavior and deciding what needs to be done to resolve the problem. You can find more information about this later in this section.

- Contact home. If a student struggles with self-regulation, ask colleagues and the other adults in their lives to support and reinforce your efforts. Early intervention, in the form of a request for help, is usually a good idea.

- Develop a behavior plan. Collaborate with paraprofessionals, last year's teachers, counselors, social workers, special education teachers, deans, or administrators to brainstorm additional strategies or support for the student. Create goals and a regular progress check for the student. Consider a Check-in, Check-out system so that someone connects with the student first and last thing in the day.

- Arrange a conference with families or caregivers. If a student's disruptive behaviors persist and you have tried several interventions with no success, then consider scheduling a conference with family members or caregivers.

- Refer a student to an administrator. You may need to make this choice when you have exhausted all other possibilities or when the behavior is severe or persistent. There is more information about how to handle referrals to an administrator later in this section.

For more specific information about how and when to intervene to handle a behavior problem, you can use the chart in Teacher Template 13.2.

TEACHER TEMPLATE 13.2

Repertoire of Responsive Discipline Options

Teachers need to know the student and the context to choose the correct response to disruptive behaviors. For example, generally students shouldn't sleep during instruction, but a child who experiences homelessness may need a nap during the school day and a plan to meet their basic needs. The severity and frequency of behavior will also determine your response. In the following chart, some behaviors include multiple options, depending on the circumstances. In this chart, you will find some behaviors that every teacher needs to manage effectively as well as a suggested level of intervention for each one. You should also consult your school's guidelines for handling specific behaviors. The level of intervention should increase to meet the seriousness of the behavior.

Behavior	Ignore the Behavior	Briefly Delay Acting on the Behavior	Intervene to Solve the Problem	Involve Other Adults
Daydreaming	X			
Lack of materials		X		
Chronic lack of materials			X	
Talking while the teacher is talking			X	
Off task and excessive talking			X	
Missing assignments or assessments		X		
Chronic missing assessments			X	
Lying to the teacher			X	
Stealing			X	X
Cheating or Plagiarism			X	X
Tardy to class		X		
Chronic tardiness			X	
Cell phone misuse in class			X	
Forged note			X	X
Lingering in the hallway		X		
Chronic requests to leave class			X	
Name-calling			X	
Intentional profanity directed at the teacher			X	X
Profanity in conversation with peers			X	
Occasional messy work		X		

(continued on next page)

(continued from previous page)

Behavior	Ignore the Behavior	Briefly Delay Acting on the Behavior	Intervene to Solve the Problem	Involve Other Adults
Chronically messy work			X	
Getting ready for dismissal early		X		
Sleeping in class			X	
Head down on the desk disengaged		X		
Talking back to the teacher			X	
Rolling eyes		X		
Horseplay			X	
Slow to settle to work		X		
Weapon possession				X
Inappropriate remark			X	
Unkind remark to a classmate			X	
Discriminatory speech			X	X
Inappropriate touching			X	X
Sexting				X
Refusal to work			X	
Refusal to cooperate with a group			X	
Off task while online			X	
Substance abuse			X	X
Explosive or Violent behavior			X	X
Insignificant vandalism			X	
Serious vandalism			X	X
Refusing to clean a work area			X	
Brief inattention	X			
Chronic inattention			X	
Out of seat frequently	X	X	X	
Unusually loud comment	X			
Challenges and confronts the teacher			X	X
Challenges and confronts a classmate			X	
Attempting to harm or bully a classmate			X	X
Rushing though assignments		X		
Negative nonverbal reaction	X			
Disrupting class, but shushed by classmates	X			
Insulting or rude to classmates			X	

Take a Problem-Solving Approach

The first step in adopting a problem-solving approach to disruptive behavior is to develop a proactive attitude to manage your own reactions. Refuse to take student behavior personally, even though you may be hurt, frustrated, and angry. Deescalate the situation and handle it in a productive way.

The following steps will help you not only solve problems, but also prevent further ones. You will find that Teacher Template 13.3 has space provided for you to write out your responses to each of the steps in the problem-solving process.

Step One: Define the problem. Step back and be clear about what happened. Be specific about observable behavior. Instead of "My class comes back crazy after lunch," define it more clearly as "Fifteen students have trouble settling back to work for the first ten minutes after they return from lunch." Specifically defining the problem will give you the detailed information you need to make rational decisions.

Step Two: Seek to understand. Gather information about the cause of the problem from the students involved. Asking a large group to verbally tell you what happened can lead to chaos, finger-pointing, hurt feelings, and loss of instruction time. Instead, ask each student to write out their version of events. Read what they wrote. Ask clarifying questions. Ask students for their solutions to the problem and if harm occurred, how to repair the harm.

Step Three: Once you have gathered information about the incident and students' proposed solutions, take the time to reteach the class agreements, procedures, policies, and consequences that apply to the situation with the students involved. You will base your next steps on the information you gathered and the expectations you have in place for the class.

Step Four: Tell your students that you will need to take some time to decide. This is especially important if you are upset about the incident. You need time to think through the issue and to arrive at the best possible solution.

Step Five: Generate as many solutions as you can. Review what your students suggested. Brainstorm a list of the possible solutions to the problem. Try to generate as many as you can while also anticipating the pros and cons of each. Consider using a generative AI tool to add to your list and then determine if any of those solutions could be helpful.

Step Six: Ask an administrator, a team member, or a colleague for advice if you are not sure of the right course of action to take. It never hurts to ask for advice from someone whose judgment you trust. Discuss your brainstormed list. It should not take long to consult one or two people who can help you make the best decision.

Step Seven: Decide on the action that will help students learn the skills they lack, repair harm caused, strengthen their sense of belonging, and prevent future disruptions.

Step Eight: Decide how you will implement the solution. Remember that your goal is for students to learn social, emotional, and behavioral skills they need for a lifetime, and for the rest of the class to pursue learning without disruption. Having selected the best option for a solution, implement it in such a way that students can learn and grow from the experience.

Problem-Solving for Challenging Behaviors

Use the step-by-step process in this template to clarify your thinking and guide your decision making as you work through the various behavior challenges that you may encounter at school.

Step One: What is the problem?

_____

_____

_____

Step Two: Seek to understand. According to the students involved, what caused the problem? What would solve the problem? What would repair any harm?

_____

_____

_____

Step Three: Which classroom agreements, procedures, or policies apply to the situation? How can you reteach them?

_____

_____

_____

Step Four: When is the best time and place to discuss the issue with your student(s)? Should you facilitate individual conferences or a group conference?

_____

_____

_____

Step Five: What possible solutions can you and your students generate?

_____

_____

_____

Step Six: If necessary, what advice have you received from your colleagues to solve the problem?

_____

_____

_____

Step Seven: Which course of action will help students learn, repair harm, and prevent future disruptions?

_____

_____

_____

Step Eight: How will you implement the solution?

_____

_____

_____

Redirection without Enacting Consequences

Your goal when redirecting students is to quickly and quietly help them get back to learning. Often all it takes is for you to move closer to the student or to make eye contact to let the student know that you are aware of their behavior. When delivering simple redirections, to ensure that instruction is not interrupted, strive to be as unobtrusive and as pleasant and supportive as possible. When you notice students behaving in unexpected ways, try these suggestions:

- Use sticky notes to write reminders and put them on the desks of students who need help focusing.
- Set a timer and give everyone a two-minute break.
- Change the pace of the assignment.
- Ask students if they would like help from you or a peer.
- Use your teacher look to remind students to keep working.
- Remind students of their long- and short-term goals.
- Ask students to restate the directions.
- Ask students to estimate how long it will take to finish the assignment.
- Count "One, two, three," and wait for everyone to pay attention to your directions.
- Move to stand near the students who are distracted.
- Have students stand, stretch, and then return to work.
- Discreetly remove distractions.
- Ask students to sit near you.
- Pleasantly remind students of the behavior you would like to see.
- Sometimes the problem is not off-task behavior, but noise. You can also establish signals such as these with your students to let them know that they need to moderate their noise level:
  - Flick the lights.
  - Fan them so that they "chill out."
  - Tell them to use a "six-inch" voice so that only someone six inches away can hear them.
  - Ring a bell or portable, wireless doorbell.
  - Wave your hands over your head.
  - Snap your fingers until students snap back.
  - Play calming classical music.
  - Raise your hand until they raise theirs.
  - Clap your hands until they clap with you.
  - Clap twice until they clap three times.
  - Stand near a noisy group.

- Give them a thumbs-up when they are quiet.
- Give them a thumbs-down when they are noisy.
- Shush the nearest group and have them pass it on.
- Place your finger over your lips and have them do the same.
- Hold up your fingers in a *V* for volume sign.

Redirection Involving Consequences

Even though you may have done everything possible to prevent a discipline issue from occurring and then exhausted an array of subtle redirections without consequences, students may continue to disrupt the classroom. When this happens, it is necessary to have logical consequences as you redirect students to move forward with their learning.

The purpose of consequences is not to punish, but to help students learn to self-regulate, and remember the classroom agreement, policy, or procedure that they should follow. Consequences should also help students understand that their behavior causes harm to their classmates' ability to learn as well as to their own success. When delivering redirections with consequences, there are a few things to keep in mind:

- Because the purpose of a consequence is not punitive, the specific consequence should match the offense in a logical way so that students see the connection between it and their actions. For example, it would not make sense to have a student clean a work area if the offense was that the student said unkind things to a classmate. Instead, a more appropriate consequence would be for that student to provide a genuine apology.
- The consequence should fit the severity of the action. For example, being moved away permanently from a work group where the student is usually happy and productive is not necessary for distracting behavior. Changing seats for the rest of the class period is more appropriate.
- Students should not be surprised that their behavior is not acceptable because of the previous work you have done to make sure that class expectations are clearly understood by all students.
- A redirection with consequences should be delivered in a quiet, calm voice. Ideally, you should be close enough to the student so that only you and the student are involved in the conversation.
- Always treat students with respect, especially as they experience consequences for their actions.
- Never threaten a student, especially when giving a consequence. Simply enact the consequence.
- Deliver the consequence in a neutral tone. If you are angry or upset, students will focus more on your emotional reaction rather than on the consequence.

- Briefly explain the reason for the consequence and what happens next. For example, if a student has repeatedly refused to work despite your interventions, you could say, "I know you're having a difficult time focusing on your work. Because this needs to be completed for you to learn the material, during choice time, you will work with me and if you finish it before choice time is over, you may join your classmates in a choice activity."
- Avoid arguing or chatting with the student when explaining the consequence. Be concise. Be serious. Stick to explaining the consequence and nothing else.
- Usually, consequences fall into three broad categories. Here are those categories with some brief examples:
  - Students make amends for behavior.
    - Apologize to a classmate they harmed
    - Repair or replace something broken
    - Revise incomplete, inaccurate, or messy work
    - Engage in learning by completing assigned tasks
  - Students take a temporary time-out to self-regulate.
    - Move to another part of the classroom designated as a calming space
    - Move to a nearby classroom where you have made prior arrangements with that teacher
    - Go to a counselor or social worker's office
    - Step into the hall for a few moments or get a drink of water and then return
  - Students lose a privilege.
    - Cannot participate in choice time or a preferred activity
    - Must sit near the teacher
    - Must walk near the teacher if in the hall
    - Cell phones sent to the office

Affirm Student Dignity When Redirecting

No matter how upset and frustrated you may feel as a result of student behavior, it is crucial that you affirm that student's dignity when you offer redirection. In your language and your actions make sure that students know you care enough to hold high expectations for their behavior and want to help them learn. You know the student is more than their behavior. You may disapprove of the behavior, but you respect and care about the student.

Never humiliate a student in the process of correcting behavior. If the purpose of a redirection is to teach skills and prevent it from happening again, embarrassing a student will not achieve that goal. Students who feel humiliated will not be able to think clearly because they will be overwhelmed by their emotions. They will not be able to listen or to focus on anything other than their own misery.

Teachers who embarrass a student in front of classmates will make that student and the whole class feel unsafe and uneasy wondering who among them will be next. This will harm a teacher's relationship with the entire group because they will lose trust in a teacher when they experience unpredictable behavior.

Embarrassing a student will also seriously harm a teacher's relationship with that student. Students with lagging behavioral skills may be accustomed to being corrected by adults and may tune out authority figures. Instead of a productive relationship, teachers who humiliate students undermine a culture of mutual respect, harm students, and escalate behavior issues.

Failing to affirm a student's dignity when redirecting will also harm that student's relationship with the rest of the class. Embarrassing a student is a sure way to damage the relationships that students need to feel connected with the group. Here are a few suggestions for what to do and what not to do when affirming a student's dignity. To affirm a student's dignity when providing redirection, be careful *to*:

- Listen attentively; take the student's concerns seriously
- Use a kind voice when talking with the student
- Be as patient and understanding as possible
- Try to be as fair as possible when redirecting
- Ask sufficient questions to be sure that you understand the incident
- Work to resolve problems and not just punish the student
- Assure the student that you believe that the behavior will not happen again
- Make every effort to see the entire child and not just their disruptive behavior

To preserve a student's dignity, be careful *not* to:

- Call a student a name, even in jest
- Compare one student to another
- Engage in a power struggle with a student
- Allow a confrontation to build in front of others
- Ignore a student who needs your attention
- Raise your voice
- Be sarcastic or insulting to a student

How to Obtain Behavior Support When You Need It

Just as teachers work in collaboration with colleagues to solve curriculum issues, they also work together to solve discipline problems. Child or Student Study Teams meet weekly in most schools to review student needs and create academic and behavior support plans. Learn about the team at your school and how to make referrals. Although you may feel overwhelmed at times, you are not alone.

It's not always easy to ask for help, especially with such an anxiety-producing topic as addressing disruptive behaviors. Because you will certainly not be the first teacher at your school to need help with behavioral issues, you will find that there are many supportive colleagues who will offer assistance if you just take the time to ask.

In fact, it is much better to ask for help and advice early when your classroom issues are easier to solve than if you wait until later in the term. Being proactive in the way you ask for help will indicate that you are aware of the problem and are willing to listen to advice.

The first person you might talk to about discipline issues is your mentor, if you have been assigned one. If you do not have a mentor, then consult a colleague who has a positive classroom culture and who seems open to extending a helping hand. Be respectful of that person's time, but be honest about the challenges you are experiencing and your determination to solve them.

One of the most valuable ways to ask for help with the way you support student behaviors is to ask several teachers or administrators to make snapshot observations while you are teaching. (See Section One for more information about classroom observations.) If you are open-minded and express gratitude for their coaching, you will develop solutions faster and deepen your collaborative relationships with colleagues.

How to Partner with Families and Caregivers to Provide Behavior Support

Families and caregivers want the best for their students. They want their students to learn and grow and be successful. There are times that you will need their support with academic goals and times when you will need their support with behavior goals. Some families and caregivers will be able to partner with you to reinforce behavioral or academic expectations at home and some may be unable to.

There are many ways to maintain open communication between school and home from apps like ParentSquare, Remind, or ClassDojo to send emails or text messages, and make phone calls. The positive and productive relationship that you want with your students' families and caregivers can be maintained if you take the time to treat them with respect when a problem arises. Here are some suggestions for how you can demonstrate your respect and still successfully solve challenging behavior problems in partnership with families and caregivers:

- Get to know the adults at your students' homes early in the year so that you can understand their circumstances and what partnership means to them.
- Contact home with positive notes about students early and often.
- Communicate early and often. Keep behavioral issues small by asking for help early in the year.
- Make it clear that you care about their child and that you want the student to achieve both academic and behavioral success.

- Ask for their help. Make it clear that you want to work with them to help their child learn and grow and do well in school.

- Start conversations from a strengths-based perspective. Say positive things about their child as a prelude to a conversation about a challenge. Separate the child from the behavior. Convey that the behavior is the problem and not their child.

- Be an active listener. Allow families and caregivers to explain their viewpoints, offer suggestions, and give you background information that can help you understand their child better.

- When you call home, be sure to ask first if they have time to talk with you. If not, arrange a time that would be good for you both. Avoid trying to cram in a phone call home when you have only a few minutes.

- If you leave a message, be brief and ask them to call you back, leaving a work phone number and the best times to reach you.

- It is typically better to call instead of email about behavior issues.

- When you describe the details of an incident, be concise and factual. Stick to exactly what happened instead of editorializing about it. Be specific and precise about what you say.

- Protect students' privacy. If other students were involved, do not mention them by name or share information about other students.

- If you are upset, wait until you are regulated before calling home so that your purpose—solving the problem—will be evident instead of your emotions.

- If a family member or caregiver becomes verbally abusive, before hanging up, calmly let them know you understand that they are upset and request that they call you the next day. Contact an administrator as soon as possible to report the phone call. It is possible that family member or caregiver may also contact an administrator.

> "If there is a tricky situation and a parent is not treating you with respect, do not hesitate to call in a supervisor. We have all been there. You need help navigating some of those tough situations. Don't be too proud to ask for that help. It will make it much easier in the long run."
>
> *Mary Landis, 22 years' experience*

How to Hold Successful Behavior Support Conferences

Student conferences focused on behavioral issues can be a powerful tool for teachers to establish a positive relationship with a student who needs additional support with prosocial behaviors. When the two of you sit down together to work out solutions to a problem, you will both benefit.

Holding a successful conference with a student who has violated classroom agreements is not difficult. Use the strategies that follow to set you both up for success and effectively work together to resolve problems:

Before the Conference

- Choose the time and place for the conference so that you affirm the student's dignity and can focus on addressing the concerns. Consider equity issues and do not require a conference, for example, when it would cause a student to miss the bus home.

- If necessary, contact home to see if a student can arrive before school or stay after school.

- Make sure that the conference time is workable and does not harm your relationship with the student by creating hardship for them.

- Arrange a place to meet that is as free from distractions as possible. While you will confer 1:1 with students informally during class, do not have a formal behavior support conference with a student while other students are in the room.

During the Conference

- Be courteous in your greeting. This will set the tone for the rest of the meeting.

- Make the area as comfortable as possible. Offer a pen and paper for taking notes, and sit at student desks or at a table. Do not sit behind your desk.

- To protect yourself from charges of misconduct and make the student more comfortable, when you are meeting one-on-one with a student, sit near the door to the room, and make sure the door remains open.

- Do not touch a student for any reason during a conference.

- Begin the meeting by stating that the purpose of the conference is to work together to support their learning and behavior and to come up with solutions to the issues. Avoid rehashing unpleasant details, blaming the student, or showing your anger.

- Ask the student to tell you why you are meeting and what they hope to get out of the conversation. Make sure that you each have a chance to state the problem as you see it.

- Listen to the student without interrupting.

- When you discuss the student's behavior, separate the child from the behavior. Convey that the behavior is the problem and not the student.

- After the student has spoken, practice active listening. Reflect on what they said and paraphrase key points. Make sure you understand the problem and express your sincere interest in solving it.

- Brainstorm solutions with the student. Ask questions about how the student can repair any harm that occurred and how they can handle the situation differently in the future.

- Agree on a plan that satisfies both of you. Make sure that you are comfortable with implementing it.

- Calmly explain the positive reinforcement or consequences of successfully completing the plan and the negative consequences if the student does not fulfill their part of the plan.

- Once again, state that you care and are committed to helping the student be successful.

At the End of the Conference

- Ask the student if there is anything else they wanted to say.

- Thank your student for taking the time to problem-solve with you.

- Add a note on your calendar or lesson plan to check in with the student in two days to see how the plan is working and give them positive or constructive feedback.

Document student conferences in a consistent way with sufficient detail. You may make a log entry in the student information system or have a document, spreadsheet, or form you use. Maintain this documentation until the end of the school year. You can use Teacher Template 13.4 to help with this task.

TEACHER TEMPLATE 13.4

Student Behavior Support Conference

Teacher Name: _____   Student's Name: _____

Date: _____   Time: _____   Location: _____

Reason(s) for the conference:

_____

_____

_____

Problems and solutions discussed:

_____

_____

_____

Next steps for the teacher:

_____

_____

_____

Next steps for the student:

_____

_____

_____

Positive consequences:

_____

_____

_____

Negative consequences:

_____

_____

_____

Check-in/Follow up date: _____

Teacher's signature: _____

Student's signature: _____

When You Need to Involve Other Adults

Sometimes your efforts to support student behavior in class will not improve their behavior or solve the problem created by disruptive behaviors. Learn about your school's Child or Student Study Team and how to refer a student to the team for additional support. Talk with administrators about discipline guidelines to know when they expect to get involved to support student behavior. Hopefully your school engages in restorative practices and responsive discipline schoolwide and involving additional adults provides increased levels of support for the student.

There are a range of interventions that involve other adults before referring to an administrator, dean, or behavior support personnel. For example, elementary colleagues may invite the student into their classroom to spend a short period of time during the day with older or younger students. Perhaps your school has a counselor or social worker who can spend time supporting the student in class or in another space. Depending on the student and the behaviors, you may need to make a referral to the dean, administrator, or student support personnel. There is no question that you should make a referral to an administrator for any of these behaviors:

- Bringing weapons to school
- Sexual harassment
- Persistent bullying and harassment
- Violence

Depending on the severity and frequency of these behaviors, you will involve additional adults:

- Persistent defiance
- Stealing
- Vandalism
- Deliberate profanity directed at the teacher
- Substance abuse
- Making threats
- Truancy
- Cheating
- Persistent disruptions

Before the Referral Occurs

- There are usually preliminary measures you have taken before you refer a student to an administrator, dean, or student support personnel. Talking with the student and contacting families and caregivers are two of the most important early interventions you should try.

- Make sure you are familiar with the school guidelines and procedures that apply to your students. Be aware of the ways the school board and your other supervisors expect you to handle student misconduct.

- Prevent disruptive behavior through building relationships with students, student-centered educational practices, and restorative practices.

- Handle routine disruptive behaviors yourself. Establish your classroom agreements, policies, and consequences early in the term and follow through when necessary. Document the methods you use to handle these routine behaviors.

- Make sure you have the necessary referral forms on hand so that you can use them if a time comes when you must refer a student to an administrator.

- If a problem with a student or situation has been brewing for a while, you probably have already been in touch with the administrator to ask for advice and support. This is a good idea so that the administrator has background context on what has been tried to develop a solution.

After the Referral Has Occurred

- Once a student's behavior has reached the point that you will refer them to an administrator, make sure you prevent a bad situation from becoming worse by maintaining the student's dignity and privacy in front of classmates.

- When you talk with a student about an incident, express your concern; don't threaten or bully the student, even if you are angry. Calmly state your policy and the consequences for the behavior.

- Calm down before you write the referral. Your language should be as professional and objective as possible. Many different people will see the referral. Use language that is focused on observable behaviors, facts and solutions. Do not state your opinion of the student's behavior or sink to name-calling or sarcasm.

- Contact the student's home before the end of the day to inform them of the incident and of your action in referring the student to an administrator.

- Make sure you also tell the student when you refer them to an administrator. The best way to do this is privately at the end of class.

- In a responsive discipline system, referring a student to a dean, administrator, or student support team engages a higher level of intervention to support the student. You are their teacher and remain central to their success, but now you have additional colleagues with additional tools to improve their behavior.

What to Do When Fights Occur

In the last few years, there has been a dramatic increase in the number of fights at school; sadly, some of these conflicts have involved the use of weapons. As an educator, you can do a great deal to improve students' self-regulation and conflict resolution skills, reducing violence and increasing safety for you and your students.

Expectations for Teachers

- Follow your school district's procedures for handling student fights.

- If you are assigned to hall duty, cafeteria duty, or any other duty, don't miss it. Be on time, bring your walkie-talkie or cell phone, and be alert. A visible adult presence deters many fights.

- Act quickly to prevent fights by reporting student rumors about fights to administrators.

- Don't leave the location of the fight. Call the office or send students to the office for help instead.

- Keep your students as safe as you can if a fight erupts.

- Take reasonable measures to stop fights without putting yourself or others in danger. This is one time when yelling "Stop!" at students is the right thing to do. Students often want an excuse to not fight and you repeatedly telling them to stop may work. Disperse the crowd, as removing the audience can also reduce their desire to continue fighting.

- Do not intervene physically in a fight. Use of force or restraint with students should be a rare intervention and one that is only done by trained staff members.

- Be prepared to provide an accurate witness report.

- Witnessing a fight may affect you and your students. Consider debriefing with students in a class conversation or a journal-writing exercise. Don't pretend like it didn't happen; process it, if necessary, and then move on with learning.

Do What You Can to Prevent Fights at School

- Teach students self-regulation and conflict resolution skills regularly.

- Facilitate class meetings so that students practice communication skills and strengthen their sense of community

- Familiarize students with your school's policy concerning students who fight at school.

- Make sure that your students are aware of their options for conflict resolution besides fighting.

- Be alert to the signs that a fight is building: rumors, a high level of excitement, and remarks about what will happen later.

- If you see that two students are beginning to square off, intervene verbally and remind them of the serious penalties for students who fight. Often students will take this as an opportunity to back down without losing face because they can claim that they do not want to deal with the consequences.

- Immediately contact an administrator about a possible fight.

- Make sure that all your students are aware of the school policy on weapons and how to report weapons to an adult.

- Teach your students about bullying and harassment. Make sure that they understand the limits they should observe when interacting with one another and what they should do if they are bullied or harassed.

- Encourage positive behavior by intervening if students insult one another, even in jest.
- Teach your students about their role as bystanders and that they have the ability to deescalate rather than encourage a fight.

If Fights Occur Near You

- Use your emergency communication tools whether that's a phone, walkie-talkie, intercom, or sending a student to get help. Do not try to restrain or step between students.
- Remove students from the area if possible, without leaving the area. Make the safety of all students at the scene your first concern.
- Raise your voice. Tell students firmly to "Stop! Now!"
- Be very careful about how you approach students who are fighting so that no one, including yourself, is injured.

If There Are Weapons Involved

- If you hear a rumor that there is a weapon in the building, contact an administrator at once. You should not attempt to handle this situation by yourself.
- When a weapon is used during a fight, do not allow other students to take it. The weapon may be used as evidence. If you can, confiscate it and turn it over to an administrator.

If There Are Injuries

- Depending on the extent of the injury, contact the office, send a student for the school nurse, or call 9-1-1. Deal first with any injured students and then with the other students at the scene. Do not leave the area.
- Assist the more seriously wounded students first. Be careful that the aid you offer does not injure students further.
- Protect yourself and others from contact with blood-borne pathogens or other bodily fluids.
- If you are even slightly injured, seek medical attention promptly.

What to Do after You Have Witnessed a Fight

- As soon as you can, record the details of what happened. As a witness to the fight, you may be called on to remember these details in the investigation and possibly in court, sometimes months after the incident, so be as specific as you can when you record your notes.
- If a fight took place while students were under your supervision, contact the families and caregivers of students involved so that you can work together to repair harm and prevent a recurrence.

- Model the calm response you want from your students. Witnessing a fight may affect you and your students. Consider debriefing with students in a class conversation or a journal writing exercise. Don't pretend like it didn't happen, process it, if necessary, and then move on with learning.

Help Students Move Forward after a Behavior Issue

Once a behavior incident has occurred in a classroom, it is up to you, the student who committed harm, and the rest of the classroom community to resolve it and help students move past the incident. This is a vital step in the process of handling all types of discipline issues successfully because without it, your relationship with the student, their sense of belonging in the community, and that student's sense of self-worth could be damaged.

Because some behavior issues are easier to handle than others, you may not need to spend a long time on this part of the process with every issue. A quick nod of the head, a smile, or a comment such as "I know you've got this" will all be sufficient to reassure the student that you still care and believe they are capable of future success.

When a behavior issue is serious or time-consuming, it is even more important to make sure that the student feels included, valued, and trusted again. Without that feeling, the student has little motivation to repair, learn, and do well in your class. Spend a few minutes with a student whose behavior caused harm, reassuring them that you have every confidence in their ability to be successful in the future. It's a step well worth the trouble.

Maintaining Behavior Documentation All Year

Keeping accurate records about the behavior issues in your classroom is a necessary professional responsibility, no matter what grade you teach. Technology makes it easy to keep a behavior log in your student information system. This way, all the adults at school who work with the student also have access to the student's behavior log. Because discipline issues can affect all aspects of a student's life and can also be a point of contention between home and school, the documents you keep about how discipline problems occur and are resolved should be accurate and up to date.

Behavior records serve several purposes. They will also allow you to see the growth of your students as the year progresses. When you review them, you will be able to see what worked and what did not; this will enable you to make informed decisions when future problems occur.

Well-maintained records will also make it easier for you to recall the details of a behavior incident long after the incident has passed. Accurate behavior documentation is also especially important if a behavior incident is serious enough that you may be asked to testify in court.

If you make it a habit to complete the records you need to maintain as soon as an incident is resolved, you will find that it is easier to recall the details of the incident when needed. One final tool that can help you identify and meet the behavioral needs of students is to reflect on the impact that each intervention had on your class. You may want to adopt forms like Teacher Template 13.5 and the ones on p444–452 to fit the needs of your teaching practice.

TEACHER TEMPLATE 13.5

Behavior Intervention Documentation

This template allows you to quickly record and analyze the behavior interventions that you have tried with a class that has many behavior challenges.

Class period: _____   Major concerns: _____

_____

_____

_____

_____

Record the success of each intervention you have tried in the last column by using these numbers:

1. Not successful
2. Somewhat successful but needs modification
3. Successful

Date of Intervention	Intervention	Level of Success/ Notes
	Recorded or videoed myself to determine how I could be contributing to the problem	
	Asked a colleague to observe the class and provide feedback	
	Analyzed the time used by students at the start of class, during various activities, and at the end of class	
	Made sure that expectations are clearly expressed in several modalities and taught to students	
	Made sure that procedures for all activities are in place and known to students	
	Made sure that students are aware of the class agreements and the positive and negative consequences connected to them	
	Held individual conferences with key students	

(continued on next page)

(continued from previous page)

Date of Intervention	Intervention	Level of Success/ Notes
	Held a brief conference with the entire class to solicit their suggestions	
	Used exit slips or other written formats to elicit student suggestions	
	Adjusted the pace and types of instruction	
	Increased student choices for instructional activities	
	Encouraged the positive behavior of the entire class	
	Made student successes as concrete and visible as possible	
	Involved other staff members in creating solutions	
	Involved students' families and caregivers in creating solutions	
	Engaged in a team-building activity to build a sense of community	
	Made sure all students have access to materials and supplies	
	Worked with individual students to set and achieve goals	
	Worked with the entire class to set and achieve group goals	
	Made sure that the level of work is neither too easy nor too difficult	
	Used all available class time in a productive way	
	Offered a variety of relevant learning activities, including games and technology-based instruction	
	Taught positive social skills to replace negative behaviors	
	Included motivational activities in the lesson to increase engagement	
	Provided positive opportunities for students to be in the spotlight	
	Established signals for students to indicate that they need help	
	Involved students in as many helpful roles in the classroom as possible	

(continued on next page)

(continued from previous page)

Date of Intervention	Intervention	Level of Success/ Notes
	Established ways for students to productively help one another	
	Offered a combination of intrinsic and extrinsic rewards	
	Taught students how to modulate their noise levels	
	Made it obvious that the purpose of class is to learn	
	Posted encouraging mottoes to remind students to stay focused	
	Have a policy for proficiency-based learning allowing students to retake a failed summative assessment	
	Communicated a strong belief in students' ability to succeed	
	Established predictable routines so that students know what to do	
	Provided various role models and mentors for students	
	Appealed to a variety of learning styles in each lesson	
	Established a calming space so that students can gain self-control	
	Made sure the lesson was as exciting as possible	
	Gave written and verbal directions that are easy for students to follow	
	Made sure the class traffic flow is highly efficient	
	Offered frequent checks for understanding to reduce frustration	
	Involved students' interests in the lesson	
	Acknowledged student effort	
	Ignored as much low-level behavior as was possible and prudent	
	Varied instructional activities to include collaboration and independent work	
	Kept expectations for academic and behavioral success high	

Questions to Discuss with Colleagues

Sharing ideas with colleagues is a helpful way to devise solutions to some of the problems that you must manage successfully at school. Here, you will find several topics to open discussions with colleagues about successful instructional practices:

1. Several of your students are easily distracted and have made it clear that they are not interested in the subject matter you are teaching. How can you intervene and redirect while treating each one with respect and dignity? What is your goal in this situation? How can you prevent this behavior from occurring in the future?

2. What are the most common negative behaviors that you observe among your students? How do the other teachers at your school handle them? What advice do they have for you as you work to establish an orderly classroom environment?

3. You would like to learn more about restorative justice and responsive discipline and how it could be used in your school. How can you and your colleagues learn more about these practices and how to integrate it into your school? Who can help you with this?

4. When students engage in negative behaviors, it is often hard to reduce the stress that a discipline issue brings with it. How can you manage your stress related to discipline? What suggestions do your colleagues offer to help you with this?

5. Although you accept that the discipline issues in your classroom are your responsibility, it is apparent that some of them are caused by the negative climate and culture at your school. What can you and your colleagues do to improve the overall discipline climate?

Topics to Discuss with a Mentor

Although the topics that new teachers need to discuss with a mentor vary from teacher to teacher and from school to school, there are some that most first-year teachers should be comfortable discussing with a mentor or a trusted colleague. You should ask your mentor about these topics from this section:

- Advice about referring students to the Child or Student Study Team
- Suggestions for redirecting students who are off task
- How to learn more about your legal responsibilities as an educator
- Information about which behaviors you should overlook and which require intervention
- Advice about how to respond to and document behavior problems

Reflection Questions to Guide Your Thinking

1. What are your skills regarding problem solving with a student who struggles with behaviors? How can you capitalize on your strengths? What can you improve about how you support students?

2. Why do students engage in negative behaviors in your class? Can you notice a pattern or a time when this behavior is most likely to occur? What can you do to prevent them from happening?

3. What plans do you have in place for handling serious student behavior, such as fighting? What is your school's policy about teacher intervention in a student fight? What can you do to keep your students and yourself safe if a fight erupts?

4. What do your supervisors recommend teachers do in terms of discipline? What do the families and caregivers expect of you? How strict or flexible do they expect you to be?

5. What attitudes can you adopt to increase your confidence in your ability to address discipline issues as learning opportunities? How can you improve your ability to address the discipline concerns in your classroom?

SECTION FOURTEEN

How-To Quick Reference Guide to Common Behavior Issues

This section purposefully comes at the end of the book after you have read all about the importance of building relationships and classroom agreements with students; after you have read about connecting with families, caregivers, and the support team at your school. It comes after all the important information about social-emotional learning, culturally responsive practices, restorative practices, and equity. All those pieces need to be in place along with facilitating student-centered engagement strategies in order for behavioral interventions to work.

All behavior is a form of communication. Behaviors, both positive and negative, meet a need. They provide attention, escape/avoidance, access to something, or provide or remove sensory input. Because of this, teachers need to understand the unmet needs that students are trying to satisfy through their behavior and teach positive social skills to replace the negative behaviors.

With all the foundational pieces in place, this section is designed to give you a few helpful strategies to address behavior issues that teachers face. Your understanding of the student and the reasons behind their behavior will guide how you choose to respond.

Even though there may be some overlap within the categories, you'll find the behaviors divided into four categories:

Category One: Behavior Involving Individual Students

In this category, the harm caused by the behavior is generally limited to the individual students.

- How to respond when students fall asleep in class
- How to respond when you suspect a student is under the influence
- How to respond when students are tardy to class
- How to help students who are chronically absent

- How to help students who repeatedly engage in negative behavior
- How to respond when students tell lies
- How to address smartphone use in class

Category Two: Behaviors Violating Class/School Agreements

In this category, the harm caused by the behavior affects additional students in the class.

- How to respond when there's a classroom theft
- How to respond when students use profanity
- How to respond when students use discriminatory language
- How to address cheating
- How to respond when students engage in sexting
- How to handle negative behavior in the hallway
- How to respond when students engage in horseplay
- How to address bullying and harassment

"One day in the cafeteria, I noticed a young man who was not his usual fun self. I walked by, stopped, and asked him quietly if everything was all right. He said yes, but I knew it wasn't. I told him he knew where I was if he needed me and then moved on. The next morning, I found a note on my desk, all folded, teen style. In the note, this young man thanked me for asking him if he was okay. He said he had been struggling with some very hard news and was really thinking of doing something stupid, but I had made him rethink his decision. I was awed at the power teachers have. As teachers, we never, ever know the full extent of our effect on those lives entrusted to us. We must truly exercise caution in how we interact with young people. I carry that note, now more than thirty years old, in my wallet every day of my life, to remind me of this moment. The good news: this young man is now a productive member of our community with a lovely wife (who was also my student) and three great children. What greater reward could any teacher desire?"

Luann West Scott, 42 years' experience

Category Three: Behaviors Disrupting Learning

In this category, harm caused by the behavior negatively affects learning for one or more students in the class.

- How to support students who refuse to engage in learning
- How to support a class that is slow to settle down and engage
- How to respond when students behave disrespectfully to a substitute teacher
- How to respond when classes are inappropriately noisy

Category Four: Negative Behaviors toward the Teacher

In this category, behaviors are directed toward the teacher and suggest a negative relationship between the teacher and student.

- How to respond when a student is disrespectful or defiant
- How to avoid and disengage from classroom power struggles

Each entry begins with a general description of the behavior so that you can easily recognize it. This description is then followed by a list of classroom-tested strategies that can guide you to make informed decisions about how to respond to these behavioral challenges should they appear in your classroom.

Category One: Behavior Involving Individual Students

HOW TO RESPOND WHEN STUDENTS FALL ASLEEP IN CLASS

Sometimes students are sleepy, but learning doesn't occur if they are asleep in class. When that happens only now and then, sleepy students are not a big concern. The behavior becomes concerning when a student repeatedly falls asleep in class or chooses to sleep to avoid work. Then the behavior is symptomatic of a larger issue that requires adult intervention and support.

Strategies That Work

- When you ask a student about sleeping in class, seek first to understand. Ask them if they are doing okay.
- Speak to students in private to find out why they are so tired. Do they stay up too late at home? Is there a medical problem? Do they have an after-school job that requires long hours? Are they bored? Is the work too challenging? Are they experiencing homelessness?
- If talking to a student does not resolve the concern, consider contacting home to elicit their support.
- When you see that a student is becoming sleepy, allow that student to stand up, move around, or get a drink of water.
- Give students a reason to stay awake with compelling lessons relevant to their interests. Sometimes if students decide that they cannot succeed in a class, they sometimes choose to sleep rather than be frustrated. Involve these students in activities in which they can be successful and that they will enjoy more than napping through class.
- If you notice that several of your students are tempted to sleep, reflect on the lesson plan and increase your use of active learning strategies.

HOW TO RESPOND WHEN YOU SUSPECT A STUDENT IS UNDER THE INFLUENCE

As a classroom teacher, it is important that you know your district's guidelines around responding to substance use by students. It is also important that you know which staff members to turn to for help if you determine that a problem exists.

Strategies That Work

- Know the signs and paraphernalia related to substance use.
- Speak with the student privately. Use "I statements," like, "I'm concerned about you," and tell them what you observed.
- Listen to the student's reply and determine if that changes your assessment that they are under the influence.
- Even if you are not sure that the student is under the influence, then at least you have let them know you care and you are observant.
- If you believe, after talking with the student, that they are under the influence, then follow your school's protocol.
- Remain fact-based. Avoid using scare tactics about the worst things that could happen due to substance use. Avoid making "always" or "never" statements about what always or never happens as a result of substance use.

HOW TO RESPOND WHEN STUDENTS ARE TARDY TO CLASS

There are many valid reasons why students might arrive late to class. Yet, tardiness can be a distraction and causes students to miss instruction. Promptness is also an important college and career readiness skill.

Strategies That Work

- When talking with students about their tardiness, let them know you care and are glad they are part of the class. Ask them what causes them to be late and what actions they can take to arrive on time. Determine if the student needs additional resources to overcome barriers.
- Find out about the lives and needs of chronically tardy students. There may be barriers that prevent them from arriving on time, like transportation, that you can help them figure out.
- Define *tardiness* for your students and be reasonable in your definition. Most teachers will agree that a student who is inside the classroom when the bell rings is not tardy.
- Make it important for your students to be on time to your class. Begin class quickly, with bell ringers and morning meetings that students will find enjoyable. Make the first few minutes of class as meaningful as the rest.
- Involve families and caregivers if a student is repeatedly tardy. This is an especially important step if the tardy student is late to school and not just late from another teacher's class.
- Follow through with your tardiness policy and logical consequences. Be aware of your school's policy for handling habitual tardiness.

- Model the behavior you expect. Your students will be very quick to point out your hypocrisy if you are tardy and then correct them for the same offense.

- Keep accurate attendance records. Tardy students often arrive after attendance is taken, so remember to change an absence mark to a tardy mark.

HOW TO HELP STUDENTS WHO ARE CHRONICALLY ABSENT

Many factors may contribute to a student's absenteeism. Get to know your students and their circumstances. Take an active role in encouraging students to attend school regardless of the reason for their absenteeism. Encouraging your students to attend school on a regular basis is one of the most important messages you can convey to students.

Strategies That Work

- When you realize that a student is not attending, do not ignore it. In addition to the office making automated calls, it is meaningful and effective for teachers to reach out to the student and contact home.

- Be aware of your students' attendance patterns. Find out the reasons for a student's absenteeism so that you can offer meaningful assistance.

- Remember that students who feel connected to their school, their classmates, and their teachers rarely miss school without good reason. Encourage regular attendance by building a strong relationship with each of your students. Students should feel that they are missed when they are absent.

- Work with the counselor or social worker to create a Check-in/Check-out system for the student to check in with someone when they arrive at school and check out just before they leave. This will create a positive and inviting arrival and departure.

- Contact home when students have excessive absences to offer to work with them on solutions.

- Maintain accurate attendance records and follow your school district's procedures for reporting and handling attendance, especially if you want to seek assistance for chronically absent students. It is not always easy to keep up with attendance records, but students and administrators need to have an accurate accounting of attendance throughout the term.

- Ask a counselor or social worker to speak to students who are having trouble with their attendance so that the students know what resources are available to them.

- Talk to students about their absences. If your students are having challenges at home or social problems, seek help for them.

HOW TO HELP STUDENTS WHO REPEATEDLY ENGAGE IN NEGATIVE BEHAVIOR

Negative behaviors come in infinite varieties of disruption, stress, and frustration. From tattling in kindergarten to wearing earbuds and listening to music when it's not appropriate to senioritis, negative behavior is something that all teachers experience. Sometimes the behavior is contained to one or two students and sometimes it is a problem involving an entire class. In either case, negative behavior requires a thoughtful and deliberate problem-solving approach.

Strategies That Work

- Attend to safety issues first. It is your responsibility to act decisively and quickly to keep all your students safe. Never allow behavior that jeopardizes student health and safety to continue.

- Be supportive and encouraging. Stay positive in your approach. Work to resolve the needs behind the behaviors instead of just reacting to the behavior.

- Set a clearly established goal for improvement and measure their progress in their journey toward it.

- Show students how they are supposed to behave. Use plenty of models, examples, and explicit details so that your students can have a clear idea of just how they are supposed to act.

- Let your class agreements, policies, and procedures do their work. Enforce them consistently and fairly.

- Engage student voice and choice in the classroom. Respect students' dignity so that they do not need to act out to have a voice. You'll send a strong message that you respect students and that the focus in your class is on learning.

HOW TO RESPOND WHEN STUDENTS TELL LIES

Behavior is designed to meet a need. A student who did not complete an assignment on time may make up an excuse to avoid embarrassment or negative consequences. One of the most difficult issues that teachers may need to address is what to do when they realize that a student has been lying to them.

Strategies That Work

- Don't take it personally while teaching the student that truthfulness serves them better.

- Speak privately with the student. Ask questions that will lead them to admit the truth.

- Have the facts before accusing a student of lying to avoid damaging your relationship with the student.

- Contact home when necessary. Sometimes it takes a united front to tackle the underlying issues that have encouraged a student to lie. Be compassionate and understanding when speaking with a family member or caregiver.

- Once you and the student have worked out the problem, assure the student that the matter is resolved and that you intend for both of you to move forward.

- Be a role model of honesty and integrity yourself.

HOW TO ADDRESS SMARTPHONE USE IN CLASS

Smartphones are powerful devices for daily living and students' addiction to smartphones is also a significant hindrance to learning. Some of the apps are useful for school, from calculators to translators. Some apps are built to be addictive and some apps harm students' mental health. Students and adults can struggle to find the rightful place for smartphones in their lives. Learning self-discipline around smartphone usage is a vital life skill.

Strategies That Work

- Follow the guidelines set forth by your school concerning student smartphones. Some schools ban them or require them to remain in backpacks or purpose-built phone lockers. Some require them to be out of sight. Some just address problem smartphone behavior as it arises.

- Model the smartphone behavior that you expect from students. Make sure friends and family members know you will have limited access to your phone. Give them alternative ways to reach you during school hours for emergencies.

- Make sure all students are aware of your policies so that they understand the times when they can use their smartphones and the logical consequences of inappropriate smartphone use.

- Be consistent in teaching students self-discipline skills with respect to smartphones.

- Many teachers have had success with reducing the distraction caused by smartphones by asking students to leave them turned off and zipped inside of backpacks. This can work well if students get into the habit of managing their smartphones at the start of class and if teachers are vigilant and consistent with the procedure.

- Still others have had success with a designated smartphone area of the room where students can stow their phones upon entering the classroom. Teachers have created cubbies or hanging pockets for parking smartphones. Some schools install purpose-built smartphone lockers to safely store student phones during the day. (Note that some students then bring two phones to school; one is a decoy to turn in.)

- Ask your colleagues, mentor, and PLN how they address smartphones in class. This will enable you to make sound decisions that are similar to what other teachers do. When there is a consistent approach like this in a school, students will find it easier to follow the guidelines.

Category Two: Behaviors Violating Class/School Agreements

HOW TO RESPOND WHEN THERE'S A CLASSROOM THEFT

Behaviors that violate classroom agreements can undermine students' sense of safety in the classroom. A student who takes what doesn't belong to them may be impulsive or have unmet needs due to poverty. Teachers have a responsibility to uphold class agreements, and teach students life skills around taking accountability and not stealing. The student who has stolen something will need to take responsibility and repair the harm that was caused by their actions. In this way, they will strengthen ties to the classroom community.

Strategies That Work

- Always lock your classroom when leaving, and never give your keys to students. Discourage students from taking items from your personal space at school. Secure your personal belongings in a locked space.

- Make it easy for the student who took an item to have a change of heart and "find" the missing object. This will allow them to save face in front of peers, minimize disruption, and encourage the positive class community you want for your class to continue.

- If you collect money from your students for any reason, secure it until you can deliver it to the office for proper accounting and depositing.

- Remind your students to secure their valuable personal items: devices, smartphones, headphones, money, jewelry, hats and more.

- To recover a stolen item you might offer a small reward for its safe return. Promise to ask no questions, and honor that promise. If the item is not returned, you will want to alert other teachers and administrators about what has happened so that they also can be on the lookout for the missing item.

- If you catch a student in the act of stealing, ask if you can help them. If you can calmly recover the item without disrupting class or searching a student's possessions, then do. If not, then report the incident immediately so that an administrator can intervene.

- After an incident, have a conference with the student. Agree on how they will repair the harm they caused.

HOW TO RESPOND WHEN STUDENTS USE PROFANITY

What is "appropriate" language in school is a complex question. The answer is influenced by culture, societal norms, and a teacher's personal limits. There is a continuum of profanity from acceptable cussing *about* something to unacceptable use of profanity *at* someone.

Strategies That Work for Unintentional Profanity

- Have an open conversation about swearing at the start of the term. Have students brainstorm reasons why this type of language is not acceptable everywhere, in all settings.

- Build students' word wealth by having them develop synonyms and replacement words for profanity.

- If a student slips and accidentally uses profanity in a conversation with another student and you overhear it, ask them to find another word or perhaps they can offer three alternatives to the word they used.

- Some teachers create a lesson around age-appropriate Shakespearean curse words and phrases to make students aware of language choices.

- If a student habitually curses, you may want to privately tally the number of times they use profanity in a class period and share the data with them.

- Pay attention if a student is genuinely remorseful and immediately apologizes. At that point, the negative consequences should not have to be enacted because the student has enough self-discipline to realize that the mistake should not have happened and has tried to correct the error. If the student continues to forget, then you should enact the consequences.

When students are highly emotional and use profane words toward you or other students this is a very different situation than unintentional use of profanity. Students are deliberately using language to try to hurt the object of their anger.

Strategies That Work for Intentional Profanity

- To affirm the dignity of all students, establish a class agreement around not using language that implies that any member of the class is less than other members of the class. This includes profanity directed at a student or teacher. Explain the rationale for your expectations to students.

- As difficult as it is, don't take it personally.

- Respond immediately and calmly. Let the student know you can see they are upset and ask them if they want to take a break and get a drink of water to calm down.

- Reinforce to them and the rest of the class that we don't do that here. We talk to each other respectfully and you'll talk with them when they calm down.

- If the student is unable or unwilling to calm down, contact the office, a counselor, or social worker to help de-escalate the situation.

- Determine if a referral to an administrator is necessary.

- Determine if contacting home is necessary and helpful.

- After the student has calmed down, start the restorative process. Talk with them about how the incident made you or the targeted student feel. Listen as the student tells you what upset them. Agree on how to repair the harm. Have the student rehearse a meaningful apology and come up with replacement strategies. Check in a day or two to make sure the agreed upon actions happened.

HOW TO RESPOND WHEN STUDENTS USE DISCRIMINATORY LANGUAGE

Teachers must respond immediately if students use discriminatory language or slurs such as racist, sexist, homophobic, transphobic, ableist, classist, anti-Semitic, Islamaphobic, fatphobic, glottophobic, or xenophobic language in school. It is of vital importance to intervene when harmful language is used. If a teacher ignores the use of such language, it causes students to feel unsafe, disrespected, and it can lead to violence. Intervention is needed whether it is casually or even "jokingly" used in conversation or directed at you or another student in anger.

- When creating classroom agreements, teach students what it means to create a safe and respectful community where each student feels a sense of belonging.

- It's important to understand the culture of your students and the concept of in-group and out-group language. Members of an in-group have a shared identity and a unique relationship. There are words that don't belong to everyone; words that when used by an in-group within that group are part of their culture. The same words used by the out-group would be considered discriminatory and harmful.

- Respond immediately letting the student know that their language is unacceptable and set a time to talk with them privately. Check in with the student(s) who experienced harm and provide any needed support.

- If the student who used discriminatory language is emotional, have them take a break and calm down. If they are angry and disruptive, refer them to the counselor or office.

- Meet with the student who caused harm after they calm down. Make sure they know why the language is inappropriate and agree on how they will repair the harm that was caused. Let the student know about consequences should they repeat this behavior.

- Ask the student(s) who were harmed by the discriminatory speech if they want an opportunity to tell the student how the behavior made them feel and how to repair the harm that was caused.

- If students want to communicate in person or in writing, facilitate that or ask a counselor or social worker to facilitate it with you.

- Determine if a referral to the office is needed.

- Contact the homes of the student who caused harm and the student(s) who experienced harm. In the case of a homophobic or transphobic comment, ask the student who was the target of the behavior for permission before calling home.

HOW TO ADDRESS CHEATING

Cheating in a school context is defined as "acting dishonestly and passing off someone else's work as one's own." It is an unfortunate part of school life that requires multifaceted solutions. Sometimes students cheat because the work is too difficult or they have a fear of failure and are not prepared for class. Still others cheat because they do not see the relevance of the tasks they are asked to perform. Internet searches and generative AI tools are available to students, making it very easy to create text and images, search for answers to questions, and cut and paste information into a document. It is important to teach students when and how to use the internet and generative AI in an ethical way, and how to cite the use of other sources and tools.

Strategies That Work

Step One: Preventing Cheating from Occurring

- Know your school's policy on student cheating and follow it. If all teachers in a school consistently enforce a schoolwide policy on cheating, then students will have consistent expectations.

- During class discussions, define *cheating* and encourage students to talk about the issue. They will surprise you with the insights and experiences they are willing to share with a concerned adult.

- Create alternative assessments that are more difficult to cheat on. For example, require in-class, handwritten essays when you want an original writing sample. Have students demonstrate their learning orally with presentations so that they must explain their thinking.

- Have students submit assignments through technology that can scan for plagiarism or AI-generated content.

- Model integrity by citing your sources on instructional materials and images and by respecting copyright laws for films, software, books, and other material.

- Help your students see cheating as detrimental to learning and negative in the big picture of life choices.

- Search "how to cheat in school" on the internet to stay current on students' strategies.

- Talk with colleagues about the tactics students use to cheat so that you can be observant. Keep desks and work areas clean so that you will notice if answers are written on them or if a cheat sheet is visible. Keep cleaner on hand to wipe away any notes or answers.

- Before a summative assessment, ask students to neatly stow away their books, papers, cell phones, and other materials as part of preparing for the test. Make it obvious that you are checking. Students can easily take photos of tests with cell phones to share with other students.

- Talk to your students about taking a commonsense approach to avoiding the appearance of cheating. Students should not turn sideways in their seats during a test. Students should also not talk to one another during an independent test or quiz.

- Don't leave tests, quizzes, or answer keys on your desk where anxious students might be tempted to peek at them.

- Any questions your students may have during an in-class independent test should be directed only to you. Walk over to the student who has a question. Students should remain seated during tests to avoid inadvertently seeing another's paper.

- Monitor your students very closely during a quiz or test. You can't do this by sitting at your desk. Move around the room frequently.

- Give several different versions of a test or quiz—even during the same class period.

- When students finish a test early, either have them keep their papers until you collect them all at once or have them turn them in and begin another independent assignment immediately.

Step Two: Addressing Cheating Once It Has Occurred

- If you have caught a student cheating, the first thing you should do is arrange a private conference with the student to discuss the reasons why they cheated. Whatever the reason, talk with the student in a calm manner to determine what went wrong and to help the student see other options that could prevent future cheating.

- When you catch one of your students cheating, contact their families or caregivers so that they can follow up with a conversation at home and so they understand the consequences.

- Follow the school's policy on cheating. Sometimes this means involving counselors and administrators.

- Unless your school's policy prohibits it, allow the student to make up or redo the assignment. This gives them an opportunity to learn from the behavior.

- If a student reports to you that another student is cheating, thank them and advise that student about the best next step. Make sure you take such confidences seriously and act with discretion to take the necessary steps to solve the problem.

- Once you have settled an incident with a student, forgive and forget. Convey this attitude to any students who cheat on an assignment, and you will provide them with an incentive to start fresh and to put their mistakes behind them.

- If a student repeatedly cheats, then additional interventions are needed and may include a conference with the student, counselor, and family or caregiver. It may involve a behavior contract, increased supervision when they are completing assignments, or more serious consequences from a dean or administrator.

HOW TO RESPOND WHEN STUDENTS ENGAGE IN SEXTING

Sexting is the act of digitally transmitting or receiving sexually explicit messages, photos, or videos. Students who share explicit content may have felt pressured to, or see nothing wrong with doing so, but sending explicit content can have serious consequences. Underage sexting is considered child pornography. The student who is the subject of the explicit content can lose control over the text or image as it is shared with others, posted online, and they become vulnerable to bullying and harassment.

Strategies That Work

- Begin by educating yourself about the problem. Sexting is widespread and can have long-lasting consequences for students.
- Make sure that you are familiar with your school district's policies on sexting and aware of the steps that are required of you. Most school districts have very clear policies about how sexting should be handled.
- When a student confides in you, do not look at or get a copy of the sexually explicit content. Do not confiscate the phone or device. Doing any of those things could have serious legal implications for you.
- Act quickly if you become aware of a sexting incident. Remain calm and follow your district's policies about how to handle the matter.

- Contact an administrator immediately to report the incident and ask them to handle these sensitive and confidential matters.
- Common Sense Media has lesson plans about the risks and consequences of sexting. These lessons can be an important part of comprehensive health education, advisory, or digital citizenship education.

HOW TO HANDLE NEGATIVE BEHAVIOR IN THE HALLWAY

Hallway challenges vary widely depending on the age of the student. In elementary school, students often move through the halls in lines with their teachers. There is rarely a passing period where the halls are crowded. In middle and high school, teachers generally stand in their doorways, greet students, monitor the halls, and urge students to be on time for their next class. Visible adults can improve student behaviors and reduce disruptive behaviors.

Strategies That Work

- Be proactive in your approach to this problem. To begin, make sure you know the expectations for hallway behavior at your school.
- Teach expectations of hallway behavior to students and practice transitions with students.
- Make it enjoyable for elementary students to follow procedures. Play games such as calling out "One, two, three, freeze!" at some point in the trip to have students form themselves into human statues. You can also find enjoyable ideas for improving hallway behavior just by searching online. Try using "lining up strategies" as a search term on the We Are Teachers website to find dozens of ideas.

HOW TO RESPOND WHEN STUDENTS ENGAGE IN HORSEPLAY

A friendly push, a quick grab from behind, running in the hall, or throwing backpacks are behaviors that are all too common when students gather. Horseplay has been a part of school life for as long as schools have been in existence. So, too, have the serious consequences associated with horseplay. In addition to the disruption and loss of instructional time that horseplay causes in a learning environment, there are other, potentially more serious concerns.

It is all too easy for students who are "playing around" to injure themselves as they knock one another about. Bystanders can also be injured when the students who are rough-housing bump into them or into furniture. Finally, the most significant detrimental effect of horseplay is that what starts as friendly fun can escalate into an unfriendly or even violent event when one of the students is injured or decides to retaliate.

Strategies That Work

- Teach students the importance of respecting others' personal space. Be explicit about explaining what is acceptable behavior and why it is important.

- Most horseplay occurs when students are in transition times, such as when they are lining up, moving through the hallway, entering class, on the playground, or in the cafeteria. Be extra careful to monitor students during these less-structured times of the school day.

- Stand at your classroom door when class starts, but position yourself so that you can monitor students in your classroom as well.

- Have clearly spelled out and well-timed dismissal procedures so that students do not have enough time to roughhouse as they get ready to leave class.

- Carefully consider the traffic flow of your classroom to eliminate unnecessary wandering. Are the paths to the trash can, the area where students pick up or turn in papers, and the pencil sharpener efficiently laid out so that students will easily take care of tasks?

- If you have students who continue to engage in horseplay even after you have warned them and enacted consequences, you may want to contact home for additional support, or consult with the counselor or social worker for additional support.

HOW TO ADDRESS BULLYING AND HARASSMENT

Bullying and harassment can take many forms and reports of bullying and harassment must be treated seriously by teachers and administrators. *Bullying* is threatening, harmful, or humiliating conduct. When that bullying behavior is directed at someone because of their identity or protected class, it becomes *harassment*.

Physical, verbal, or emotional bullying and harassment can take place in person or online. Harmful behaviors may occur one time or be ongoing. The impact of these behaviors is to intimidate students and create an unsafe environment for learning. As an educator, you have significant responsibilities to prevent and intervene in the face of bullying and harassment:

- You must know your school's policy about bullying and harassment as well as your responsibilities for handling it.
- You are expected to take necessary steps to prevent bullying and harassment by getting to know your students and building a supportive community of learners.
- Teach your students about bullying and harassment and supervise them adequately.
- Because bullying and harassment are such serious issues, schools typically require that teachers involve counselors, social workers, administrators, families or caregivers, and other support personnel. Follow your school's policy.

Strategies That Work

Before an Incident Occurs

- Get to know your students. Build a supportive, respectful community.
- Teach social skills and the vital role of bystanders to intervene in an incident of bullying or harassment. Brainstorm how bystanders can take action and become upstanders. Encourage students to speak up or step in to disrupt an incident.
- Teach social skills as part of your class curriculum, no matter how old your students are.
- Be alert for the early or subtle signs of bullying. Listen carefully to what students say both to and about one another. For example, if you notice that several students have targeted one of their classmates or that a student is having trouble adjusting, intervene and be alert that more may be going on than what you see.

When an Incident Occurs

- If you witness or receive a report of an incident of bullying or harassment, act immediately. Intervene to stop the students committing harm and protect the target of bullying or harassment. This is a powerful statement to students. Share the information with an administrator to follow up if an investigation is needed.
- Because of the serious nature of bullying and harassment, you should not attempt to manage this without administrative help. As soon as you are aware of an incident of bullying or harassment, quickly put the school's procedures into action by formally reporting the incident to an administrator. Be accurate, factual, and specific in your reporting.
- Respect the confidentiality of the students involved, sharing the incident only with those who need to know.
- Support the student harmed by bullying. Often, just talking with an adult will help the target of bullying relieve some of the anxiety that they are feeling.

- Talk with the student who engaged in behavior that harmed other students,

- To learn more about what you can do to prevent and respond to bullying and harassment, including cyberbullying, explore this helpful site for educators maintained by the U.S. Department of Health and Human Services: StopBullying.gov.

Category Three: Behaviors Disrupting Learning

HOW TO SUPPORT STUDENTS WHO REFUSE TO ENGAGE IN LEARNING

Students disengage for many reasons. Some lack the skills to participate and need additional support to continue learning. Others may have issues outside of school, affecting their ability to focus. Some students may want attention from their peers and refusing to work in defiance of the teacher may be the way they are trying to get that attention. In any case, the work refusal harms the student's learning and can affect the rapport you have with your entire class as well as the individual students.

Strategies That Work

- Ask the student if they are okay and find out what's going on. Listen to their response and act accordingly to remove any barriers to their learning.

- Be encouraging and supportive, but also clear with your expectations.

- Prevent as much work refusal as you can by designing instruction that is collaborative and active-learning experiences that are student-centered, meaningful, and relevant.

- Set small, achievable goals with students so that they can see their progress toward reaching a goal.

- Work on your relationships with students who refuse to work. Make sure that they know you care and are willing to help them succeed.

- Teach students how to collaborate in small groups to create a social context for learning.

- Consider assigning study buddies to all students. When students can turn to friendly peers for support, it will be easier for them to stay on task and to complete their work.

- If the problem persists after you have offered help and made your expectations clear, then you must enforce your logical consequences.

- You may also seek additional solutions from colleagues, counselors, or social workers.

- Call home to enlist the support of families and caregivers when you see a pattern developing. Working as a team with other supportive adults is often an effective way to address the issue of work refusal.

HOW TO SUPPORT A CLASS THAT IS SLOW TO SETTLE DOWN AND ENGAGE

Classes that are slow to settle down often enter the classroom energized from a previous class or an active event in their day. Returning to the room after lunch, recess, or physical education class can be particularly difficult for some classes who struggle with transitions.

Strategies That Work

- Don't miss the opportunity to have fun at the beginning of class by providing students with a series of opening exercises. The opening routine may include a bit of focusing movement or a high interest topic like current events that will help them transition into a learning frame of mind.
- Be patient when trying to solve this problem. Classes that are slow to settle down and engage will not learn to focus in just a day or two. Be persistent.
- Make sure that the expectations you have for the time it takes your class to settle down are realistic. It takes a large class longer to settle down than a smaller one. It is reasonable for students to chat as they get ready for class.
- Does the traffic flow of your class allow students to settle down quickly, or do they need to move around the room to pick up materials and supplies from different places? Make it easy for students to find their seats and the resources they need.
- Discuss the issue with students and ask for their suggestions to solve the problem. Because it is a problem that affects the entire class, it should be a problem that the entire class can solve by working together.
- Have consistent routines and procedures in place so that students can confidently anticipate what is expected of them at the start of class.
- Set a class goal for the time that it should take all students to settle down and engage. Post this goal in a conspicuous place and remind students of it as they enter the room. Chart their progress on the board so that they can have a visual representation of their own progress.

HOW TO RESPOND WHEN STUDENTS BEHAVE DISRESPECTFULLY TO A SUBSTITUTE TEACHER

Teachers may refer to substitute teachers as guest teachers to encourage students to remember to treat them as guests in their classroom. There are times when you need to be absent from work and still the unexpected change in routine can throw students off. It is important for learning to continue in your absence and for students to behave in a manner that is safe, respectful, and responsible even with a guest teacher.

Strategies That Work

- Prepare students at the start of the year talking about behavior expectations remaining the same, even with a guest teacher. You can find more information about how to prepare for your absence from school in Section Three.
- Create lesson plans for a substitute that are engaging and easy for the teacher and students to implement.
- Develop relationships with a couple of substitute teachers you can get to know and trust. If at all possible, request substitutes in advance to provide students the same guest teacher any time you need to be absent.
- If a substitute teacher left a note about disruptive student behavior, be sure to seek clarification about what happened before acting. One way to do this is to ask a few students to give you their version of events privately. Another strategy is to ask the entire class to jot down their thoughts about what happened, what went well, and what can be improved.
- Once you determine what happened, decide if there is a need for more conversations or consequences.
- Use the students' feedback to revise your plans for the next guest teacher.

HOW TO RESPOND WHEN CLASSES ARE INAPPROPRIATELY NOISY

Each teacher has unique teaching methods, classroom leadership styles, and learning philosophies. Learning can be purposefully loud and messy. Still, there are times when students individually or collectively create unacceptable noise levels. The noise level in a class must be appropriate for the activity or learning suffers and so does the classroom next door.

Strategies That Work

- Teach quieting signals. Never talk over students or shout to be heard in your classroom.
- Ask for suggestions from your students about how to manage noise levels.
- Teach your students about how to choose their vocal levels, when to use a whisper, a six-inch voice, or project their voices for a presentation. Make sure they know that it is not acceptable to talk across the room to classmates, to shout at any time, or to talk during a presentation.
- When you plan activities that have the potential to be noisy, consider moving to a part of the building where you can't disturb other classes.
- Don't plan group activities without teaching students how to control the noise level of their groups. One way to do this is by using distances as noise measurements. For example, students should find a one-foot voice useful for working in

pairs and a three-foot voice useful for working in groups. When you give directions for an assignment, tell students the acceptable noise level for the activity.

- Model the noise level that you want from your students. If you speak softly, your students will follow your lead. If you shout, you will dramatically increase the noise level in your class.

- Help your students feel they can succeed in your class. Students who feel they are part of a worthwhile experience have a reason to stay on task and to cooperate with you. They show respect for themselves and for their classmates when they have a reason to engage. Students who do not care about their work, your expectations, and their classmates have no reason to respect the class agreements and talk at appropriate noise levels.

- If you have a group that likes to talk, capitalize on this by getting them talking productively about the lesson. If you are successful at doing this, their need to interact with one another will also result in learning.

- If your students tend to talk when they have finished an assignment and are waiting for the rest of the class to finish, sequence your instruction so that there is always an activity for early finishers.

- Sometimes when students are very excited, allow them to spend a minute or two talking to clear the air so that they can focus on their work. Be clear in setting brief time limits and timers when you do this.

- Stay on your feet when your class has a problem with talking and excessive noise. Eye contact, proximity, and other nonverbal cues will help. Persistent and careful monitoring will encourage students to stay focused on their work rather than on conversation.

- Shifting gears from one activity to another is difficult for many students. Make transition times as efficient as possible in your class to avoid this problem.

- Use good-natured but firm signals to indicate that students should stop talking. Some signals that are appropriate include the following:
  - Saying a code word that your students recognize
  - Ringing a portable, wireless doorbell, chime, or other sound
  - Saying, "If you can hear my voice, take a deep breath," and repeating this as many times as necessary for quiet (and calming)
  - Counting backward from ten
  - Flicking the lights
  - Turning music on or off
  - Putting your finger to your lips
  - Holding your hands over your ears
  - Projecting a timer countdown on the board or screen
  - Holding your hand up and counting by folding your fingers
  - Standing in the front of the room obviously waiting
  - Having them put their pens down or close their devices when you call for attention

Category Four: Negative Behaviors toward the Teacher

HOW TO RESPOND WHEN A STUDENT IS DISRESPECTFUL OR DEFIANT

A student may behave in a disrespectful or defiant way for many reasons. Most likely, they want to feel seen, significant, and empowered. Their behavior, however conflicts with a teacher's need to be respected and the leader of the classroom. It's difficult to remain calm and difficult to avoid a power struggle, but that is exactly what you must do in the face of defiant behavior.

Defiance and disrespect can be angry, loud, abusive, and confrontational, or it can sound like something muttered under one's breath accompanied by an eye roll. Whatever its form, it is disruptive to learning and to a climate of mutual respect.

Strategies That Work

- Develop strong relationships with students. Connect with students daily. Give them positive encouragement. Make sure they know you care and you will reduce the likelihood of defiant behavior.

- Teach students to disagree respectfully with each other or with you, using sentence stems like:

  - "I feel that...."
  - "I suggest that...."
  - "I would like to add...."
  - "I respectfully disagree with ___ because ____."
  - "I have a different idea about that...."

- Give students leadership roles in the classroom so that they feel a sense of agency.

- Greet students at the door as they arrive and take a temperature check. If you see that a student is frustrated or upset, offer help and support as quickly as you can.

- Although you should take an angry outburst or other signs of defiance seriously, remain calm and start to deescalate the situation. Acknowledge to the student that you see they are upset. Ask the student if they want to take a break or get a drink of water.

- If the student remains agitated, quietly and calmly ask them to leave class. Have established locations that students can go to cool down. This may be a calming space in the classroom or the counseling office.

- After the incident, debrief with the student. Ask them to share how they felt and what they need. Listen without interrupting. Share how the student's behavior affected you and the other students. Problem-solve how to avoid future incidents and how to repair the harm that was caused.

- If the situation persists, involve the student's family or caregivers, the counselor or social worker, and an administrator. Meet with them and the student to work out a plan to solve the problem.

- Continue to work on your relationship with a defiant or disrespectful student. A positive relationship with this student will go far in preventing potential conflicts.

- When students are disrespectful to their teachers, there could be issues with classroom leadership and with teacher-to-student relationships that need to be addressed. It's important to reflect on your actions to consider if they contributed to the student's behavior.

- Make an agreement with students who feel the need to talk back. Tell them that you want to hear what they have to say and are willing to listen but that they need to speak to you respectfully. When you take this attitude, you offer students a chance to approach you in a positive manner, a way to deal with frustrations, and an opportunity to learn how to resolve conflicts respectfully.

HOW TO AVOID AND DISENGAGE FROM CLASSROOM POWER STRUGGLES

Frustration can often lead to power struggles and escalating behaviors. Power struggles involve teachers trying to use threats, force, or coercion in the face of a student's disruptive behavior. It can sound like, "Do this or else. . ." as both student and teacher vie for control. Avoid power struggles and if you find yourself in one, disengage from it because no one wins a power struggle.

- Don't take it personally. Even if a student is saying hurtful things to you, it's not about you (unless you have done something unfair or hurtful to the student, then you should take accountability and apologize). It's about the circumstances and the stresses of their lives and a need for control. You happen to be a nearby authority figure who becomes a target of their frustration.

- Remain calm. It is easier for students to self-regulate if they are in the presence of a regulated adult.

- Provide choices for a student to give them a sense of agency. Would you like to take a break in the calming corner or in the counselor's office?

Strategies That Work

- Turn negative student leaders into positive ones with a delicate touch. What they want to do and are already pretty good at doing is simple: leaders want to lead. Give them plenty of constructive opportunities to do so. Here are just some of the small actions you can take that will allow leaders to be productive instead of destructive influences in your classroom. Class leaders can:
  - Have a class job: Teacher's Assistant, Pencil Manager, Guest Greeter, Line Leader
  - Lead a class discussion

- Be the reporter for small-group discussions
- Take class votes, and assume responsibility for issuing books or distributing papers
- Run errands and pick up supplies
- Be the helper when there is a substitute
- Be as overwhelmingly positive with your (formerly negative) class leaders as you can.
- Reinforcing positive behaviors is the best strategy you can take with students who have previously tried to engage in a power struggle with you. You will gain their cooperation as well as the approval of the entire class when you make it clear that you want everyone in the class to succeed.

Questions to Discuss with Colleagues

Sharing ideas with colleagues is a helpful way to devise solutions to some of the problems that you must manage successfully at school. Here, you will find several topics to open discussions with colleagues about successful instructional practices:

1. One of your students is chronically late to school because a parent drops him off late many mornings. You have tried talking over the situation with the parent, but the child is still late. What should you do?

2. Two of your students turn in research reports that are very similar. You believe that one student copied another's paper or they both used generative AI to create the reports. However, you do not have any proof. What are your school's policies about how you are to handle this? What steps could you take to determine if cheating occurred? To whom can you turn for help?

3. You have a class right after lunch that has a difficult time settling down. How can you help them focus and get engaged with the lesson? To whom can you turn for help?

4. Students continue to be distracted by smartphones, checking them in their pockets or under desks during class. It's disruptive to learning and you want to do more to address it. What do other teachers do? How can you get students' buy-in? What should you do?

5. You suspect that some of your students might be harassing another student, but you have not actually caught them. The student who appears to be the target of the harassment denies any concerns. What, if anything, should you do? Who can help you with this?

Topics to Discuss with a Mentor

Although the topics that new teachers need to discuss with a mentor vary from teacher to teacher and from school to school, there are some that most first-year teachers should be

comfortable discussing with a mentor or a trusted colleague. You should ask your mentor about these topics from this section:

- Advice about the disruptive behaviors you can expect to encounter
- How to learn your school's policies regarding tardiness and absenteeism
- How to prevent the problems that you may be experiencing from becoming worse
- Advice about defiant or disrespectful students
- How to address student smartphone use

Reflection Questions to Guide Your Thinking

1. What is the most serious behavior issue that you have faced to date? How well did you handle the situation at the time that it occurred? How well did you take steps to prevent it from occurring again? What did you learn from the experience that you can use in the future?

2. How are you and your students doing with building a culture of mutual respect? Are you satisfied with the way you are building positive relationships? What areas would you like to work on? Who can help you with this?

3. A student who is normally respectful and well prepared is suddenly rude to you. How should you respond? Do you have a plan in place to respond to students who are defiant or disrespectful? How do you look beyond the behavior to discover what caused the behavior?

4. A student gets frustrated easily and his behavior escalates quickly, causing significant disruptions in your classroom. What can you do to discover the root of his frustration? Who are the specialists you can collaborate with to improve his behavior skills? What do other teachers in your school do to address situations like this?

5. What is your biggest worry regarding classroom behaviors? What can you do to address not only the issue itself but also your stress levels regarding it? How can you use your personal strengths as a classroom teacher to respond to disruptive behaviors? What areas for growth are you aware of, and how can you improve your knowledge and skills in those areas?

A Final Word

As a first-year teacher, you are on the threshold of an exhilarating time in your life—a meaningful career path that stretches far into the future. You will have many good days at school, and like every other educator, you will also have some tough days.

Maintaining a healthy work-life balance is one of the most important responsibilities that you have as an educator—and as a human. Be proactive about managing your stress. You are worth it. To help you with this, I have one more strategy to share with you. It's one that I learned during my own first year and that I continued every year since. I am so glad I did. You will be too, because after 30 years, they provide joy and inspiration still. Here's my final advice to you.

Find a cookie jar or an old shoebox and label it "Goody Jar," "Positives," "Good Vibes," "Treasure Chest," "Warm Fuzzies," or any other positive title that works for you. In that box, store all the expressions of gratitude and other encouragement that come your way: thank-you notes, student-crafted cards, notes from colleagues, endearing artwork, and precious homemade gifts that students give you. Store the mementos that touch your heart and remind you why you became a teacher.

When you come home after a tough day, get out your treasure trove of positive messages and let the contents renew your faith in yourself. Soon you will not only be surprised by how many good things come your way, but also by how much you have learned and how much you have grown as an educator. You'll be able to put those tough times in perspective because they are just one small part of your school life.

Your container of positive messages will remind you of the impact you have on the lives of students, colleagues, families, caregivers, and the community. With each note, you will remember that being a teacher is changing lives and helping students achieve their dreams. It's important to always remember that you matter and what you do matters a great deal.

Michelle Cummings

TEACHER TEMPLATE
Suggested Competencies

Consider some of these competencies appropriate for first-year teachers as you assess your strengths and the areas of your professional practice you would like to improve.

First-year teachers should be able to

1. _____ Set up and organize a classroom for maximum student achievement
2. _____ Collaborate effectively with colleagues and parents or guardians
3. _____ Take ownership of their professional development
4. _____ Manage professional responsibilities and duties
5. _____ Maintain a consistent work-life balance
6. _____ Manage stress with appropriate strategies
7. _____ Work with students from diverse cultures
8. _____ Teach students with various types of special needs
9. _____ Use student prior knowledge and preferred learning styles to differentiate instruction
10. _____ Plan lessons that align to state standards and district curriculum
11. _____ Vary teaching strategies to appeal to all learners
12. _____ Use data from formative assessments to inform instruction
13. _____ Engage students in student-centered learning activities
14. _____ Provide meaningful feedback to students and parents
15. _____ Adopt a problem-solving approach to resolve problems
16. _____ Appropriately assess student mastery of mandated content
17. _____ Establish an orderly discipline environment
18. _____ Prevent almost all discipline problems from occurring
19. _____ Use appropriate strategies when discipline problems occur
20. _____ Integrate available technology into instruction when appropriate

Be Proactive about Your Professional Growth

To guide you as you take ownership of your professional growth as a teacher, consider using this quick template.

- If you have already used a method in the list, write *Complete* in the blank.
- If you plan to use one of the methods but have not yet done so, write *Yes* in the blank.
- If you do not want to use a method, write *No* in the blank.

1. _____ Use action research to inform classroom decisions
2. _____ Attend conferences
3. _____ Participate in an edcamp
4. _____ Join professional organizations
5. _____ Read professional journals
6. _____ Investigate the National Board for Professional Teaching Standards
7. _____ Explore educational websites
8. _____ Establish your own personal learning network
9. _____ Take learning walks and snapshot observations
10. _____ Set and achieve professional goals
11. _____ Create a professional portfolio

Planning Template for the First Day

Although not all these items may be applicable to your class and to your students, this template can give you some idea of how to plan for your first day.

Opening welcome exercise (Time allotted: _____):

_____

_____

Supplies, materials, and books to be issued (Time allotted: _____):

_____

_____

Student information forms and inventories to be used (Time allotted: _____):

_____

_____

Rules, policies, and procedures (Time allotted: _____):

_____

_____

_____

_____

_____

_____

_____

Introduction of self (Time allotted: _____):

_____

_____

Welcome activity (Time allotted: _____):

_____

_____

Forms to be sent home (Time allotted: _____):

_____

_____

(continued on next page)

(continued from previous page)

Fees to be collected (Time allotted: _____):

_____

_____

Activities to help students connect (Time allotted: _____):

_____

_____

Lesson (Time allotted: _____):

Teacher input:

_____

_____

_____

_____

_____

_____

_____

_____

Student activity:

_____

_____

_____

_____

_____

_____

_____

_____

Closing (Time allotted: _____):

_____

_____

_____

_____

_____

_____

_____

_____

Student Learning Profile

Student name: _____ Date: _____

Learning Styles

Please rank the ways that you prefer to learn new material in this order:
Place a 3 in the blank before the way you like best.
Place a 2 in the blank before the way you like next.
Place a 1 in the blank before the way you like least.

_____ Auditory learning (I learn best by hearing.)
_____ Visual learning (I learn best by seeing.)
_____ Kinesthetic learning (I learn best by doing.)
_____ Combination of learning styles _____ and _____

Additional notes or explanation of learning styles:

_____

School Work Habits

I would describe my school work habits as:

_____

Interests

My interests include:

_____

School Experience

My favorite subject is _____ because: _____

_____

My least favorite subject is _____ because: _____

_____

Strengths and Weaknesses

My strengths include:

_____

I want to get better at:

_____

I learn best when I:

_____

My goals in life are:

_____

Behavior Incident Report

Use this form to record your notes about the details of a behavior incident so that you will have a clear record of the event.

Teacher: _____ Student: _____

Date and time of incident: _____

Place of incident: _____

Information shared by the student:

_____
_____
_____
_____
_____
_____
_____
_____

Actions taken by the teacher/Results of those actions

_____
_____
_____
_____
_____
_____
_____
_____

Parent or guardian contact:

_____
_____
_____
_____
_____
_____

Notes:

_____
_____
_____
_____
_____
_____

Behavior Observation Form for a Class

This template is a useful tool for helping you gather the data that you need to make discipline decisions because it will allow you to record specific behaviors quickly. After you have made your observations, you should then be able to use the recommendations column to jot down the ideas you have for remediating problems. As an alternative, you could ask a colleague to make the observations while you teach.

Date: _____   Class: _____

Number of students in the class: _____

Observed Misbehaviors	Number of Students	Recommendations
Tardy to class		
Lack of materials		
Talking while the teacher is talking		
Off task and excessive talking		
Missing assignment		
Cheating		
Cell phone use in class		
Unintentional profanity		

(continued on next page)

From *The First-Year Teacher's Survival Guide, 5th Edition*, by Michelle Cummings. Copyright © 2024 by John Wiley & Sons, Inc. Reproduced by permission.

(*continued from previous page*)

Observed Misbehaviors	Number of Students	Recommendations
Intentional profanity		
Sleeping in class		
Disrespectful to the teacher		
Disrespectful to classmates		
Horseplay		
Refusing to work		
Misuse of materials or equipment		
Negative verbal reaction		
Negative nonverbal reaction		
Disorganized work space or materials		
Asking to leave room		
Distracting other students		
Distracted		

Behavior Observation Form for an Individual Student

Use this form after you have already determined a student's specific behaviors that you want to observe. You can either do the observations yourself or have a colleague observe your students as you teach.

Observer: _____ Student: _____

Date and time: _____

Targeted Behavior 1 _____

Frequency:

_____

Level of disruption: Self   Nearby students   All students

Possible triggers:

_____

_____

Teacher response:

_____

_____

Result of teacher response:

_____

_____

Insights or reflection:

_____

_____

Next steps:

_____

_____

(continued on next page)

From *The First-Year Teacher's Survival Guide, 5th Edition*, by Michelle Cummings. Copyright © 2024 by John Wiley & Sons, Inc. Reproduced by permission.

(continued from previous page)

Targeted Behavior 2 _____

Frequency: _____

Level of disruption: Self   Nearby students   All students

Possible triggers:

_____

_____

Teacher response:

_____

_____

Result of teacher response:

_____

_____

Insights or reflection:

_____

_____

Next steps:

_____

_____

Behavior Intervention Documentation for an Individual Student

This form is suitable for documenting the responses you have made to a student's behavior so that you can be sure that you have a complete record of the steps you have taken to help the student succeed.

Student:_____ Class period:_____

Major concern(s): _____
_____
_____

Level of Success

Record the success of each intervention you have tried in the last column by using these numbers:

1: Not successful
2: Somewhat successful but needs modification
3: Successful

Date	Behavior or Concern	Intervention	Level of Success

Index

Page references followed by *fig* indicate an illustrated figure.

Black on Black Education podcast, 5, 202, 206
Blended learning, tech resources to support, 295
Blogs, educational, 5–6. *See also specific blogs*
Bloom's Taxonomy, 315
Body language:
    leadership persona and, 92–93
    teacher nonverbal signals and, 92–93
Book Creator, 241
Bookmarks, interactive, 233
Book recommendations, AI-generated, 36
Boss, Suzie, 281
Boundaries:
    healthy, 74, 162, 170, 172, 174–175
    setting, 25, 27–28, 52
"Brain breaks," 370–371
BrainPop, 278, 301
Brainstorming, using AI for, 38
Breakout.edu, 94, 105
Breaks, taking, 29
Breathing exercises, 32, 199
Bucket Filler activities, 198
Buddy Reading, 266
Bulletin boards, creating quick and effective, 132–133
Bullying, 206
    cyberbullying, 297, 432
    how to deal with students engaged in, 430–432
Burk, Connie, 212
Burnout, avoiding teacher, 26
Burns, Jennifer, 77, 143, 238, 346
Burns, Ken, 304
Bye Bye Plastic Bags initiative, 284

C

Cabral, Joshua, 6
Call-and-response, 96
Calm (website), 31
Calm assumption of cooperation, 356–357
Calming classroom space, creating a, 132
Canva, 39, 56, 198, 241, 278, 294, 301
CapturingKidsHearts.org, 336
Career Readiness Standards, 266
Career worries, 25
Caregivers, *see* Families and caregivers;
    Parents/guardians
Caring for yourself, 26–28
CASEL.org, 188–189, 266
Case studies, 233
CAST.org, 213
CDC (Centers for Disease Control), 212
Celebrating mistakes, 102–103
Cell phones, *see* Smartphones
Center for Black Educator Development, 8
Centers for Disease Control (CDC), 212
Center for Talented Youth at Johns Hopkins University, 218

CER (Claim-Evidence-Reasoning), 288–290
CES (Coalition of Essential Schools), 8
Chain of command, 77
Chalk talks, 233
Changing Lenses–A New Focus for Crime and Justice (Zehr), 340
ChatGPT, 35–36
Cheating, 406
    addressing, once it has occurred, 428
    strategies to prevent, 427–428
Check-in, Check-out systems, 391
Checklists, student, 116
Childhood trauma, 210–212
Children and Adults with Attention-Deficit/ Hyperactivity Disorder, 218
Child Study Team notes, 58
Child Trauma Toolkit, 212
Chiu, Yen-Yen, 284
Choice boards, 232
Chromebooks, 298–300
Chronic absenteeism, 421
Chunking, 233
Circle within a Circle, 151
Civil discourse, class discussions toward, 288–291
Claim-Evidence-Reasoning (CER), 288–290
Clarity of purpose, in lesson planning, 258–261
Clark, Holly, 41
Class(es). *See also* Classroom(s)
    first ten minutes of, 117–119
    handling when slow to settle down and engage, 433
    how to use any time left at end of, 123
    inappropriately noisy, 434–435
    keeping on task while working with small groups, 366
    last ten minutes of, 120–123
    managing smartphone use in, 423
    power struggles in, 437–438
    students who are tardy to, 420–421
    students who sleep in, 419
Class agreements, discipline related to enforcement of, 418
Class discussions:
    before, during, and after, 289–291
    toward civil discourse, 288–291
ClassDojo, 298, 401
Classist language, 426
Class meetings, learning about students' interests during, 227
Class-related templates:
    Behavior Intervention Documentation, 411–413
    How Well do You Use Class Time?, 109–110
    Plans for Ending Class Effectively, 122
    Plans for Starting Class Effectively, 119